Third Edition

Kellogg
on
Marketing

The Marketing Faculty of the
Kellogg School of Management

Edited by
Alexander Chernev
Philip Kotler

WILEY

For general information on our other products and services or for technical support, please contact our Customer Care Department within the United States at (800) 762-2974, outside the United States at (317) 572-3993 or fax (317) 572-4002.

Wiley also publishes its books in a variety of electronic formats. Some content that appears in print may not be available in electronic formats. For more information about Wiley products, visit our web site at www.wiley.com.

Library of Congress Cataloging-in-Publication Data is Available:

ISBN: 9781119906247 (cloth)
ISBN: 9781119906254 (ePub)
ISBN: 9781119906261 (ePDF)

Cover Design: Wiley
Author Photos: © Evanston Photo

SKY10042768_021323

Contents

Preface

The term *marketing* came into use in the early 1900s to describe company activities taking place in markets. The early marketing textbooks were written by economists who felt that economics textbooks spoke mainly about price, demand, and supply and left out many other variables that influence buying and selling decisions. Economics textbooks failed to say much about how sales, advertising, distribution channels, product development, wholesaling, retailing, or branding influenced the economic outlook. Marketing textbooks did a better job of describing real-world economics, and a number of specialized books appeared on specific marketing functions such as advertising, sales, promotion, and retailing. While early marketing textbooks were largely descriptive of these activities and the institutions engaged in them, the writers also occasionally offered prescriptive ideas on how these activities and institutions could be improved, at times citing the results of scholarly studies on effective selling, pricing, and advertising.

The breakthrough in the development of marketing theory came in 1967, when Philip Kotler, then a rising star at Northwestern's Kellogg School of Management, published a new textbook, called *Marketing Management* (now in its 16th edition). The book's analytical approach synthesized ideas from economics, behavioral science, organization science, and mathematics. The theory outlined in the book argued that marketing should be customer focused, not product focused. Customers and their needs, rather than the attributes of the company's products, should be the focal point of managers' efforts. It further argued that the strategy, broadly defined as a process of identifying target customers and developing a value proposition, should guide a company's tactical activities—including product design, pricing, promotion, and distribution. Because of its deep insights, *Marketing Management* became the leading marketing text in business schools around the world and has remained so for many decades. It helped shape marketing as a business discipline and also helped shape the way in which the Kellogg marketing faculty views marketing and its role in an organization and society.

Building on Kellogg's tradition of marketing leadership, *Kellogg on Marketing* presents the current developments in marketing theory and practice. Combining cutting-edge research with real-world insight, expert authors—the marketing faculty at the Kellogg School of Management— outline the fundamental marketing concepts and show how the practical application of these concepts can help companies gain and sustain market position. With a focus on customer centricity and value creation, the ideas presented in this book can help managers design bestselling products and services, develop impactful communication campaigns, and create effective distribution channels. Insightful and practical, *Kellogg on Marketing* is the essential reference for everyone seeking to achieve market success: from entrepreneurs to managers working in large companies, from junior market-ers to senior executives, from engineers designing a company's next offerings to creative teams developing the communication campaign promoting these offerings.

The information presented in this book is organized into seven parts. Part One, *Marketing Strategy and Tactics*, focuses on the big-picture issues in mar-keting: the recent changes in the business environment and their impact on marketing practice, the role of strategic value creation, and the importance of a systematic approach to market planning. In the first chapter, Alexander Chernev and Philip Kotler discuss some of the key changes in the current business environment. These range from the emergence of new technologies, the exponential growth of available data, the increasing reliance on data ana-lytics and artificial intelligence to complex sociocultural dynamics, mounting environmental challenges, and unpredictable market disruptions. This chap-ter further outlines the main marketing trends that have emerged from the rapidly changing market environment.

In the next chapter, Alexander Chernev and Philip Kotler address the drawbacks of focusing only on the tactical aspect of marketing management without devising a sound strategy to guide a company's actions. They further argue that managers are better served by going beyond the four Ps to develop a strategy that clearly articulates the value that the company aims to create in its target market. Building on the concept of value management, in the following chapter, Alexander Chernev advances a framework for marketing manage-ment centered around the concept of creating and capturing value. Dubbed G-STIC after its key components—goal, strategy, tactics, implementation, and control—this framework provides a roadmap for a company's actions and en-sures that these actions are aligned with the company's overarching goal.

Part Two, *Marketing as an Engine of Business Growth*, focuses on the cen-tral role of marketing in the organization and the primary driver of company value. In Chapter 4, Lakshman Krishnamurthi and Rebecca Devine explore the essence of market disruptions. Specifically, they examine how changes to a product and the way it is brought to the market can create significant value for the company and can even change the way an industry operates. In the next chapter, Tom O'Toole underscores the role of customer centricity as a business strategy. He argues that because digital media allow companies to address their target customers individually—and at scale—a company's customer strategy is the key to market success. In Chapter 6, Greg Carpen-ter delineates the difference between market-driven and market-driving ap-proaches to managing growth. In this context, he argues that firms can gain competitive advantage by shaping consumers' thinking through the timing of their entry, the means used to distinguish their brands, and the admiration they achieve among their peers. Finally, Chapter 7, by Tim Calkins, explores an important and often neglected part of marketing: defensive strategy. Spe-cifically, he argues that when companies fail, it is often because they could not hold on to market share when attacked by new entrants, and he outlines the key defensive strategies that can enable companies to mount a viable response to competitive threats.

Part Three, *Developing a Winning Marketing Strategy*, examines some of the key issues involved in defining the ways in which a company identifies markets in which it will compete and defines the value it will create in these markets. This part starts with a chapter by Julie Hennessy, in which she discusses the process of identifying target customers and the importance of deciding which customers to serve and which to ignore. This chapter further argues that precision targeting is a key component of a company's strategy to grow a company's sales and profits.

In the following chapter, Kent Grayson specifies four steps that a company must take when segmenting a market for both new and existing products. Using examples for consumer and business-to-business marketing, he highlights potential segmentation misunderstandings and pitfalls that companies should try to avoid. Building on the concepts of segmentation and targeting, in Chapter 10 Kevin McTigue discusses the importance of crafting a unique strategy to win and retain customers. He further identifies the key principles of crafting a winning positioning strategy and shows how to fight value-destroying price competition by becoming a better choice for target customers.

Part Four, *Creating Value with Brands*, examines the role of brands as an important source of value for both companies and their customers. This part starts with a chapter by Alexander Chernev on the role of brands as a key driver of customer and company value. He outlines the function of brands as a marketing tool, the importance of creating a meaningful brand image, the ways in which brands create customer and company value, and the role of brand equity and brand power in brand valuation.

In Chapter 12, Neal Roese delineates the essence of brand image, how best to quantify it as a key performance indicator, and how best to build it. This chapter further explains the importance of strategizing through the lens of brand image. In the chapter that follows, Jonathan Copulsky outlines strategies that enable brands to survive, persevere, and thrive in an ever-changing digital world. He describes some of the main threats facing brands and provides a framework that gives brand stewards a means for anticipating and responding to threats that might undermine the brand value they have worked so hard to build.

Part Five, *Crafting a Successful Communication Campaign*, focuses on the process of communicating a company's offerings to its target audience. The chapter by Derek Rucker offers a framework for successful planning, implementation, and evaluation of a company's advertising activities. Rich in original insights and practical suggestions, this chapter is a quintessential primer on developing great advertising that derives its creative solution from a sound marketing strategy.

Chapter 15, by Kevin McTigue, outlines the core principles of developing an impactful communication campaign and shows how to leverage a customer-centric approach to design and implement a successful communication campaign. This chapter further offers a systematic approach to navigate the Who, When, Where, and What of communication planning and offers a practical approach to creating actionable communication campaigns. In the following chapter, Mohan Sawhney offers an enlightening vision of how the metaverse will lead to further major changes in the marketing landscape. This chapter defines the essence of the metaverse, outlines some of the key marketing opportunities it offers to trendsetting companies, and discusses how it can become a viable platform for marketing initiatives.

Part Six, *Designing Effective Distribution Channels*, addresses the ways in which companies deliver their offerings to target customers, the importance of creating an effective omnichannel strategy, and the integral role of the sales force in this process. This part starts with a chapter by Julie Hennessy and Jim Lecinski, who discuss how channels create value for both firms and customers. They further present alternative models that can help marketers design channel structures that match the needs of their target customers. This chapter also explores the retail, wholesale, and direct-to-consumer routes to marketing, and discusses the advantages and limitations of each approach.

In Chapter 18, Jim Lecinski unpacks the two main elements required to deliver a true omnichannel experience: a front-end customer interface and a back-end technology that powers it. Taken together, these two elements offer a roadmap for managers to successfully create and manage an effective and cost-efficient omnichannel customer experience. In Chapter 19, Craig Wortmann describes how sales professionals and marketers can become more persuasive and boost sales by capturing, distilling, and sharing powerful stories. He outlines two practical tools—the Story Canvas and the Story Matrix—that help people tell the right story at the right time for the right reasons.

Part Seven, *Data-Driven Marketing*, discusses the ways in which companies can use market data to design and implement effective marketing campaigns. This part starts with a chapter by Eric Anderson and Florian Zettelmeyer, in which they discuss how managers can use data analytics and artificial intelligence to improve their marketing actions and drive value. They argue that nowadays having a working knowledge of data science is a prerequisite for most, if not all, marketing functions within the organization, and that the implementation of data-driven decision making is a leadership challenge that must be addressed at the C-suite level. In Chapter 21, Aparna Labroo outlines frameworks and case studies that spotlight how marketers can leverage opportunities arising from technological changes to better manage customer experience. These frameworks can be used to consider future opportunities and challenges that may arise as technology continues to develop.

Chapter 22 by Derek Rucker and Aparna Labroo outlines a novel framework that enables managers to use predictive data analytics based on psychological insights into consumer behavior. This chapter lays out the perils of reactive managerial responses to data and advances a theory-based predictive testing approach based on a set of clearly articulated, managerially relevant hypotheses. In the last chapter, Tom O'Toole discusses the recent developments in implementing customer centricity on the individual customer level. Specifically, he examines the role of predictive analytics in enhancing a company's ability to detect specific needs, desires, and preferences, and proactively customize effective marketing programs for each individual customer.

Overall, the chapters contained in this book provide an insightful overview of the current state of marketing theory and practice. Whether you are new to marketing or an experienced marketer, *Kellogg on Marketing* can deepen your knowledge by offering strategic insights as well as practical illustrations of how to design actionable marketing programs that create value for your target customers in a way that benefits your company and collaborators.

—*Alexander Chernev*
Philip Kotler

Acknowledgments

This book has benefited from the wisdom of many of our current and former colleagues at the Kellogg School of Management at Northwestern University: Chethana Achar, Nidhi Agrawal, Jim Anderson, Robert Blattberg, Ulf Böckenholt, Galen Bodenhausen, Miguel Brendl, Moran Cerf, Yuxin Chen, Anne Coughlan, Patrick Duparcq, David Gal, Kelly Goldsmith, Sachin Gupta, Karsten Hansen, Dipak Jain, Ata Jami, Robert Kozinets, Angela Lee, Eric Leininger, Sidney Levy, Michal Maimaran, Eyal Maoz, Blake McShane, Vikas Mittal, Ilya Morozov, Vincent Nijs, John Sherry, Jr., Louis Stern, Brian Sternthal, Jacob Teeny, Artem Timoshenko, Rima Touré-Tillery, Anna Tuchman, Caio Waisman, Rick Wilson, Song Yao, Philip Zerrillo, and Andris Zoltners. Special thanks are due to Bobby Calder, Dawn Iacobucci, and Alice Tybout, who served as editors of the previous editions of *Kellogg on Marketing*.

Several people warrant special mention for the key roles they played in the writing of this book. Joanne Freeman and the team at Cape Cod Compositors did an outstanding job of relentlessly editing this text. They provided practical feedback and insightful suggestions that helped shape and streamline the content of this book. We would also like to thank the Wiley team, and in particular, our managing editor, Deborah Schindlar. Special thanks are also due to Richard Narramore, the executive editor at Wiley, for encouraging us to undertake this project and for supporting us throughout the entire process.

—*Alexander Chernev*
Philip Kotler

PART 1

Marketing Strategy and Tactics

CHAPTER 1

Marketing in the Age of Disruption

Alexander Chernev and Philip Kotler

Marketing has evolved dramatically over the past few decades. No other discipline has changed so rapidly in such a short period of time. These changes encompass both the strategic and tactical aspects of marketing and influence how companies conceptualize the process of creating value in their target markets and the ways in which they design specific offerings for these markets. In this context, understanding the new market realities, identifying the key marketing trends, and understanding their driving forces can help companies better design and manage their offerings to ensure sustainable market growth.[1]

The New Market Realities

The business environment is going through a period of profound changes. These range from the emergence of new technologies to the exponential growth of available data and the increasing reliance on data analytics and artificial intelligence to complex sociocultural dynamics, mounting environmental challenges, and unpredictable market disruptions.

Technological Disruption

The technological environment may influence the way companies operate in two ways: by producing *sustaining technologies* that lead to improvements in a company's operations within the boundaries of its current business model and by introducing *disruptive technologies* that facilitate the creation of entirely new business models.

The impact of *sustaining technologies* can influence a company's performance by heightening the effectiveness and cost efficiency of the value-creation process. Improvement in the *effectiveness* of a company's ability to create viable market offerings is associated with the development of new technologies that enable the creation of better-performing products and services. In addition to improving a company's products and services, technological developments have facilitated the ability of companies to effectively interact with their customers by uncovering new means of communication and strengthening the effectiveness of existing ones. Furthermore, technological developments have improved existing distribution systems by enhancing their availability, speed, and accuracy.

Along with improving the effectiveness of the company's operations, technological developments have contributed to improving the *cost efficiency* of these operations by streamlining various aspects of a company's distribution channels such as packaging, transportation, and inventory management. The cost savings stemming from lower manufacturing, communication, and distribution costs have helped many companies improve their bottom line as well as enhance the customer and collaborator value created by their offerings.

In addition to optimizing a company's existing products and services, technology influences a company's market success by breaking the standard industry operating mold and creating new market offerings and a novel business model. Such *disruptive technologies* have fundamentally changed many industries. For example, the development of the internet revolutionized retailing (Amazon), auctions (eBay), communication (Twitter), social networking (Facebook), information search (Google), transportation (Uber), hospitality (Airbnb), and entertainment (Netflix).

The current technological environment is characterized by the rapid emergence of new technologies in virtually all industries, including energy, pharmaceuticals, healthcare, communications, manufacturing, and education. Not only are new technologies being developed at an increasing rate but the cycle from invention to business application has been significantly shortened. This rapid adoption of new technologies is facilitated by increasing rates of global collaboration and transfer of technologies that stem from the global expansion of production, marketing, and research activities. These factors contribute to the ever-increasing impact of the technological context on a company's business activities.

The Data Revolution

Over the course of the past few decades, the discipline of marketing has fundamentally changed as a result of the availability of vast amounts of data that can be used to inform managerial decision making. In particular, there are three major factors that have contributed to the expanding importance of data in marketing management: greater availability of up-to-date market data, increased data processing capabilities, and advancements in machine learning and artificial intelligence.

The amount of *readily available data* is exponentially increasing such that companies have access to vast amounts of real-time market information about the company's target customers, its collaborators and competitors, as well as the effectiveness and cost efficiency of the company's own operations.

Of particular importance is the availability of customer-specific individual-level data aggregated from multiple sources. Some of this information is based on customers' direct interaction with the company, such as visiting the company website, using the product app, and interacting with the company's sales associates. Another source of customer data is the entities collaborating with the company to design, communicate, and deliver its offerings (this information is often referred to as second-party data). For example, a company can obtain information about customer activity on its Facebook page, Instagram profile, and Twitter account. Customer data can also be obtained from aggregators such as Oracle Blue Kai, Adobe, Acxiom, and Experian, which continually compile individual-level customer information from various sources (this information is often referred to as third-party data).

The vast amount of available data is complemented by increased *data-processing capabilities* that stem from several major developments. The first development is exponentially increasing computing power. More than half a decade ago, Intel's co-founder Gordon Moore predicted that the number of transistors on a microchip (which roughly corresponds to computing power) would double every two years, while the cost of computers would be halved. This prediction, often referred to as Moore's Law, holds, at least in principle, even today as computing becomes more powerful and less expensive.

In addition to intensified computing power, the *types of data* that can be processed have multiplied as well. Whereas in the past, information processing was largely limited to structured data, today an increasing amount of information is unstructured. Unlike structured data—information arranged in a highly ordered fashion and typically involving text or numerals organized in rows and columns—unstructured data do not involve text or numerals presented in an organized format. Examples of unstructured data include text, images, sounds, and movement. This expansion of the type of data that can be processed is particularly important because most of the data that we encounter on a daily basis are unstructured.

Another factor contributing to the revolutionary role data play in today's business world is the development of complex *data analysis algorithms*. One such algorithm is natural language processing that involves analyzing streams of recorded or written text and interpreting the meaning of document contents, including the contextual nuances of the language used. For example, an algorithm might analyze freeform text to understand the sentiment of the communicator—a technique commonly referred to as sentiment analysis and used to gauge popular sentiment on social media associated with the company's products, services, and brands. In addition to natural language processing, there has been significant progress in developing algorithms dealing with object recognition, planning, reasoning, and emotional intelligence.

The ubiquity of data in marketing management is also facilitated by the *growth of data-analytics platforms* that enable companies to gather insights from the available data without necessarily having to develop core competence in data analytics. Platforms such as those by Microsoft, Oracle, IBM, Salesforce, and SAS enable companies to outsource data analysis at relatively low cost and without acquiring specialized expertise. The ability to analyze data without making a major investment in facilities, technology, and human resources has propelled the use of data analytics beyond large companies that have traditionally been the primary users of market data to medium- and small-size companies that otherwise would not have been able to benefit from the data.

The advancements in *machine learning and artificial intelligence* have further accelerated the widespread use of data across all industries and business functions. Artificial intelligence involves machine learning, where data analytics and implementation algorithms are not guided by humans. Machine learning is at the heart of artificial intelligence; without self-guided learning there would be no artificial intelligence. Machine learning is different from basic automation in which a human provides a set of instructions that tell a machine what to do in order to produce a given outcome. In contrast, machine learning enables the program to constantly improve performance on a given task without explicitly being programmed and told what to do. Because machine learning is based on experience, it improves as more data become available. Given the rapid proliferation of market data, the speed with which machine learning improves is increasing exponentially, which in turn is driving its adoption by companies seeking to incorporate complex, real-time market data into their decision-making processes.

Sociocultural Dynamics

The sociocultural environment is important to a company's success in both domestic and global markets. A company's market success depends not only on understanding the specifics of the sociocultural environment in which it operates but also on its ability to predict the likely changes in this environment. Understanding and acting on key sociocultural trends enables a company to develop a successful long-term marketing strategy.

The past several decades have been marked with the emergence of several important sociocultural trends that are likely to have a significant impact on the ways in which companies create market value. Some of the key trends include the rapid growth of the middle class in many countries, increased emphasis on social responsibility, widespread transition to a digital lifestyle, and the increasing fragmentation of the social fabric.

One sociocultural trend of global consequence is the *rapid growth of the middle class* in many newly industrialized countries, including China, India, and Brazil. The speed of growth of the middle class, particularly in China and India, has increased so dramatically that the Asian middle class is becoming the world's new pillar of consumption, helping to offset the stagnation of the middle class in developed countries and establishing itself as a key driver of global growth.

Another important sociocultural development is the increased emphasis on *social responsibility*. The notion that individuals and organizations have a duty to act in the best interests of society as a whole has become an important aspect of self-identity of many consumers and an integral aspect of the corporate culture of numerous companies. As a result, a growing number of investors and consumers are factoring in a company's commitment to socially responsible practices when making an investment or purchase. Responding to this trend, many companies have made social responsibility an integral part of their business models. And they have accomplished this without compromising their bottom lines. The emphasis on prosocial behavior is furthered by the combined efforts of various government entities and nonprofit organizations to develop policies that promote an ethical balance between the dual mandates of maximizing profitability and benefiting society at large.

Yet another notable sociocultural change spurred by the technological revolution and turbocharged by the global pandemic is the widespread adoption of a *digital lifestyle*. Pandemic-related lockdowns have forced both consumers and businesses to abandon traditional in-person modes of interaction and rapidly transition to conduct most activities online. Consumers who previously have been reluctant to shop online now have been forced to rely on e-commerce. Brick-and-mortar retailers that used to generate most of their revenues from foot traffic have had to transform their business models to adjust to online traffic. In the same vein, many workplaces have evolved from a more structured office environment requiring in-person presence to a more flexible remote work environment based on virtual collaboration. The pandemic has broken through technological and sociocultural barriers that prevented remote work in the past, creating a structural shift in where and how we live and work.

The growing popularity and continuous customization of social networks has contributed to the growing *fragmentation of the social fabric*. Individuals increasingly rely on their social contacts rather than on mass media to obtain relevant information, form opinions, and decide how to act. Thus, while providing greater interconnectivity and consensus among the public, social networks and their ability to fit content to a person's needs and preferences can foster more extreme beliefs, preferences, and behaviors. This increasing fragmentation of society calls for further customization of the ways in which companies design, communicate, and deliver value to their customers and also makes it more challenging for public policy makers to create and implement programs designed to benefit society as a whole.

The Environmental Challenge

Climate change—the long-term change in the average weather patterns that define local, regional, and global climates—is one of the major challenges facing humanity. Climate change has been attributed to human activities, particularly the burning of fossil fuels, which increases heat-trapping greenhouse gas levels in the atmosphere. The increase in the levels of greenhouse gas in turn leads to an increase in Earth's average surface temperature—an effect commonly referred to as global warming.

Even though the terms *climate change* and *global warming* are used interchangeably, the latter does not accurately convey the profound impact of rising temperatures on all aspects of human life. In fact, from a marketing perspective, the popularization of the term *global warming* was a major miscalculation, in part because the general public often does not draw the distinction between climate and weather. As a result, many have interpreted global warming as referring to short-term atmospheric conditions (the weather) and, consequently, disbelieve the phenomenon when confronted with streaks of extreme cold weather. In this context, climate change is a more accurate description of the detrimental impact of human activities on the long-term weather patterns in different regions of the world.

The impact of climate change on human life is profound and goes far beyond the increase in the Earth's average surface temperature. In addition to rising temperatures, climate change leads to an increase in the carbon dioxide levels in the atmosphere, rising sea levels, and more extreme weather. These changes, in turn, have broad-reaching consequences, including extreme heat, severe weather events, poor water quality, greater air pollution, degraded living conditions, and forced migration, as well as the exacerbation of existing social, economic, and health inequities.

In addition to these fundamental changes affecting humanity as a whole, climate change can have a direct impact on a company's business activities. For example, an increase in the average annual temperature can lead to lower yields of fruits and vegetables that thrive in cooler temperatures and higher yields of warm-climate plants. As the cold season shortens, winter sports are likely to suffer, whereas warm-weather activities are likely to thrive. In addition to climate changes, which reflect the more stable weather patterns, daily weather conditions can also influence a company's business. For instance, ice cream consumption is likely to increase when it is hot and decline as the weather cools down. Abnormal weather conditions can disrupt the production and delivery of a company's products.

Global warming, although crucial, is not the only environmental challenge faced by society. Environmentally destructive trends such as deforestation, air and water pollution, natural resource depletion, lowered biodiversity, and increased waste production have become critically important, attracting the attention of consumers, businesses, and government agencies. As a result, many companies have made significant investments in the development of environmentally friendly technologies, striving to decelerate and, when possible, reverse the detrimental environmental impact created by traditional methods of production that prioritize short-term company profits over the long-term societal impact of environmental destruction.

Unpredictable Market Disruptions

As the business world has become more complex, it has also become less predictable. Market disruptions, big and small, occur more frequently than they have in the past. These disruptions challenge business models, forcing companies to be more agile and pushing into oblivion those companies that are unable to adapt. There are three major sources of such market disruptions: economic downturns, changes in government policies and regulations, and changes in the physical environment.

Economic downturns are not a new phenomenon. But as more complex financial instruments proliferate, major trading strategies are implemented in milliseconds, and an increasing number of financial decisions are made using newly developed computer algorithms, the unpredictability of financial crises and the speed with which they are likely to unfold increase dramatically. Factors such as limited money supply and credit availability associated with an economic downturn may not only curb a company's expansion plans but also threaten the company's very existence.

Changes in government policies and regulations can send shockwaves through global economies. As people's political views become more polarized, so do the policies of the political parties representing these views. This, in turn, leads to more extreme geopolitical, social, and economic agendas advanced by government as different parties take charge. These agendas might be internally focused, such as anti-monopoly legislation designed to foster competition and protect consumer interests, or they might be global in nature, such as tariffs, trade wars, and embargos. For example, the U.K. decision to exit the European Union and impose tariffs on a variety of imported goods have had a significant impact on the value-creation models of companies affected by these actions.

An increasingly important factor that can contribute to major market disruptions involves changes in the *physical environment*. For example, natural disasters associated with extreme weather conditions such as floods, hurricanes, and forest fires are becoming more frequent as a result of global climate change. In the same vein, with the increasing globalization of travel, contagious diseases that in the past were more localized are now more likely to reach pandemic status. The COVID-19 pandemic is a vivid example of the extent to which changes in the physical environment can unsettle business, social, and political life across the world. And while it is true that over time society will develop more effective strategies to mitigate the impact of these changes in the physical environment, their unpredictable nature can create major market disruptions that will require many companies to reengineer their business models.

The Key Marketing Trends

During the past several decades, there have been a number of significant technological, economic, regulatory, and social changes that have had a profound impact on the way companies do business. These new realities have resulted in a dramatic shift in how companies develop and implement their marketing strategies. This shift is represented by several marketing trends that reflect the fundamental changes in today's marketing environment.

From Customer-Centric to Customer-Driven Marketing

The notion of customer centricity, prominent in the writings of Peter Drucker, was the marketing mantra of the twentieth century. The basic premise of customer centricity is that instead of focusing only on technologies and products, companies should focus on identifying and fulfilling customer needs. The concept of customer centricity can be illustrated by the words of Apple's CEO, Tim Cook: "Our whole role in life is to give you something you didn't know you wanted. And then once you get it, you can't imagine your life without it." Reflecting this view, Apple's strategic vision revolves around customer centricity, such that its offerings, processes, and policies are designed to deliver superior value throughout the entire consumption experience.

The importance of focusing on customer needs has not changed and remains a fundamental marketing principle. What has changed, however, is the increased role of customers in defining a company's marketing strategies. Rather than being passive observers of marketing activities, consumers are now empowered to voice their opinions, thereby taking over some aspects of marketing. Customer-driven marketing implies value co-creation, such that both customers and the company are actively involved in designing, producing, and promoting the company's offering. In today's networked world, customers have become co-creators of market value.

For instance, brand building—an activity that until recently was controlled almost exclusively by the company—is increasingly shared by companies and their customers, whose collective voice can significantly strengthen or undermine the desired positioning of company brands. In the same vein, value co-creation can include the development of the actual products and services; this can range from designing open-source software, developing mobile apps, and creating videogame modules to co-designing apparel and accessories. Value co-creation can begin even before the company has developed its products and services through crowdsourcing, with companies reaching out to customers to generate and validate new ideas. As companies increasingly rely on customer input to develop new market offerings, value co-creation is becoming an integral aspect of their business models.

From Company-Focused Models to Collaborator Networks

The focus of marketing has evolved from maximizing the value of each individual transaction to optimizing the entire value-delivery process. This has propelled companies to introduce new business models in which the traditional roles of companies and customers are often reversed. Years ago, realizing that consumers are unlikely to pay to search for information, Google revolutionized the search engine business model by deriving revenues from the entity being searched rather than the one initiating the searching. By doing so, Google has created a value network in which its collaborators rather than customers are the key source of revenues and profits.

The creation of collaborator networks is facilitated by the growing number of platforms enabling companies to outsource the capabilities they do not have by partnering with entities explicitly designed for the purpose of "renting out" such capabilities. Business model platforms have emerged that create value by utilizing large, scalable networks of users and resources and facilitating exchanges between the networked entities.

With the growth of cloud-computing services, the concepts of "platform as a service," "infrastructure as a service," and "software as a service" have gained popularity. Companies like Dropbox, HubSpot, Salesforce, Mailchimp, and Slack have built their business models on the concept of providing software platforms that their customers can use to develop their offerings. And companies like Adobe, Microsoft, and Intuit have transitioned from selling their software as a product to offering it as a subscription service.

The abundance of collaborative platforms that do not require complex setup and can be easily integrated into a company's operations has contributed to the growing tendency of many companies to outsource the aspects of their business where scalability can lead to significant cost savings and specialized expertise is rather difficult to acquire. The proliferation of such value-sharing models is further encouraged by the increasing complexity of the marketplace and the need for closer integration of different players in the value-delivery chain. Value-driven collaborator networks are becoming the modus operandi of forward-looking, market-savvy companies.

From Static to Real-Time Targeting

With the advancement of online communications, the shift from mass marketing to developing customer-specific offerings has been one of the predominant marketing trends. The unprecedented growth of online communications in the past years not only has accelerated this trend but also has markedly enhanced a company's ability to identify its target customers. This fundamental change stems in part from the ability of search engines like Google, social networking sites like Facebook, and retailers like Amazon to provide insights into customer needs and to link these needs with the profile of a particular customer. The ability to directly reach customers is revolutionizing the way companies identify their customers, enabling them to tailor their marketing strategies to the needs of individual customers.

With an increasing number of individuals always online with their smartphones, tablets, or wearable devices, companies have been able to gain deep insights into consumers' preferences, choices, and behaviors and reach them across different channels. This level of addressability emanates to a large degree from the advances in geolocation that enable companies to gain a better understanding of the needs and behaviors of their customers. Using geolocation and predictive analytics, companies are able to reach their target customers with customized messages and offers based on their current needs and physical location.

The ability to gain deeper insight into customers' minds and to reach customers at different points in their decision process have enabled marketers to look beyond individual interactions with customers to managing their entire experience with the company's offerings. This runs the gamut from creating awareness of the company's offering to creating a preference, facilitating purchase, promoting usage, and encouraging customers to repurchase the offering. Understanding and managing the decision journeys of each and every customer has become the new mantra of creating market value.

From Stand-Alone Offerings to Customer Ecosystems

With technology permeating all aspects of our lives, compatibility has become a primary concern for consumers and businesses alike. As a result, the focus has shifted from developing individual products designed to meet customer needs to developing product platforms that function as customer ecosystems, ensuring seamless functionality between diverse sets of offerings.

Consider Apple's ecosystem, which offers unique compatibility across a portfolio of offerings that not only enhances product functionality but also keeps competitors from making inroads into Apple's customers. In fact, Apple has been strategically proactive in building its ecosystem. Following the introduction of the iPhone, it opened its software platform to enable independent software developers to create a variety of applications that enhance the iPhone's functionality, thus creating switching costs for customers considering leaving its ecosystem.

Examples of customer ecosystems are abundant. Think of companies like Amazon, Microsoft, Google, Alibaba, and Tencent that over time have evolved their flagship offerings into ecosystem-driven business models. By serving as hubs within networks of customers, suppliers, and producers of complementary offerings, ecosystems enable companies to create seamless product integration that translates into a streamlined and immersive customer experience. By creating superior value for customers across multiple offerings, ecosystems make it more difficult for customers to switch brands, thus fostering customer loyalty and creating value for the company. As a result, a growing number of companies are moving beyond developing individual offerings to creating sustainable product ecosystems.

From Rigid Processes to Agile Systems

Marketing has evolved not only in substance but also in the speed with which companies are able to react to changes in the environment. The era of static designs and prices is over, giving way to dynamic models in which products and prices are constantly evolving based on up-to-the-minute supply and demand. Taking advantage of the latest technological innovations, product development cycles have been dramatically compressed, leading to new production, promotion, and distribution models.

Agility is the ability of a company to reinvent itself and adapt to an uncertain and rapidly changing environment. Agility does not imply lack of stability. On the contrary, agility requires a stable foundation that does not change over time. Building on this foundation, agility allows dynamic adaptability of the company's business model to changes in the market environment. And while agility is innate for startup companies, established organizations with established legacy systems can find it difficult to remain agile. Yet, these companies often can benefit the most from retaining agility in order to avoid having their market success disrupted by more agile competitors.

Consider Airbnb, the online vacation rental marketplace. Before the pandemic, it concentrated on adding hotels to its platform, focusing largely on densely populated urban areas. Several months into the pandemic, the company observed an uptick in reservations in areas that were within driving distance of the guest's location. Based on this insight, Airbnb modified its recommendation algorithm and began to promote predominantly local stays. This timely pivot enabled the company to reverse its declining revenue trend by attracting and creating new experiences for a different type of customer.

Rapidly evolving market realities call for flexible business models that enable the company to adjust its value-creation processes to the changes in its target markets. As market dynamics constantly accelerate, agility—both in terms of business processes and managerial decision making—has become a crucial aspect of a company's marketing activities and an essential ingredient in its future success.

From "Gut Feel" to Data-Driven Marketing

Today's marketing is data intensive. Companies have access to endless amounts of data about their current and potential customers. They also have an ever-increasing arsenal of tools at their disposal to analyze the available data, and can take advantage of the sophisticated techniques developed to measure the effectiveness of their marketing campaigns. This mandates that managers not only need to know marketing theory but also need to be able to identify, procure, and analyze the relevant data. This need has made data analytics an integral part of marketing.

Data guide key business decisions and offer metrics for tracking the success of the company's marketing activities. Data-driven decision making can facilitate a more accurate measurement of the effectiveness and cost efficiency of the company's marketing actions, providing ever higher levels of transparency and accountability for marketing actions. This increased level of transparency helps shift the conventional view of considering marketing expenses as a cost to considering them as an investment in the company's future.

An important aspect of data-driven decision making is experimentation. Conducting meaningful experiments is crucial in today's complex environment because experimentation is the most effective way to establish a causal relationship between the company's actions and the actual market outcomes. Amazon designs and runs thousands of experiments every day, varying virtually all aspects of its offerings: the location of the items, their description, the availability and the magnitude of sales promotions, cross-promotions, and price. Even though larger companies are often more likely to conduct experiments, experimentation is not restricted to large companies with vast marketing resources such as Amazon. The advancement of digital technologies and online retailing has made experimentation much easier, faster, and cost efficient. As companies realize the importance of experimentation, it is becoming the norm rather than the exception.

From Human Decision Making to Artificial Intelligence Algorithms

Many decisions that used to be made by managers are now made by artificial intelligence and data-driven algorithms. Artificial intelligence's automated judgment and decision making based on self-guided and constantly improving processing helps sift through vast amounts of diverse customer data in real time. It can also anticipate customers' future behaviors along with changes in the marketing environment in which the company operates.

Many of the tactical functions that used to be performed by marketing managers—such as designing different versions of an advertising campaign for different markets, purchasing the media, and allocating the ads across different media channels to ensure that they target the right audience—are typically done using sophisticated algorithms that are faster, more effective, and more cost efficient than the managers they are replacing.

Increased reliance on artificial intelligence requires that managers have a working knowledge of the capabilities of artificial intelligence and machine learning to ensure the seamless implementation of the selected strategy. Thus, even though the role of marketing managers is increasingly strategic, focusing on fundamental questions such as identifying target markets and developing value propositions for these markets, they must understand the key principles, capabilities, and limitations of artificial intelligence algorithms in order to design a viable strategy and effectively carry it out.

As more companies realize that they can increase revenue and reduce costs by acting on data faster and with greater precision, artificial intelligence is gaining ground in the business world. Its ability to process staggering amounts of data in real time gives artificial intelligence a prominent position in managers' toolkits, helping them gain a better understanding of the market, identify the key alternatives, compare the likely outcomes of different strategies, and streamline managerial decision making.

From Hands-On Implementation to Marketing Automation

Marketing automation involves a set of tools designed to streamline the implementation of well-defined marketing tasks by delegating tasks typically done by humans to computer algorithms. In its most basic form, marketing automation is guided by predefined algorithms that provide a set of instructions telling a machine what to do to produce a desired outcome. More advanced forms of marketing automation rely on artificial intelligence in which machine learning enables the algorithm to constantly improve performance on a given task without the need for further programming.

Marketing automation is permeating all aspects of marketing, from using individual consumer data to set customized dynamic prices to creating real-time sales promotions based on geolocation information. Marketing automation is increasingly used to manage the customer experience, with chatbots using voice-recognition software enhanced with sentiment analysis to provide intuitive, responsive, and dynamic one-on-one interaction. Automation is also gaining ground in different aspects of designing and managing marketing communication, real-time content creation and personalization, dynamic targeting across diverse media platforms, selection of the optimal media, and measurements of advertising effectiveness.

Consider, for example how *The Washington Post* (owned by Amazon's Jeff Bezos) utilizes artificial intelligence to generate and manage its content and grow its customer base. In partnership with Google, the newspaper developed an algorithm to customize its online content based on individual profiles of its readers in order to attract new readers and retain existing ones. Its Heliograph algorithm can write article content in cases containing structured data, such as election results, sports scores, and corporate earnings reports. The ModBot algorithm moderates online user comments received by the newspaper, and a ViralityBot algorithm predicts the likelihood that a given story will go viral, which is then used to decide how to promote this story.

From Profits to Purpose

Consumers are becoming increasingly concerned about societal issues and are voting with their wallets for products and brands that conduct their business in a socially responsible way. In the same vein, the company employees, business partners, and investors are becoming increasingly cognizant about the social impact of companies. As a result, companies are experiencing mounting pressure to reevaluate their role in society.

Responding to the rising importance of social responsibility, companies are increasingly looking beyond sales revenue and profit to consider the legal, ethical, social, and environmental effects of marketing activities and programs. When Ben Cohen and Jerry Greenfield founded Ben & Jerry's, they divided the traditional financial bottom line into a "double bottom line" that also measured the environmental impact of their products and processes. That later expanded into a "triple bottom line"—people, planet, and profits—to reflect the societal impact of the firm's entire range of business activities.

An increasing number of companies, including Warby Parker, Bombas, and Kind, have managed to blend social responsibility initiatives with their profit-focused activities. In fact, many of the foremost companies in the world have already committed to abide by high standards of business and marketing conduct that dictate serving the interests of society in addition to their bottom line. For these companies, corporate social responsibility is a central principle guiding all business activities, including the ways in which a company sources, produces, and distributes its products, as well as ways in which it interacts with its customers, collaborators, employees, and stakeholders.

Conclusion

The marketing trends outlined in this chapter are substantive in nature and have a profound impact on companies' marketing actions. Never before have there been so many fundamental changes in the market environment, business models, and marketing strategies in such a short period of time. These rapid developments are forcing many managers to play catch-up to remain in step with the technological, social, and regulatory changes and the rapidly evolving competition.

Along with changes come opportunities. Managers who are able to correctly identify the key business trends and develop strategies that take advantage of them will enjoy market success. Those who develop their strategies by looking in the rearview mirror and relying on decades-old business strategies in the belief that their company is immune to the ongoing global changes will slowly but surely fade into oblivion.

To paraphrase a popular saying: *When it comes to the future, there are three kinds of people: those who make it happen, those who let it happen, and those who wonder what happened.* Understanding the key marketing trends that have emerged from recent changes in the business environment is the first step toward building a successful and sustainable business and making the future happen.

Author Biographies

Alexander Chernev is a professor of marketing at the Kellogg School of Management at Northwestern University. He holds a PhD in psychology from Sofia University and a PhD in Marketing from Duke University. Dr. Chernev has been ranked among the top ten most prolific scholars in the leading marketing journals and serves as an area editor and on the editorial boards of many leading research journals. He teaches marketing strategy, brand management, and behavioral science and has received numerous teaching awards, including the Top Professor Award from the Executive MBA Program, which he has received fourteen times. Dr. Chernev has written numerous textbooks on the topics of marketing strategy, brand management, and behavioral science, and has worked with Fortune 500 companies to reinvent their business models, build strong brands, and gain competitive advantage.

Philip Kotler is the S. C. Johnson & Son Distinguished Professor of International Marketing (emeritus) at the Kellogg School of Management at Northwestern University. He received his master's degree from the University of Chicago and a PhD from MIT, both in economics. Regarded as "The Father of Modern Marketing," Dr. Kotler is one of the world's preeminent marketing authorities, and his co-authored book, *Marketing Management*, now in its 16th edition, is the world's leading textbook in marketing. Dr. Kotler has published 90 books and has received numerous awards, including 22 honorary degrees from abroad. He has consulted with major companies and has taught extensively abroad. Dr. Kotler has been a member of the Advisory Board of the Drucker Foundation and the Board of Trustees of the School of the Art Institute of Chicago.

CHAPTER 2

The Fall of the Four Ps and the Rise of Strategic Marketing

Alexander Chernev and Philip Kotler

As a fundamental business discipline, marketing for many years has been lacking a clear strategic foundation to provide managers with an overarching rationale to guide their marketing actions. Instead, the scope of marketing has been relatively narrow, focusing on issues that are tactical in nature without necessarily considering their underlying strategic purpose. As a result, managers often think of marketing in terms of the four Ps—the four attributes that define the company's offering—without addressing the issue of whether and how these attributes will create value in the market in which the company aims to compete. In this chapter, we suggest that this is a rather myopic view of marketing and advance a strategic approach to marketing management that should guide all of a company's market actions.[1]

The Four Ps and the Seven Ts

One of the key concepts in marketing is that of the *marketing mix*, which refers to the attributes defining a company's offering. The term "marketing mix" stems from the notion that when creating a company's offering, a manager is faced with several key decisions that determine this offering's success or failure in the market. This view is based on the belief that there are several main types of marketing variables defining a company's offering and that a manager's role is to create the perfect combination of these variables that will appeal to the company's target customers.

The concept of the marketing mix was developed in conjunction with identifying the key managerial decisions that define a company's offering. An early conceptualization of the marketing mix, which over time became the prevalent approach to defining an offering's tactics, is the 4-P framework, introduced by Jerome McCarthy in the 1960s.[2] This framework identifies four key decisions that managers must make with respect to a given offering: (1) what features to include in the *product*, (2) how to *price* the product, (3) how to *promote* the product, and (4) in which retail outlets to *place* the product. These four decisions are captured by the four Ps: product, price, promotion, and place (Figure 2.1).

The 4-P framework is simple, intuitive, and easy to remember—factors that have contributed to its popularity. Despite its simplicity, the 4-P framework has a number of limitations that significantly limit its relevance in the contemporary business environment. One such limitation is that it does not distinguish between the product and service aspects of the offering. The fact that the 4-P framework does not explicitly account for the *service* element of the offering is a key drawback in today's service-oriented business environment in which a growing number of companies are switching from a product-based to a service-based business model.

Another important limitation of the 4-P framework is that the *brand* is not defined as a separate factor and instead is viewed as part of the product. The product and brand are different aspects of the offering and can exist independently of each other. An increasing number of companies such as Lacoste, Prada, and Disney outsource their product manufacturing in order to focus their efforts on building and managing their brands.

The 4-P framework also comes up short in defining the term *promotion*. Promotion is a broad concept that includes two distinct types of activities: *incentives*, such as price promotions, coupons, and trade promotions; and *communication*, such as advertising, public relations, social media, and personal selling. Each of these two activities has a distinct role in the value-creation process. Incentives enhance the offering's value, whereas communication informs customers about the offering without necessarily enhancing

FIGURE 2.1   The 4-P Framework

its value. Using a single term to refer to these distinct activities muddles the unique role that they play in creating market value.

The limitations of the 4-P framework can be overcome by defining the market offering in terms of seven, rather than four, attributes: product, service, brand, price, incentives, communication, and distribution. These seven attributes reflect the combination of specific activities employed to execute the offering's strategy and are the tools that managers have at their disposal to create market value (Figure 2.2).

The ultimate goal of a company's offerings is to create value in the markets in which it chooses to compete. Yet, there is no single button that managers can press or a lever they can pull to create market value. Instead, value is created by a combination of factors—the marketing mix—that ultimately determine the value that the company offering will create for its target customers. The seven attributes that define the market offering can be defined as follows:

1. The *product* aspect of an offering reflects the benefits of the good with which the company aims to create market value. Products can be both tangible (e.g., food, apparel, and automobiles) and intangible (e.g., software, music, and video). Products typically entitle customers to permanent rights to the acquired good. For example, a customer purchasing a car or a software program takes ownership of the acquired product.

2. The *service* aspect of an offering reflects the benefits of the good with which the company aims to create value for its customers without entitling them to permanent ownership of this good (e.g., movie rental, appliance repairs, medical procedures, and tax preparation). The service aspect of the offering is closely related to its product aspect such that some offerings might be positioned as either a product or a service. For example, a software can be offered as a product, with customers purchasing the rights to a copy of the program, or as a service, with customers renting the program to temporarily receive its benefits. Many offerings involve both product and service components. For example, a mobile phone offering includes a product component—the physical device that

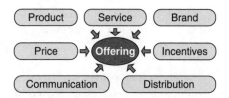

FIGURE 2.2   The 7-T Framework: The Seven Tactics Defining a Company's Offering
Source: Alexander Chernev, *Strategic Marketing Management: Theory and Practice* (Chicago, IL: Cerebellum Press, 2019).

customers acquire—as well as a service component that includes wireless connectivity and device repairs.

3. The *brand* is a marketing tool that informs customers about the source of the products and services associated with the brand. The brand helps identify the company's products and services, differentiate them from the competition, and create unique value beyond the product and service aspects of the offering. For example, the Harley-Davidson brand identifies its motorcycles; differentiates these motorcycles from those made by Honda, Kawasaki, and Yamaha; and elicits a distinct emotional reaction from its customers, who rely on the Harley-Davidson's brand to express their personality.

4. The *price* is the amount of money the company charges its customers and collaborators for the benefits provided by the offering.

5. *Incentives* are tools that enhance the value of the offering by reducing its costs and/or by increasing its benefits. Common incentives include volume discounts, price reductions, coupons, rebates, premiums, bonus offerings, contests, and rewards. Incentives can be offered to individual customers, the company's collaborators (e.g., channel partners), and the company's employees.

6. *Communication* informs the relevant market entities—target customers, collaborators, and the company's employees and stakeholders—about the specifics of the offering.

7. *Distribution* defines the channel(s) used to deliver the offering to target customers and the company's collaborators.

For example, in the case of Apple's iPhone, the *product* is the actual phone, defined by its physical characteristics and functionality. The *service* is the wireless connectivity provided by the telecommunications companies as well as the assistance offered by Apple in using and repairing the phone. The *brand* is the iPhone identity marks (e.g., its name and logo) as well as the associations that it evokes in people's minds. The *price* is the amount of money Apple charges for the iPhone. *Incentives* are the promotional tools such as temporary price reductions that provide additional value for iPhone customers. *Communication* is the information conveyed by press conferences, media coverage, and advertisements that inform the public about the iPhone. *Distribution* encompasses the channels—Apple's own stores and authorized resellers—that make the iPhone available to the public.

We refer to this view of the marketing mix as the *7-T framework*, as it defines the *seven marketing tactics* delineating the company's offering. The 7-T framework can be viewed as the current and more comprehensive version of the 4-P approach, which affords managers greater precision when

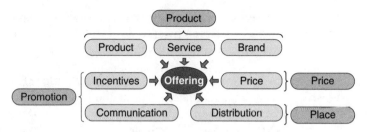

FIGURE 2.3   The Seven Ts and the Four Ps
Source: Alexander Chernev, *Strategic Marketing Management: Theory and Practice* (Chicago, IL: Cerebellum Press, 2019).

designing their offerings. In fact, the four Ps can be easily mapped onto the seven attributes defining the market offering, whereby the first P comprises product, service, and brand; price is the second P; incentives and communication are the third P; and distribution is the fourth P (Figure 2.3).

The fact that the four Ps do not explicitly include some of the key attributes defining the company offering is not the biggest challenge with the 4-P framework. A much larger concern is that managers tend to use this framework without having an overarching strategy and without a clear vision of how their offerings will create value in the market in which they aim to compete. This myopic approach is problematic because without a meaningful value-creation strategy to guide the development of the company's offering, market success is difficult to achieve. A company's tactical activities should always be guided by a sound marketing strategy.

From Tactical Marketing to Strategic Value Management

A company's success is determined by its ability to create value in its chosen market.[3] To create value for its customers, a company must clearly identify the target market in which it will compete, develop a meaningful set of benefits for its customers, and design an offering that will deliver these benefits to the target market. These activities define the two key components of a company's actions: strategy and tactics.

Marketing strategy articulates the logic of the value-creation process. Strategy guides tactical decisions to ensure that the company's offering creates value in the market in which it aims to compete. Without a clearly articulated strategy, an offering cannot reliably create market value. *Marketing tactics*, on the other hand, define the specific attributes describing the actual good that the company deploys to fulfill a particular customer need. Whereas a company's strategy defines the *value* a company seeks to create for its customers, tactics determine the specific *offering* that will deliver the value outlined in the strategy.

A company's strategy is invisible, meaning that it is not readily observable by its customers and competitors. Strategy reflects the way in which a company views a particular market: which customers it decides to target, which companies it chooses to collaborate and compete with, and the way in which it aims to create superior value for its customers. In contrast, a company's tactics can be readily observed: its customers (as well as its competitors and collaborators) can readily observe a company's products, services, and brands; the price that it charges for its products and services; the sales promotions it provides; its communication campaigns; as well as the distribution channels that carry the company's offerings.

The concepts of strategy and tactics are not particular to marketing; they have a long history that stems from military planning. The term *strategy* comes from the Greek *stratēgía* (meaning "generalship"), which was used in reference to maneuvering troops into position before a battle. Likewise, the term *tactics* comes from the Greek τακτική (meaning "arrangement"), which was used in reference to the deployment of troops during battle from their initial strategic position. The same way in which military strategy involves positioning the troops, marketing strategy focuses on identifying the market (the battlefield) in which it will compete and the way in which it will create market value (the positioning). And the same way military tactics involve deploying the troops into the battle, marketing tactics reflect the way the company will make this strategy a reality by arranging the attributes of its market offering. Thus, not unlike the way military success is determined by the soundness of the strategic vision and the degree to which the tactical actions reflect this vision, marketing success is determined by a company's vision of the value it must create in the market and the degree to which its tactics logically follow from this strategic vision.

The invisible nature of the marketing strategy is, in part, the reason why it is often ignored by many managers, who jump to decisions related to the specific attributes defining the company's offering without carefully considering the strategic impact of these decisions. The problem with this approach is that without understanding customers' needs and the value that the offering can provide to these customers, it is impossible to create an offering that will succeed in creating superior value for these customers. Strategy aims to identify market opportunities to create value and define a value proposition to take advantage of these opportunities.

To be effective, strategy requires trade-offs. This is because selecting a particular course of action inevitably requires rejecting alternative action paths. In marketing, the key strategic trade-offs involve the choice of target customers and the development of a value proposition for these customers.

Deciding to target a particular set of customers means ignoring other customers. Likewise, selecting a particular value proposition for target customers implies rejecting alternative ways to create customer value. Failure to make strategic trade-offs is likely to lead to confusion when articulating the tactics that aim to make this strategy a reality.

One of the most common strategic decisions that require managers to make trade-offs is the choice of target customers. Deciding which customers to target and which to ignore is important because it defines all other aspects of the company's actions. In this context, a common problem when selecting target customers is managers' reluctance to narrow down the segment by explicitly identifying customers whom the company will not target. Many companies have failed because they were unwilling to sacrifice market breadth to focus only on those customers for whom their offering can create superior value. Thus, the development of a viable marketing strategy involves identifying not only customers that the company aims to serve but also those it chooses deliberately *not* to serve.

Inability to make the strategic decision to ignore certain potential customers typically leads to targeting customer segments that are heterogeneous, meaning that customers vary in their needs and preferences. This customer heterogeneity has a direct impact on the *degrees of freedom* that the company has when developing its offerings for this market. The more homogeneous (uniform) a given customer segment is, the fewer degrees of freedom a manager has in designing an offering for this segment. Conversely, the presence of multiple degrees of freedom during development of an offering typically stems from the fact that the company's target market is composed of customers with diverse needs and preferences.

To illustrate, when deciding on an offering's price, if there are valid reasons to set both a low price (so that the offering is affordable for some customers) and a high price (because some customers are not price sensitive), this indicates that the target market is heterogeneous and comprises customers that vary in price sensitivity. Likewise, if when designing the product an argument can be made in favor of developing both a simple version (for customers who seek basic functionality) and a more complex version (for advanced users), it is likely that the target market contains customers with different needs who require different offerings.

In this context, marketing strategy can be viewed as a process of reducing of the degrees of freedom of the marketing tactics. The presence of multiple degrees of freedom when developing the company's offering suggests that the underlying strategy is unfocused, such that the target market consists of customers with diverse needs and preferences. To address this, managers must further narrow down the target market by focusing on some customers while excluding others. A meaningful targeting is achieved when there is little or no ambiguity (and, hence, few degrees of freedom) regarding the benefits sought by customers in this segment.

Creating Customer Value

Customer value is the worth of an offering to its customers; it is customers' assessment of the degree to which an offering fulfills their needs. The value an offering creates for its customers is determined by three main factors: (1) the needs of these customers, (2) the attributes of the company's offering, and (3) the attributes of the competitive offerings these customers can use to fulfill their needs. To create customer value, an offering should be able to fulfill the needs of its target customers. And to create *superior* customer value, this offering should be able to fulfill customer needs better than the competitive offerings (Figure 2.4).

A company's ability to create customer value is defined by the answers to three key questions:

1. *What need does the offering aim to fulfill? What is the profile of the customers with this need?*

2. *What are target customers currently doing or considering doing to fulfill this need?*

3. *Why would these customers change their behavior and choose the company's offering?*

The first set of questions identifies the company's *target customers*. Understanding customer needs is important because to create customer value a company must design an offering that fulfills target customers' needs. Identifying the profile of these customers—their demographics, psychographics, and behaviors—is important so that the company can reach these customers in an effective and cost-efficient manner. Clearly identifying the customers for whom the company will optimize its offering, as well as those whose needs the company is not going to address, is the cornerstone of developing a sound marketing strategy.

The second question identifies the company's *competitors*—that is, the means that target customers can use to fulfill the focal need. Competitive

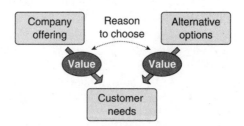

FIGURE 2.4 The Framework for Creating Superior Customer Value
Source: Alexander Chernev, *Strategic Marketing Management: Theory and Practice* (Chicago, IL: Cerebellum Press, 2019).

offerings do not have to be from companies in the same industry; any offering that can fulfill the same need of the same customers is likely to be a competitor, regardless of the industry from which it comes. Furthermore, competitors are not only offerings created by commercial enterprises; any makeshift means that customers use to fulfill their needs is a de facto competitor to the company's offering. This is because to start using the company's offering, customers will have to eventually give up their current means of fulfilling the focal need.

The third question identifies the company's *value proposition*—that is, the reason why customers will change their behavior and choose the company's offering over the current means they use to fulfill the focal need. Providing customers with a reason to change their behavior is important because of the inertia involved in the way customers think and act. Without a compelling reason to choose the company's offering, customers are unlikely to change their behavior, and without a change in customers' behavior the company's offering cannot gain market share. Thus, the company's offering must not only be able to meet customers' needs but it also should have a clearly articulated value proposition that is superior to the value they are receiving from the alternative means they are using to fulfill that need.

A company can create customer value on three dimensions: *functional, psychological*, and *monetary*. Understanding the key value drivers on each of these dimensions and prioritizing these dimensions in terms of their relative importance to target customers is essential for ensuring the market success of the company's offering. These three value dimensions are illustrated in Figure 2.5 and outlined below.

1. *Functional value* reflects the benefits and costs directly related to an offering's practical utility such as performance, reliability, durability, compatibility, and ease of use. The functional value of an offering is given by the answer to the question: *How does the offering's functionality create value for target customers?*

2. *Psychological value* reflects the mental benefits and costs of the offering, such as the emotional experience provided by the offering and the

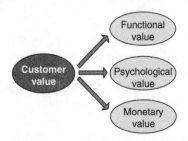

FIGURE 2.5   The Three Dimensions of Customer Value
Source: Alexander Chernev, *Strategic Marketing Management: Theory and Practice* (Chicago, IL: Cerebellum Press, 2019).

offering's ability to signal a customer's social status and personality. The psychological value of an offering is given by the answer to questions: *How do target customers feel about the offering? What signal does the offering send about these customers' self-identity?*

3. *Monetary value* reflects the financial benefits and costs of the offering, such as its price, fees, discounts, and rebates, as well as the various monetary costs associated with using, maintaining, and disposing of the offering. The monetary value of an offering is given by the answer to the question: *What is the monetary impact of the offering on target customers?*

Consider, for example, the customer value created by Apple's iPhone. The *functional value* of the iPhone is defined by its mobile connectivity; its ability to make phone calls, send text messages, and take pictures; and the benefits offered by millions of productivity and entertainment apps. Its *psychological value* stems from the satisfaction of using an aesthetically pleasing device, from peace of mind that the iPhone will function as described, and from the iPhone's ability to convey one's personality and social status. Finally, the iPhone's *monetary value* is defined by its price and any available promotional incentives.

The three dimensions of customer value are not universally positive. Because value stems from both benefits and costs, on a particular dimension costs might outweigh the benefits. In most cases, the functional value and psychological value, which reflect the core benefits of the offering, are positive, whereas the monetary value, which involves the price paid by consumers for the offering, is negative. To create customer value, the benefits across all three dimensions should outweigh the corresponding costs.

Marketing as a Process of Designing, Communicating, and Delivering Value

The value-based approach to marketing implies that a company's actions should be directly related to this company's ability to create value for its target customers. In this context, the seven marketing tactics—product, service, brand, price, incentives, communication, and distribution—can be viewed as a process of *designing, communicating,* and *delivering* customer value. Here, the product, service, brand, price, and incentives are the aspects of the offering that define its value; communication is the process of communicating the offering's value; and distribution is the value-delivery aspect of the offering (Figure 2.6).

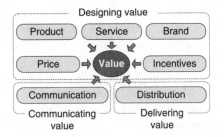

FIGURE 2.6   Marketing as a Process of Designing, Communicating, and Delivering
Customer Value
Source: Alexander Chernev, *Strategic Marketing Management: Theory and Practice* (Chicago, IL:
Cerebellum Press, 2019).

Because they define the key benefits and costs, the product, service,
brand, price, and incentives are the *key value drivers* of the offering. Specifically, the product, service, and brand aspects of the company's offering
are the key source of customer benefits and the reason customers buy the
company's offering. The price, on the other hand, reflects the monetary cost
associated with the offering. Finally, incentives modify the value created by
the offering, with price discounts, coupons, and rebates aiming to lower the
monetary costs of the offering and bonus offerings aiming to increase the
offering's benefits.

Communication and distribution, on the other hand, are the *channels*
through which the benefits created by the first five attributes are communicated and delivered to target customers. Thus, communication informs customers about the functionality of a product or service, builds the image of its
brand, publicizes its price, apprises buyers of sales promotions, and advises
them about the availability of the offering. Likewise, distribution delivers a
company's products and services, delivers customer payments to the company, and delivers the offering's promotional incentives to customers and collaborators.

Consider, for example, the way in which Apple's iPhone creates customer
value. The *value-design* component of this Apple offering involves development of the actual product (the iPhone) and service (Apple's own service and
that of the wireless carriers), the creation of the iPhone brand (crafting the
iPhone name, designing the logo, and defining the image that Apple wants
to be associated with the iPhone in people's minds), setting the price, and
deciding on the type of incentives to use to promote customer demand. The
value-communication component of the iPhone involves communicating the
features and benefits of the phone and the related services, communicating
the elements of the iPhone brand, as well as informing customers about the
iPhone price and incentives. Finally, the *value-delivery* aspect of the iPhone

involves physically delivering the phone to buyers, servicing the phone, delivering the brand-related information, collecting payments, and delivering the incentives.

So far, we have discussed the value-creation process from a company's viewpoint, whereby the company aims to design, communicate, and deliver value to its target customers. In addition to defining the value-creation process from a company's perspective, managers can also benefit from evaluating the impact that the company's actions have on its target customers. In this context, the company's ability to create customer value can be described in terms of *attractiveness, awareness,* and *availability* of its offering. Here, attractiveness reflects the value—benefits and cost—that the offering creates for target customers; awareness reflects the extent to which customers are aware of the offering and its benefits and costs; and availability reflects the degree to which the offering is accessible to customers.

Thus, from a customers' perspective, an offering's ability to create value is determined by the answers to the following three questions: *Is the offering attractive to target customers? Are target customers aware of the offering? Are target customers able to acquire the offering?* The answer to the first question outlines the customer benefits and costs associated with the product, service, brand, price, and incentives aspects of the offering. The answer to the second question outlines the way in which the company will communicate the specifics of the offering to its target customers. The answer to the third question outlines the way in which the company will make the offering available to its target customers. Thinking about value creation from a customer's perspective by focusing on the *attractiveness, awareness,* and *availability* of the company's offering can complement the managerial approach of *designing, communicating,* and *delivering* value to target customers.

Conclusion

Marketing is first and foremost a process of designing, communicating, and delivering market value. Therefore, the success of a company's offering is determined by this offering's ability to fulfill customer needs better than the competition and, by doing so, create value for the company and its collaborators. This market value principle should guide all of the company's actions, including the design of the marketing mix, which reflects the combination of attributes defining the company's offering. Without a clearly defined strategy, a company's actions are likely to be ineffective at best and counterproductive at worst. The vital role of strategy in defining tactical decisions is well captured in the words of the Chinese military strategist Sun Tzu: *Tactics without strategy is the noise before defeat.*

Author Biographies

Alexander Chernev is a professor of marketing at the Kellogg School of Management at Northwestern University. He holds a PhD in psychology from Sofia University and a PhD in marketing from Duke University. Dr. Chernev has been ranked among the top ten most prolific scholars in the leading marketing journals and serves as an area editor and on the editorial boards of many leading research journals. He teaches marketing strategy, brand management, and behavioral science and has received numerous teaching awards, including the Top Professor Award from the Executive MBA Program, which he has received fourteen times. Dr. Chernev has written numerous textbooks on the topics of marketing strategy, brand management, and behavioral science, and has worked with Fortune 500 companies to reinvent their business models, build strong brands, and gain competitive advantage.

Philip Kotler is the S. C. Johnson & Son Distinguished Professor of International Marketing (emeritus) at the Kellogg School of Management at Northwestern University. He received his master's degree from the University of Chicago and a PhD from MIT, both in economics. Regarded as "The Father of Modern Marketing," Dr. Kotler is one of the world's preeminent marketing authorities, and his co-authored book, *Marketing Management*, now in its 16th edition, is the world's leading textbook in marketing. Dr. Kotler has published 90 books and has received numerous awards, including 22 honorary degrees from abroad. He has consulted with major companies and has taught extensively abroad. Dr. Kotler has been a member of the Advisory Board of the Drucker Foundation and the Board of Trustees of the School of the Art Institute of Chicago.

CHAPTER 3

The Framework for Marketing Management

Alexander Chernev

Imagine you are a manager in charge of a new offering. Like many other managers in a similar situation, you are faced with a plethora of business decisions. Some of these decisions concern the specifics of the offering—a product or service—that is being readied for market launch. For example:

What features should the new product include?

What services should the company offer?

How should the offering be branded?

At what price should it be offered?

What, if any, sales promotions should it involve?

How will potential customers know about the offering?

How will the offering be delivered to these customers?

Other questions are more general and focus on the market in which this offering will compete and the value it aims to create in that market:

For which customers should the company develop an offering?

Why would these customers buy this offering?

What other offerings are available to these customers?

What resources must the company have to create an offering that fulfills this customer need?

Whom should the company partner with?

How will new technologies influence the ways in which the company creates value for its customers?

How will economic conditions and government regulations influence the company's ability to create a successful market offering?

Overwhelmed by the complexity of some of these questions and by the sheer number of issues to be addressed, many managers tend to ignore such questions, hoping that the answers will emerge naturally over time. They rarely do. In fact, most products fail because managers neglect to consider the relevant issues and address them in a way that will ensure the success of the company's offering. What many failed products are missing is a sound business model and an action plan that clearly delineates how the company's offering will create value in its chosen market.

A practical way to ensure that managers consider all relevant issues when managing their offerings is to use a systematic approach, or a framework, to guide their decisions and actions. Frameworks can benefit managerial decision making in several ways. By helping identify alternative ways of thinking about the decision task, frameworks provide managers with a better understanding of the problem they aim to address. In addition to helping formulate the problem, frameworks provide a generalized approach to identifying alternative solutions. Frameworks further help organizations by providing a shared vocabulary with which to discuss the issues, thus streamlining communication among managers involved in the decision process.

Marketing frameworks build on already existing generalized knowledge to facilitate future company-specific decisions. Thus, by relying on the aggregated business knowledge captured in frameworks, a manager can sidestep the trial-and-error-based learning process. This chapter outlines an overarching marketing framework that can help managers develop viable value-creation models and design actionable marketing plans that produce results.[1]

The G-STIC Framework for Marketing Management

A company's future hinges on its ability to develop successful market offerings that create superior value for target customers, the company, and its collaborators. Market success is rarely an accident; it is typically a result of diligent market analysis, planning, and management. To succeed in the market, a company must have a viable business model and an action plan to make this model a reality. The process of developing such a business model and an action plan is facilitated by the G-STIC framework outlined below.

The G-STIC framework is based on the notion that to achieve market success, a company must have a well-articulated marketing plan that delineates the goal that the company aims to achieve and a course of action to reach this goal. This action plan is defined by five key activities: setting a *goal*, developing a *strategy*, designing the *tactics*, defining an *implementation* plan, and identifying a set of *control* metrics to measure the success of the proposed action. These five activities compose the G-STIC framework, which is the cornerstone of strategic marketing management. The individual components of the G-STIC framework and the relationship among them are depicted in Figure 3.1 and summarized below.

- The *goal* identifies the ultimate criterion for success; it is the result that a company aims to achieve. The goal has two components: the focus, which defines the metric delineating the desired outcome of the company's actions, and the performance benchmarks quantifying the goal and defining the time frame for it to be accomplished.
- The *strategy* defines the value that the company aims to create in the target market. A company's strategy is defined by its target market and its value proposition in this market. The strategy is the backbone of the company's business model.
- *Tactics* define the attributes of the company's offering, namely its product, service, brand, price, incentives, communication, and distribution. These seven tactics are the tools that the company uses to create value in the chosen market. The tactics are the actionable component of the company's business model.
- *Implementation* defines the processes involved in creating the market offering. Implementation includes developing the offering and deploying the offering in the target market.

FIGURE 3.1   The G-STIC Framework for Marketing Management
Source: Alexander Chernev, *Strategic Marketing Management: Theory and Practice* (Chicago, IL: Cerebellum Press, 2019).

- *Control* provides mechanisms for safeguarding that the company is on the right track for achieving its goal. The control component of the action plan involves evaluating the company's performance and monitoring the changes in the market environment in which the company operates.

By defining the key elements of a company's marketing planning process and outlining a logical sequence of organizing these elements, the G-STIC framework offers an intuitive approach to streamlining a company's activities into a logical sequence that aims to produce the desired market outcome. The individual components of the G-STIC framework are addressed in more detail in the following sections.

The discussion of the G-STIC framework is organized into three main sections. First, we discuss the process of setting a company's *goal* and address the focus and the benchmarks associated with the goal, as well as the specific market objectives involved in achieving this goal. Next, we discuss the company's business model—that is, the *strategy* and *tactics* that the company employs to achieve this goal. Specifically, we focus on the ways in which the company aims to create value in the market in which it will compete and articulate the market value principle that must guide all of the company's actions. Finally, we discuss the ways in which the company aims to *implement* its strategy and tactics, and the way in which it will *control* this implementation by monitoring the company's performance and the changes in the market in which it competes.

Setting the Goal

The development of an action plan starts with defining the goal that the company aims to achieve. This goal then becomes the beacon that guides all company activities. Without a well-defined goal, a company cannot design a meaningful course of action and evaluate its success. The importance of having a clear goal is captured in the words of the English mathematician and author of *Alice's Adventures in Wonderland*, Lewis Carroll: *If you don't know where you're going, any road will get you there.* This insight is also relevant in business: Without a set goal, a company is like a ship without a rudder.

Defining the Goal Focus and Performance Benchmarks

Setting a goal involves two key decisions: identifying the focus of the company's actions and defining the performance benchmarks to be achieved.

The *focus* identifies the key criterion for a company's success; it is the metric defining the desired outcome of the company's activities. Based on their focus, goals can be monetary or strategic. *Monetary goals* involve monetary outcomes such as net income, profit margins, earnings per share, and return on investment. Monetary goals are the primary performance metric in for-profit enterprises. *Strategic goals* involve nonmonetary outcomes that are of strategic importance to the company. Common strategic goals include growing sales volume, creating brand awareness, increasing social welfare, enhancing the corporate culture, and facilitating employee recruitment and retention. Strategic goals are the main performance metric for nonprofit enterprises as well as for offerings of for-profit companies that have the primary function of supporting other, profit-generating offerings.

Monetary goals and strategic goals are not mutually exclusive: A company might aim to achieve certain strategic goals with an otherwise profitable offering, and a strategically important offering might contribute to the company's bottom line. In fact, long-term financial planning must always include a strategic component in addition to setting monetary goals. In the same vein, long-term strategic planning must always include a financial component that articulates how achieving a particular strategic goal will translate into financial benefits.

Performance benchmarks outline the quantitative and temporal criteria for reaching the goal. Consequently, there are two types of performance benchmarks that work in concert to define the company goal. *Quantitative benchmarks* define the specific milestones to be achieved by the company with respect to its focal goal. For example, goals such as "increase market share by 2%," "increase retention rates by 12%," and "achieve annual sales of one million units" involve specific benchmarks that quantify the set goal. *Temporal benchmarks* identify the time frame for achieving a particular milestone. Setting a timeline for achieving a goal is a key decision because the strategy adopted to implement these goals is often contingent on the time horizon. The goal of maximizing the next quarter's profits will likely require a different strategy and tactics than the goal of maximizing long-term profitability.

Overall, the company goal must address three main questions: *what* is to be achieved (goal focus), *how much* should be achieved (quantitative benchmark), and *when* it should be achieved (temporal benchmark). To illustrate, a company might set the goal of generating net income (goal focus) of $50 million (quantitative benchmark) in one year (temporal benchmark). Answers to these questions capture the essence of the company's goal and serve as a beacon that guides the company's strategy and tactics.

Setting Market Objectives

Goals vary in their level of generality. Some goals reflect outcomes that are more fundamental than others. Therefore, a company's goals can be represented as a hierarchy headed by a company's overarching goal, which is implemented through a set of more specific goals referred to as *market objectives.* Unlike the overarching goal, which is typically defined in terms of a company-focused outcome, market objectives delineate specific changes in the behavior of the relevant market factors—customers, collaborators, the company, competitors, and context—that will enable the company to achieve its ultimate goal.

- *Customer objectives* aim to change the behavior of target customers (e.g., increasing purchase frequency, switching from a competitive product, or making a first-time purchase in a product category) in a way that will enable the company to achieve its goal. To illustrate, the company goal of increasing net revenues can be associated with the more specific customer objective of increasing the frequency with which customers repurchase the offering. Because in most cases customers are the main source of a company's revenues and profits, a company's goal typically involves a customer-focused objective.

- *Collaborator objectives* aim to elicit changes in the behavior of the company's collaborators, such as providing greater promotional support, better pricing terms, more seamless systems integration, and extended distribution coverage. To illustrate, the company goal of increasing net revenues can be associated with the more specific collaborator objective of increasing the shelf space available for the offering in distribution channels.

- *Company objectives* aim to elicit changes in the company's own actions, such as improving product and service quality, reducing the cost of goods sold, improving the effectiveness of the company's marketing actions, and streamlining research-and-development costs. For example, the company goal of increasing net revenues can be associated with the more specific internal objective of increasing the effectiveness and cost efficiency of its communication.

- *Competitive objectives* aim to change the behavior of the company's competitors. Such actions might involve creating barriers to entry, securing proprietary access to scarce resources, and circumventing a price war. For example, the company goal of increasing net revenues can be associated with limiting competitors' access to target customers by creating exclusive distribution agreements with retailers serving these markets.

- *Context objectives* are less common and usually implemented by larger companies that have the resources to influence the economic, business, technological, sociocultural, or regulatory context in which the company operates. For example, a company might lobby the government to adopt regulations that will favorably affect the company by offering tax benefits, providing subsidies, and imposing import duties on competitors' products.

Defining market objectives is important because without a change in the behavior of the relevant market entities, the company is unlikely to make progress toward its goal. To illustrate, a company's goal of increasing net income by $100 million by the end of the fourth quarter can involve different objectives. A customer-specific objective might be to increase market share by 10% by the end of the fourth quarter. A collaborator-related objective might involve securing 45% of the distribution outlets by the end of the fourth quarter. And a company's internal objective might call for lowering the cost of goods sold by 25% by the end of the fourth quarter.

Designing the Strategy and Tactics

A company's ability to achieve its goal is determined by the degree to which its offerings can create superior value in the market in which the company aims to compete. The way in which an offering creates value is determined by the company's business model and its two building blocks: strategy and tactics. The key aspects of developing an offering's strategy and designing the tactics are outlined in the following sections.

Designing the Strategy: Defining the Target Market

The target market is the market in which a company aims to create and capture value. The choice of the target market is a crucial decision that can determine the viability of the company's market strategy. The target market is defined by five factors: *customers* whose needs the company aims to fulfill, *competitors* that aim to fulfill the same needs of the same target customers, *collaborators* that work with the company to fulfill customers' needs, the *company* managing the offering, and the *context* in which the company operates. The five market factors are often referred to as the *five Cs*, and the resulting framework is referred to as the *5-C framework* (Figure 3.2).[2]

FIGURE 3.2   Identifying the Target Market: The 5-C Framework
Source: Alexander Chernev, *Strategic Marketing Management: Theory and Practice* (Chicago, IL: Cerebellum Press, 2019).

Target customers are the entities (individuals or organizations) whose needs the company aims to fulfill. Because a key goal of a company's offerings is to create customer value, identifying the right customers is essential for market success. In business-to-consumer markets, target customers are typically the end users of the company's offerings. In business-to-business markets, target customers are other businesses that use the company's offerings. The choice of target customers is determined by two key principles: Target customers should be able to create value for the company and its collaborators; and, vice versa, the company and its collaborators must be able to create superior value for these target customers relative to the competition.

The selection of target customers determines all other aspects of the market: the scope of the competition, potential collaborators, company resources necessary to fulfill customer needs, and the context in which the company will create market value. A change in target customers typically leads to a change in competitors and collaborators, requires different company resources, and is influenced by different context factors. Because of its strategic importance, choosing the right target customers is the key to building a successful marketing strategy.

Competitors are entities that aim to fulfill the same need of the same customers as the company. Because the success of a company's offering hinges on its ability to create superior customer value, identifying the competitive offerings that customers will consider when making a choice is essential to a company's ability to gain and defend its market position. Competitors are defined relative to customer needs rather than the industry within which they operate. For example, digital camera manufacturers do not only compete with one another; they also compete with the manufacturers of smartphones because both digital cameras and smartphones can fulfill the same customer need of capturing a moment in time. By defining competitors based on the customer needs they aim to satisfy rather than a particular category, a company can gain a better understanding of whom their current and future competitors are likely to be.

Collaborators are entities that work with the company to create value for their customers. Common types of collaborators include suppliers, manufacturers, distributors (dealers, wholesalers, and retailers), research-and-development entities, service providers, external sales force, advertising agencies, and marketing research companies. The choice of collaborators is driven by the complementarity of the resources needed to fulfill customer needs. Collaboration involves outsourcing the resources that the company lacks and that are required to fulfill the needs of target customers. Thus, instead of going through the risky and time-consuming task of building or acquiring resources that are lacking, a company can "borrow" them by partnering with entities that have these resources and can benefit from sharing them.

The *company* is the entity that develops and manages a given market offering. The company can be a manufacturer that produces the actual goods being sold, a service provider, an entity engaged in brand building, a media company, or a retailer. A company's motivation and ability to create market value can be defined by two main factors: goals and resources. *Goals* reflect the outcome that the company aims to achieve with a particular offering. Resources, on the other hand, reflect the company's assets and competencies that determine its ability to create market value and a sustainable competitive advantage. A company's resources include factors such as business facilities; suppliers; employees; know-how; existing products, services, and brands; communication and distribution channels; and access to capital.

Context describes the environment in which the company operates. Understanding the context is important because even small changes in the market environment can have major implications for the company's business model. The context is defined by five factors: *sociocultural context*, such as social and demographic trends, value systems, lifestyles, and beliefs; *technological context*, such as new technologies, skills, and processes for developing, communicating, and delivering market offerings; *regulatory context*, such as taxes, tariffs, embargoes, regulations, and intellectual property laws; *economic context*, such as the overall economic activity, inflation, and interest rates; and *physical context*, such as natural resources, climate, and health trends. Unlike the other four Cs—customers, competitors, collaborators, and company—which describe the different market players in the value exchange, the context defines the environment in which the value exchange takes place. Consequently, changes in the context can influence all market participants and the ways in which they create and capture market value.

Designing the Strategy: Defining the Value Proposition

To succeed, a company must create value for three market entities: target customers, the company, and its collaborators. Accordingly, a company must consider all three types of value: customer value, collaborator value, and company value (Figure 3.3). This is the *market value principle:* The company

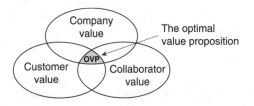

FIGURE 3.3   The Market Value Principle
Source: Alexander Chernev, *Strategic Marketing Management: Theory and Practice* (Chicago, IL: Cerebellum Press, 2019).

must create superior value for its target customers and collaborators in a way that enables it to achieve its goals. All company activities must be guided by this principle. Failure to create superior value for any of these entities inevitably leads to an unsustainable business model and a failure of the business venture.

The market value principle can be visually represented as a Venn diagram, where the intersection of the three types of value defines the optimal value proposition—the scenario in which the company's offering creates value for all relevant entities: the company, its customers, and its collaborators. Offerings creating value that falls outside of the optimal value proposition, meaning that at least one of the relevant entities does not benefit from this offering, are unlikely to enjoy sustainable market success. The three types of value—customer value, collaborator value, and company value—are summarized below.

- *Customer value* is the worth of an offering to its customers; it is customers' assessment of the degree to which an offering fulfills their needs. The value an offering creates for its customers is determined by three main factors: the *needs* of these customers, the intrinsic value created by the company's offering, and the value created by the alternative means (competitive offerings) these customers can use to fulfill their needs. The customer value proposition is given by the answers to the following questions: *What value does the offering create for its target customers? Why would target customers choose this offering? What makes this offering better than the alternative options?*

- *Collaborator value* is the worth of an offering to the company's collaborators; it is the sum of all benefits and costs that an offering creates for collaborators. The collaborator value proposition reflects an offering's ability to fulfill collaborator goals better than the alternative offerings. The collaborator value proposition is given by the answers to the following questions: *What value does the offering create for the company's collaborators? Why would these collaborators partner with the company? What makes the company's offering better than the alternative options available to collaborators?*

- *Company value* is the worth of the offering to the company; it is the totality of all benefits and costs associated with an offering. The value of an offering is defined relative to the company's goals and the other opportunities to achieve these goals available to the company (e.g., alternative offerings in the company's portfolio). The company's value proposition is given by the answers to the following questions: *What value does the offering create for the company? Why should the company invest resources in this offering? What makes this offering superior to the alternative options available to the company?*

The market value principle and the concept of the optimal value proposition can be illustrated by examining the value proposition of the iPhone. Its *customers* receive the functionality and prestige of the iPhone, for which they offer Apple and its collaborators monetary compensation. *Collaborators* (wireless service providers) receive the strategic benefit of associating their service with a product that is in high demand and likely to promote greater usage of wireless services. In return, these collaborators invest resources in making their services compatible with the iPhone. Another set of collaborators (retailers) receives monetary benefit (profits) from selling the iPhone as well as the strategic benefit of carrying a traffic-generating product. Retailers then invest monetary and strategic resources (shelf space, inventory management, and sales force) to ensure that the iPhone is available to its customers. In return for developing, advertising, and distributing the iPhone, the *company* (Apple) receives monetary compensation from consumers purchasing the iPhone as well as the strategic benefit of strengthening its consumer brand and its ecosystem of compatible Apple products.

Another example of developing an optimal value proposition is Starbucks. Its *customers* receive the functional benefit of a variety of coffee beverages as well as the psychological benefit of expressing certain aspects of their personality through the choice of a customized beverage, for which they deliver monetary compensation. Starbucks *collaborators* (coffee growers) receive monetary payments for the coffee beans they provide and the strategic benefit of having a consistent demand for their product, in return for which they invest resources in growing coffee beans that conform to Starbucks' standards. By investing resources in developing and offering its products and services to consumers, the company (Starbucks) derives monetary benefit (revenues and profits) and the strategic benefit of building a consumer brand and enhancing its market footprint and portfolio of offerings.

Defining the Tactics: Developing the Market Offering

Marketing tactics define the company's offering by delineating the specific attributes describing the actual good that the company deploys to fulfill a particular customer need. Whereas a company's strategy determines its target market and the value it seeks to provide to relevant market participants, tactics determine the specific offering that will deliver the value outlined in the strategy. The tactics are the means that managers have at their disposal to execute the offering's strategy and create market value.

A company's offering is defined by seven attributes: product, service, brand, price, incentives, communication, and distribution. These seven attributes, also called the 7-T framework (referring to the seven attributes defining the marketing tactics), can be defined as follows. The *product* and *service* aspects of the offering define the core benefits of the company's offering. The *brand* helps identify the company's offering, differentiate it from the competition, and create unique value beyond the value created by this offering's product and service aspects. The *price* is the amount of money the company charges for the benefits provided by the offering. *Incentives*, such as volume discounts, price reductions, coupons, rebates, premiums, and contests, enhance the value of the offering by reducing its costs and increasing its benefits. *Communication* informs the relevant market entities—target customers, collaborators, and the company's employees and stakeholders—about the specifics of the offering. Finally, *distribution* defines the channels used to deliver the offering to target customers and the company's collaborators.

Consider, for example, the attributes defining Starbucks' offerings. The product is the variety of coffee and other beverages, as well as the selection of food items and coffee accessories. The service is the assistance offered to customers prior to, during, and after purchase, along with the use of its space and amenities. The brand is captured in Starbucks' identity elements, such as its name and logo, as well as the associations these identity elements evoke in customers' minds. The price is the monetary amount that Starbucks charges customers for its offerings. Incentives include Starbucks' loyalty program as well as the coupons and temporary price reductions it uses to provide additional benefits for its customers and, thus, increase its sales. Communication is the information disseminated via different channels—advertising, social media, and mobile communication—informing the public about Starbucks' offerings. Distribution includes the Starbucks-owned stores and Starbucks-licensed retail outlets through which Starbucks' offerings are delivered to its customers. Working in concert, these attributes define the value created by Starbucks' offerings.

A company's strategy and tactics are intricately related. The strategy defines the target market and the value the company aims to create in this market, whereas the tactics define the attributes of the actual offering that creates value in the chosen market. Because tactics logically follow from the company's strategy, they should be designed and evaluated with respect to the market value principle—that is, their ability to create superior value for target customers in a way that benefits the company and its collaborators (Figure 3.4). Without knowing the offering's strategy—whose needs the offering aims to fulfill, what those needs are, and what the competing options are for fulfilling these needs—it is virtually impossible to develop an offering that can create market value.

Different marketing tactics play different roles in creating market value. Because they define the key benefits and costs, the product, service, brand, price, and incentives are the *key value drivers* that define the design of the offering. Specifically, the first three attributes—product, service, and brand—define the core benefits that the offering delivers to its customers, the price is the primary cost associated with the offering, and the incentives typically reduce the cost of the offering by modifying the price. Communication informs

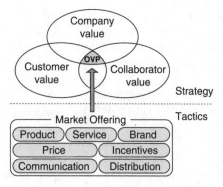

FIGURE 3.4   Creating Market Value: Strategy and Tactics
Source: Alexander Chernev, *Strategic Marketing Management: Theory and Practice* (Chicago, IL: Cerebellum Press, 2019).

customers about the offering's value, and distribution involves delivering the offering to target customers. Regardless of the different ways in which they create market value—by contributing to the design, communication, or distribution aspect of the offering—the seven marketing tactics must be consistent with the overarching marketing strategy as well as aligned with one another in a way that helps create value for target customers, the company, and its collaborators.

Managing the Implementation and Defining Controls

Setting a goal, defining the strategy, and designing the tactics reflect the way in which the company *thinks* about its offering. Indeed, these three aspects of marketing management, although crucial to the development of a successful offering, are only mental exercises that do not automatically create market value. To have market impact that will help the company achieve its goal, the company must implement its strategy and tactics and, at the same time, monitor the market performance of its offering. The processes of managing the implementation and defining marketing controls are discussed in more detail in the following sections.

Managing Implementation

Marketing implementation is the process that turns a company's strategy and tactics into actions and ensures that they accomplish the company's goal.

Implementation directly follows from a company's strategy and tactics, such that each decision is translated into a set of actions that make this decision a market reality. Implementation involves three key components: developing the company resources, developing the offering, and commercially deploying the offering.

Developing the company resources aims to secure the deficient competencies and assets necessary to implement the company's offering. Resource development can involve developing business facilities such as manufacturing, service, and technology infrastructure; ensuring the availability of reliable suppliers; recruiting, training, and retaining skilled employees; developing relevant products, services, and brands that can serve as a platform for the new offering; acquiring the know-how needed to develop, produce, and manage the offering; developing communication and distribution channels to inform target customers about the company's offering and deliver the offering to them; and securing the capital necessary to develop these resources.

Developing the market offering involves the process of creating the actual good that the company intends to launch in the market. Offering development involves managing the flow of information, materials, labor, and money to create the offering that the company will deploy in the market. Thus, offering development involves designing the product (procurement, inbound logistics, and production) and service (installation, support, and repair activities); building the brand; setting retail and wholesale prices and incentives (coupons, rebates, and price discounts); designing the means of communication (message, media, and creative execution); and setting the channels of distribution (warehousing, order fulfillment, and transportation).

Commercial deployment involves the process of introducing the offering to the target market and includes activities such as setting the timing of the offering's market launch, defining the resources involved in the launch, and determining the scale of the launch. Commercial deployment logically follows the process of developing an offering by delineating the process of bringing the offering to market. The deployment of the offering can be selective, initially focusing on specific markets to assess customers' reaction to the offering, or it can involve a large-scale rollout across all target markets.

Defining Controls

The constantly changing business environment requires companies to be agile and continuously realign their actions with market realities. Controls help a company ensure that its actions are aligned with its strategy and tactics in a way that will enable the company to achieve its goal. The primary function of controls is to inform the company whether to proceed with its current course of action, reevaluate its actions and realign the underlying strategy and tactics, or abandon its current course of action and develop a different offering that better reflects the current market realities. Controls involve two key components: evaluating the company's performance and monitoring the market environment.

Evaluating performance involves tracking the company's progress toward its goal, as defined by its focus and benchmarks. In this context, performance evaluation involves comparing the desired and actual performance metrics, such as sales revenues, profit margins, and market share. Performance evaluation can reveal one of two outcomes: adequate goal progress or a discrepancy (performance gap) between the desired and the actual performance. When the progress is adequate, the company can stay the course with its current action plan. In contrast, when performance evaluation reveals a gap whereby a company's performance lags behind the benchmarks set, the company's action plan must be modified to put the company back on track toward achieving its goal. Evaluating performance also includes experimentation and testing— theorizing, experimentation, generalization, application.

Monitoring the environment aims to identify market opportunities and threats. It enables the company to take advantage of new opportunities such as favorable government regulations, a decrease in competition, or an increase in consumer demand. It also alerts a company of impending threats such as unfavorable government regulations, an increase in competition, or a decline in customer demand. Once the key opportunities and threats have been identified, the action plan can be modified to take advantage of the opportunities and counteract the impact of threats. Because it aims to align a company's actions with the changes in the market in which it operates, monitoring the environment in which the company operates is a prerequisite for sustainability of the company's value-creation model.

Developing a Marketing Plan

The marketing plan is the tool for directing and coordinating a company's marketing efforts. It is a tangible outcome of a company's strategic planning process, outlining the company's goal and the ways in which it aims to achieve this goal. The marketing plan serves three main functions: delineate the company's goal and proposed course of action, inform the relevant stakeholders about this goal and course of action, and persuade the relevant decision makers of the viability of the goal and the proposed course of action.

Most marketing plans suffer from a common problem. Rather than fulfilling their vital mission of steering a company's actions to attain a stated goal, they are frequently written merely to fulfill the requirement of having a document filed in the company archives. As a result, instead of outlining a meaningful course of action, marketing plans often comprise exhaustive analyses of marginally relevant issues and laundry lists of activities without delineating whether and how these activities will benefit the company. This lack of internal logic and cohesiveness often leads to haphazard actions that fall far short of helping the company achieve its goal.

An effective marketing plan must outline a sound goal, propose a viable action plan to achieve this goal, and communicate this goal and action plan to the target audience. To successfully guide the company's marketing activities, the marketing plan must be relevant, actionable, clear, and succinct. This can be achieved by organizing the marketing plan around the G-STIC framework. Accordingly, the core of the marketing plan involves a clear goal, a meaningful value-creation strategy, well-articulated tactical aspects of the offering, an actionable implementation plan, and a set of control measures to monitor the offering's progress toward its goals. The G-STIC section of the marketing plan is preceded by an executive summary and a situation overview and is followed by a set of relevant exhibits. The key components of the marketing plan and the main decisions underlying each individual component are illustrated in Figure 3.5 and summarized below.

The *executive summary* is the "elevator pitch" for the marketing plan—a streamlined and succinct overview of the company's goal and the proposed course of action. The typical executive summary outlines the key issue faced by the company (an opportunity, a threat, or a performance gap) and the proposed action plan.

The *situation overview* section of the marketing plan provides an overall assessment of the company and identifies the markets in which it competes. The situation overview typically involves two sections: (1) the *company overview*, which outlines the company's history, culture, resources, and its portfolio of offerings (e.g., SWOT analysis); and (2) the *market overview*, which outlines the markets in which the company operates and could potentially target.

The *G-STIC* section is the core of the marketing plan. It identifies (1) the *goal* the company aims to achieve; (2) the offering's *strategy*, which defines its target market and value proposition; (3) the offering's *tactics*, which define the product, service, brand, price, incentives, communication, and distribution aspects of the offering; (4) the *implementation* aspects of executing an offering's strategy and tactics; and (5) *control* procedures that evaluate the company's performance and analyze the environment in which it operates.

Exhibits help streamline the logic of the marketing plan by separating the less important or more technical aspects of the plan into a distinct section in the form of tables, charts, and appendices.

The ultimate purpose of the marketing plan is to guide a company's actions. Accordingly, the core of the marketing plan is defined by the key elements of the G-STIC framework delineating the company's goal and the proposed course of action. The other elements of the marketing plan—the executive summary, situation overview, and exhibits—aim to facilitate an

Executive Summary		
What are the key aspects of the company's marketing plan?		

Situation Overview		
What are the **Company** company's history, culture, resources, offerings, and ongoing activities?	What are the key **Market** aspects of the markets in which the company competes?	

G-STIC Action Plan

Goal		
What is the key **Focus** performance metric the company aims to achieve with the offering?	What are the criteria **Benchmarks** (temporal and quantitative) for reaching the goal?	

Strategy		
Who are the **Target market** target customers, competitors, and collaborators? What are the company's resources and context?	What value does the **Value proposition** offering create for target customers, collaborators, and company stakeholders?	

Tactics		
Market offering		
What are the product, service, brand, price, incentives, communication, and distribution aspects of the offering?		

Implementation		
How is the company **Development** offering being developed?	What processes will be **Deployment** used to bring the offering to market?	

Control		
How will the **Performance** company evaluate the progress toward its goal?	How will the company **Environment** monitor the environment to identify new opportunities and threats?	

Exhibits		
What are the details/evidence supporting the company's action plan?		

FIGURE 3.5 The Marketing Plan
Source: Alexander Chernev, *Strategic Marketing Management: Theory and Practice* (Chicago, IL: Cerebellum Press, 2019).

understanding of the logic underlying the plan and provide specifics of the proposed course of action.

Once developed, marketing plans need updating to remain relevant. Marketing planning is an iterative process in which the company executes its strategy and tactics while simultaneously monitoring the outcome and modifying the process accordingly. Continual monitoring and adjustment enable the company to assess its progress toward the set goals as well as account for the changes in the market in which it operates. The dynamic nature of marketing planning is ingrained in the G-STIC framework, where the control aspect of planning is explicitly designed to provide the company with feedback on the effectiveness of its actions and the relevant changes in the target market.

Conclusion

The increasing complexity of the environment in which companies operate calls for using a systematic approach to marketing management that is centered around the concept of creating market value. Such a systematic approach is provided by the G-STIC framework, which outlines the company's goal, its business model delineating the strategy and tactics to achieve this goal, and an action plan to make this model a reality. The core of the G-STIC framework is the market value principle stating that an offering must create superior value for its target customers and collaborators in a way that enables the company to achieve its goals. The G-STIC framework also serves as the backbone of a company's marketing plan to provide a roadmap for a company's actions and ensure that these actions are aligned with the company's overarching goal.

Author Biography

Alexander Chernev is a professor of marketing at the Kellogg School of Management at Northwestern University. He holds a PhD in psychology from Sofia University and a PhD in marketing from Duke University. Dr. Chernev has been ranked among the top ten most prolific scholars in the leading marketing journals and serves as an area editor and on the editorial boards of many leading research journals. He teaches marketing strategy, brand management, and behavioral science and has received numerous teaching awards, including the Top Professor Award from the Executive MBA Program, which he has received fourteen times. Dr. Chernev has written numerous textbooks on the topics of marketing strategy, brand management, and behavioral science, and has worked with Fortune 500 companies to reinvent their business models, build strong brands, and gain competitive advantage.

PART 2

Marketing as an Engine of Business Growth

CHAPTER 4

Creating Value to Disrupt Markets

Lakshman Krishnamurthi and Rebecca Devine

Most products and services are changed incrementally: Features are added, prices decrease. However, every so often we are presented with something that changes the status quo in a significant way: for example, the ability to use phones instead of desktop computers for browsing the internet and go to a local pharmacy instead of a doctor's office for a vaccination. This is market disruption. It can be a tremendous source of growth for new entrants and established firms alike and can impact all aspects of the business environment, from competition and pricing to regulation.

In this chapter, we explore issues such as: What are market disruptions? How do we best prepare to introduce a new product or rethink an existing product? How can we create the type of value that allows for market disruptions? What are the types of market disruptions? The frameworks introduced in this chapter will allow us to observe changes in the competitive landscape and determine whether new or updated products are merely novel or have the potential to change the way we do business in a more significant way.

What Are Market Disruptions?

All new products and product innovations at some level address customer pain points, but very few disrupt markets. In our definition, a market disruption should change the status quo by doing one or more of the following in a significant way: (1) influence customer behavior, (2) impact market and/or technological evolution, (3) provoke significant competitive response, and (4) bring new players into the market.

Disruptors can be new entrants or established players. Disruptive innovations are often driven by new entrants, typically smaller companies targeting overlooked customer pain points. As explored by Clayton Christensen, many incumbents are unable to fend off these smaller disruptors because of organizational inertia.[1] But disruptors need not only be smaller or new entrants. As an example, the healthcare delivery market is ripe for market disruption. Major players like CVS and Walgreens, who are neither small nor new, are making a big push to deliver a wider range of diagnostic care more conveniently and affordably than the traditional doctor's office.[2]

Disruptors can impact any industry. Disruptive innovation often occurs when existing products do not meet the needs of the existing market. But disruption need not only be aimed at the unserved or underserved market. For example, electric vehicles are a major disruption of the existing combustion engine vehicle market. The early entrant Tesla, as well as the other automobile companies rushing into this market, did not start at the low end of the market or target non-consumers.

Two key conditions make existing markets vulnerable to disruption:

1. *High market prices.* These could result from concentrated market power, product complexity, high input factor costs, and so forth.

2. *Low experience value* for some segment of customers. This could be due to a high price relative to the experience, and/or existing products that do not address the needs of this segment.

The implied value proposition that addresses these two pain points is lower prices and a better customer experience. This is conceptually simple but difficult to implement successfully. One can always sell at a lower price, but how does one make money? It could be that products or services would have to be completely reimagined, which incumbents may not want to do, or that the organizational transformation needed to make changes may be too challenging to enact.

How Do We Best Prepare to Introduce a New Product or Rethink an Existing Product?

Any new product, whether disruptive or not, must have a sound marketing plan to enhance the chance of success. All marketers need to ask and have answers to these questions before introducing a new product or rethinking an existing product.

- Who is the *target* customer?
- What are the *goals* of the customer?
- What are the *needs* of the customer?
- What *pain points* does the customer face?
- What is the company's *value proposition* that will address customer goals and needs and solve customer pain points better than the next best alternative?

How does the marketer assemble the data to answer these questions? By applying the five-step marketing planning framework briefly illustrated in the following sections.

Step 1: Analysis of Market Attractiveness

This is an analysis of the market environment (the context), the company, competition, and collaborators.[3]

Step 2: Customer Analysis

This 360° look at the customer consists of background variables and current purchase behavior, including what they buy, why they buy, where and how they buy, when they buy, and so forth.

Steps 1 and Step 2 are popularly known as the *5Cs analysis*. Note that market attractiveness should be evaluated before conducting a deep dive into customers for a pragmatic reason: The data needed to evaluate market attractiveness can usually be obtained more easily than customer-level data.

Step 3: Value Proposition

A value proposition involves value creation, value communication, and value delivery (discussed in the next main section). Since value is relative, the combination of creation, communication, and delivery must be superior to that of the competition. Among the customer's consideration set, product 1 is judged superior to product 2 if value (1) – price (1) > value (2) – price (2).[4]

Steps 4 and 5: Tactics and Implementation

Tactics involve selecting product options, branding, pricing, promotions, communication choices (such as media weight and allocation), distribution options, levels of service, and so forth. Implementation involves the monitoring and adjusting of prices, communication, and distribution, promised service levels, delivery system (e.g., removing bottlenecks), and so on to maximize the value proposition.

How Can We Create a Value Proposition?

Value is what a customer thinks an offering is worth,[5] which is the same as a willingness to pay for that product. Value is formed over time from use, word of mouth, advertising, the convenience of acquisition, peer recognition, sense of self-worth, and so on. *Whether the disruption is sustainable or short-lived depends on the value received by the customer.* There are four components of value: creation, communication, delivery, and capture.

How can we create value?

1. Create Better Products

Value creation is embodied in the physical product, service, app, or NFT. One should distinguish between objective value and subjective value. *Objective value* is a function of the product specifications, while *subjective value* is represented by the brand. The important thing to note is that two brands could have essentially identical objective values but different subjective values. For example, store-brand aspirin and Bayer Aspirin are functionally equivalent, but Bayer Aspirin is priced higher because of higher subjective value based on brand identity.

2. Let the Consumer Know

Value communication involves creating awareness of the product and explaining or demonstrating the value proposition of the product. This is key not only to promoting trial but also to creating loyalty. Customers are less likely to consider switching to the competition if you can convince them of the superiority of your value proposition.

3. Get the Product to the Market

Value delivery is accomplished by the seller making product acquisition easy (and perhaps even pleasant) through availability, accessibility, and elimination of the friction that is usually inherent in the process. For example, Warby Parker eliminated the hassle of going to a physical store to try on eyeglasses by creating a visual try-on app.

4. Make It a Good Deal

Value capture. To influence customer choice, the difference between the total value of the product through creation, communication, and delivery must be greater than the price charged for the product. The seller can lower the price to provide a positive surplus and/or raise the value of the product above the price.

Trends in Value

Value creation of all types, from products to services to apps, has become more feasible at lower cost because of globalization. It has never been easier or quicker to go from an idea to a finished product because of technology that facilitates communication and the exchange of ideas. Design and manufacturing of all types of products can be outsourced to collaborators in lower-cost locations.

Value communication is theoretically cheaper with the wide use of social media platforms such as Facebook, Instagram, Twitter, Pinterest, Snapchat, and the increasing ubiquity of TikTok. Many companies host channels for free on YouTube. Although this reads like a lower-cost way of creating awareness and educating target customers about the value proposition, the reality is different because of the crowded nature of—and the difficulty of establishing trust within—these channels.

Value delivery has been disrupted through direct distribution, both physical and streaming, and through hosting on the cloud. These options are not new but have become more accessible with improvements in technology and logistics, as well as more supply choices. The Covid pandemic, which began in 2020, also influenced many customers, both business-to-business (B2B) and business-to-consumer (B2C), to accept and eventually embrace remote transactions.

Finally, many of the consumer companies selling their products direct-to-consumer (DTC) online are pricing below mainstream competitors to *capture value.* The expectation is that many existing customers in the target market as well as new customers will be attracted by the lower price of products advertised through channels that are considered to be more convenient and make product research easier. The lower price, of course, can reduce value capture for the companies pricing aggressively and can also bring market prices down.

Technology by itself cannot disrupt markets. While technology can provide the impetus—the spark—customers must fan the flames for there to be a fire. This depends on whether technology or market shifts in general solve important pain points for customers. In most cases, the pain point exists, and the customer is eager to adopt the new technology. Think of the first word processor making the typewriter obsolete. In other cases, customers discover pain points they did not know they had. They put up with inconveniences without giving them much thought. Consider the Amazon Echo powered by Alexa. It is not clear that anyone was missing a digital assistant or a smart speaker. However, the availability of the product itself stimulates curiosity and new activities: It creates value.

Different Types of Market Disruptions

We classify market disruptions, somewhat imperfectly, on the basis of three dimensions:

1. The *degree of complexity* required to bring the offering to market, such as technical or manufacturing difficulty, the number of collaborators needed, or the level of investment required;
2. The *extent of change* in product newness—from bringing an existing product to the market in a new way to creating an entirely new market; and
3. The current and potential *value of the market*.

Typically, complexity and product newness are correlated, but not perfectly so. Disruptive value can be defined as equaling complexity × change × market.[6] The figure plots a number of different product markets on the complexity–change axes. Market value, either in unit size or in dollars, is not comparable across very different product markets. For example, the razor market, which was disrupted by Dollar Shave Club, is bigger in unit size than the mined-diamond market now facing disruption from gem-quality lab-made diamonds, but it is smaller in dollar value. Market size matters when evaluating entry as it affects the potential return on investment.

Disruptors may introduce new products to existing markets, deliver traditional products in a new way, or create an entirely new market. For example (as illustrated in Figure 4.1):

- New delivery systems, such as DTC models, cause disruptions in established markets like those for razors, eyeglasses, and mattresses, although the products offered are not significantly different from available options.
- New products, such as plant-based meat substitutes and lab-made diamonds, disrupt existing meat and diamond markets.

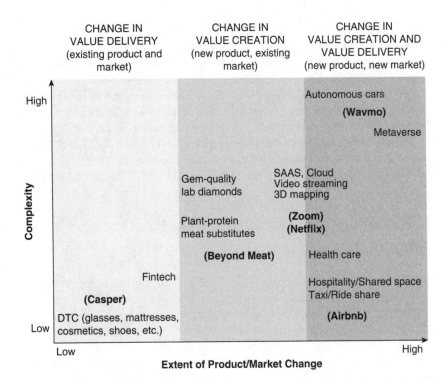

FIGURE 4.1 Examples of Market Disruptions

- The hospitality and taxi industries have been disrupted by platforms that connect customers to existing resources and create new product categories: shared-space vacation rental and ride-share services.
- Electric vehicles constitute a new product category that is changing the automotive industry, in addition to other markets, as the need for gas stations, oil changes, and so forth decreases.
- Disruptors in some cases create products that are so innovative that they become new markets. Examples include cloud computing, autonomous vehicles, and the metaverse.

How to Analyze Market Disruptions— A Case-Based Approach

The discussion of value and target customers' goals, needs, and pain points, together with the steps involved in marketing planning, provide the foundation for evaluating the success or failure of market disruptions. We will illustrate these frameworks by looking at some examples in more detail.

It is important to note that the companies and products mentioned in the examples that follow may or may not survive. Market disruption is not determined by the survival or profitability of a particular product or company but by whether the path blazed takes root and changes market dynamics in the form of customer behavior, market evolution, incumbent response (either singly or in combination), and the entry of new players following the initial disruptor. To avoid repetition, different aspects of the five-step planning process and the four value components are highlighted in each of these examples.

Low Level of Complexity, Change Mostly in Value Delivery

Over the course of a decade, starting in 2010 with the launch of Warby Parker, several entrants have attempted to disrupt established markets like eyeglasses, mattresses, razors and blades, luggage, and cosmetics with a DTC model. Overall, consumer welfare increases; this is a hallmark of successful disruption.

The value proposition is *lower prices and greater convenience of purchase* than the well-known brands. The start of the online DTC revolution was fueled by millennials who showed an increasing interest in a different purchasing experience—one that was more transparent and fit better in their busy lifestyles. This target was more willing to experiment with new brands and was less impacted by more traditional marketing. The playbook followed by these DTC players is a fairly standard one, made possible by outsourcing: Find a low-cost manufacturer, start a website, and sell direct. This addresses value creation and value delivery. This is the relatively easy part; the hard part is creating awareness. Almost all these DTC companies were started by younger entrepreneurs challenging large companies in well-established markets. Initially each started with an online-only model.

Case #1: Casper Mattress   Casper entered the mattress market in the United States in 2014. Unlike earlier entrants, Casper secured a significant amount of VC money to turbocharge its awareness and growth. The company raised $70 million in 2014 and 2015, and $270 million over the next four years, for a total of $340 million. The initial funds helped Casper create a lot more awareness for its mattress product than the competition, and the later funds helped to expand the product portfolio and its distribution footprint.

Context: Just like buying glasses online from Warby Parker was a novelty, buying a mattress online was an even more difficult idea for consumers to grasp. Traditionally, a mattress was a long-term purchase made at physical retailers that carried a wide selection, with many options priced at over

$1,000 or $2,000. Service included delivery and setup and taking the old mattress away. Many consumers had particular sleep habits that mattress brands advertised they could satisfy, a big driver of the large number of products leading to customer confusion.

Value creation and delivery: The initial value proposition of Casper was eliminating customer confusion by selling a single, comfortable mattress. Made of a combination of latex and foam, with the claim of providing good back support, the mattress was launched at an affordable price point of $500 to $950, depending on size. Purchase risk was mitigated with a 100-day in-home trial, with free returns.[7] The product came in a box and blossomed into a real mattress when unboxed. The mattress product line eventually expanded to include duvets, mattress protectors, bed frames, lamps, and other accessories. Like many DTC players, Casper is no longer just an online seller. It first expanded distribution through Amazon and followed that with pop-up stores, a partnership with Target, and at the time of this writing owns more than 60 retail locations. Casper is also available in Canada and a few European countries.

Casper went public in February 2020. Revenue was $497 million in 2021 and $436 million for the first three quarters of 2021, but the company has not been profitable. A private equity firm acquired Casper in November 2021.

Summary: It is estimated that there are over 100 online mattress companies operating now, nearly all of which started after Casper and mimicked Casper's strategy. When Casper entered the market in 2014, reportedly more than 90% of mattresses were purchased from retail stores. Eight years later, the awareness of online mattresses is high, and recent statistics show a significant increase in online mattress sales. Amazon, Walmart, and the dominant brick-and-mortar retailer Mattress Firm now sell their own bed-in-a-box mattress brands. The large, established mattress company Serta Simmons acquired Tuft and Needle, one of the earliest DTC bed-in-a-box companies. Even though Casper was not the first online player, one can credit Casper with revolutionizing and reconfiguring the mattress industry by paving the way for many more DTC entrants and forcing established players to play catch-up.

It should be pointed out, however, that the products sold by many of these DTC players are not complex. Value creation may not match that of high-quality established players, so the value proposition is largely about capitalizing on the pain points of customer confusion and high prices to launch an attractive option at a price lower than the market. Low complexity means entry barriers are low, other than the critical issue of raising money. There is also little to prevent incumbents, whether brick-and-mortar or e-retailers, from sourcing similar products from outsourced manufacturers. Finding that an online-only DTC model comes with limited awareness and high customer acquisition costs, many companies have shifted to a hybrid strategy, which changes the cost structure significantly. Consequently, it is not surprising that financial success has been difficult to achieve for many of these DTC disruptors.

So, why is online DTC featured as a disruption? First, it expanded consumer choice and influenced consumer behavior. Second, it caused market prices to come down. Third, it forced the established disrupted incumbents to adapt to the business model of the disruptors.

Medium Level of Complexity, Change in Value Creation

In the DTC examples, while the products sold required some development (e.g., Warby Parker curated appealing styles, and Casper figured out how a mattress could be mailed in a box), the disruptors are still selling glasses and mattresses that are in well-understood and well-developed product categories. Developing an alternative to an existing product can be much more complex.

For example, naturally occurring diamonds are formed by extremely high temperatures and pressures about 150 miles beneath the Earth's surface. Although synthetic diamonds for industrial use have been available for decades, making in a lab gem-quality diamonds that are chemically equivalent to natural mined diamonds is much more difficult.[8] Players in this field were willing to make the large R&D investment because the diamond market is so large in value. Companies like Diamond Foundry[9] and Lightbox, owned by the diamond giant De Beers, are disrupting the diamond market with gem-quality lab-grown diamonds that can be made in a variety of colors. The first part of the value proposition is the price, which is less than the cost of equivalent mined diamonds. Lightbox, in particular, prices its lab diamonds significantly lower than mined diamonds of the same carat size. The second aspect of the value proposition is that lab diamonds are ethically sourced. The third aspect, being environmentally friendly, is under scrutiny.

Likewise, there is technical complexity in creating plant-based protein substitutes that mimic the taste of meat, and the go-to-market is complex as well because of the need for collaborators. The meat industry, specifically beef and chicken producers, is concerned about the disruption from plant-based protein substitutes. We highlight the *context* (Step 1) and the *customer* (Step 2) of the planning process to examine the impetus for the disruption.

Case #2: Beyond Meat   *Context:* Over the past decade, the health and livability of the planet has become an important concern for many citizens and governments alike. It culminated in the Paris Climate Agreement of 2015, which almost all of the countries of the world signed.[10] The concrete goal of the agreement was to limit the rise in the global temperature to less than 2° centigrade. Achieving this goal requires a substantial drop in emissions.[11] Among many other contributors to global warming, livestock raised for production of meat is a major source. It is estimated that land used for grazing and growing crops for livestock accounts for over 75% of all agricultural land acreage. But this allocation produces less than 20% of the world's supply of calories.[12] Consequently, this is a very inefficient use of land. Cows emit a significant amount of methane, which also contributes to global warming.

Consumers: The percentage of Americans who are vegetarians and vegan is small but growing.[13] The public is now better educated and more knowledgeable about the foods they consume, in particular about the negative health effects of heavy red meat consumption. The drumbeat of news about the environment is raising consumer knowledge of the link between livestock farming and global warming. Consumers are also becoming increasingly aware of the cruel ways in which animals are raised for food. Social media is playing an important role in creating awareness of ecological, sustainability, and animal welfare concerns.[14]

Value creation: The first entrant to make a splash was Beyond Meat, which launched in 2009. The company strove to produce a plant-based burger that tastes close to a beef burger—with a better nutritional profile. Over a period of several years and multiple iterations, the taste of the product has improved.

Target and positioning: The value proposition is different depending on whether the consumer targets are vegetarians and vegans or meat eaters. The positioning statement for vegans and vegetarians could be:[15]

- For vegetarians and vegans, who prioritize their own health and that of the planet, Beyond provides a tasty meatless food option with about the same amount of protein as meat that is sustainable because it is plant based.

The positioning statement for meat eaters could be:

- For people who enjoy the taste of meat but are conflicted about eating healthy, Beyond offers a plant-based meat alternative that tastes as good as meat but is healthier because it contains 35% less saturated fat than an 80% lean beef burger.

One concern is that targeting just the vegan/vegetarian market is not a viable business proposition because it is a small market. Making central the value proposition of being better for the environment is unlikely to be compelling enough to attract a large customer base. Also, leading with an environment positioning for a food product may result in an unintended perception that it is not flavorful. Hence, from the very beginning, Beyond focused on meat eaters interested in an alternative as their primary target.

Value communication and delivery: To reach meat eaters, Beyond has worked diligently to place their burger patties and ground product in the same retailer refrigerated meat case as regular burgers, with varying success. Beyond also signed partnerships with the big fast-food chains and is working on other partnerships.[16]

Competition: Impossible Foods followed Beyond in 2011. Overall, its strategy has been similar to Beyond in securing retail and fast-food chain distribution. The biggest meat producer in the United States, Tyson Foods, recently introduced plant-based burger patties and ground "meat" as well as chicken nuggets and tenders in supermarkets. Tyson has enormous distribution clout, so it could make plant-protein meat alternatives more widely available.

Value capture: At present, plant-based alternatives are priced at a premium relative to equivalent meat products, which could inhibit trial. However, one would expect price differences to narrow as the scale increases.

Summary: Beyond initially tapped into existing consumer concerns about environmental sustainability and eating healthier food. For the disruption to succeed, however, meat eaters must change their preferences, which is not an easy matter. Changing preferences will depend on superior value communication and value delivery to influence a large enough fraction of consumers to choose these options as part of their diet. Predictions are that the plant-based meat alternative market will continue to grow, based on the expectation of a large shift in consumer behavior. If this prediction does turn out to be true, plant-based meat protein substitutes should lead to a significant reduction in livestock farming—and global warming.

Low Level of Complexity, Change in Value Creation

While Warby Parker and Casper tweaked the products they brought to market, and Diamond Foundry and Beyond Meat created alternatives to existing products, companies like Airbnb and Uber created new markets that gave access to resources that already existed.

Case #3: Airbnb Although VRBO started a decade earlier, it is Airbnb that disrupted the hospitality industry by creating a new market opportunity for property owners to monetize living spaces of all types and for travelers to access unique accommodations.[17] Airbnb has now outstripped VRBO in popularity and has many more active listings worldwide.[18]

Value creation and delivery: Airbnb initially started as an opportunity for any property owner to rent a space, whether it is currently occupied or not. This is the concept of a "shared space."

- Increasingly, people are interested in visiting (and perhaps even working from) places that are less well traveled or smaller towns that often do not have a hotel or other lodging options. Airbnb (and VRBO and others) provides these unserved or underserved markets an entry into the hospitality market.

- In regions where hotels are available, renting a single room through Airbnb is usually cheaper than a hotel room.[19] Airbnb rentals can also be much bigger than a hotel room and/or have additional amenities, including kitchen facilities.
- Airbnb also offers unique hospitality options like cabins, boats, castles, treehouses, lighthouses, igloos, yurts, and so forth, in addition to more traditional apartments and homes.

It is easy to write out the goals, needs, and pain points for the vacation traveler. The value proposition of Airbnb is in providing a trusted worldwide platform that provides two-sided matching of property owners and travelers, facilitates payment, and establishes the rules of engagement. The superiority of the platform is manifested in the loyalty of users—both "hosts" and renters—which reinforces the value proposition.

Summary: Airbnb reports 4 million hosts, 6 million listings, and 1 billion guest arrivals in over 100,000 cities and towns in almost every country and region in the world.[20] Where it has a strong presence, Airbnb has put pressure on hotel room rates and has impacted the number of hotel room nights occupied. Major hotel chains like Marriott have reacted to Airbnb by offering vacation homes. Boutique hotels have started to list on Airbnb as a way of increasing visibility. Some studies have found that Airbnb has decreased the number of rental units in cities, driving up rents. As a result, some local city governments are creating and enforcing rules such as requiring registering as an Airbnb host, showing proof of insurance, paying a tax, limiting the number of rental days in a month or year, or banning the rental of private rooms (but not entire apartments) as in Barcelona, Spain in 2021. The hospitality market has been disrupted when governments start to enact restrictions!

Higher Level of Complexity: Change in Value Creation and Delivery

While Uber and Airbnb invested primarily in their delivery platforms to create a new market using cars and living spaces that already existed, some disruptors needed to invest more heavily in R&D to create a product that addresses customer pain points. The complexity of bringing offerings such as streaming, video conferencing, SaaS, cloud computing, and electric vehicles to market is high from a technology and investment point of view. The value derived by customers lies both in the value created by offerings that provide greater functionality at reduced cost as well as in new modes of value delivery.

Case #4: Zoom—Changing Education and More *Company and customers:* Is Zoom a disruptor? It has certainly transformed the

video-conferencing market. Whether the company would have been as impactful without the Covid pandemic is an open question. Zoom was founded in
2011—the same year that Microsoft bought Skype—by Eric Yuan, one of the
founding engineers of Cisco's Webex. Covid allowed Zoom an entry opportunity that it seized with both hands: namely, the university market, which was
an underserved market in early 2020. The *goals* for schools and universities
were to not shut down, the *needs* were technology that easily allowed online
teaching and interaction, and the *pain point* was that educational institutions,
with few exceptions, were simply incapable of providing online education to
large numbers of students with their existing systems.

Value creation and communication: Zoom's web-based app was easy to set
up, and the pricing was affordable. Students using Zoom introduced it to their
parents, who then also began using the platform. Of course, it helped that
Zoom had a free option, which attracted a lot of users outside of their work
environment. The awareness of Zoom skyrocketed.

Value delivery: For a couple of reasons, Zoom has been more successful
than incumbents Cisco and Microsoft, although they both have significantly
more resources. Both Cisco's WebEx and Microsoft Teams targeted the business enterprise market, and neither product is the company's core business.
Zoom, on the other hand, *is* the company and so was able to focus on addressing the market shift, learning from its user community and adding relevant
functions and features quickly. In addition, Zoom is a stand-alone product,
whereas Teams is part of Microsoft Office365 and so is less accessible. Zoom
is now pushing into the enterprise space.

Summary: To qualify as a market disruption, it does not matter whether
Zoom wins or loses, or whether Zoom was simply lucky because of the
pandemic. Zoom succeeded in changing the conversation around video
conferencing, brought the technology into the hands of millions of people
worldwide, impacted the need to travel for short business meetings, and created awareness among large numbers of young people. It is significant that
Zoom is better known than Teams or WebEx by this group, which bodes well
for its future. Of note, value capture is unclear; this may derail the company.

Case #5: Netflix—Streaming Disrupts the Cable TV Market

Context: Technology, in the form of the internet, has changed consumer
behavior regarding video entertainment. The internet became available in
the 1990s, and Wi-Fi was released to consumers in 1997, but speeds available
to the average consumer were painfully slow. It wasn't until the mid-2000s
that Wi-Fi speeds were fast enough for downloading large files, which was
critical for video use. The launch of smartphones, such as the iPhone in 2007,
Android phones like Samsung soon after, and tablets like the iPad in 2010,
brought the power of the internet to the palm of one's hand. Taking advantage
of these changes, Netflix, which launched as a competitor to Blockbuster in

1997, offered online streaming of movies via a subscription model in 2007. This disrupted the pay TV (cable) market.

Value creation and delivery: For cable's traditional point-of-entry target (those making independent expenditure decisions for the first time, such as college students and recent graduates),[21] cable appears both old-fashioned and exploitative since streaming directly over the internet is cheaper and provides more freedom to watch the programming of their choice when convenient and on the device of their choice. This group is also influencing their parents to drop cable subscriptions in favor of paying only for what they want to watch via streaming. As one would expect, cable penetration rates are higher with older consumers. And many consumers have not completely cut the cord but have augmented their cable subscriptions with streaming options.

Summary: Cable penetration peaked in 2010 at 88% of all TV households and, due in large part to Netflix's disruption, has steadily fallen since 2015. The number of households with a cable subscription has decreased from over 100 million in 2010 to about 78 million in 2020 and is expected to fall to 60 million in 2025.[22] AT&T, which bought DirecTV (the largest satellite pay TV provider) in 2015, spun off the company after a significant loss of subscribers. Comcast, the largest cable provider, has endured subscriber losses as well and has changed its growth strategy.

The success of Netflix also paved the way for new players to enter the market. There are at present too many streaming services, causing confusion among consumers. Netflix and others like Amazon, Hulu, Disney, and Apple also produce original content to reduce churn. Content creation is an expensive and high-risk endeavor, and it is hard to see how these streaming services and content providers can reliably produce hits that consumers want to watch. So, value capture is becoming very difficult for these players, which is evidenced by significant losses for Disney+ and the hammering of Netflix's stock price in 2022. Going forward, consumers should expect higher subscription prices for both streaming services and content. Now we are back to the question of value and willingness to pay. One can expect both retrenchment and consolidation in this industry. Streaming, however, will be increasingly mainstream as more powerful Wi-Fi and cellular data access becomes the norm.

Higher Levels of Complexity, Change in Value Creation and Value Delivery: Greater Uncertainty about Market Value

The distinguishing feature about these disruptions is that the value proposition is not as clear as in the other cases. These products and services involve high technical complexity, lengthy development times, and significant capital investment—with much greater uncertainty in market outcomes. However, given time, they have the potential to cause significant market disruption, leading to the creation of new markets and new market boundaries.

Case #6: Driving with Your Eyes Closed: Autonomous Cars

Context: One of the leading causes of death in the United States for ages 1–54 is vehicle-related injuries. Annual U.S. vehicle-related fatalities have averaged in the mid-30,000s for several years, peaking at over 38,000 in 2020. In addition, over 4 million individuals are seriously injured, requiring medical attention. Worldwide, the numbers are 1.35 million deaths and 20–50 million nonfatal injuries that require medical attention.[23]

Value proposition: The value proposition of autonomous cars is manifold.

1. Improved safety, accomplished by eliminating driver error, which is responsible for nearly all vehicle-related accidents.
2. Reduction in medical costs associated with accidents.
3. Upgraded urban planning, as fewer parking spaces will be needed. Autonomous cars could wait at designated locations and pick up passengers on demand. Parking garages and lots can be repurposed into green spaces or communal spaces.
4. Better use of driving time.
5. Enhanced mobility and quality of life for those with impaired vision or other disabilities that inhibit driving.

Google started to work on autonomous cars as early as 2009, and created a new division called Waymo in 2016 to continue the work. The vision of Waymo is a fully autonomous car, which means no driver, no steering wheel, and no operating pedals. Waymo's view is that a fully autonomous car is safer than one in which the driver must engage. Since Google's entry, Tesla as well as many of the legacy car manufacturers like GM, Ford, Volvo, Audi, and Mercedes have all invested in this market.

Summary: The concept of a fully autonomous car with no driver intervention may seem too far-fetched. Cars have gotten much safer with improvements in active safety technology. Many drivers may like the thrill of driving. So, a fully autonomous car is not likely to address pain points that are currently salient for most of the existing market. Where this concept could be more appealing is to a younger generation that is not of driving age yet and are far more comfortable with technology than their elders. The impediment here, of course, is *value capture*, because it is this target that has the least ability to pay. An on-demand or subscription pricing model may ease entry.

Case #7: You and Your Avatar   *Metaverse:* The metaverse is an amalgam of the physical world in which we live and the virtual world in which we can participate through our avatars. It can be considered a three-dimensional version of the internet. Versions of the metaverse already exist in gaming. An example is *Second Life*, the simulation game in which people create a virtual life through their avatars. The current vision of the metaverse, however, is broader in that the physical and virtual worlds can interact. Roblox, an online gaming platform whose customers are about evenly split among children and teens, has held several virtual concerts in which the hologram avatar of the artist performs, and the concert attendees participate in much the same way as in a live concert. It has a virtual currency called Robux, which can be used to buy branded products for one's digital avatar.

Value creation: The building blocks of the metaverse already exist in the form of virtual reality (and augmented reality) and blockchain technology to store and authenticate digital assets. The challenge, however, is to find commercial applications that have scale. Various scenarios have been floated, such as shopping, attending parties and concerts, interacting with family or romantic partners who are physically distant, and, of course, gaming. One can think of digital metaverse subscriptions to monetize some of these activities.

Value communication: Does this concept of the metaverse address existing or latent customer pain points? It is not clear that individuals have a good understanding of what the metaverse is and how it will benefit them. So, the challenge of companies like Facebook, now called Meta, is to create awareness and educate consumers about the possibilities that await them. Despite the building blocks that exist, the technical challenge of building a hyperrealistic and immersive experience in which individuals will want to engage in a sustainable way is quite daunting. If the metaverse vision of the physical and the digital worlds seamlessly interacting plays out, it will be a transformative experience. As with many other digital technologies, it will be the younger generation who will be the first consumers.

Conclusion

One can provide a lot more examples, but the key takeaway is that a disruption must change customer behavior and market evolution to have long-lasting effects. The key to disruption is the creation of value, whether it is in the seamless delivery of a product, improving a product, or creating a new market to address a consumer need.

Any new product—whether disruptive or not—must have a sound marketing plan to enhance the chance of success. In some cases, technology can lead consumers to try an offering, but success can only be assured if customers believe they are better off than before. This is an obvious statement, but many companies rush into markets without a clear understanding of who their target customers are and what pain points they are solving. And, of course, when multiple companies enter the same market space, the pressure to be top of mind and differentiate unravels the economics of many of the players.

Whether a company is established or looking to enter (or even create) a market, its efforts at disruption begin with analyzing the status quo to determine the best path forward. This chapter provides some tools and frameworks to help consider a proposed or existing change, and determine if it is merely an incremental change or if it has the power to be disruptive. That is where true progress lies.

Author Biographies

Lakshman Krishnamurthi is the A. Montgomery Ward Distinguished Professor of Marketing at the Kellogg School of Management at Northwestern University. He holds degrees in engineering from IIT Madras, an MBA from LSU, and an MS in statistics, as well as a PhD in marketing from Stanford University. He has won several teaching and research awards and has consulted for a number of companies such as Pearson, Medtronic, and the Chicago Tribune, among others. He has also conducted executive education seminars for DuPont, Microsoft, Abbott, ExxonMobil, Johnson & Johnson, ThyssenKrupp Elevators, and several others. Krishnamurthi is co-author, with Rakesh Vohra, of the book *Principles of Pricing: An Analytical Approach*, published by Cambridge University Press.

Rebecca Devine is a program leader and instructional associate at the Kellogg School of Management at Northwestern University involved with a variety of courses including Marketing Strategy, Advertising Strategy, Critical Thinking in Digital and Social Media Marketing, Negotiations, and Organizational Growth and Transformation. She holds a BS in business administration from SUNY College at Buffalo and an MBA from Kellogg School of Management. In addition to teaching, she works as a project manager at a commercial construction materials company and provides growth strategy consulting to a variety of entities from small businesses to colleges. Her experience includes over 20 years of management, finance (portfolio management), entrepreneurship, consulting, and marketing.

CHAPTER 5

Customer Centricity as a Business Strategy

Tom O'Toole

From the roots of modern business until well into the twentieth century, companies grew largely through product strategies—by offering better products. Then, in the mid-twentieth century, and particularly after World War II, mass media and mass marketing gave rise to the era of brand strategy. People didn't just buy products, they bought brands that were positioned, as companies built awareness, created identities, and targeted mass market segments. For decades, the study and practice of marketing was largely about brand strategy.

That all began to change toward the end of the twentieth century. Fragmenting markets, data use, and digital media required and enabled increasingly targeted marketing, focusing on more tightly defined sets of customers that were identifiable and reachable through addressable media. This shift progressed steadily in the first decades of the twenty-first century, accelerated and enabled greatly by mobile devices, data analytics, and social media.

Today, the practice of marketing is well into a new era. Markets are very heterogeneous and becoming more so. Customer data systems enable identifying and knowing customers at the individual level. Predictive analytics, artificial intelligence, and machine learning inform proactive marketing that is highly individualized. Thanks to digital media, customers can be addressed individually—and at scale. As a result, *customer strategy today is more important than brand strategy.*

That statement may seem heretical for a chapter in *Kellogg on Marketing*, given that the Kellogg School of Management, known worldwide for brand strategy, is where much of the leading work was originally created and continues to be advanced. Nonetheless, I firmly believe that this assertion is not only true today but is becoming more so, with a growing range of examples across industries.

The purpose and aim of a strategy, by definition, is to achieve an objective. What is the objective of customer strategy? The objective of customer strategy is to *grow customer value*—at both the aggregate level (i.e., all customers) and, particularly, at the individual customer level. Today's advances—digital media, customer data systems, predictive analytics, AI, new forms of loyalty programs, and more—are used to achieve this objective. The framework of marketing today, into which all these methods and pieces fit and in which they are utilized, aims to grow customer value, primarily at the identifiable individual customer level. As this chapter discusses, *a customer-centric business strategy is foundational to a customer strategy that maximizes and secures customer value*. In short, customer centricity is all about growing customer value.

Focusing on customers is not a new idea. Peter Drucker, the legendary management theorist, famously said, "The purpose of business is to create a customer."[1] In Drucker's view, every business enterprise could be reduced to two basic functions: marketing and innovation. Regarding marketing, Drucker said, "The aim of marketing is to know and understand the customer so well the product or service fits him and sells itself."[2]

Today, I would update Drucker's statement. *The aim of marketing is to create enduring customer relationships that grow in value*. In other words, the role of marketing is to create loyal customers. That objective is best achieved through a customer-centric approach.

What Is Customer Centricity?

Peter Fader, in his book *Customer Centricity*,[3] which led much of today's thinking on the subject, defined customer centricity as: "a strategy that aligns a company's development and delivery of its products and services with the current and future needs of a select set of customers in order to maximize their long-term financial value to the firm."[4] For the purpose of this discussion, we define customer centricity as:

> The practice of differentiating customers and managing customer offerings, investment, and engagement in order to maximize customer value.

In this definition, the most important words are *differentiating* and *customer value*. Those words are not just about marketing. They anchor customer centricity as a business strategy.

Admittedly, the term "customer centricity" can sound like an abstract academic buzz term du jour. Thus, it's important to observe that an entire company has been built on the aim and practice of customer centricity. That company is Amazon. Founder Jeff Bezos has stated for years, and as recently as 2020, that, "We have always wanted to be the Earth's most customer-centric company."[5]

There are two observations about Amazon that are most relevant to our discussion of customer centricity. First, while a customer-centric business approach is not a novel concept today, Bezos was focused on it and talking about it virtually since the inception of the company in the 1990s. Second, Amazon has progressed from selling just books to becoming a mega-retailer of a wide range of product categories and a marketplace for other sellers; to introducing the Kindle, Amazon Web Service (AWS), and Alexa-enabled devices; to building an enormous advertising business and pioneering an unprecedented distribution system; to much more. But, at its core, underneath it all, throughout its history and to the present day, Amazon has been about:

- Maintaining a *customer-centric* business strategy
- Using *data, predictive analytics*, and, today, leading-edge *artificial intelligence* and *machine learning*
- *Personalizing* customer interaction, *optimizing*, and growing *customer value* at the individual customer level

Amazon illustrates the fundamental point that customer centricity isn't just a marketing strategy; it's a *business strategy*.

The Three Centricities

To further the understanding of customer centricity, we can compare and contrast it with different approaches: product centricity and brand centricity. Let's start by highlighting different imperatives that a company focuses on under each, as shown in Figure 5.1. (This certainly isn't an exhaustive list.)

Product Centric	Brand Centric	Customer Centric
Product development	Brand awareness	Customer differentiation
Product features	Brand identity	Customer value
Product portfolio	Brand positioning	CRM
Product innovation	Brand value	Customer life cycle
Sales	Brand (market) share	Customer journey

FIGURE 5.1   Different Approaches Focus on Different Imperatives

When these different approaches are described and contrasted, students typically respond, "Yes, but can't a company use more than one?" Certainly, companies can and do need to attend to all three. Amazon is a customer-centric company but manages its brand carefully and is constantly exploring product and service innovation, as well as new categories (should it sell cars or get into the travel business?) Apple is arguably product-centric, but it has created one of the world's most admired brands and doesn't try to offer a product for everyone (such as a very low price or a disposable phone). Distinguishing the primary business approach—product centric, brand centric, or customer centric—of a company doesn't mean that a company attends exclusively to one of the three approaches. All companies need to attend to all three as part of their business strategy.

The three centricities can be better understood by looking at the same company from the viewpoint of each. Take the example of Mercedes, a global manufacturing company with more than 100 years of history. Mercedes has been a product leader since the invention of the automobile, and its brand is synonymous with the world's best quality.

If we look at Mercedes from a product-centric viewpoint, what would we focus on? We would probably start with its engineering. Its products are known for the finest technical design, engineering, performance, and reliability in every part and detail. Or we consider its product design and the careful evolution of its vehicle silhouettes. We would certainly focus on its grille design. We would look at the technology in its engines, brakes, headlights, and more. Today, we'd also focus on its cabin electronics and the company's technical advances in the shift to hybrid and electric vehicles.

Now, let's switch to a brand-centric point of view. Here the focus is on brand awareness, brand identity, brand positioning, brand value, and perceived quality. We'd start by looking at the iconic Mercedes logo that has become a worldwide symbol of brand quality. We'd focus on the careful attention to brand standards and to how the brand is presented. We'd consider the aesthetics expressed in the brand experience in Mercedes dealers worldwide. We'd study Mercedes' brand structure, model designations, and the positioning of the AMG performance brand. We'd observe their top-tier and successful position for decades in Formula One racing and other motorsports, plus their intentional and impeccably executed sponsorships in golf, fashion, and other affluent sports and lifestyle activities. We'd gauge the perceived brand value and brand premium that Mercedes commands. In short, we'd admire Mercedes as a textbook example of brand strategy that has been crafted and well executed for decades.

Now, as we think about the future of the company in the global market of today's customers and potential customers, in both mature and, especially, emerging markets, let's examine Mercedes' business from a customer-centric viewpoint. What do we focus on now? Instead of looking at product features or brand identity, we focus instead on different types of customers. We compare a young woman in India with a young family in Colombia, with business professionals in Germany, with wealthy Chinese entrepreneurs, with affluent empty nesters in California, with high-performance aficionados worldwide, and more. It's a world of different customer profiles with different needs, wants, and desires in different countries, with different customer values and different growth rates.

For whom is Mercedes designing cars? For whom is the Mercedes brand positioned? How important are adaptive headlights? In-vehicle Wi-Fi hot spots? Self-driving vehicles? Engine technology? Horsepower? Price? Luxury? Performance? In each case, the question must be followed with *"For whom?* . . . *For which customers?"* To some customers, the answer is that a particular feature is completely irrelevant. The customer neither knows nor cares about it. To other customers, it is very important, a key brand criterion and essential to their sustained loyalty. And so, the decision of which sets of customers to focus on, and which not, becomes critical to Mercedes' business strategy across its product strategy, brand strategy, and much more. In other words, a customer-centric business strategy becomes critical.

The shift from a product-centric to a customer-centric strategy can be, and often is, a wrenching change, with myriad practical implications for legacy companies. This is often particularly true for companies with a strong heritage of engineering, which have proudly built their businesses through product leadership. And yet it's a shift that more and more companies face.

Not many businesses have the scale, resources, and brand of Mercedes, however. Thus, readers who lead or work in small and mid-sized businesses may wonder how this applies to them. So, let's take a completely different example of looking at a business from product-centric, brand-centric, and customer-centric viewpoints.

Eric Hemphill and Silviu Gansca are the founders and co-owners of Redefined Fitness in Wilmette, Illinois. Eric is my personal trainer. Redefined Fitness has one location. By my estimate, it has about 10 employees, almost all of whom are personal trainers. The fitness and personal training business is highly competitive, with an expanding range of competitors, from national chains to local studios to virtual trainers, offering a widening range of locations, services, and prices, and featuring the latest fitness trends and methods. Eric and Silviu are entrepreneurs who have built and sustained an award-winning business of excellent trainers with a loyal clientele.

Let's look at their business from product-centric, brand-centric, and customer-centric viewpoints. Looking at Redefined Fitness from a product-centric approach, we see that they offer individual and small group training. Their approach is, broadly defined, functional fitness, spanning strength, core, cardio, mobility, and more. Their clients, many of whom have been with them for many years, include young parents, middle-aged individuals dedicated to being fit and healthy, and seniors wanting to stay strong and flexible. They have a legacy of expertise in rehabilitative techniques and training student athletes. Now, however, new competitors and methods abound. Should they expand into children's programs? Yoga classes? Massage? Physical therapy? High-intensity interval training? New types of equipment? Virtual personal training became popular during the Covid-19 shutdown and continues growing. Should they offer personal training via Zoom? Through a mobile app? Should they be concerned about competitors offering fitness classes or exercise facilities at lower prices? These are all product questions.

Taking a step back and looking at Redefined Fitness from a brand-centric viewpoint, we focus on their excellent reputation and the Redefined Fitness brand; the word-of-mouth advocacy of their clients; their position in the local community, including successive years of winning "Best Personal Training" in local polls; their reviews on Yelp and other rating sites; and their presence on Instagram, Facebook, and other social media, which further enhances their brand. Should they raise their profile in the community? Should they do more PR? Should they introduce branded merchandise? Should they open more locations? Should they franchise Redefined Fitness? Should they create a Redefined Fitness YouTube channel?

Finally, taking a customer-centric view of Redefined Fitness, we focus on whom they serve—and whom they want to serve. Affluent families? Young parents? Healthy middle-agers? Student athletes? Ironman competitors? Social young adults? CrossFit enthusiasts? Therapeutic clients? People looking to get started and get healthy? And, whom *aren't* they looking to serve—or are not well suited to serving?

Whether it is Mercedes or Eric and Silviu, businesses face the same questions:

- How can we gain and retain customers?
- What is most important to our customers?
- What drives customer engagement?
- What produces customer loyalty?
- How can we grow customer value?

All of these questions require us to answer with the question: "For which customers?"

What Customer Centricity Is Not

No doubt many readers have had the experience of hearing their CEO or another senior leader say, or have even said themselves, often in a big company meeting, something along the lines of, "We're going to organize this entire company around the customer. Our whole company is going to be focused on delighting the customer." Typically, this statement is accompanied by a graphic with "Customer" in the center, surrounded by different functions with arrows all pointing to the customer. That's all well and good; after all, what's not to like when it comes to having satisfied customers? But that's not what we mean by customer centricity.

Customer centricity is about customer differentiation. And the need for customer differentiation follows from customer heterogeneity.

"The Customer" Does Not Exist

Customer centricity is built on understanding that customers are heterogeneous. As Fader said, "the customer" does not exist.[6] Given the wide array of customer profiles, types, needs, expectations, desires, behaviors, and, particularly, value, talking about them as a homogenous aggregate doesn't provide the practical specificity and insights needed for business purposes. To illustrate this, picture the front door of your neighborhood Walgreens (or any large pharmacy). Think of all the people who walk through the door of that Walgreens on a typical day. It could be a woman from out of town who realizes she forgot to pack her makeup. She will probably never return to that specific Walgreens store. There's the man who comes to the store with his two small children to buy some cough medicine, along with juice and a bag of potato chips. He and his family live nearby and are regular customers for everything from prescriptions to diapers to greeting cards to soft drinks. A woman who has diabetes heads straight to the pharmacy to pick up her insulin prescription, which she depends on and needs to be refilled regularly. She hopes that her insurer has approved filling her new prescription and that it's been done properly. She may buy a few other things while she's in the store. These and myriad others may walk through that Walgreens front door in an hour on any given day. To talk about all these people as if they were the same "customer" really doesn't tell us much that's useful.

Not only are these customers different, but they are not all of equal value from Walgreens' viewpoint. This observation can be misinterpreted, as it was by a group of healthcare system executives a few years ago during a presentation that included customer differentiation. Some reacted negatively and vigorously. They recoiled from the assertion that not all customers are created equal because they interpreted it as meaning that they would or should give some patients better care than others. That's not at all what it means.

All this statement means is that different customers have very different profiles, needs, wants, and behaviors, and different values for the business. That is not to say that some customers have greater value as human beings or that the health and well-being of any customer or group are more important than another's. Airline customers who pay more for their flight don't receive more safety than others. Restaurants don't have different food safety and cleanliness standards for customers who eat there weekly compared to customers who only come in occasionally.

Some customers are more valuable to a business than others because of the nature and patterns of their purchase behavior: the frequency of their purchases, the mix of products they buy, their loyalty, their total revenue, their profitability, and other factors. For example, my wife and I both shop at Target, but from Target's viewpoint, she is a more valuable customer than I am. She shops there more often, buys more product categories (food, children's clothes, household supplies, home furnishings, and more), while I buy items from time to time in men's apparel. That my wife is the more valuable customer for Target doesn't mean a less frequent shopper who generates smaller sales (like me) doesn't matter. Target still wants me to find what I'm looking for, have a good checkout experience, and, if I need to make a return, for it to go smoothly. All customers should have a good experience. Nor should lower-value customers be disregarded. They still produce significant revenue that the company doesn't want to lose (and that can probably be grown). The practical reality, though, is that not all customers are of equal value; some customers are more important than others and, thus, not all customers warrant equal investment.

As this shows, *customers are heterogeneous. Customer heterogeneity is foundational to customer centricity.* This is more important than ever because *customer heterogeneity is increasing* in a wide range of businesses. Customer heterogeneity might be obvious with retail customers. But let's look at an entirely different industry: electric utilities. Every household in the neighborhood gets the same electricity, right? It would seem that an electric utility has about as homogenous a customer base as you can imagine. And yet, there is growing heterogeneity even among electric utility customers.

Consider the most basic dynamic, that electricity historically went in only one direction—from the utility to the customer. Now there are customers who want their electricity to flow in two directions. Owners of the Ford F-150 Lightning can use their vehicles to generate electricity that they can resell back to the electric grid. This is in addition to the growing number of residential customers who have installed solar panels and generate their own electricity that they can use to offset their utility electric usage and/or sell back. Electric utilities now have customers who are "prosumers"—producers and consumers. And, they want to use, or not use, the electric utility at the times they choose. Then there is the elderly homeowner who, far from wanting to produce her own electricity, just wants to be sure her power is reliable because she depends on her breathing machine. Some customers now expect to be able to manage their household electricity usage remotely using a smartphone app. Others don't care about mobile apps but just want low prices and utility bills that are simple and easy to read. Still others want their power to be produced by renewable generation methods. Today, the electric utility industry is experiencing customer heterogeneity as never before, with more to come and with resultant practical implications. The same holds true for a wide variety of industries.

Next, we'll see how customer centricity based on *customer heterogeneity* leads to the related topics of *customer segmentation, customer differentiation,* and, ultimately, *customer valuation.*

Customer Segmentation: The Truck Stop

To explore the concept of *customer segmentation,* let's use an example that's probably familiar to anyone who has ever driven along a highway—truck stops.

If we look at the typical truck stop, we can see three types of customers. One is a family on a trip that stops to use the restroom and then buys a Coke and lunch for everyone before hitting the road again. In the parlance of the travel industry, these are *individual leisure travelers.* Another group is the businesspeople who spend much of their workweek on the road—for example, covering a sales territory from Chicago to Dayton to Cleveland to Detroit and back again. Driving from place to place, the businessperson uses a truck stop to get gas and a coffee. Then there are the professional truck drivers who transport loads over long-distance routes across multiple states and often coast to coast. These truck drivers come to the truck stop to eat, take a shower, restock supplies and sundries, and fill up their tractors with diesel.

Looking at these three groups—or segments—of customers, we can differentiate them quantitatively in multiple ways. For example, based on traffic and transaction volume (the number of people walking through the front door and paying at the cash register), the family of leisure travelers may account for 50%, the businesspeople on the road for 30%, and the professional truck drivers for the remaining 20%. Traffic and transactions, however, while measures of customer activity, aren't the same as customer value. A family's Cokes and snacks and a truck driver's 100 gallons of diesel fuel are each one transaction, but obviously those transactions have greatly different customer values to the business.

When we go a step further and segment customers based on the revenue each group generates, a different picture emerges. The leisure traveler segment (families buying snacks and gas) may produce 15% of revenue. Business travelers (coffee, lunch, and gas) account for perhaps 30% of revenue. Professional truck drivers (buying 100 gallons of diesel at every fill-up) could well be 55% of revenue. We can add additional steps to further refine our value estimation by asking what the profit margin is for each segment. Professional truck drivers buy a lot but at a substantial discount. How often do they stop (their purchase frequency), how big is the segment, how fast is it growing (or shrinking), and so on?

This is a very simple example, but it introduces customer differentiation based on customer value as the basis for determining which customer segment(s) the business chooses to target. Again, that doesn't mean ignoring customers in other segments; but they're not who we're designing the business for. A more complex example of customer differentiation is provided by the airline industry.

The Airline Passenger

Envision a typical passenger concourse at a busy airport such as Chicago, New York, Atlanta, London, Frankfurt, or Tokyo. It is a sea of humanity. Looking at that throng of all types of people traveling for all types of reasons illustrates how referring to them categorically as "the customer" doesn't really tell us much; while it's not visible, their customer value varies greatly. How can the airline management team differentiate their value? If we apply a few basic criteria, sharp differences in customer value become evident. First, are they *business travelers* or *leisure travelers*? Second, how *frequently* do they travel? And third, how much average *yield* (the industry term for revenue per mile flown) do they produce? In other words, do they fly longer distances at higher fares? By applying those basic criteria to the mass of humanity in the airport concourse, airline passenger segments emerge.

At one extreme is the very high yield, very frequent business traveler—for example, the lawyer who lives in Chicago and travels monthly (first class) to meet with her client in Singapore. At the other end is the college student who goes to Daytona Beach once a year for spring break on the cheapest ticket he can find. In between, obviously, is a range of customer segments with very different values depending on their respective combination of travel patterns and characteristics, frequency, and yield, with higher-end segments of business travelers producing a disproportionate share of the total value (i.e., revenue and profitability).

Now, while everyone is welcome on the airline, all should get good service, and everyone must arrive safely, if you're an airline executive, you can't design and optimize the airline for everyone in all customer segments. This doesn't imply that there's a single right answer. Southwest Airlines and Singapore Airlines are both successful airlines that target different customer segments. The same applies to Lufthansa and easyJet. Common to all is the fact that if you're an airline executive, it's essential to be strategic and disciplined in differentiating and identifying your target customer segment(s) based on customer value when making business decisions such as where to fly, how much to invest in your product, your customer experience design, and the incentives in your frequent flyer program. The same concepts, among others, apply to credit cards, hotels, retailers, and many other businesses in both business-to-consumer (B2C) and business-to-business (B2B) sectors.

From Differentiation to Valuation

A popular statement in business is that "customers are our most important asset." So, then, how do we value that asset? We said that the objective of customer strategy is to grow customer value. How do we measure (and project) customer value?

This brings us to another fundamental concept of a customer-centric business strategy: *customer lifetime value*. Fader described customer lifetime value as "the very unit of measurement upon which customer centricity and customer-centric firms are built."[7] As Kellogg colleague Florian Zettelmeyer has pointed out, "Customer centricity provides an analytical framework to think about marketing decisions by quantifying customer value."

Our entire discussion of customer centricity has been leading us to focus on customer value and, at the individual customer level, *customer lifetime value* (CLV). When we say that our objective is to grow customer value, what we ultimately mean is to grow CLV. CLV is *the present value of the total profit—past and future—from a customer.* Two points in that definition bear highlighting at the outset. First, CLV is based on *profit*, not revenue. Second, CLV is *prospective* (i.e., forward-looking), not just historical or retrospective, and includes both *past and future* profit (Figure 5.2).

The past element of customer value is known. In practice, we may not be able to track it at the identifiable individual customer level, for either or both of two reasons. First, we may not know the identity of end-user purchasers or be able to associate purchase value with identifiable individuals. Second,

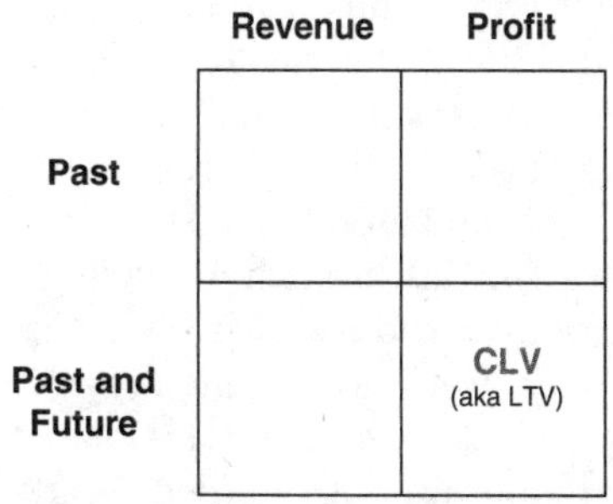

	Revenue	Profit
Past		
Past and Future		CLV (aka LTV)

FIGURE 5.2 Measuring Customer Value

even if we are able to identify our end-user customers and their respective purchases, our information systems may not yet enable tracking at this individual level. However, the profit that an individual customer has generated in the past has, in fact, occurred.

Projecting the future value component of CLV is probabilistic. It is a prediction of the customer's *expected future value* (i.e., profit from that customer). We project and predict how much value (profit) the customer is likely to produce going forward. A full explanation of the methodology for projecting CLV, and doing so as accurately as possible, is well beyond the scope of this chapter. However, the basic elements that are used to project the customer's future value are the following:

- *Projected duration of relationship.* How long do we expect to retain the customer? A different way to say this is the churn rate. How likely are we to lose the customer each year?

- *Projected frequency of transactions.* How often do we expect the customer to purchase?

- *Projected value of each transaction.* How much value do we expect each transaction to generate?

These are the most basic elements that we use to project the customer's future value. Then, we can add the historical value to estimate the individual's CLV.

There are many refinements of the basic CLV formula that are relevant in practice. Ideally, we should use the present value of the future profit from the customer in computing CLV at a given point in time. In other words, we need to discount the future profit stream back to the present.

CLV is calculated somewhat differently for contractual and noncontractual businesses. In a contractual business, such as a cellphone contract, we know when the relationship ends (i.e., the customer doesn't renew, or "churns"). In a noncontractual business, such as a retailer or airline, we don't know if and when we've lost the customer. Plus, the frequency and size of transactions are much more variable.

Tallying the average CLV of all customers in the aggregate is typically of limited usefulness and, more important, can be misleading. CLV typically varies significantly by customer segment. (Think, for example, "heavy users," "average users," and "light users.") Therefore, calculating CLV at the segment level is much more accurate and useful. Similarly, for a business that acquires its customers in cohorts, such as through marketing campaigns, calculating and comparing CLV by cohort is key (e.g., credit cardholder acquisition). Another factor that is often useful is differentiating CLV by source of acquisition (i.e., how the customer was acquired). This chapter doesn't go into detail on the methodology for projecting CLV; rather, the intention here is twofold:

(1) that you understand the basic concept of CLV and its elements, and (2) that you start to think about and look at your business strategy and your customers in terms of CLV.

CLV is important to a customer-centric business because it informs our understanding and decisions on many practical questions. We can determine the worth of a given customer or customer segment and differentiate and compare customers and segments based on their value. We can make decisions about which customers and segments warrant investment. More important, we can determine how much investment in a given customer or segment is economical. How much should we invest to acquire a customer? How much should we invest to retain this customer? How much should we invest to grow this segment? CLV enables us to assess the value generation of marketing investments and optimize our marketing activities accordingly—and more.

CLV in the Real World

When chief marketing officers in various companies and industries are asked, "Are you using CLV in your company?" the answer is often a variation of "We're working on it." Some businesses are partially there; they can track CLV for some of their customers. For example, they typically can track and project CLV for members of their loyalty program but often not for customers who are not in the loyalty program. This occurs, for example, in retail and travel. Or they may be able to tally the CLV of customers who purchase through certain distribution channels but not through others. Think, for example, of an athletic wear brand that can track the CLV of customers for direct purchases through their website or mobile app but not for purchases that these same customers make at a sporting goods store. In that case, they can know part of the CLV for a customer, but not that customer's whole value. Loyalty programs are a mainstay way to overcome this problem. Plus, there are other ways (such as the credit card used) that can be employed to identify and track customer value.

Another practical challenge in putting CLV into practice at the individual customer level is information systems. Building a customer data system that enables tracking and projecting the value of individual customers, and then analyzing and using that data, is an undertaking, particularly in companies with legacy IT systems. Fortunately, cloud-based systems make this more doable than ever for companies of all sizes.

So, for all these reasons, most companies are on a journey to using CLV at the individual customer level. Additionally, the structure of some businesses means that there are impediments to getting identifiable individual customer data, and they may never do so. Some businesses sell through distributors (as do many B2B businesses) and others through retailers. In these cases, the brand manufacturer typically doesn't get the identity, transaction history, and purchase value of specific customers. If Fairlife sells milk through Target, for example, it probably can't get the specific data that Customer X buys two half-gallons every Saturday; nor can it market directly to that customer, suggesting other Fairlife products. Again, loyalty programs can be key to solving this problem; but there are other ways around it, and data provision is getting better. Nonetheless, some businesses will always face inherent difficulties in getting to identifiable end-user customer value.

Often, the best that a business can do is to get to the customer-segment level. In other words, it can determine the total value of a group of customers (e.g., people who buy lawn equipment for farms compared to people who buy lawnmowers for homes), but can't identify the individual customers. A very revealing method can be differentiating customers by source of acquisition (i.e., through the channel the customer was acquired). If you know the number of customers in the segment, you can approximate the average customer value by segment.

Projecting CLV by customer segment and calculating the average customer CLV for each segment isn't the ideal for multiple reasons, but it's a lot better than not differentiating based on customer value and can still be very useful. Getting to the absolute and technically perfect CLV calculation is less important at the start than using the concept and approach as a framework for customer centric-thinking about your business strategy and making business decisions based on customer value. Do your best to get to individual customer value measures, start to differentiate your customers by value, and put this data to use, while steadily improving your data and methodology as you work to progress.

To recap briefly, a customer-centric business strategy is based on differentiating customer value. Doing so provides the foundation and basis for a wide range of important practical decisions: which customers to target, how much to invest to acquire and retain a customer, how to most effectively grow customer value, how to optimize marketing investments and activities, and more. CLV provides a framework for thinking about a business in this way. It also provides a methodology for projecting and maximizing the value of customers individually.

Let's return to the example of a small business, Redefined Fitness. While Eric, the co-owner, doesn't have a customer data system that enables him to calculate CLV, he can still use this concept as a framework for a customer-centric approach to thinking about his business and customers and making decisions. Eric can observe, for example, which types of customers tend to remain for years and which wane. He can relate this to individuals' reasons for working out. He can consider which customers tend to increase their frequency of working out over time, as well as which ones tend to shift from group sessions to individual sessions. He can associate all of this with the initial acquisition source of the customer. Were they recommended by a physical therapist, or were they a walk-in who lives in the neighborhood? We could easily expand this list of questions. Eric can probably get relatively specific about gauging and projecting the CLV of his customers, by profile and individually, without an elaborate customer data system. And all of this can provide very practical, useful guidance for him to grow his business. I often ask MBA students: "If you were Eric, and a person whom you've never met before walked in the door of Redefined Fitness and said that they'd like to start working out there, and you could ask them three questions to project their likely CLV, what three questions would you ask?"

Customer-Centric Business Valuation

Thus far, we've said a customer-centric business strategy is based on customer differentiation, particularly differentiation of customer value, and that its aim is to grow customer value. We've also discussed CLV at individual and customer-segment levels and that customer value can also be tallied at the aggregate level for all customers. The total value of all the customers of a business (in other words, the total of all individual customer CLVs) is known as its *customer equity*. Customer equity is the financial value of the customer base.

Customer-based corporate valuation (CBCV) projects the value of a business based on its customer equity. The basic rationale for CBCV is that the value of a business depends on the value of its customers (i.e., the CLV of its customers and their aggregate customer equity). As McCarthy and Pereda[8] explain, while there are many methodological issues still to be worked out, CBCV holds great promise. By extending customer centricity to corporate valuation, CBCV advances the integration of marketing and finance, thus raising the credibility and accountability of the practice of marketing.

This brings us back to Drucker at the beginning of this chapter. The purpose of a business is to create a customer. The aim of a customer-centric business strategy is to grow customer value. Doing so in turn grows the value of the business.

Conclusion

Customer centricity, which differentiates customers and manages customer offerings, investment, and engagement, should be a business strategy, not just a marketing strategy. It is foundational to a customer strategy that maximizes and secures customer value at both the aggregate level (i.e., all customers) and at the individual customer level. Customer centricity is based on *customer differentiation* and follows from *customer heterogeneity*, which is foundational to customer centricity. An essential criterion for differentiating customers is their value. *Customer lifetime value* (CLV) provides a framework for thinking about a business in terms of customer value. CLV is based on *profit*, not revenue, and *is the present value of the total profit—past and future—from a customer*. It is *prospective* (i.e., forward-looking). In other words, it incorporates a measure of the customer's value to date and a prediction of the customer's *expected future value* (i.e., profit from that customer). CLV informs our understanding and decisions on many practical questions, such as how much to invest in acquiring or retaining a customer. The total value of all customers of a business (in other words, the total of all individual customer CLVs) is known as *customer equity*. *Customer-based corporate valuation* (CBCV) projects the value of a business based on its customer equity. Thus, CBCV extends customer centricity to corporate valuation. Carrying the practice of customer centricity all the way to the individual customer level leads to *personalization*, the subject of Chapter 23.

Author Biography

Thomas F. (Tom) O'Toole is the associate dean for Executive Education and Clinical Professor of Marketing at the Kellogg School of Management at Northwestern University. He previously served as the executive director of the Program for Data Analytics at Kellogg. His work and teaching focus on customer value growth and related subjects. He developed and teaches a popular Kellogg MBA course on customer loyalty strategy and practices. He is the author of "Branding Services in the Digital Era" in *Kellogg on Branding in a Hyper-Connected World* (Wiley, 2019). O'Toole is a senior advisor for McKinsey and Company. He has served and currently serves on the board of directors of public and private companies in a range of industries. He writes for *Forbes* on subjects spanning academia and business. Until his retirement, O'Toole was chief marketing officer of United Airlines and president of its MileagePlus business unit. Before United, O'Toole was chief marketing officer and chief information officer of Hyatt Hotels Corporation.

CHAPTER 6

Emptor Cognita: Competitive Advantage through Buyer Learning

Gregory S. Carpenter

In 1954, Peter Drucker wrote that the purpose of business is "to create a customer,"[1] and from this foundation the concept of a market orientation bloomed. Market-oriented firms understand customers' needs, share information they learn with the firm, and respond to customers.[2] This approach has become known as being *market driven* or *customer centric*. Scholars have developed the concept, investigated the organizational culture associated with a market-driven approach, and outlined the process by which organizations become more market-driven.[3] Empirical studies demonstrate that a greater market orientation is associated with superior financial performance,[4] as firms have amply demonstrated. For example, Amazon and Toyota illustrate the power of the customer-centric approach.

Despite the compelling logic and mounting evidence of the success of a market-driven approach, Steve Jobs famously pursued a different approach: "Some people say, 'Give the customers what they want.' But that's not my approach. Our job is to figure out what they're going to want before they do . . . People don't know what they want until you show it to them."[5] Head of product development for BMW Dr. Wolfgang Reitzle essentially agreed with Mr. Jobs when he said, "We know what a BMW is. We don't have to ask our consumers."[6] Howard Schultz expressed a strikingly similar view when he wrote, "Don't just give the customers what they ask for. If you offer them something they're not accustomed to, something so far superior that it takes a while to develop their palates, you can create a sense of discovery and excitement and loyalty that will bond them to you. It may take longer but . . . you can educate your customers to like it rather than kowtowing to mass-market appeal."[7] Apple, BMW, and Starbucks illustrate a *market-driving* approach.[8]

Although the success of a market-driving approach may appear to be a recent phenomenon, Austrian economist Joseph Schumpeter laid the intellectual foundation for such an approach over 90 years ago: "Innovations . . . do not as a rule take place in such a way that first wants arise spontaneously in consumers," he wrote. "The producer . . . initiates change, and consumers are . . . taught to want new things."[9] The ability of firms to shape customer thinking appears obvious, yet the strategic thinking within firms remains rooted in a market-driven approach. A small but growing number of studies over many years explore how firms drive market by shaping consumer tastes.[10] But the strategic import of the mechanisms these studies identify remain underdeveloped. In this chapter, we will explore three studies that suggest new avenues to create enduring competitive advantage through shaping buyer learning.

Buyer Learning

The market-driving approach raises a fundamental question: With so many demands on our time, why do we devote cognitive resources, time, and effort to learning about dish detergent, life insurance, motor oil, and thousands of other products? The simple answer is that we believe doing so will, in some meaningful way, improve our lives. The more complete answer is that throughout our lives we pursue *goals*—a desired future state of being. Our goals can be simple and easily achievable in the short term, such as enjoying a nice cup of coffee this afternoon. We might pursue lifelong, complex goals such as being part of a loving family. We pursue personal, professional, simple, complex, short- and long-term goals. We seek to achieve some outcomes (e.g., fame and fortune) and avoid others (e.g., failure and humiliation). Achieving some goals is extremely important, whereas achieving other goals is less meaningful. Each of these goals creates a problem to solve, and solving those problems, achieving goals, creates value for consumers.

To solve problems, we learn. Research suggests that consumers engage in a five-stage process. First, we formulate and recognize that we have a goal, which creates a problem to solve. Second, we search for alternative solutions, discovering brands and learning to understand the benefits they deliver.

Third, for options that survive the initial screening, we develop a logic for comparing alternatives. Fourth, consumers develop a strategy for choosing among the surviving candidates. In some cases consumers are careful, thoughtful, and deliberate in making choices, but in others consumers choose based on emotion or without careful consideration. Fifth, with a choice made, consumers evaluate the outcome. In some cases, the feedback is clear and unambiguous. For example, did the plumber stop the leak in the faucet? In other cases, feedback is ambiguous, noisy, and difficult to interpret.

Consumers learn a great deal as they solve problems, but four types of knowledge are key. First, consumers learn how to categorize options. Categories form the basis for competition among brands. Second, within each category, consumers learn perceptions: the thoughts, feelings, and associations that define each member of a category. These perceptions define how consumers draw comparisons between brands and thus make trade-offs, creating patterns of competition among brands. Third, consumers learn how to value these differences, forming preferences. Preferences determine consumers' willingness to pay and thus directly influence the fortunes of firms. Finally, consumers learn how to choose. The logic consumers use can be comprehensive, considering all the factors at play, but more likely consumers will rely on a simpler strategy that excludes much relevant and possibly crucial information.

Although what consumers learn may ultimately determine the fortunes of competitors, firms nevertheless play a central role in what consumers learn. Firms create markets, differentiate their brands, and launch new products. Each of these actions—and many more, of course—influence what consumers observe, what they experience, and, therefore, what consumers learn. Rather than simply satisfying consumers, market-driving firms shape the information available to consumers, which influences the learning process. By shaping what consumers know, market-driving firms create competitive advantage. But how do firms influence the process to gain advantage? We explore three avenues through which firms shape consumer thinking and thus embrace a market-driving strategy.

Market Pioneering

After venturing to San Francisco following the gold rush of 1849, Levi Strauss opened a retail store to supply miners. With Jacob Davis, a tailor from Reno, Nevada, Strauss formed Levi Strauss & Company and launched 501 jeans in 1873, featuring Davis's unique design: copper rivets securing the pockets. Levi Strauss & Company's revenues topped $7 billion more than a century later, Levi's 501s remain iconic jeans, and Levi Strauss & Company's market capitalization recently surpassed $7 billion.

Influencing Consumers

Market pioneers like Levi Strauss & Company play a special role in consumer learning. Prior to the pioneer, there is no category; consumers lack perceptions, have yet to form preferences, and have no reason to develop a logic to choose among brands. For example, before 1873, consumers had, at best, limited understanding of the concept of blue jeans. By creating a new market, the pioneering brand can become strongly associated—even synonymous—with the category. Red Bull and Uber are obvious examples. Psychologists describe such brands as *prototypical*. As such, pioneers can become the very definition of the product category. The pioneer has the opportunity to define the product category, establish the dimensions of consumer perceptions, shape the preferences consumers develop, and influence the strategies consumers use to choose among brands.

In a series of experiments, Kent Nakamoto and I explored the impact of market pioneering.[11] In one experiment, subjects learned about down quilts, a product category they were unfamiliar with at the time. We designed four different products based on four attributes: the type of down fill (mixed goose and duck down or exclusively goose down), the type of cover (cotton or synthetic), the fill rating (a numerical indicator of warmth), and price. Half the subjects viewed brand A as the pioneer, while the other half viewed brand B as the pioneer. After we presented subjects with the pioneer, they viewed the other brands and indicated their preferences.

The results showed that subjects preferred brand A or B more when it was the pioneer compared to the case in which it was not. Moreover, subjects preferred the attributes of the pioneer over the attributes of other brands. For example, if the pioneer offered exclusively goose down, subjects preferred goose down to mixed goose and duck down. If the pioneer offered a cotton cover versus a synthetic cover, subjects preferred cotton to synthetic and vice versa. The impact of pioneering in consumer preferences creates an advantage for pioneers. Buyers simply learn to prefer it.

Competitive Advantage

Empirical analyses show that pioneers' advantage can endure for years or even decades.[12] Different studies report different results based on different definitions of pioneering and different types of data. For example, some studies use historical data that includes failed entrants,[13] while others use data over shorter periods of time.[14] Despite these differences, studies demonstrate that *surviving* pioneers outsell *surviving* later entrants. For example, Glen Urban and his colleagues[15] demonstrated that, holding other factors constant, second entrants earn on average 71% of the market share of the pioneer, third entrants earn 58%, and so on up to the sixth entrant, which earns less than half the market share of the pioneer.

This pattern of results suggests that later-entering competitors with equally attractive products and similar strategies earn *a smaller* market share than the pioneer simply by virtue of their order of entry. To achieve the same share as a pioneer with the same strategy, later entrants must spend more on advertising, be priced below the pioneers, be available in more outlets, or adopt a more attractive brand position. The evidence reveals something very important about consumer behavior and entry timing. Consumers apparently think about pioneers and later entrants differently, and this difference creates an advantage for pioneers. Research suggests that pioneers continue to benefit from early entry for at least three reasons:

1. *Awareness and recall.* By entering first, the pioneer becomes better known. Being better known, a pioneering brand is easier to recall and is therefore simply recalled more often than later entrants. You may easily remember that Charles Lindbergh was the first pilot to successfully fly solo across the Atlantic. But who was second? (Answer: Amelia Earhart.) Pioneering brands enjoy a similar advantage. Being better known, the pioneer will be considered more often and, as a result, chosen more often, all else being equal.

2. *Low risk.* After the pioneer creates a market, some consumers will try the pioneer and become satisfied, even loyal, customers. For people with experience with the pioneer, later-entering brands remain untested and therefore risky. So long as the risk difference exists, the pioneer will remain a safer and thus more attractive option.

3. *Setting the standard.* By creating the category, the pioneer can set the standard or simply define the ideal product. The existence of a standard creates a dilemma. All late entrants are judged in comparison to the pioneer. If the later entrant adopts a position similar to the pioneer, it has little differentiation. The pioneer remains the preferred choice. If the later entrant chooses to be very different from the pioneer, the later entrant will also be seen as less attractive. Thus, later entrants struggle to establish an appealing position when one brand sets the standard.[16]

Summary

Although the popular view expressed by Drucker and so many others implies that consumers have established tastes, research across many fields suggests instead that individuals *learn* their preferences. Virtually all tastes are acquired. We are born with poorly defined tastes. Market pioneers play a special and unusually powerful role in shaping the categories, consumer perceptions, preferences for brands, and the strategies consumers use to choose. As a result, market pioneers can shape the competitive process to create long-lived, powerful competitive advantages.

Brand Differentiation

Budweiser launched its famous American-style lager in 1876. A low-calorie alternative, Miller Lite, entered in 1973. Just five years later, Coors introduced Coors Light, and the number of new entrants continued to grow. By 1997, more breweries operated in the United States than in Germany.[17] Despite intense and growing competition, Coors Light reached the number-two position in revenue behind Bud Light in 2018.[18] What fueled the rise of Coors Light?

Coors Light uses a unique brewing process, described as "frost brewing." According to Coors' advertising, "Coors Light's unique frost-brewing process locks in a taste as cold as the Rockies." Brewers filter beer at cold temperatures to remove impurities, a less expensive alternative to heat pasteurizing, but one writer described frost brewing as "fairly meaningless."[19] Can a brand differentiate itself from 7,000 rivals and rise to the number-two best-selling beer in the United States using a feature that is distinctive but possibly meaningless?

Consumer Learning

In a series of experiments, Rashi Glazer, Kent Nakamoto, and I explored that question.[20] We designed profiles of brands of down jackets, pasta, and compact disc players. In the case of down jackets, for example, we created a set of eight different jacket brands based on three attributes (temperature ratings, type of shell cover, and type of stitching). One group of subjects viewed the eight different jackets that we described as offering regular down fill. A second group of subjects viewed the same set of jackets except we described one option, the so-called target brand, as offering "alpine-class down fill." We provided no explanation as to the meaning of features. We repeated the experiment for another group of subjects, but for this group we revealed that "alpine-class down fill" was no different than regular down fill. After reading the descriptions, all subjects expressed their preferences for each of the jackets.

Subjects' preference for the target brand with regular down fill averaged 3.1 on a scale of 1 to 10, with 10 being most preferred. But when that same jacket included alpine-class down fill, subjects' preference climbed to 9.1. When subjects learned that alpine-class down fill was a meaningless difference, subjects' preference for the target brand averaged 4.3; when the same jacket included alpine-class down fill, subjects preference was 8.4. In both cases these differences are statistically significant, suggesting that people unambiguously preferred the jackets with alpine-class down fill whether or not they knew it was irrelevant.

What about the case in which the differentiated brand varies in price from the other brands? In another experiment, we varied the price of the target brand jacket with alpine-class down fill. Subjects viewed the same jacket at either $150, the price in the first experiment, $120, or $180. Again, we left some subjects in the dark about the meaning of alpine-class down fill, but we revealed the attribute's irrelevance to other subjects. When the jacket offered only regular down fill, raising its price reduced preference for it. But when that same brand offered alpine-class down fill, raising the price *increased* consumers' preference for the jacket.

Competitive Advantage

Why would consumers value an attribute they know or suspect to be irrelevant? Can an irrelevant difference create an enduring competitive advantage for the differentiated brand? Research on consumer psychology suggests four intriguing possibilities:

1. *Hypothesis testing.* Consumers may view the novel attribute as proposing a hypothesis. The firm is essentially suggesting that the attribute is valuable. Why else would they include it? One logical reaction for a consumer is to buy the product and test the firm's claim. In many cases, testing is difficult or ambiguous. Is the jacket with alpine-class down fill warmer than the one with regular down fill? How is a consumer to *objectively* determine the difference? When a test is ambiguous or uninformative, consumers have a tendency to *confirm* a hypothesis. Confirming the value of an irrelevant attribute simply reinforces its importance. Brands that lack the attribute are, therefore, perceived as inferior and at a competitive disadvantage.

2. *Pragmatic communication.* By including a novel attribute, the firm is communicating something to consumers. But what? Every communication has two dimensions: the *semantic or* literal meaning of the communication, and the *pragmatic* meaning or the reason for the communication. An irrelevant attribute, however, has little literal meaning. When a communication lacks literal meaning, individuals look for pragmatic meaning. A consumer would ask, "Why are they telling me about this feature?" A consumer could reasonably conclude that the firm included it because it must be valuable. Why else would they offer it?, a consumer might reason.

3. *Novelty.* An irrelevant attribute is, by design, novel. Consumers give greater weight to novel information compared to redundant information. When comparing two brands of shampoo, for example, consumers look

for what distinguishes one brand from the other. Differences that might be small become more important in that situation. Differences that are irrelevant can become valuable and, as long as they remain novel, they can be the basis for meaningful differentiation.

4. *Simplifying choice.* Choosing among similar brands is a difficult process. Finding the superior brand of coffee, jacket, or motor oil is challenging, given that many similar alternatives exist. Humans are cognitive misers, spending as little effort as possible to make a choice. By being unique, a novel, though irrelevant, attribute creates the opportunity for a consumer to construct a simple and logical reason to choose one brand over another. This simple logic becomes part of our routine and, once established, changes slowly.

If consumers value an attribute, why will they continue to do so after learning that it is indeed irrelevant? If a consumer learns that an attribute is, in fact, irrelevant in that it does not affect the product performance as one might conclude, the evidence suggests that consumers will continue to value it. Experience may "confirm" its value in hypothesis testing by consumers, even if those "tests" are ambiguous and inconclusive. The irrelevant attribute still has pragmatic value; it remains novel, and it will continue to simplify choice. Thus, even knowing that an attribute is irrelevant does not eliminate its influence. It remains a unique source of value and thus a source of competitive advantage.

Summary

Brand differentiation is a classic marketing strategy. Achieving differentiation is a central goal of many marketing efforts. The logic for doing so often rests on finding an overlooked source of difference. The research on irrelevant attributes suggests, in contrast, that unique, distinctive, yet irrelevant differences can serve effectively as sources of differentiation. In markets where brands offer similar value and essentially offer the important, meaningful benefits, consumers can find choosing among the options challenging. Differentiating a brand with an irrelevant attribute can, ironically, simplify consumer choice and create a meaningfully distinct brand.

Brand Status

After making wine for many years in Bordeaux, France, Christian Moueix produced his first vintage of Dominus Estate in Napa Valley, California, from the 1983 harvest. Years before, two Napa Valley pioneers—Chateau Montelena and Stag's Leap Cellars—had captured the world's attention in 1976 when a panel of wine luminaries ranked their wines above legendary French wines in the famous blind tasting known as the Judgment of Paris. After emulating the great French wines, Napa Valley producers developed a unique style, producing richer, fruit-driven, more opulent wines. Although these so-called New-World-style wines sold well and commanded high prices, some experts described them as excessively alcoholic "fruit bombs." When asked about this New-World style, Mr. Moueix was distinctly unequivocal: "I hate the fruit bomb." He shuns the approach his thriving Napa Valley neighbors developed to produce it. Instead, Mr. Moueix relies on methods he developed making Pétrus, one of the most expensive wines produced in Bordeaux. Furthermore, when asked how he thinks of the consumer when making wine, he replied simply, "I don't. I make what pleases me." Even without consumer input, Dominus Estate wines have a devoted following. One critic described the 2016 vintage of Dominus Estate as "beyond perfection," and some retailers sell a single bottle for over $800.

The Status Game

How do firms succeed with consumers even as they reject consumer input? Ashlee Humphreys and I studied the U.S. wine market,[21] examining firms selling wine in the United States, including U.S. producers and producers in France and Italy. We interviewed, observed, and analyzed the behavior of dis tributors, retailers, and consumers, seeking to understand their motives and how they succeed. We discovered that firms create high-status brands using an approach that differs in significant ways from the process used to create successful mass-market brands.

Successful mass-market firms start with the consumer, as Peter Drucker advocated so many years ago. Firms analyze customer needs and seek to discover powerful drivers of what buyers value. Buyer insight is the foundation of successful mass-market brands. But in the wine industry, firms view customers as being uninformed and having inconsistent and difficult-to-predict preferences. From this perspective, consumers are poor guides to firms' decision making and a weak foundation for strategy. Rejecting consumer input, a firm develops a creative vision, which becomes the primary roadmap guiding the firm.

Based on the roadmap, the firms develops products. In mass-market firms, the winemaker is very much like an engineer. Fruit is grown or purchased, fermented, and blended to meet consumer tastes, the profile requested by a retailer, or the tastes of a powerful critic. Firms look for trends, seeking new growth opportunities. For market-driving firms, however, producing wine is more like creating art. Winemakers transform simple fruit into something extraordinary in a process that can transcend logic. The winemaker is like a musician, a sculptor, or a chef. More than a simple illusion, the winemaker performs magic.

For mass-market firms, reaching consumers through the existing distribution system is essential to access retailers, restaurants, and, ultimately, consumers. Distributors and retailers are especially powerful because of the extensive network of state and federal laws governing the sale of alcohol in the United States. Mass-market firms build relationships with retailers, seeking to gain greater access to their shelves for their wines. The retailer is a critically important and powerful customer. Some firms even develop products to meet retailer requests.

In contrast, firms building high-status brands reject input from retailers and use retail outlets as a stage to perform their magic. High-status brands stage events at retailers and elsewhere. During these events, the winemaker takes center stage, typically shares their vision of the wines, offers a broader perspective on wine in general, and conducts a tasting. Through such events, high-status brands attract new consumers, court loyal buyers, and share their vision with members of the retail staff.

As with movies, restaurants, and so many other product categories, critics and other voices on social media influence consumers. Hundreds of writers, critics, and magazines review and discuss wine. Although the quality of a wine may be ambiguous, critics have created a simple but powerful metric. In a review, a critic describes the wine and assigns a score (typically between zero and 100). By one estimate, every additional point from the most powerful critic can add 2.80 euros to the price of each bottle; a perfect score of 100 can fuel a three- or fourfold price increase.[22] For many market-driven firms, the power of critics creates an irresistible opportunity. Some firms produce wine with the explicit goal of earning a high score. By pleasing the critics, they reason, consumers will follow.

In the status game, however, critics are potential allies to *persuade* the public. Winemakers cultivate relationships with critics, sharing their knowledge and persuading critics of the wisdom of the winemaker's vision. Critics provide consumers with a language for the sensations of consuming wine, describe benchmarks, and provide needed structure to help consumers develop preferences,[23] even if the experience is highly ambiguous.[24] Rather than customers being satisfied, critics become advocates for a vision.

Market-driven firms see consumers as central to a winemaker's success as a commercial enterprise. Firms succeed by satisfying consumers. But in the status game, firms shape consumers' tastes to reflect the vision of the firm. Making wine to respond to consumer tastes violates industry norms. Producers risk losing their very legitimacy among other producers by being market driven. Instead, firms advance their vision in a battle for status; some win and others lose. Winners gain the respect and admiration of those with influence in the industry. Winners earn status, which consumers value. Wine lovers hunt for high-status wines and search for obscure, yet-to-be-discovered producers; buyers compete for the right to purchase wines from firms with limited production. Consumers research producers to develop their expertise, build networks to create a community, and pay premium prices for high-status brands.

Competitive Advantage

Our analysis of the wine industry suggests that status leads to power, power provides influence, and influence creates competitive advantage. But do these advantages endure? Do the premium prices high-status brands command reflect an enduring advantage over lower-status rivals? It would seem that competitors could produce high-quality alternatives, price them below high-status alternatives, and gain market share. In mass markets, such a process is to be expected. But our research suggests that high-status brands compete following a very different process. Competition follows a *social logic* rather than a market logic, as in the case of mass markets. Winners of the status game may or may not produce the best quality product, according to market logic. Losers may make fine, even excellent wines in the eyes of some consumers, but the consensus among those with influence is that they are inferior. The logic that separates winners and losers is based on social rivalry.

Can status create an enduring competitive advantage? The historical evidence suggests that differences in pricing between high- and low-status brands can be remarkable and can endure.[25] Sociologist Robert Merton dubbed this *the Matthew effect*,[26] after a verse in the New Testament. According to the Matthew effect, low-status brands are doubly disadvantaged. They start with fewer resources and subsequently have access to fewer opportunities and thus more limited access to resources. High-status brands, in comparison, have more resources and more opportunities to add to their resources. For example, high-status wines command premium prices, attract more attention from critics, gain shelf space more easily, and have access to resources that lower-status rivals do not. A low-status firm may duplicate the taste of a high-status wine, but gaining the same level of status can be challenging. The Matthew effect has been demonstrated in a variety of industries.[27] Status, it appears, creates enduring advantage.

Conclusion

Although the market-driven approach is deeply ingrained in many successful firms, the power of the market-driving approach is undeniable, as Apple, BMW, Starbucks, and so many others illustrate. How firms succeed with that approach, shaping what buyers learn, raises many important questions and suggests the need for a range of new strategic thinking. Fortunately, scholars have been studying learning for decades, providing a rich source of insight. Drawing on that extensive knowledge can reveal new avenues for creating enduring advantage. This chapter has suggested that firms shape consumer thinking through the timing of their entry, the means used to distinguish their brands, or the admiration they achieve among their peers. Surely, this is the tip of an iceberg in new strategic thinking.

Author Biography

Gregory S. Carpenter is Harold T. Martin Professor of Marketing and director of the Center for Market Leadership at Northwestern University's Kellogg School of Management. His research focuses on marketing strategy, how organizations become more customer centric, and luxury brands. His most recent book, *Resurgence: The Four Stages of Market-Focused Reinvention*, examines how firms transform their culture to become more customer centric, and his research has been recognized with the William F. O'Dell Award, the Paul E. Green Award, the Donald R. Lehmann Award, and the Sheth Foundation/*Journal of Marketing* Award from the American Marketing Association. A former Academic Trustee of the Marketing Science Institute and chair of the Kellogg Marketing Department, he served on the faculties of UCLA, Yale University, and Columbia University.

CHAPTER 7

Defensive Market Strategy

Tim Calkins

Google, FedEx, Apple, Lipitor, Patagonia. These are all tremendous businesses. They are leaders in their category, wildly profitable, and respected the world over. They are also late entrants. Apple wasn't the first company to make computers, and Lipitor wasn't the first statin. FedEx wasn't the first company shipping packages, and Google wasn't the first search engine. Despite showing up late, however, they managed to become successful firms. They found a way into the category.

For every successful late-entrant firm, however, there is another firm with another ending: the company that had all the market share and couldn't hang on to it. As the new competitor appeared, the established player lost customers and revenues. The market slipped away.

When we consider defensive strategy, the question is simple: How can you prevent this from happening to you? There are few things that are certain in this world, but here is one: If you have a profitable, successful business, you can be quite certain that competitors would like to get a piece of it. The better your business, the more profitable your firm, the more competitors will attack.

Defensive strategy is a critical but rarely discussed part of marketing. In this chapter, we will define defensive strategy and then walk through the process of developing a defense plan.

Defining Defensive Strategy

Defensive strategy is taking action to blunt the impact of a competitor's move. Offensive strategy, growth strategy, is focused on taking action to move the firm forward, to build revenue, profit, and market share. Defensive strategy is reacting to what competitors are doing in order to protect your business.

People often make this observation: "The best defense is a good offense." You have probably heard this. It is a catchy phrase and appealing in its simplicity. It is also supremely comforting: It suggests that all we have to do is focus on our growth efforts. If we do this well, everything will be okay.

There is just one problem with the statement: It isn't true. On the contrary, the statement is completely wrong. The best defense is not a good offense. The best defense is a good defense. What are typical offensive moves? How do companies grow their profits? Firms might implement a price increase or go after new customers, or enter a new market segment, or optimize spending. What should a company *not* do when it is under attack from a competitive threat? Well, all these things. In most situations, effecting a price increase just as a new entrant appears is a terrible thing to do. Going after a new segment of the market while under attack is completely wrong: You should be protecting your customers and business, not going after someone else's business.

The most common type of defensive situation is based on a new product launch. A competitor is introducing a new product in a bid to get a piece of your business. But firms can defend against any sort of competitive move: a price change, a new advertising effort, a loyalty program. Any time a company is reacting to a competitive move, it can be considered to be using a defensive strategy.

Defense Is a Hidden Strategy

Firms defend all the time: In many categories there are constant competitive battles. And defensive strategy is incredibly important. The survival of the firm depends on its ability to protect its market. If a growth strategy fails, what happens? The company doesn't grow. The firm might miss its profit target, and profits might decline for the year. You try something different. If a defensive strategy fails, the business might completely collapse.

Despite its importance, defensive strategy receives little attention. People don't talk about it very much. There aren't many books on the topic. Corporate executives don't bring it up. A few years ago, I kept track of the business executives giving talks at Kellogg. In particular, I studied the topics. Out of perhaps 200 guest speakers, not a single person talked about anything related to defensive strategy.

There are two likely reasons for this strange dynamic. First, acting defensively is rough. When you are defending your business, your goal is to push back the new entrant. You want the attacker to fail and exit the market. Executives logically don't want to discuss this; it sounds unfriendly and inhospitable. When business leaders speak at a business school, they are likely to stick to positive, happy topics like the servant leader, innovation, and big data analysis.

Second, there are antitrust concerns. This is the sphere of competition law. Government regulators around the world track what might be considered anti-competitive behavior. On occasion, defensive strategy can be considered anti-competitive. The rules surrounding this aren't clear, so to be safe executives avoid the topic entirely.

The reality is that defensive strategy is legal and accepted practice. It is just part of business. Should firms fight hard to hang on to customers? Absolutely. Should companies react to changes in the market? Yes! Should firms work to expand their market share? Of course.

Still, the rough nature of defense and the risk of appearing anti-competitive means that defensive strategy isn't mentioned much. But it is incredibly important and common.

Three Important Things to Remember About Defense

There are three things to remember when thinking about defensive strategy.

Every New Product Is Based on a Business Proposition   When considering a competitive attack, it is important to remember that behind the new product is a set of financial numbers, and these numbers make sense. People only launch new products and services if they believe the initiative will make money. The numbers have to make financial sense. Losing money is never the goal.

This insight has two important implications. First, when you see a new product, you should ask yourself, "What do they see?" Clearly, the new entrant believes that the new product is a good idea. What are the beliefs behind this assessment?

Be particularly careful if a competitor's move doesn't seem to make sense. If it seems like a bad idea, pause. Clearly, the competitor thinks it is a good idea. Perhaps it is! Maybe there is an underserved segment of the market or a new technology that has the potential to transform the industry.

The second implication is that if you want someone to stop attacking you—if you want someone to give up—you just have to ensure that their numbers no longer work. When a leader loses faith in the figures, when there is no apparent route to profits, they will give up and cancel the initiative. The figures don't actually have to stop working. You just have to convince the attacker that the numbers won't work.

Every New Product Has to Go Through the Same Five Phases
Every new product in the world has to go through the same five phases in

order to successfully enter a market. This is true for both consumer and business markets.

The first phase is testing and development. In this phase the company is developing the idea, formulating the launch plan, and preparing for the introduction.

Gaining distribution is the second phase. For consumer products, this might involve getting distribution in retail stores. In business markets, gaining distribution might involve signing agreements with key distributors. On occasion, this step will require government approval; it is impossible to sell a pharmaceutical product in many countries, for example, without regulatory permission.

The third phase is building awareness. It is a simple but important truth that if someone is not aware of your product, they are not going to buy it. Ensuring that customers know about the new product is a critical step for anyone involved in launching a product.

Trial is perhaps the most important and challenging phase in the process. This is when customers actually purchase and try the new product. Gaining trial can be exceptionally expensive, and this step is the focus of extensive marketing efforts.

The final phase is securing repeat. This is when customers return to buy a product a second or third time. By this point they are aware of the new product, they've tried it, and they are back for a repeat purchase.

Each part of the process is essential; a new product will only succeed if it can complete all the steps. If a new product can't get access to a market, for example, it won't succeed. Similarly, a product that fails to generate significant trial rates will not succeed. Understanding these phases is important because it is possible to defend at every step in the process.

People Generally Believe They Are Correct   One of the remarkable things about people is that we all have an incredible ability to convince ourselves that we are right: Whatever we believe is correct.

As we move through the day, we evaluate different pieces of information. If something is consistent with what we believe, we tend to hold on to it. "I knew it!" we might think. If something is inconsistent with what we believe, we often discard it. "Now that is a flawed study," we might say, or "That is not a very convincing piece of information."

Understanding this bias is important when it comes to defense for two reasons. First, when someone enters our industry with a new idea, our first response is likely to be, "Wow, what a dumb idea! That will never work."

In most cases, you have already considered the idea. You evaluated it and decided it wasn't a good idea. When a competitor shows up with the idea, you will quickly say, "That will never work!" and ignore the threat. This is a dangerous response!

Attackers also think they are right; they believe in their new idea. As a result, new entrants will be slow to give up on their idea. A half-hearted defense just isn't likely to be successful. If you want someone to go away, to stop attacking you, you need an overwhelming defensive effort. Otherwise, they are going to continue to attack, believing that they are right.

The Three Key Steps in Defense

Defending a brand consists of several distinct steps. The first step is identifying the threat and then learning about it. Once you have some knowledge, then the focus shifts to a decision: Defend or not? This is a critical question. If a defense is needed, then it is time to develop the plan the initiatives and tactics call for.

Step 1: Learning About the Threat

It is impossible to create a defense plan unless you know something about the threat. It is hard to defend against a ghost. Defense begins when you learn about a threat.

Information Needs   To make a smart decision, you need a lot of information about the competitor. Here are just a few of the pieces of information you will want to gather:

- Positioning: What is the new brand's positioning? Who is the brand targeting? What is the primary benefit?
- Marketing mix: What does the launch plan look like? What is the product, the pricing, the distribution strategy, and the promotion plan?
- Source of volume: Where will the revenue likely come from? Will the new entrant attract new users to the category or increase purchase rates in the category? Or will the new entrant likely steal share from existing players in the category? If so, which ones?
- Timing: When does the new product launch?
- Who: There are two dimensions here. First, who is the company? What sort of resources do they have? Second, who is the person? There is always a person responsible for a move. Who is this? What is their background? How well do they know the business?

- Rationale: A key question: Why is this company attacking my business? What is the rationale?
- Financials: What is the competitor's financial proposition? What are they looking at? Every new product is based on a set of financials; the new venture has to make financial sense. So what is the competitor considering?

Competitive Intelligence   There are many ways to learn about a competitor; the world of intelligence is vast and complicated.

Some techniques are obvious. You can purchase the competitor's product and look at it. You can visit their website and watch the advertising. You can review press releases and listen to talks by company executives. This list goes on and on.

Other techniques are less obvious. Both suppliers and distributors, for example, can be tremendous sources of information. Suppliers often sell to many of the players in a category, so they know what is happening. Distributors, too, know what is happening because they carry products from many different companies.

Your customers are often a tremendous source of competitive information because they will often hear from the new entrant and know the pitch. Job postings can be informative. If a competitor is hiring a certain type of programmer, you can make assumptions about their intentions. An effort to hire a large number of salespeople tells you something about the competitive approach to the market.

Social media also can be a rich source of competitive information. Reviewing LinkedIn postings, for example, can be highly informative. Following your competitor's social media posts can be interesting, too.

Government documents are often a particularly useful—but often overlooked—source of information. Patent and trademark filings, for example, are all public information. In many countries, import records are available for review. Environmental filings can be helpful, too; a company discharging a particular chemical is likely using a product process that involves that chemical.

Competitive intelligence is a swirly world, both legally and ethically, so it is essential to be thoughtful and intentional about how you approach it. There are many things you could do that are simply not appropriate. Bugging your competitor's computer, for example, is not appropriate. Sneaking into someone's offices after hours and paying an insider for confidential information are also not acceptable.

Step 2: Deciding Whether or Not to Defend

Eventually, defensive strategy comes down to a decision: Is a defensive effort necessary? This is a critical question. If the competitive threat warrants a response, then the path is clear: Quickly assemble and implement a defense plan.

There are reasons to defend a business and reasons not to. Each situation requires consideration and study.

Reasons to Defend   There are multiple reasons to defend a business. The most obvious reason is to protect market share, revenue, and profit. If a new entrant is likely to take significant business from you, then you'll of course work to prevent this from happening. The bigger the potential loss, the more urgent the need for a defense.

There is also the chance that the new entrant has a good idea! Clearly, the people behind the new product think it is a good idea, and they are presumably smart and capable people. Perhaps they have found a compelling new technology, or identified an underserved segment, or figured a different want on which to structure the value proposition. Regardless, if your competitor has come up with a good idea, you should take advantage of their good thinking.

Another reason to defend a business is to send a signal to ward off potential future threats. If you defend your brand aggressively against a competitive attack, other firms will take note, which will dissuade future attacks. Remember that the financials behind every new product have to work, so if you have a reputation for making life difficult for attacking companies, it makes it harder for future entrants to justify encroaching on your territory.

A defensive effort often makes good sense from a personal career perspective. Rallying the team to defend a business is a chance to show leadership and initiative. People tend to pull together when under attack. Leading the team through a defensive battle is a chance to show your leadership potential.

Defending is also a safe action. If the new product fails, you can declare victory: "We did it!" If the new product succeeds, you can say, "We did what we could; defending was definitely the right move." Or, perhaps more compelling, "Just think how bad it would have been."

If you don't defend and the new entrant fails, you don't get any credit. The new entrant just failed, and you didn't do anything. But if the new entrant succeeds, then you will get the blame for the share and profit declines and the missed opportunity. Perhaps you will go down in history as the person who didn't defend and let the brand suffer such losses.

Reasons Not to Defend   Still, a defensive effort is not always the best move. A defensive effort can be costly and disruptive, and it will often force you to shelve your growth efforts.

One reason not to defend is that the threat is simply too small. Perhaps a company is launching a competitive brand in a different geography. Perhaps the company is tiny, just a small startup with little money and little chance of securing funding. In these situations, it may be best to simply monitor the new entrant. If it starts getting traction, then a defensive effort might be appropriate.

Another reason is that you might want a competitive brand. Perhaps you are in an emerging category and having a second player in the market would help establish the new segment, or you have such a high market share that regulators might accuse you of having too much market power. A new competitor could reduce this concern.

And then there is the fact that you might not be able to win. If a new entrant has a compelling idea and vast resources, you might find yourself in a somewhat hopeless position. If this is the case, then perhaps a strategic retreat would make more sense, as you shift your resources to other opportunities. Spending money trying to defend a brand when there is little chance of success is not a wise move.

The Risk: Missing the Defense Window   In general, companies defend too little. This is how successful brands get into trouble; they fail to react to competitive threats.

People don't defend for several reasons. Sometimes the established player doesn't recognize the threat or discounts the risk. More often, perhaps, the established player has exciting growth plans. Canceling the growth efforts to fund a defensive push seems like a fearful move.

One of the great risks for firms is that successful leaders have a tendency to become optimistic and discount potential threats. Derek Rucker, my colleague at Kellogg, studied this dynamic with other researchers. In a series of experiments, they tested what happened when people felt powerful. The results were striking. When people felt powerful and in control, they discounted risks and were more likely to engage in risky behavior.[1]

The learning is quite clear: The more successful a firm, the more likely it will fail to respond to a competitive attack.

Step 3: Assembling the Plan

Once the competitive analysis is done and the decision to defend has been made, the focus shifts to creating the defense plan. This is the phase when the brand leaders create the marketing plan and consider goals, strategic initiatives, and tactics.

Speed is of the essence when developing a defense, so it is critical to move quickly. In this way, offensive strategy and defensive strategy are very different. Offense—or growth—strategies can happen at your timing. There isn't any critical timing, beyond the need to grow your business and perhaps respond to seasonal concerns. Defense is different. Every day is critical. The sooner you start to defend, the more likely you will be successful.

Every competitive move will require its own defensive strategy. A pricing change, for example, will likely involve a different response than a service enhancement. But there are ways to respond to every situation.

The classic defense scenario—and perhaps the most concerning—is when a competitor is launching a new product to attack your business. So let's dive into that specific scenario and consider ways a company can defend.

The best way to defend against a new product is to consider where the new product is in its launch process. As discussed earlier, every new product has to go through the same five steps. It is possible to defend at each step in the process.

Defending in Phase 1: Development and Commercialization

In the first step, the competitor is developing the launch plan. The company might be doing R&D, hiring a team, securing necessary funding, or figuring out the supply chain. Often at this stage the threat will appear as a rumor—perhaps "Did you hear that Firm X is considering entering your market?" or "I heard Firm Y is hiring developers who work on our type of software."

The goal at this stage is very simple: Ensure that the competitor doesn't proceed with the launch. As Sun Tzu observed many years ago, "The best battle is the battle we never fight."

How can you prevent a company from launching a new product? There are many different options. One of the simplest ways is to signal an aggressive defense. If you let the new entrant know that you will fight hard to protect your market share, the new entrant will have to do two things: reduce their market share and revenue forecasts, or increase their spending to overcome the likely defense. In either scenario, the financials deteriorate and it becomes harder to justify the launch.

There are many ways to send a defensive signal to a competitor. One of your company executives could make a comment at an industry analyst meeting, or you could put something in a quarterly earnings release. Competitors are always watching each other. Firms don't say, "We are going to kill you!" or "Die, you dog!" This would seem inappropriate. Instead, a company might say, "We are going to spend whatever it takes to maintain our market share this year," or "We are going to increase our marketing spending in this industry by 150%."

Another way to defend at this stage is to block the competitor by launching the idea first. New entrants rely on PR and buzz to build awareness. A new idea is exciting. So to stop a competitive launch, one option is to simply introduce the competitor's product first. If you find out that the competitor is planning to introduce a blue product, then you go ahead and launch a blue product first. When the competitor's product comes out, people might then say, "Oh, another blue product."

Messing up a competitor's market research efforts is another option at this stage of the process. In most cases, a company will only move forward with a launch if the market research results are positive. Finding a way to block these results, then, is a good way to defend.

One example of this comes from the bleach industry. Clorox, the leader in bleach in the United States, one day learned that Procter & Gamble was planning to test a line of bleach in a test market in Portland, Maine. Concerned about the idea of P&G entering the bleach market, Clorox decided to give away free bleach to the entire city of Portland. This effectively destroyed the test market, and signaled that Clorox was willing to take dramatic steps to protect its business.[2]

There are also legal avenues to consider. Perhaps you find out that the competitor is violating one of your patents or trademarks or crossing other legal lines. If so, a strong legal attack could slow the competitor. This works particularly well with new, small companies. These firms are often short on two things: time and money. By filing suit, you can use up their time and money in a costly legal fight.

Defending in Phase 2: Gaining Distribution   A new product won't sell if customers can't buy it. A product has to be available to generate sales. This seems obvious, but in some categories the challenge of gaining distribution is significant indeed. Getting grocery stores to stock a particular product, for example, can be costly and challenging.

As a result, this phase of the launch is a promising place for a defensive effort. If an established brand can successfully block or limit distribution, the new product will fail. There are many different ways to block distribution. One way is to provide incentives for key channel partners: retailers and distributors. When food giant Conagra decided to launch a line of cheese, for example, established player Kraft went to retailers and offered them a significant amount of money to simply maintain the number of Kraft items on their shelves. This move made it much more difficult for Conagra to gain space. There is only so much room in a refrigerated section of a store, and if the retailer wants to maintain Kraft's presence, then there just isn't much space for the Conagra products.

Another tactic is to secure government support. When Italian pasta giant Barilla entered the U.S. market, for example, the established players accused Barilla of dumping and secured a major tariff on imported pastas. This made all the Barilla pastas much more expensive.[3]

The iron ore industry provided another example of using government support to defend. Mining giant Vale at one point came up with the strategy of building a fleet of large, efficient ships to transport iron ore from Brazil to China. The company constructed a fleet of enormous ships, spending billions in the process. Unfortunately for Vale, Chinese firms had previously done all the shipping, and as the first of these large ships approached China, the Chinese Ministry of Transport announced that the large ships were simply too big. They were dangerous for workers and as a result were not allowed to dock in China. So the Brazilian ships would have to anchor offshore and unload into smaller ships. This highly inefficient transition meant the venture made no economic sense. The numbers no longer worked.

Eventually Vale decided to abandon the venture and sold the ships. It turns out that Chinese firms acquired the ships. Shortly after, the Chinese Ministry of Transport announced that, upon further analysis, the ships actually were safe and could land in China.[4]

Defending in Phase 3: Building Awareness

Every new product needs to gain awareness, for the simple reason that if customers don't know about a product or service, they won't buy it. New entrants spend a lot of money on awareness building: advertising, PR efforts, and social media efforts with influencers.

The key to defending in this step is to limit the impact of the new entrant's spending. One simple approach is to dramatically increase your spending. Your share of voice, or share of spending in a category, has a big impact. If the new entrant is spending $5 million on building awareness, you spend $25 million. Customers will see much more of your messaging than your competitor's.

Another approach is to create clutter. If there is a lot happening in a particular category, customers will get distracted and the impact of each particular initiative will fall. So, if a competitor is bringing interesting news to a category, you follow along. Perhaps you introduce a new product as well, or roll out a big and unexpected promotion, or host a very special event that attracts a lot of attention. Perhaps you do all these things at the same time.

Simply copying the competitor's move will limit their awareness, too. If a competitor embraces a health message, you embrace a health message. The key is to take away any significant news from the competitor.

Computer chip giant Intel did this when defending against the much smaller yet very capable AMD. At one point AMD announced that it would be holding a press conference to introduce its latest new product: a new, remarkably fast computer chip. Intel, obviously concerned about this, then announced that it would be holding a press conference on the same day.

At the events, AMD announced its new chip. Intel announced that it had a new technology that would let its current chips run event faster! The news stories focused then on all these fast chips coming to market from Intel and AMD. Only later was it revealed that Intel didn't actually have a new technology. It never launched it. Intel had an idea.

Still, by the time the reality became apparent, the news had faded away.

Defending in Phase 4: Gaining Trial

The most important part of a new product launch is gaining trial. This the step where customers actually experience the new product. It is an essential step: If people don't try a new product, they certainly won't turn into repeat purchasers.

Trial is difficult! Getting people to spend money for something new and unproven is not easy. One way to overcome this is to make the new product completely free, but this becomes very expensive. As a result, most new product introductions include a huge amount of marketing spending focused on driving the trial with sampling, promotional offers, and major incentives.

For a defender, this is a critical moment. Anything that will slow down the rate of trial will limit the risk. The goal at this step is to blunt the impact of the trial spending, to do things that will slow down trial rates. The goal isn't to completely stop the new product; this would be almost impossible. The task is to simply reduce it. Bringing trial rates from 8% to 6% is a huge accomplishment—it is a 25% reduction in the number of customers trying the new product that will turn into a 25% reduction in long-term purchasers.

There are many ways to limit trial. One of the most powerful tactics is to load up customers. If you can get customers to buy a lot of product—three jugs of laundry detergent, for example—then they don't need to purchase more. This makes it harder for a new detergent brand to get a trial purchase.

Long-term contracts are another great way to block trial. If you can get customers to commit for several months, you ensure that they won't try a new product. A cell phone provider, for example, could offer major discounts in return for a six-month commitment just as a new provider enters the market. When the program ends, the new entrant may well have spent all their trial-building resources.

You can also offer the same benefit. If a new entrant is going to position around the idea of convenience, you could also talk about convenience. If the new product is embracing cause marketing, you can embrace cause marketing. By simply using the competitor's language, you reduce the incentive for customers to try something new. If everyone in the category is talking about causes, then there is no advantage for one brand over another.

A more controversial approach is to raise questions about the new entrant. With this approach, the established player communicates something negative about the new entrant. Perhaps the new entrant uses an unpopular ingredient or has certain risks. By highlighting concerns around the new product, it is possible to limit trial. It is just another barrier for the new entrant to get over.

Defending in Phase 5: Securing Repeat   The final step in the new product launch process is securing repeat. At this point the new entrant has developed the product, gained access to the market, built awareness, and secured trial. The challenge for the defending brand: Ensure that customers don't return to purchase the product or service again.

This is a difficult time to fight a defensive battle. How do you stop someone from buying a product they liked? This is not easy. Still, there are things that a defender can do at this point.

One option is copying the new entrant. If the new product has a particularly interesting and appealing feature, the established player just copies it. In the process, the defender takes away the reason to buy the new product. Meta is employing this strategy as it responds to TikTok; the new Reels feature copies many of the features of TikTok.

Blocking distribution continues to be an option at this phase of the battle. With enough spending, perhaps the established player could make it difficult for the new entrant to hold on to the shelf space.

Dominating share of voice is another strategy; a massive wave of spending from the established player can overwhelm the new entrant's spending. If the new entrant is spending $10 million, a $200 million investment by the established player will limit the impact.

Spending can cause problems for the new entrant in other ways, too. A hiring campaign designed to pull over key employees from the new entrant can create critical gaps in their team.

Massive spending combined with a distribution push can be an effective one–two punch. The spending slows sales of the new product, and then the distribution effort encourages retailers or channel partners to discontinue the now-slowing new product.

And then there is the last resort: You just buy the new entrant. This is what Facebook did when confronted with fast-growing Instagram, and what Google did with Waze. An acquisition is a costly approach; you will likely be paying a high premium for the product. Still, it may be the only good option left to stop the new entrant.

It is important to note that defensive acquisitions are different than offensive acquisitions. Most acquisitions can be considered offensive, with the acquisition a way to drive growth. In this scenario, the cost of the acquisition can be compared to the forecast upside. Is there enough incremental growth to justify the spending required?

A defensive acquisition involves a different calculation. The question isn't "How much upside is there?" The question instead is "How much loss will this help us avoid?"

Keys to Success

Brand management requires understanding the drivers and impediments to defending a company's market position. In this context, there are several factors that marketers must consider to successfully defend the brand.

Be Paranoid

If you are managing a strong brand, you just can't be too concerned about competition. As Intel CEO Andy Grove observed, "Only the paranoid survive." A brand leader should be constantly watching the competitive landscape. What are my competitors doing? More important, perhaps, is watching trends. What is happening in the market? What are my customers focused on? Where might someone attack me? The best way to prevent a competitive attack is to ensure that there isn't an opportunity to attack you. Remember: a new entrant will only enter a market if the numbers work, and the numbers will only work if there is an opportunity.

Move Quickly

New products are a bit like people: They are most vulnerable when they are young. A two-year-old isn't particularly threatening. A 20-year-old is a different thing. This is true for companies as well. At the start, new entrants aren't very strong. Cash is usually scarce. Awareness is low. There is no revenue. Over time, the company becomes stronger. As a result, it is harder to defend against.

When defending, the key is to move quickly. The sooner you start defending, the more options you have and the less expense you will incur. Before a company launches, there are ways to defend that are virtually free. After the new entrant reaches trial and repeat, the cost can be exceptionally high.

Of course, new entrants don't look scary at the beginning. It is only over time that a new idea begins to seem concerning.

This is the trap of defensive strategy: Early on, it is easy to defend but things don't look scary. By the time threats are fully developed, your ability to defend is limited. The best approach: Defend early and often.

Defend Like You Mean It

A half-hearted defense is a problem for two reasons. First, it isn't likely to work. You won't convince someone to go away with a little bit of spending. Second, it sends the signal that you don't defend aggressively, which will encourage other companies to attack you.

When faced with a threat, defend with intensity. A defensive effort needs to be priority #1. Profit targets will need to decline—it is costly to defend—but it is also essential if a brand is going to protect its place in the market.

Conclusion

Businesses only endure when they can hold back competitive attacks. This makes defensive strategy the most important job for any leader. Remember that if your growth strategy fails, you don't grow and will have to try a different approach. If your defensive effort fails, your business will likely suffer sustained harm. There are many ways a company can defend. The first and most important step is finding and evaluating the threat. A firm that moves with speed, focus, and commitment can limit the risk posed by even the most fearsome competitors.

Author Biography

Tim Calkins is associate chair of the Marketing Department and clinical professor of marketing at Northwestern University's Kellogg School of Management. He teaches Marketing Strategy and Biomedical Marketing. In addition, he works with companies on marketing strategy projects. He is the author of several books including his latest, *How to Wash a Chicken: Mastering the Business Presentation*. He began his career at Kraft Foods, where he spent 11 years managing brands including Miracle Whip, Taco Bell and Parkay.

PART 3

Developing a Winning Marketing Strategy

CHAPTER 8

Target Market Analysis: How to Identify the Right Customers

Julie Hennessy

This chapter introduces a very central and important concept of marketing: the importance of targets. We'll get into the details of the "how-tos" of target selection in a little bit. But first you'll need a little background to understand why making decisions about who your target is, and even who your target is not, is so important. Before we get to work on picking targets, let's consider how the situation you will face as a marketer today is fundamentally different from the one you would have faced as a marketer in the 1960s or 1970s, the era that saw the birth of many of today's consumer mega brands. This is important because the rules for success seem to be changing before our very eyes.

Today's Marketer Is Not an Adman

Let's start with a question, one I've asked my students many times: "When you think of the word marketing, what comes into your mind?" Now, I don't know for sure what you thought, but I can guess. I bet more than a few of you thought "advertising" or "selling," and this isn't surprising. That's because to a lot of the world, marketing means advertising.

To those people who are not in the field, the work of marketing is the work of the advertising agency. They picture a client bringing their product in and advertising people devising clever, maybe even manipulative, ways to get the consumer to know and want and buy something that they might not otherwise know or want or buy. Now, while this sort of thing certainly falls under the umbrella of marketing work, it's not the smartest, the most effective, or even the most ethical way to get the job done. Instead of starting with a product or service that is already conceived and designed and attempting to coerce folks into buying it, smart marketers start with a problem to be solved or an opportunity to be capitalized on.

LaCroix attempted to give thirsty customers a healthier version of what they refer to as "fun beverages." This was about the fizzy freshness of carbonated soda without the calories and chemicals. Peloton started with engaging instructors teaching spin classes to help people stick with a workout routine long enough to have an impact. And Grainger sought to be a plant manager's best resource, organizing in one place the thousands of products and parts that might be needed at a moment's notice to keep a manufacturing plant up and running. So, here's the key. Effective marketing shouldn't start with thoughts about advertising and persuasion. It should start with in-depth knowledge about customers.

Not only is this "advertising first" way of thinking about marketing not the smartest way, it often doesn't work. Companies get in the habit of over-relying on advertising to solve problems that are not fundamentally a communication problem. When sales or profits are down, they fire their ad agency. Burger King is a great example. For two decades, through most of the 1960s and 1970s, Burger King ran their iconic "Have It Your Way" campaign, with a clear emphasis on customization as a relevant contrast to McDonald's focus on speed and efficiency.

To this day, those of us who are old enough to remember the 1970s can still rattle off the memorable jingle: "Hold the pickle, hold the lettuce, special orders don't upset us. All we ask is that you let us serve it your way." Late in the '70s, though, Burger King felt a need for fresh news. And for the past 40 years, they've been a revolving door of agencies and approaches. Consumers no longer have any idea what Burger King stands for, and the results show this lack of direction.

Just as bad is the dilemma that occurs when your advertising, while well crafted, doesn't match the product or service that you're trying to sell. The financial return on United Airlines' "Friendly Skies" advertising had to be pretty low in 2009, while over 20 million consumers were watching YouTube's top trending video, "United Breaks Guitars." Expecting advertising to convince consumers that United was friendly when customer service was downright surly wasn't likely to work. So, marketers must make sure that products and services and experiences are what customers want and need before they work on communicating their benefits. The "advertising first" approach just doesn't get the job done.

This truth has huge implications for organizational structure. Marketing jobs that are just about communication with no jurisdiction over product design and service can be problematic. This troubled relationship helps explain why chief marketing officers, or CMOs, have the highest turnover in the C-suite. According to an analysis by Korn Ferry, they stay in their jobs for 4.1 years on average, while CEOs average over 8 years.

So, if marketing is not synonymous with advertising, what is it? Well, I work with a lot of technology firms in many different areas. These R&D (research and development) powerhouses span different industries—classic technology firms like Microsoft or pharmaceutical giants like AbbVie, or aviation and defense firms like Textron, which builds Cessnas and Bell helicopters. None of these firms think of themselves as big advertisers, but they are trying increasingly to be savvy marketers.

For firms like these, the focus is not on advertising. So why, then, do they care about marketing? They care about marketing because it helps them more efficiently turn their R&D into cash. While these firms don't care a lot about advertising, they spend billions collectively in R&D. If understanding their customers better can help them more readily turn their R&D investments into real value and advantage, they become very, very interested.

Modern marketing is about understanding what your customers want, what their problems are, and how to design your products and services to be their best choices. Products that address real customer needs are easy to advertise, easy to sell, and generate high returns. And that, even more than designing clever advertising campaigns, is exactly what we as marketers should want to do.

The Target Imperative

Let us start with a story. Once upon a time, a long time ago, the competitive landscape in many markets was different. In the United States, there were three main TV networks: ABC, CBS, and NBC, with a little bit of PBS for the TV snobs. There were three main diaper brands: Pampers, Luvs, and Huggies, and two were made by the same parent company. The domestic beer industry consisted mostly of Budweiser, Miller High Life, and maybe a little Pabst Blue Ribbon. Country after country, market after market were dominated by a few large brands with broad distribution, big TV and print ad budgets, and mass consumer followings. But today, the world is different.

ABC, CBS, and NBC are still with us, but they compete with Netflix, Disney+, Hulu, and, increasingly, YouTube, Instagram, and TikTok for consumers' screen entertainment time. Pampers and Huggies are still market leaders, but new parents are more intrigued by Honest Diapers, Seventh Generation, Andy Pandy, and Charlie Banana. And the beer market has exploded in a way that insiders call the "wine-ification" of beer. Now we see a dizzying set of craft brews: IPAs, ciders, stouts—literally thousands of options. And it's not just TV content, diapers, and beer. Marketers in nearly every market are experiencing more competition—actually, hypercompetition—than they ever dreamed of.

So, what does this mean? Well, it changes the game in many ways, but one in particular. Hypercompetition sets what I'm going to call the "trap of customer satisfaction." Now, maybe this is confusing. How can satisfying customers be a trap? Isn't that what we all set out to do? Well, for decades it was. But you know what? Today, customer satisfaction is not going to cut it. Let me explain what I mean.

Right now, I've got a basic bottle of water in my hand. Its label just says: "Pure Water." And it's fine. If someone were to ask me if I was satisfied with this water, I'd say, "Well, of course." And if it were my only option for water, then that would be just fine, too. But the problem is, it's often not my only option. Increasingly, I have lots and lots of choices. There's tap water. In many locations, tap water is fine, too, and it's free. And there's Smart Water, which costs a lot more. But there's not just Smart Water. There's also Evian, supposedly a geological miracle from the French Alps. Then there's VOSS from Norway. And of course, there's Fiji. I've never been to Fiji, but for only $3 I can get 16.9 ounces of the genuine Fiji experience. And that's just for the water without carbonation.

If we want a little bubbly, we've got to add in LaCroix, in tons of flavors like key lime and pamplemousse. And then there's the brand Bubly, which, by the way, is bottled by Pepsi. The list goes on and on. Eventually, I get so invested in the water itself that I've got to go shopping to find the best of 25 different options in water bottles to carry this precious hydration with me throughout my day.

Now, what happens when we face hypercompetition? Well, it means that the basic water, the one that I started with, which was perfectly satisfactory, is going to have a hard time competing. That's because while it's completely satisfactory, it's not my favorite. What's my favorite? Well, that depends. If I'm feeling cheap, tap water is my favorite. If I really wanted Coke but I'm trying to be healthier, I'll pick a LaCroix lime. And if I'm feeling indulgent, maybe the Fiji, the one with the really pretty three-dollar bottle. Our perfectly satisfactory bottle of water is in trouble here. I'm happy with it if there are no other options. But often, there are many other options. This will be a surprise to that basic bottle's marketers, who asked the consumer before they put it on the market how satisfactory it was. Disappointed with their sales, they'll be tempted to drop the price. And for brands, that's often the beginning of the end. After all, the tap water they compete with is free.

What does this mean? Well, increasingly, *customer satisfaction is nowhere near enough*. Today, if you want to win, you need to be perfect for someone.

When you're perfect for someone, amazing things start to happen. These are things that just don't happen when people are merely satisfied. When your product or service is perfect for someone, they don't look at the price. They come back again and buy and, better still, maybe even sign up for a subscription. And, best of all, they tell their friends. And when they tell their friends, they do that old advertising job for you at no charge, more convincingly than even the best advertising agency.

But here's the conundrum. It's impossible to be perfect for all people in all situations. So, to be perfect, we have to pick. The choice we make in picking is called our target. We can sell to other people in other situations, but I'll repeat again: We design to be perfect for our target. And if we don't, we risk the satisfaction trap. In today's market, this is what we call the target imperative.

Strategic Segmenting to Facilitate Target Selection

Let's now talk about the challenge of segmenting a market in order to pick the targets that we will be perfect for. Remember that it's important to have a very clear and specific design target. While in most cases we will do business with customers that fall outside of our target, it's critical to have someone in mind for whom we optimize. In order to define our targets (and by omission to define our non-targets), it's important to divide the total addressable markets (sometimes called TAM) into segments. But how do we best segment the market? This is a challenge. For most markets worth serving, I can think of literally hundreds of ways to segment the market. Let me give you an example.

If I'm in the business of roofing, I could break the market up by geography, East Coast versus West Coast, or urban versus rural. Or I could break it up by the type of customer, maybe residential versus commercial customers. Or by the roof size in terms of square feet covered or the roofing style (flat roofs versus pitched roofs versus gables). I could segment by the type of job (take off the old roof or cover it over), or the skill level needed to install, or the roofing material. The list goes on and on. In a way, segmentation options can be overwhelming.

So, here are the rules for segmentation. There are no absolute right or wrong ways to segment, but your goal is to segment in a way that helps you separate good opportunities from not-so-good opportunities. So, what's a good opportunity? What's a good target? Well, there are three criteria. First, a good target likes what's good about you. Second, a good target doesn't actually mind what others would find bad about you. And third, a good target is not so well served by other providers like your competitors. In other words, a good target has an addressable need gap.

These rules for target selection give us some direction in terms of how to segment a market. We want a segment to clearly separate folks who care about our best benefits from those who don't. We want to separate markets that are already very well served by other providers from those that are not. And we want to be left with a clear, well-defined, and homogeneous target to design for.

For example, traditionally, firms segmented their potential customers demographically by gender, education level, or age if we are talking about a consumer market. They segmented by customer size and growth rate or industry verticality if we are talking about a business customer. Demographics or firmographics were the original way of segmenting markets. There were two reasons for this.

First, it was pretty easy to do. These are discrete variables that provide for relatively simple classification of potential customers. Second, remember that the old definition of marketing was about advertising, and media companies use demographics to classify their audiences. Therefore, since you could "buy" women from 24–55 years of age in terms of media delivery, it made sense to segment the market by demographics.

However, it turns out that these demographics or firmographics alone often don't deliver on our segmentation goals. They don't clearly separate potential customers who care about my best benefits from those who don't, and they don't separate the already well served markets from the market opportunities. So, increasingly savvy marketers use more than demographics and firmographics to segment. They layer in attitudinal orientations. So, now I'm separating the women 25–54 who care a lot about health from those who are convenience oriented from those who are primarily bargain hunting. These women all share the same age demographic but not the same motivations.

Additionally, I could layer in behavioral segmentation variables on top of demographic, firmographic, and attitudinal factors. What products in the category do these consumers currently use? How frequently do they use them? Are they loyal to a single product or do they switch around? What's their purchase process like? Do they buy impulsively or research thoroughly first? You get the idea. Building in these attitudinal and behavioral variables can make my target definition much clearer and more specific than just demographics.

Now, why is that important? It's important because it gives me significantly better guidance on what products to build for these customers, where to find them, and what to say to interest and engage them. In a sense, the right segmentation choices are crucial to my having a useful target.

The advent and growth of online purchasing has supercharged our ability to productively segment markets. When customers are researching and often buying online, they leave remarkable data trails to be mined by marketers. Google and Amazon have built mammoth businesses on harnessing and harvesting this data. Marketers don't have to settle today for knowing that the purchasers of a weight-loss app like Noom are more likely to be female than male and have an average age of 42. They can specifically target individuals who have searched for audio books on weight loss or bought exercise equipment recently or investigated the SkinnyLicious menu at Cheesecake Factory. This ability to target individuals based on their actual individual online behavior instead of the demographic, attitudinal, and behavioral buckets they fall into has led to many talking about segments with an $n = 1$. And while this is accurate from an algorithmic perspective, it's still useful for human marketers to understand the demographic, attitudinal, and behavioral tendencies that describe their best customers as a group. New legislation that protects consumer privacy and limits the ability of companies to target directly based on search history will in some ways limit companies' abilities to use behavioral targeting, but not completely. These precision targets are here to stay.

Some Key Tools for Smart Targeting

I want to share with you three tools for smart targeting decisions. One is the concept of customer lifetime value. The second is the use of personas. And the third is the customer journey.

Key Tools for Smart Targeting— Understanding Customer Lifetime Value

Building on this orientation toward using data to make targeting decisions, let me introduce a really useful concept. This tool is called *customer lifetime value*, or CLV for short. Historically, marketers tended to gravitate toward the largest targets in terms of incidence and population size. CLV helps us make better decisions. It does this by considering the fact that members of different target groups may not be equally valuable. Therefore, 10 members of customer target A may not be more valuable than 7 members of target B. Let's look at an example. This time, we'll consider a business-to-business targeting decision. Let's say that you are a manufacturer of paints and coatings that are particularly scratch resistant. You're debating whether to focus on automotive companies, aircraft manufacturers, or the makers of industrial equipment. It's an important decision because buyers in each of these industries look for different features. It would be hard to be perfect for all three customers.

To calculate customer lifetime value, we will first model the typical annual revenue and profit for a customer in each of these different segments. What's the value of goods and services that each customer will typically buy in a year? Next, we will estimate the variable margin that will be earned on that revenue for each group. This is our first measure of what this customer is worth. But looking at one year's revenue and profit is just the beginning.

Now we have to factor in the cost of activities to make that prospect a customer: the customer acquisition cost, or CAC. Think about your typical customer acquisition activities—things like advertising online, sending catalogs, providing samples, or making sales calls. What sales activities will be needed to close the deal? What will these activities cost, and what's the likely response rate to our actions? These are the things we must know to estimate the CAC.

Finally, we need an estimate of customer retention or attrition. How long will this customer, once acquired, be likely to stay with us? What's the likelihood that they will leave the category or defect to another supplier? Estimates of retention or attrition rates have a huge impact on customer lifetime value.

These streams of projected cash flow going in and coming out of the firm are all weighted to factor in the time value of money. Typical CLV models estimate the value of a customer over many years. This results in an estimate of customer lifetime value for each of these customer types under consideration.

As you would suspect, we can actually spend a lot to acquire a customer who buys frequently, uses high-margin products, and stays with us for a long time. Having a few of these valuable customers may actually be more profitable than having a higher number of customers who buy infrequently, favor our lowest-margin items, and are highly fickle.

Customer value models are extremely useful in quantifying the impact of these factors, adding another tool to our bag of tricks for assessing potential targets.

Keys to Smart Targeting— Creating Personas

Customer lifetime value is a terrifically useful tool. However, some critics comment that reducing customers, human customers, to a measure of their financial worth over time is more than a little bit objectifying. While it is useful to understand what a customer is worth and to use financial metrics to compare one target to another, there are also some problems with thinking about customers in this way.

Being objective about target choice is a good thing, but it also has a downside. Your target customers may become just a collection of data instead of real people. Why do we care? Well, because part of the job of marketers is to get into the minds and hearts of the people we market to in order to understand their challenges, empathize with their problems, and ultimately gain satisfaction from coming up with solutions.

For this reason, many companies find it useful to create relatable human personas, fictional representations of our target to help employees—those in marketing but also in R&D, customer service, or operations—relate to and empathize with the customers we seek to serve. Let me give you an example to demonstrate the difference between a dataset and a persona.

Let's take a look at the real estate company Zillow, and one of their key customer segments. We will look at a Zillow profile for their professional realtor broker. We'll start with the data that Zillow had about their established experienced realtors. They called these customers master residential realtors, and they knew them by their demographics, usage behaviors, needs, and lifetime value. In this case, a typical master residential realtor was between 40 and 50 years old or older. More than likely this broker was female with over 15 years in residential real estate in her location. She had a bachelor's degree, was married with two to three children, and lived in the area in which she worked. She was employed by a major real estate firm like Coldwell Banker or Keller Williams, and she used email and texts to communicate with her clients, often on an iPhone or a laptop. Now, take a couple of minutes and jot down from the data I just gave you an idea or two about what Zillow could do to successfully build their business with the master realtors I just described. Come back in a couple minutes, and while I hope you have a good idea or two, we will see what we can do to make your ideation a little more productive.

Hopefully, you came up with an idea you like. But let's turn that target profile into a persona and see if we can make it easier for you to empathize with this broker. To create a persona for a target profile, we ask three simple questions: (1) What does our target want? (2) What does our target need? And (3) What does our target fear? We will also give the target a name and a face.

Meet Gretchen; let's get to know her better. We'll look at her wants first. Gretchen wants job security, increasing compensation, and the ability to work into her retirement. She also wants recognition as a professional and as the ultimate expert on her residential market. Next come her needs. These are slightly different. She needs tech management and analytic skills. Her job used to be very relationship based and she was good at it, but that's not enough anymore. She also needs better information systems to monitor client and property activities. And then there are her fears. These are surprisingly useful. Gretchen has nightmares about her role being replaced by one of those online residential platforms like Zillow. She resents her lessened role in the residential property search process: She used to be the first way that some of her customers knew about a new property on the market. And she fears looking like she's behind the times.

Now, with these insights about wants and needs and fears, you can really empathize. So, pull that pad of paper out again and get to thinking. If you're like most people, it will now be much easier to come up with ways for Zillow to be a help and not just a threat to brokers like Gretchen. Understanding her wants, needs, and fears makes all the difference.

The Keys to Smart Targeting—The Journey Is Half the Fun

Let's look at two more tools for selecting and understanding targets. Both of these tools involve journeys, but they are different. One of these tools is an older one: the marketing funnel, a look at the marketing process from the point of view of the marketer or advertiser. The second is the customer journey. Customer journeys look at the process of considering, researching, making a purchase, and using a product or service from the perspective of the consumer. These are different perspectives, but both can be very useful.

Before customer journeys, marketers tended to think about the marketing process as a *marketing funnel*. There was a set of sequential objectives that looked like this: (1) Build awareness; (2) Generate interest; (3) Drive purchase; (4) Incentivize product usage; and (5) Repeat and recommend. Marketers think of this as a funnel (see Figure 8.1). That's because you need to have a lot of potential consumers who are aware of your product to get some of them to try it. Fewer still will like your product and come back, and even fewer will tell their friends.

Marketers think about this funnel mathematically and calculate conversion rates from each step to the next. In the digital world, our ability to track these dynamics increases enormously. Data-rich firms, especially technology firms, think in terms of metrics around each of these steps in the funnel.

Web advertisers frequently measure the productivity of their work in terms of impressions or eyeballs or the number of times a particular ad has been viewed. An even more crucial measure, linking to our earlier discussions of customer lifetime value, is cost per acquired customer (CAC). This measures the amount of awareness-building and trial-incenting activity needed on average to produce a first purchase. Later on, there are measures of retention—whether an acquired customer comes back and purchases again or stays with

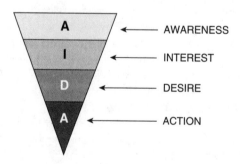

FIGURE 8.1 The AIDA Model

the product in a subscription model—and of advocacy—whether a customer shares positive information with others.

Customer journeys are a little different from the marketer's funnel. That's because in customer journeys we take a look at the customer experience, not the process the marketer goes through. This puts the customer right at the center.

The use of customer journeys actually originated maybe 25 years ago in the marketing of pharmaceuticals. Pharma marketers realized that there was a need to understand a customer's (or patient's) experience way before they started taking a medicine. Instead of focusing on the moment of purchase, it was important to start empathizing with the patient as they experienced the first symptoms and questions to be answered, through multiple steps toward diagnosis, through treatment and maybe even afterward. Depending on the condition, there can be many steps in this process. Nonmedical steps are often explored as well, such as the need to get medical insurance or the need to take time off work for treatment.

This approach is used widely in healthcare marketing, from the relatively simple patient journey for someone with the common cold to the very complex patient journey for a living donor kidney transplant patient. At some point, marketers outside of healthcare realized that this patient journey mapping could be really useful for them as well. Think about the process of dreaming about, researching, purchasing, and taking a vacation, followed by sharing your envy-inducing pictures on Instagram. Or, less fun, the process of having hail damage to your home, filing an insurance claim, and getting your roof and water damage repaired.

Marketers love customer journeys because they create sets of potential touchpoints. Each one of these touchpoints is a point in time or an occasion when a company or brand can reach out and have an impact on the customer decision. In the process of planning and booking a vacation, for example, consumer touchpoints might include any sources of information that a company might provide or that consumers might consult for places to go, activities to do, places to stay, or restaurants to visit.

Understanding where consumers are in their journey turns out to be important. As a company, you treat consumers differently when they are in the "dreaming and idea-gathering" stage than when they are "ready to book" a trip to a specific location. A totally different approach is needed when your customer is actually "on vacation" and wanting immediate support or help.

Different marketers use different formats for mapping a customer journey, but they all tend to look something like Figure 8.2.

In all journeys, the key is to identify and map the different stages in the journey, and to think about the customer goals, needs, and feelings at each stage. The format provided here is simplified. Some journeys have complicated loops and branches and look more like decision trees than the simple visuals you see here.

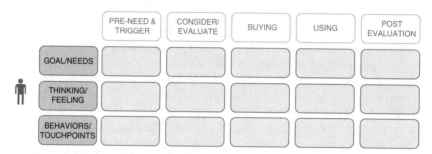

FIGURE 8.2   Mapping a Customer Journey

But journeys help us build on the basic decision of who your target is. To be effective, we need to determine not only whom we are targeting, but also at what stage in the journey we want to reach out and meet our target. Understanding and empathizing with your target customer is crucial, but so is meeting them exactly where they are in the customer journey.

Then, for each stage of the journey, a marketer thinks about how their brand can usefully engage—what media and messaging to use to try to reach out, and how to help consumers along their journey. Skillfully using both the marketer's funnel and the customer's journey can help make for both successful marketers and consumers meeting their own goals.

Pulling It All Together

We've spent quite a bit of time here understanding the importance of selecting targets, considering the trade-offs between targets that seem big and inclusive versus specific and precise, and thinking about how we pick targets for whom we can be the clear best choice. We've talked about some tools for quantifying the value of different target segments, for deepening organizational empathy with your target, and for thinking about where we meet our target customer along their purchase and usage journey.

This is a lot to accomplish within a chapter. I'd like to leave you with just a few summary pieces of advice:

Remember that targeting is not just about media and advertising. Targeting decisions will impact how you design your products and services, how you price and capture revenue, and how you bring your product to market through distribution channels.

While it is great to be inclusive, it is important to be perfect for someone. Consumers in most markets have lots of purchase options. You need to be the clear best choice for someone. It's hard to be best for a large group with heterogeneous preferences. Therefore, it's useful to pick a specific, homogeneous target and to design to be perfect for them.

This doesn't mean that our target customers need to "look" homogeneous from a demographic perspective. While demographics can be useful targeting tools, they are usually not enough. Instead, as sophisticated marketers we use attitudinal and behavioral data to describe our target customers. We define targets not just by who they are demographically but by what they think, how they feel, what they do, and what their goals are.

Beyond just counting members of a target group to pick one target over another, it's useful to quantify the value of a potential relationship with a target customer from start to finish, from the point of acquisition of a customer through their full relationship with a brand. Measures of customer lifetime value can be a useful metric for doing this.

Customer personas and customer journeys are also crucial tools in a marketer's toolkit. Use personas to deepen your organization's understanding and empathy for your target customer. Use mapping of the customer journey to understand the process a customer goes through in their relationship with your category and brand. Think about where your customer is in their journey as you plan for a set of appropriate touchpoints to help your customer reach their goals.

Author Biography

Julie Hennessy is a clinical professor of marketing at the Kellogg School of Management at Northwestern University. She teaches Marketing Management, Marketing Strategy for Growth and Defense, and Marketing Consulting Lab. She is also actively involved in executive education, with recent work with McDonald's, Coca-Cola, Crate & Barrel, Textron, UPS, Wayfair, Uber, John Deere, Nike, Athletico, Medtronic, and AbbVie. She twice received Kellogg's prestigious Lavengood Professor of the Year award and has also been a frequent recipient of Student Impact and the Core Marketing professor awards. She has written numerous business cases that are used in top business schools around the world.

CHAPTER 9

Defining Customer Segments: Four Steps for Successful Market Segmentation

Kent Grayson

Three activities are fundamental for developing a winning marketing strategy: segmentation, targeting, and positioning (STP). *Segmentation* is the process of dividing your customer market into different groups. *Targeting* is the process of choosing which segment or segments you will focus on. *Positioning* is the process of deciding what general approach is most likely to convince customers in your target segment to switch from their current solution to your product or service. Good STP decisions are important for marketing success, whether you are developing a strategy for an existing product or service or for a new one.

The previous chapter focused on targeting, and explained why the marketing strategy for a product or service should focus on only a subset of customers in a market, rather than on most or all of the customers. As that chapter pointed out, a product or service will be successful only to the extent that it is perfect for a specific group of customers (or at least more perfect than the competition). Why does being perfect require you to focus on only a subset of customers? Because customers in any market are *heterogeneous*—their preferences differ from one another. As a result, a product that is perfect for some customers is almost certain to be imperfect for others. Imperfect products create dissatisfied customers, which makes life harder for you and makes it easier for competitors to steal your customers.

Before you can choose which segment to target, you have to decide *how* to segment the market. Although segmentation is a necessary first step in STP, decisions about segmentation, targeting, and positioning are always interrelated. As a result, when marketers make segmentation decisions, they are usually also considering or anticipating the likely implications of these decisions for targeting and positioning.

A market segment is a group of customers who have a common need, problem, or goal—or a common set of needs, problems, or goals. Therefore, segmentation is the process of figuring out how best to divide up the customer market into different groups with different needs, problems, or goals. This chapter presents a four-step process for doing this. These steps are equally applicable to marketers in business-to-business and consumer marketing contexts, and this chapter uses examples from both contexts to illustrate the main points. These steps are also equally applicable whether you are already competing in a market or thinking of entering a new market.

Step 1: Understand Customer Needs, Goals, and Problems

To create and sell a product or service that is perfect for a group of customers, you need to first understand what "perfect" means to those specific customers. Marketers often refer to this understanding as "customer insight." Developing customer insight begins with identifying what relevant needs, problems, or goals your customers have. (A *relevant* need, problem, or goal is one that can be addressed, solved, or achieved with the help of a product or service you currently offer or might offer in the future.) Market segmentation approaches that begin with gaining customer insight are sometimes referred to as "needs-based segmentation," and this is the approach that is strongly recommended in this chapter.

Customer needs, problems, and goals can be generally categorized into three types. One type centers on *practical* aims, such as removing mildew from tiles, carrying a baby safely while riding a bike, or increasing the efficiency of a manufacturing process. A second type of problem or goal is more *experiential*. These relate to the process of buying or using a product or service; for example, some customers may prioritize a buying process that is enjoyable or effortless or a service that is fun or exciting. Third, customers can have problems or goals that are related to the meaning of what they are buying. These *symbolic* aims often center on how a customer's product choice will influence the way the customer (or the company) is seen by others. For example, hiring a well-known consulting firm to help solve a company problem can send a different symbolic message than choosing a little-known firm.

When customers purchase a product or service, they often consider all three types of goals, and many products or services can help customers achieve all three. For example, a tile cleaning product may serve not only the practical goal of stopping mildew growth in the bathroom but also the experiential goal of having a nice-smelling bathroom and the symbolic goal of having a bathroom that guests recognize as being clean.

However, customers also frequently prioritize some goals more than others. For instance, some customers don't notice or care about how a tile cleaner smells and focus more on how effectively it cleans. Others pay more attention to the fragrance of a tile cleaner than to its cleaning effectiveness. Business-to-business buyers are often assumed to prioritize practical goals, but that is not always the case. For example, a purchasing manager at a manufacturing firm may be willing to buy a lower-durability component (which does not optimally serve the practical goal of product longevity) if the supplier offers an easier ordering and delivery experience than the competition. These examples highlight that being perfect for a customer does not always mean being perfect on all dimensions, especially in a marketplace where no competitor optimally addresses all three goals. Instead, being perfect can often mean being perfect on the dimension that matters most to target customers.

Researching Customer Needs, Problems, and Goals

Marketers usually learn about customer needs, problems, and goals by doing customer research. But which customers should you research? If your product is already being offered in the market, it makes sense to start with your product's existing customers, as well as customers who purchase from your direct competitors. Alternatively, if you are launching a new product, many new products are developed to solve a problem (or address a need) better than some existing solution, in which case, your market research should start with customers who purchase the existing solution. In both of these scenarios, the starting point is relatively narrow, and you may, therefore, miss learning about customers who could benefit from your product but who are not currently on your radar. However, most companies do not have the resources to research the entire customer market in an effort to get a comprehensive map of all potential segments. Even companies with the budgets to do this usually do not research all customers in a market. For example, a company that sells manufacturing assembly lines would have no reason to research high school students because no high school students are purchasing assembly line equipment.

There are many research methods available to help managers gain customer insight and segment a market. These methods include surveys, customer interviews, and customer observation. Because each research method has its own benefits and best practices, it can be helpful to hire a market research firm or consultant to assist you. Hiring a firm not only will save you time (because the firm will do most of the work) but also will allow you to benefit from their expertise and experience. However, customer insight and segmentation research can be expensive. If you work at a firm that does not have the resources or priorities to hire a third-party vendor, you can still make good progress toward understanding customers by doing the work yourself. If you have not had significant exposure to market research options, you can gain a good working knowledge of the available techniques by reading books on market research, watching online videos, or taking online courses.

Regardless of whether you do the research on your own or with help from a market research firm, customer insight and segmentation projects usually start with an exploratory phase. The main aim of exploratory research is to understand the full range of relevant needs, problems, and goals that different customers have. Even when two customers prioritize the same type of goal—for instance, experiential goals—they may prioritize different things. Consider customers who purchase energy drinks. One type of customer may prioritize the experience of how the drink tastes, while another may prioritize the experience of being able to conveniently find the drink at most nearby retail locations. Exploratory research usually involves asking open-ended questions (such as "tell me about how you came to purchase this product"). As you do your exploratory research, it's important to keep an open mind; to watch for new or unexpected needs, problems, and goals; and to try not to be influenced by previously held assumptions.

Identifying Your Segments

After you have researched a sufficiently wide range of potential customers, the next step is to turn your attention to how their needs, problems, and goals are similar or different, and how they can be grouped into segments. Kellogg marketing guru Philip Kotler recommends that your goal for segmentation should be to group customers so that those in the same segment have goals and problems that are *very similar to other customers in the same segment* but that also are *clearly different from customers in other segments*. For example, imagine that you have been asked to segment the market for a new protein drink. After talking with people in the market, you find that some people are interested in building muscle mass and that they know that accomplishing this goal requires a high-protein diet. You also find that other people are interested in losing weight, and these people believe that a high-protein diet will curb their appetite. In this example, people who are interested in *building muscle* have a shared similar goal that is relevant to protein drinks. People who are interested in *losing weight* also have a shared similar goal. However, the goals of people in each of the two segments are quite different—some want to gain weight while others want to lose it.

As another example, suppose you work for a company that manufactures tackifiers, which are chemical compounds that make things sticky. After researching businesses that might be interested in tackifiers, you find that some organizations make products that *adhere to things*, such as medical tapes and patches that must to stick to a patient's skin. You also find that other potential customers (such as farmers) are concerned about soil erosion due to wind, and they want something that will *keep the soil from blowing away*. In this example, companies with products that need to adhere to skin have a shared goal that is relevant to tackifiers. Those interested in keeping soil from blowing away also have a similar shared goal. However, the goals of organizations in each of the two segments are quite different.

After identifying needs-based segments using exploratory research, some companies implement a more quantitative follow-up study that aims to test or confirm the exploratory findings. The questions for research like this are usually more narrow, and focus specifically on the segmentation dimensions identified via exploratory research. This kind of quantitative data can be collected via surveys, third-party sources, or company websites or databases. Companies analyze this data using multivariate statistical analysis, machine learning, or other computational techniques that investigate how many clusters of customers are likely to exist—and often also test the defensibility of any findings. Depending on how these quantitative studies are implemented, they can be helpful not only with testing and refining the segments identified by more exploratory research but also in understanding customers' current solutions (Step 2 of your segmentation project), estimating segment size (Step 3), and finding segment indicators (Step 4).

Step 2: Understand Customers' Current Solutions

Once you have identified key needs-based segments in your market, it's essential to develop a more sophisticated understanding of each of the identified segments. This usually involves dividing each needs-based segment into smaller subsegments, based on your answers to four key questions.

First, within each needs-based segment, *what solutions are customers currently using* to meet their need, solve their problem, or achieve their goal? Customers within any segment can be usefully classified into three types, depending on the solution they are currently using.

1. Customers who primarily use a product that is similar to yours. These are the customers of your direct competitors. In the protein drink market, these would be the customers who are consuming a brand of protein drink that is not yours.

2. Customers who primarily use a solution that is in a different category than your solution. For example, some bodybuilders do not buy protein drinks at all and instead get their protein exclusively from fresh foods or from protein snack bars.

3. Customers who primarily purchase products from your company. In our protein drink example, this type of customer would be relevant only if your company already sells a protein drink.

Although customers within the same segment have the same need, problem, or goal, you will likely have to use a different marketing approach depending on what existing solution the customer is using. For example, trying to attract a customer who currently gets their protein from a competitor's protein drink will likely require a different product, price, and social media campaign than trying to attract a customer who currently gets their protein from fresh foods.

Second, investigate *how important the relevant need, problem, or goal is* to the customer. You can investigate this from two perspectives. One perspective involves making comparisons *between* customers in the different needs-based segments you have identified. For example, imagine you are thinking of selling tackifiers in a region of the world where erosion due to wind is a minor annoyance but not a serious problem for farmers. In that region, the problems that tackifiers can address for farmers are likely to be less important than the problems they can address for medical supply companies, where the health of a patient depends on whether a medical patch remains affixed. The second perspective involves making comparisons *within* each of the needs-based segments, based on whatever current solution the customer is using. Is the problem or goal more important for those who are purchasing from a competitor, buying from you, or using a product from a different category? For example, a marketer may discover that farmers who already buy tackifiers in a particular region tend to be much more concerned about wind erosion than those who use other solutions, such as wind barriers.

Third, *what sources of dissatisfaction* do customers have with their current solution, and how frustrating, annoying, or costly are these sources of dissatisfaction? For example, a company selling protein drinks may find that a common complaint among customers is that the protein drinks currently available in the market have too much sugar. The company may also find that this concern is more frustrating and annoying for those who are drinking protein drinks to reduce hunger cravings than for those who are drinking protein drinks to build muscle. Sources of dissatisfaction with existing solutions present opportunities for your product or service to be more perfect for the customer—as long as you can convincingly address these sources of dissatisfaction.

Fourth, *what do customers really like or love* about their existing solution that they would miss if it were not offered by your product or service? While customers are usually willing to consider switching to a new solution that addresses a source of dissatisfaction, their willingness to switch will be dampened if the new solution does not offer some of the prized benefits that their existing solution offers. Being more perfect on one dimension but less perfect on another does not necessarily make your product or service more perfect overall.

Recall that the first step in your segmentation process involves identifying needs-based segments in your market. If, at the end of this step, you have identified quite a few needs-based segments, then answering the four questions for the second step in each of the segments could be quite time-consuming. For example, if you identify five needs-based segments and divide each of those into three subsegments (competitors' customers, customers buying outside the category, your current customers), you would be faced with trying to analyze sources of dissatisfaction for 15 potential subsegments. Furthermore, if there are already a lot of competitors in your category, the sources of dissatisfaction may differ from competitor to competitor, making your analysis even more challenging. A further challenge is presented by the fact that the need, problem, or goal will be more important for some customers than for others. One way to simplify your analysis is to rank your needs-based segments (and/or subsegments) by a rough assessment of how attractive you think they are likely to be. Which segments (if targeted) are more or less likely to contribute to company goals? You can do this based on a provisional consideration of the factors specified in Step 3, such as segment size and likely conversion rate. After prioritizing, you can focus your time and energy on understanding only the top two or three needs-based segments.

Step 3: Assign a Value to Each Segment or Subsegment

Segmentation involves not only dividing the market up into groups of customers with similar needs, problems, and goals, but also helping your company to assign a likely value to each group. In most cases, a segment's value to a firm depends heavily on the likely sales or profits that would be earned if the segment is targeted. Four key numbers/inputs are important when estimating the value of a segment. In some instances, a firm will have sufficient resources and documentation to be able to specify each of these four numbers with a high degree of certainty. However, in most cases, marketers use available information as a basis for making educated inferences about these inputs.

The first input is your estimate of *how many customers are in the segment*. If you have implemented a quantitative study of customers as part of your segmentation research, the results from that survey will likely give you a firm basis for estimating segment size. In addition, marketers can access free online information that can help them estimate segment size. For example, at the time of writing this chapter, **statista.com** provides free data on how many farms there are in different countries around the world. This information would be a helpful starting point for a company that is trying to estimate the size of the segment of customers in a country or region who are interested in buying tackifiers to minimize soil erosion. When free online information is not available, companies sometimes purchase segment size reports from online data brokers such as **Euromonitor.com**, **marketresearch.com**, **statista.com**, and **mintel.com**. For example, currently **marketresearch .com** is selling a report on the size of the protein drink market. This information would be a helpful start for a company that is thinking of trying to convert customers who already purchase protein drinks.

The second input is the *revenue or gross profit you anticipate earning per customer*. Revenue is the money that the customer will spend for your product or service. Gross profit is revenue minus any variable costs required to serve the customer. (For example, to produce and deliver a protein drink, a company has to pay for drink ingredients, the bottle that holds the ingredients, and the labor to produce and deliver the drink.) When estimating revenue or gross profit per customer, you will also need to consider what time frame is appropriate. For products that are purchased daily, weekly, or monthly, companies will calculate or estimate the value of a customer's business over a particular time period, such as a quarter or a year. In contrast, when a company sells big-ticket items that are infrequently purchased, customer revenue and gross profit are calculated on a per-purchase basis. When a company's customers tend to be loyal for more than a year, firm managers will also often calculate the total revenues and gross profit they expect to earn during the entire time the customer is expected to remain as a customer. (This is called customer lifetime value, or CLV.) Regardless of the time frame you pick, revenue per customer is calculated by multiplying the number of purchases the customer makes during the time period specified by the average price charged per purchase (total revenue per customer), or by average unit margin per purchase (total gross profit per customer).

The third input is your estimate of the *likely conversion rate for each segment*. "Conversion rate" refers to the percentage of customers in the segment you think will switch from their current solution to purchasing your product or service. Another way to think about conversion rate is what you think your likely market share will be among customers in the target segment. The best way to estimate a conversion rate is to do market testing. To implement a market test, you will need to identify a position for the product (remember, positioning is the "P" in STP), and market testing often involves testing and comparing the effects of different positions. If you do not have the time or resources to implement a formal market test, you can informally try out your product and positioning ideas through surveys, focus groups, or customer interviews and use that information to make your best assessment of the likely conversion rate. Marketing managers who do not implement market testing sometimes estimate a best-case and worst-case prediction for conversion rate (e.g., "the conversion rate will be between 2% and 4%"), and they make sure their firm is prepared for any outcome within that range.

The fourth and final input are any *one-time or recurring fixed costs* that will be needed to target and serve a particular segment. These may include R&D costs to develop product features required to convert target customers, the cost to adjust or expand your firm's manufacturing capabilities, and sales training costs.

Once you have calculated or estimated these four inputs, the likely value of each segment can be estimated using any or all of the following equations:

Total segment sales = Segment size × Conversion rate × Revenue per customer

Total segment gross profit = Segment size × Conversion rate × Margin per customer

Total segment net profit = Total segment gross profit − Fixed costs

Some marketers are surprised to encounter these calculations, because terms like margin per customer and net profit are more commonly associated with finance and accounting than with marketing. However, the most successful marketers can evaluate and communicate the financial impact that their proposed strategies will have on their company's bottom line. If you are unfamiliar with the terms listed above, the concepts behind them are simpler than they appear, and it is fairly easy to learn about them via free online materials.

Why and How Value Differs from Segment to Segment

As you think about the four inputs in relation to each of the segments and subsegments you have identified, use your knowledge of the marketplace to estimate which segments hold the most (and least) promise for achieving company goals. Each of the four inputs will play a role in your decision making. Let's first consider *segment size*. All other things (such as conversion rate and fixed costs) being equal, larger segments are more attractive than smaller segments. For instance, if your conversion rate is 10%, then converting 10%

of a larger segment will generate more customers (and more revenue) than converting 10% of a smaller segment.

However, all things are not usually equal between segments and subsegments. First, your product's *conversion rate* will likely differ due to a number of factors that you examined in the second step of your segmentation analysis. Two of the most influential factors center on how motivated the customer will be to switch from their existing solution to a new solution. First, if your product or service addresses a problem or goal that is not especially important to customers in a segment, your conversion rate will likely be lower than if you address a more vital problem or goal. Second, if customers in a particular segment do not have a significant source of dissatisfaction with their existing solution, you will have a harder time convincing them to switch. The influence of these two factors on your conversion rate emphasizes how important the first and second steps of your segmentation research are. Your success with a product or service will depend in large part on how effective you are at identifying significant problems, goals, and sources of dissatisfaction that customers have. This discussion also re-emphasizes why being perfect for a subset of customers can be so beneficial to firms. The more satisfied a company's customers are, the less likely they will be to switch to a potential competitor.

A third important factor that will influence your conversion rate is your company's skills and assets. These allow you to compete more effectively for customers with certain needs, goals, and problems and less effectively for customers with other needs, goals, and problems. Thus, even if you identify a customer segment that has a significant source of dissatisfaction with their existing solution, you will not be able to get them to switch unless your company has the creativity and capability to produce a product or service that mitigates or eliminates it. The less effectively your product addresses the source of dissatisfaction, the lower your conversion rate is likely to be.

Segments also can differ from one another due to *revenue per customer.* Customers are likely to pay more for a product or service that addresses a problem or goal that is important to them, and they will pay more for a product or service that solves a particularly frustrating source of dissatisfaction. Also, the financial status of customers in different segments may differ. As a result, even if a product or service is more perfect than the competition's, customers may face income or budget constraints that can reduce their likelihood of conversion. Note also that the price you charge will often affect the conversion rate. A higher price will be less affordable for customers in a segment, causing conversion rates to go down.

Last, *margin per customer* and *fixed costs per segment* will differ between segments. Because customers differ from segment to segment, different materials and activities will be needed to develop a product or solution that effectively addresses the problems in different segments. For instance, imagine that a protein drink company finds that the main source of dissatisfaction for one target segment is that low-sugar protein drinks don't taste very good, and that the main source of dissatisfaction for another target segment is that consuming high amounts of protein makes them feel bloated. Figuring out the solution to each of these problems may require different levels of investment in R&D; also, once a solution is identified, producing a product that addresses each source of dissatisfaction may have a different impact on manufacturing costs and the cost of raw materials. Marketing and sales costs will also likely be higher if the problem your product solves is not very important to the customer or if the product does not address a significant source of dissatisfaction; converting lukewarm customers usually requires more advertising or more visits from your sales team.

Step 4: Find Reliable Segment Indicators

One of the biggest challenges with needs-based segments is that it is not always obvious how to identify different customers in different segments. For example, if you are marketing a protein drink to customers who are interested in losing weight, it is not immediately obvious how to detect customers who have this problem or goal. This can create a number of practical challenges for your marketing activities. For example, how can you make sure that customers in your target segment see messages that explain why your product is more perfect than the solution they are currently using? How do you decide what retail locations are most convenient for members of your target segment? In business-to-business settings, how will your sales representatives identify which firms they should visit to sell your product? One way to address these challenges is to advertise, sell, and distribute very broadly. However, your return on these investments would be dampened by the fact that your messages will reach a lot of people who are not interested in your product, your product will be sold in places where your target customers do not shop, and (in business-to-business markets) your sales representatives will call on customers who are not in the target segment.

Often, a more efficient approach is to find *reliable segment indicators*. Segment indicators are easy-to-measure attributes of customers that allow you to identify customers in the segment. For example, if a consumer product company knows that its customers tend to fall within a particular age range or tend to live in certain parts of a city, then age and zip code can be used to focus their marketing spending and increase the return they get on that spending. In a business-to-business setting, if a firm knows that its customers tend to produce products in a particular industry or tend to have a certain number of employees, they can focus their marketing and sales efforts on companies that have these characteristics.

When identifying segment indicators, you are looking for measurable attributes of customers that (to use a statistical term) are *correlated* with having a particular problem or goal and, therefore, are good predictors of what needs-based segment a customer is in. No correlation is 100%; in other words, no indicator will perfectly predict a customer's membership in a segment or likelihood of purchase. The purpose of indicators is to increase the chance that a customer who gets your marketing message or shops in a retail location will be a member of your target segment, increasing the likelihood of a customer response (such as a purchase).

There are three primary ways to find segment indicators. One is to use your knowledge of the customer to *make your best conjecture*. For example, imagine that a pharmaceutical company has recently received government approval to market a new drug for leukemia, a type of blood cancer. The drug helps doctors and their patients achieve the goal of decreasing the likelihood that the patient's cancer will get worse; however, the drug is effective only when the patient's leukemia has particular characteristics. The company wants to inform the right medical professionals about the drug and its effectiveness, but how can the company's managers find doctors who are likely to have a patient whose leukemia can be effectively treated by this medication? One idea might be to focus on the doctor's job title—information that is usually publicly available. For instance, the pharmaceutical company might focus its social media and sales efforts on doctors whose job titles include "oncologist." Oncologists are doctors who diagnose and treat cancer, so this title is a good indicator (or predictor) of being in the right target segment for this product. Not all oncologists treat leukemia, and some doctors who treat leukemia do not have "oncologist" in their job title. But focusing on oncologists increases the chances of finding customers who have goals that are relevant to this new pharmaceutical product.

Another way is to *quantitatively test or identify indicators* by implementing the kind of quantitative survey described earlier—a survey that allows the firm to research the needs, problems, or goals that customers have and identify clusters (or segments) of customers with similar needs, problems, or goals. These surveys can also include a number of other questions about potentially useful segment indicators. Some of these questions may be selected based on the kind of conjecture just described. For example, a protein drink company may anticipate that having a gym membership is a good predictor of having a need, problem, or goal that can be solved by their product. Including a question about gym memberships on a survey can help test the accuracy of that conjecture. In addition, quantitative surveys can include questions about a variety of different customer characteristics (such as automobile ownership, number of children in the home, or marital status), which do not necessarily have a logical or obvious connection with the need, problem, or goal, but that marketers include in the hope they will find something that correlates with having the goal, problem, or need. For example, a quantitative survey may find that those who buy protein drinks to build muscle are also more likely than other groups to use public transportation. Although the survey is unlikely to reveal *why* customers who are trying to build muscle tend to use public transportation, a protein drink company can still use this correlation as evidence in favor of advertising their product on public transportation. (And, firms can do follow-up research with customers to better understand why public transportation is a good indicator.)

A third way to identify good segment indicators is to *use what are sometimes called "lookalike audiences."* This term has been used and promoted by the Facebook social media platform, but a number of other online platforms use a similar approach. A foundational assumption behind the logic of lookalike audiences is that the customers who currently buy from you are very likely to be in your target segment. This assumption is often reasonable: Customers rarely buy a product or service that does not help them achieve a goal or solve a problem. To create a lookalike audience (that is, a target audience that "looks like" your current customers), a company provides a "seed list" of existing customers to an online platform, and the platform tries to identify what the people on this seed list have in common and how they may differ from other people on the platform.

Because most online platforms have considerable information about their customers (as well as the capabilities to process this data in a useful way), they can often find indicators that might not otherwise be known to the company and might not be obvious predictors of purchase. In fact, the platform will likely identify a *set* of indicators that, when occurring together, are good predictors of being interested in a product. Once these indicators are found, the platform can create an audience that "looks like" existing customers (or shares key indicators with existing customers). Then, the company (in partnership with the platform) can send a marketing message to the lookalike audience and assess the response rate. Based on that response rate, the platform can further refine its understanding of the indicators that are more or less likely to predict interest in a product.

As is true for the correlation approach mentioned previously, firms will not know *why* a lookalike audience responds better to their marketing messages. But they will have the ability to identify customers who do respond. (Note: Lookalike audiences can be created and used in other ways. For example, the seed list can be people who follow you on social media or people who have a particular characteristic such as the oncologist job title mentioned earlier—and then that seed list is refined in similar ways.)

Segment indicators play a vital role in needs-based segmentation because they help firms find customers in targeted segments and, therefore, increase the efficiency and effectiveness of marketing activities. Segment indicators are also essential for assessing how customers in the target segment respond to marketing activities. However, indicators are not merely signs of a customer's membership in a segment. They can also help firms refine their understanding of customer goals, increase the sophistication of their customer insight, and better tailor their marketing tactics. For example, a tackifier supplier may learn that farms that grow and harvest *corn* are more vulnerable to soil erosion (and, therefore, are more concerned about it) than farms that grow other crops. In other words, growing and selling corn is a good indicator of having a problem or goal that tackifiers can address. Once this indicator has been identified, the firm can further use the indicator to improve their marketing. For example, the firm's sales representatives could learn more about corn farmers—for instance, what problems (other than soil erosion) these farmers face, what motivates them to grow corn, and what special terms or slang these farmer may use. This knowledge will enhance the sales representatives' ability to explain why tackifiers can be helpful for corn farmers in particular and, more generally, to build rapport with their target customers. Even more fundamentally, the firm may learn about unique soil erosion problems that corn growers face and might adjust its tackifier product so that it is even more ideally suited for solving those particular soil erosion problems. On a more superficial level, the company's website may feature pictures of corn farms (rather than generic farms or oat farms), which signals to corn farmers that the company has products and services that target them.

A similar logic applies to consumer marketing contexts. For example, a protein drink company may discover that customers between the ages of 20 and 30 years are significantly more likely to be interested in building muscle than customers in other age brackets. Knowing this, the company may tailor its marketing to the interests and values of customers in this age bracket—for instance, by choosing celebrity endorsers that are admired by this group and offering flavors that are especially appealing to customers in this age bracket.

Approaches to Segmentation That Are Not Needs Based

If you search online for ideas about how to segment markets, you will find a variety of recommended market segmentation approaches that are not explicitly needs based. Three commonly recommended segmentation approaches are "geographic" segmentation (which divides customers based on where they live or work), "demographic" segmentation (which divides customers based on certain vital statistics such as gender, age, income, and education), and "firmographic" segmentation (which, in business-to-business contexts, divides customer firms based on certain vital statistics such as industry type, revenue, and number of employees). On the surface, these recommended approaches are not needs-based. There is no reason to target people in a particular area and no reason to target firms with particular characteristics unless these attributes are useful indicators of having a particular need, problem, or goal. For example, a firm that sells tackifiers to help with soil erosion may find that larger farms tend to be more concerned about soil erosion than smaller farms are. In this case, the firmographic dimension of farm size is a good indicator of the likelihood of having a problem that can be solved by a tackifier. However, this target segment is *not defined* by farm size; it is defined by customers who really want to solve the problem of soil erosion. In this example, farm size is a useful indicator (or predictor) for firms that have this problem.

Another commonly recommended segmentation approach is "behavioral segmentation." Behavioral segmentation divides customers into different clusters depending on how they behave toward the company. One behavioral segmentation approach that marketers have used effectively for decades is based on *RFM*, which refers to *recency* (how recently the customer has purchased), *frequency* (how often the customer has made a purchase over a given time period), and *monetary value* (how much the customer has spent during that time period). For example, a company may identify customers with high recency, high frequency, and low monetary value and may implement a campaign that tries to encourage these customers to increase their monetary value—that is, how much they spend when they make a purchase. Another behavioral segmentation approach involves grouping customers based on how they interact with the company website. Some firms undertake a sophisticated analysis that clusters customers based on their "customer journey" on the site. This approach might identify "browsers," who visit a variety of pages on the company website but rarely purchase, and "category experts," who tend to visit only the pages that relate to a particular product category. Other firms take a less sophisticated approach to behavioral segmentation by grouping customers based on just one behavior. For example, customers may be placed in a targeted segment if they download a white paper about a particular topic or if they put a product into their online cart but do not purchase that product. Yet another behavioral segmentation approach is to use past purchases as a basis for recommending future purchases ("recommended for you").

It is important to keep in mind that—like geographic, demographic, and firmographic segmentation—behavioral segmentation approaches use potential *indicators* of customer needs, problems, or goals. Sometimes customer behaviors are indeed clear indicators of their needs, problems, or goals. For example, if a customer downloads a white paper about how to solve a specific security problem for a large computer network, it is reasonable to assume that this customer is facing a problem like this or anticipates that they will be facing it at some point. On the other hand, consider an RFM segment— for example, customers who spend a lot per year with a firm (high monetary value) and purchased in the last month (high recency) but who buy from the company only once a year (low frequency). Based only on this information, it is hard to know what need, goal, or problem the customer solves by purchasing from the company and what source of dissatisfaction they may have with the company. This requires a deeper analysis.

Another approach to segmentation is "psychographic" segmentation, which involves segmenting customers based on their values, interests, and/ or lifestyle. This approach is similar to demographic segmentation because it is based on characteristics of the customer. However, psychographic segmentation focuses more on how the customer generally thinks and feels. Psychographic segmentation can also overlap with needs-based segmentation because a customer's general attitudes can directly relate to the customer's needs, goals, and problems.

For instance, imagine that a psychographic segmentation approach discovers three distinct segments in a market: customers who care about art and fashion, customers who care about tradition and family, and customers who care about nature and the environment. Based on this information only, it would be reasonable for a firm that sells solar panels (or ecologically friendly cleaning supplies) to anticipate that targeting the "nature and environment" segment will result in a higher conversion rate than targeting the "art and fashion" segment. This is because the lifestyle segment has clear implications for what product-related goals the customer had. In contrast, a firm selling protein drinks may find it hard to decide, based on these segment definitions alone, which customer segment is likely to have the highest concentration of people who have needs, problems, or goals that can be solved by a protein drink. It may be that membership in one of these three segments is a good predictor of having a relevant need, problem, or goal, but more research would be needed to confirm.

Deciding How Narrowly to Segment

When making market segmentation decisions, marketers often face the question of how broadly or narrowly to segment. As a way to think about potential answers to this question, consider the example of a firm that sells technology for monitoring the behavior of people who are driving vehicles. The technology sold by this firm might include small cameras that are easy to mount inside vehicles; a software program that collects, stores, and analyzes driver data; and an onscreen interface that gives managers the ability to watch drivers in real time. A firm that sells this kind of technology could segment its potential customers very broadly into two segments: organizations that want to monitor the behavior of drivers and those that do not. Alternatively, the firm could take a more narrow approach to segmentation by dividing customers who want to monitor their drivers into smaller groups. For instance, the firm could group customers by industry: taxi/rideshare organizations, delivery organizations, law enforcement organizations, public transportation organizations, and car rental organizations. Which segmentation approach is better—broader or narrower?

The equations presented earlier in this chapter can provide a helpful guide for making this decision. Two key variables in these equations were *segment size* and *segment conversion rate*. The decision to segment more narrowly or more broadly almost always has an effect on *segment size*. Relative to segmenting more narrowly, segmenting more broadly results in larger segments. Considering segment size alone, one might conclude that a broader segmentation approach is always better because it targets more customers. However, a broader segmentation approach often involves grouping customers together that are more different from one another, which increases the heterogeneity of customers in the segment. This heterogeneity makes it harder to be perfect for all customers in the segment because the needs, goals, and problems of these customers differ. In such cases, increasing segment size will cause the average conversion rate to decrease.

Importantly, a lower average conversion rate does not necessarily mean that total sales will also decrease. A lower conversion rate (for example, 3%) of a larger segment (200,000 customers) can sometimes produce more converted customers than a higher conversion rate (5%) of a smaller segment (100,000 customers). So the decision of whether to segment more broadly or narrowly requires answering two questions. First, *will segmenting more narrowly allow a company to create a more tailored product or service for some segments?* The answer to this question will hinge on the quality of the company's customer insight and its ability to produce a product or service that can address the insight. A driver monitoring company may decide to focus more narrowly on law enforcement organizations. But, if the company does not deeply understand the unique needs, goals, and problems of organizations in this industry, it is unlikely that the company can produce an offering that is more perfect than the competition's.

If the answer to the first question is "yes," then the second question is: *Will the more tailored product significantly increase the company's average conversion rate?* The answer to this question will hinge on how important the need, problem, or goal is to the target customer and/or how dissatisfied the target customer is with the current solution.

Imagine that a driver monitoring company conducts customer research and learns that public transport organizations and taxi/rideshare organizations have similar goals for monitoring their drivers: Organizations in both industries want to record driver interactions with the public so that documentation is available if and when customers complain or are injured. This finding suggests that a driver monitoring company could target both public transport organizations and taxi/rideshare organizations with the same marketing approach. Combining the customers from these two industries into one segment does not increase customer heterogeneity with regard to the reason for wanting to monitor drivers.

However, imagine that customer research also reveals that taxi/rideshare companies are dissatisfied with existing driver monitoring technologies because existing technologies don't include a system for tracking the customer ratings (and reputations) of its drivers. Because of this, taxi/rideshare companies have to purchase two systems (monitoring and reputation management), which do not always integrate well. This is not a need for public transport companies, which do not ask customers to rate drivers. This finding suggests that it may be beneficial for the technology firm to expand the capabilities of its monitoring technology to include the management of driver reputation information. By doing this, the firm could increase the conversion rate of taxi/rideshare customers, but not public transport customers. The big question for this firm is whether addressing this need will increase conversion among taxi/rideshare companies to justify the narrower focus (and likely higher fixed costs for developing the technology).

Companies that are considering how broadly or narrowly to segment should also consider how their segmentation decision (and the associated targeting decisions) may affect their vulnerability to competitors. As mentioned earlier, a product that is not perfect for a customer makes the customer more vulnerable to a competitor whose offering is more perfect for the customer. A company that emphasizes its ability to monitor driver–customer interactions for taxi, rideshare, and public transportation organizations may be vulnerable to a competitor that specializes more narrowly in monitoring driver–customer interactions in public transportation contexts. However, as is true for any more narrow (versus more broad) segmentation strategy, a competitor's ability to succeed with this strategy will depend on whether the competitor firm can address the unique needs, problems, or goals of public transportation organizations better than a firm that segments more broadly.

As you explore the topic of segmentation, you may encounter the term *micro-segmentation*. The term is used in different ways by different companies and commentators, but it almost always refers generally to identifying a customer's unique characteristics (or circumstances) and then tailoring the company's marketing to match. Because segmentation and targeting are defined as dividing a market into subgroups of customers and tailoring marketing for one or more of these subsets, "micro-segmentation" is sometimes just another way to say "segmentation and targeting." In many other circumstances, micro-segmentation refers more narrowly to sending personalized *marketing communications messages or content* to different customers in a needs-based segment. Thus, this approach to micro-segmentation does not subdivide customers based on different needs, goals, or problems except as they relate to the kinds of messages they prefer or are most likely to respond to.

A wide variety of criteria are available as a basis for personalizing marketing communication. The behavioral segmentation approaches described earlier are all potential bases for micro-segmentation. For instance, the message that a company sends to a customer who left a product in a cart will be different from the message that a company sends to a customer who abruptly stopped purchasing once a week. Another micro-segmentation approach is to group customers based on where they are in the decision process (the customer decision process is sometimes called the "marketing funnel"). For example, if a customer has never heard of a company, then this person is at an early "awareness" stage of the decision process. On the other hand, if a customer has evaluated the available options and has narrowed their choice to two options, this person is very nearly at the "action" stage. Although customers in each of these stages may have the same needs, goals, or problems, they will likely respond better to marketing communication messages and other content that is tailored for their decision process at that time. Experts in email marketing also often use micro-segmentation approaches by testing and identifying the different kinds of content and messages that different customers on the email list tend to respond to. For example, an email marketer may know that some customers on their list tend to open emails that have helpful checklists, while others tend to open emails that include industry news. This knowledge helps the marketer to ensure that customers in each micro-segment get messages and content that are valuable to them.

Of note, micro-segmentation approaches like these presume that the company has already performed a needs-based segmentation of the market, has already targeted a particular needs-based segment, and has developed a general position for the segment. Therefore, although messages sent to different customers may be personalized for their particular interests or circumstances, the overall position (and benefits emphasized) do not change from customer to customer.

Conclusion

Every segmentation strategy is just one way of understanding and perceiving customers in a market. If two competing firms follow the four steps recommended in this chapter, they will inevitably reach different segmentation decisions, even if they compete for the same customers in the same category. During Steps 1 and 2, the two companies will ask different exploratory questions and will interpret the answers in different ways, in part because they will see different opportunities based on the different skills and assets they have. The two firms, therefore, will likely develop different customer insights and cluster customers in different ways, resulting in different perspectives on customer problems, goals, and sources of dissatisfaction. Even if two companies segment the market in exactly the same way, their valuation of segments in Step 3 will differ because each firm's skills and assets will differentially affect the likely conversion rate, gross margin, and fixed costs associated with targeting different segments.

However, while there is no single right way to segment a market, there are many wrong ways, which can create problems rather than opportunities for firms. For example, a segmentation strategy that is not based on customer insights can result in segmenting and targeting customers based on dimensions that do not helpfully inform the development and choice of marketing activities and, therefore, do not convert target customers. As another example, a segmentation strategy that does not identify useful segment indicators will have a challenging time identifying target customers and tracking their responses. Although the four steps recommended in this chapter sometimes require significant time and resources, following them can ultimately enhance company profitability by sidestepping these potential problems and maximizing the company's return on marketing spending.

Author Biography

Kent Grayson is an associate professor of marketing at the Kellogg School of Management at Northwestern University. He holds a PhD in marketing from Northwestern University. Dr. Grayson has been teaching marketing fundamentals to MBA students for nearly 30 years—first at London Business School and then at Kellogg. Since 2003, he has also been teaching segmentation principles to executives in Kellogg's business-to-business marketing program. He has worked on segmentation challenges with firms in a variety of industries, including consumer electronics (Sony), automotive (Nissan), packaged foods (Sigma), hospitality (Hilton International), and pharmaceuticals (Abbvie).

CHAPTER 10

Crafting a Positioning Strategy: Capturing the Customer Mindshare

Kevin McTigue

Since the early 1980s, when Al Ries and Jack Trout popularized the concept,[1,2] marketers have applied innumerable frameworks to crack the positioning code for their brand and "own" a valuable space in consumers' minds—a singular benefit most strongly associated with their brand, distinct compared to competitive offerings and important to customers. Volvo could own "safest," Coca-Cola "most refreshing," Apple "most creative." This positioning strategy was first designed to act as the basis for firms' advertising campaigns in which they reinforced this unique benefit and strengthened customers' associations. The concept of positioning was extended further to guide a brand's entire offering strategy across pricing, distribution, product features, service levels, branding, innovation, and even incentives.

But is this idea still relevant in today's marketing world? Brands have never produced more content across more channels than they do today. So how do we manage the purity of the single-minded positioning and the practical need to create massive amounts of different, compelling content? We also see many brands moving to "purpose-driven" communication in which they seek to move past product-oriented benefits and associate themselves with higher-order human benefits or charitable causes. Across B2C, even B2B, and on both sides of the political spectrum we can find examples. And now with artificial-intelligence-driven personalization, we can adapt the message to the individual and frequently modify the pricing and product features the same way. I think we can simplify the conversation by simplifying "positioning," and the easiest way to approach it is to think of it as explaining "who we're for" and "why we're better."[3]

An augmented reality technology company, Magic Leap, was preparing for launch and wanted to define their positioning. The world had seen disappointing attempts at immersive virtual reality from Google Glass, but this was entirely new. Through a mechanism that projects light into the wearer's eyes, the user can "see" digital content overlaid on their actual physical world. For instance, your calendar could appear in the top right corner of your vision. You could watch a video that seemingly appears in the air over your desk. You can play a video game chasing virtual three-dimensional monsters through your own home. There are many applications, from education to medical to B2B to entertainment.

If we ask ourselves who we're for (our target) and why we're better (our positioning), then on this project the company had an abundance of choices. They could be for B2B companies that wanted to help clients diagnose issues on complicated machines, for gamers who wanted the thrill of being in the video game, for physicians who could leverage real-time information in their line of sight as they operated, for entertainment seekers who wanted immersive storytelling, for teachers and students who wanted to see education in a new way . . . . So many things. Is having so many choices a blessing or a curse? In positioning, it can be both.

The market opportunity was enormous, and so Magic Leap launched across seven targets and the associated seven competitive sets and seven differentiating benefits. Even with $3.5 billion in funding, the company could not successfully develop seven solutions. Firms fail when they lack focus. Frequently, we think of positioning as a tool for advertising and it is, but it's also a tool for corporate strategy. With seven focal areas, you have no focal areas. The attention and resources of the firm are spread too thin. Think through the implications. As you prioritize product development, which features are most important? As you pursue partnerships, with whom should you start? As you hire expertise to develop content, on which areas do you focus? As a sales force is deployed, against which customers? And, yes, as you advertise the brand, what do you say? The brand faltered over the years after launch as they struggled to gain a foothold in any market. In late 2021, they received another round of funding and publicly stated that their focus would be on healthcare. One target, one set of competitive choices, and one differentiating benefit. Have they abandoned all these other wonderful opportunities? Absolutely not. But now, by progressing in order starting with the most likely market for success, they enable the team to concentrate efforts and win, one market at a time. This focus helps firms prioritize the space where they can win and helps consumers prioritize their choices within a given competitive set. We call this focus "positioning."

The basic goal of marketing is to have a set of customers choose our offering over other options. It's facilitating a value exchange in which our customer benefits and we benefit. At its core, positioning is simply defining why someone would choose us over the competition. Then, with consistent reinforcement of this "reason to choose," customers develop strong memory linkages between brand and benefit. So when the time comes to choose and memories are accessed, the brand and associated reason for choice come easily, and our offering is chosen. This makes it a very simple idea and also, typically, the most difficult task marketers undertake—particularly when a brand is "blessed" to have multiple positive benefits and associated multiple different segments that might choose it.

The Classic Positioning Statement

To (strategic target segment), our brand is the (frame of reference) that provides (most compelling benefit) because of (reasons to believe).

Deceivingly simple and still incredibly useful. Embedded in the positioning statement are four questions that are among the most difficult to answer (see Figure 10.1). Answer well and we have the strategic underpinning of our entire marketing strategy. Answer poorly and we will fruitlessly chase tactical solves, endlessly debate different choices, and watch as a more focused competitor takes our business. Let's break it into its pieces and unlock the value.

Strategic Target

Segmentation and targeting were covered in Chapter 9, but we need to start with the fundamental understanding that "beauty is in the eye of the beholder": What you value is different than what someone else values. And,

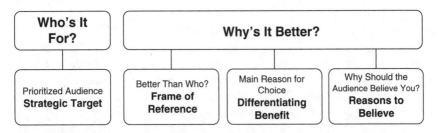

FIGURE 10.1   The Positioning Statement Framework

therefore, you can't be best in everything for everyone. I was teaching this concept in Copenhagen, Denmark, and a student raised a hand in protest. "Professor, we have a store here that makes the perfect pants." I had to see this. After class, I walked over to the boutique in anticipation of decades of marketing theory being washed away (perhaps not really). Sold at a store called Shaping New Tomorrow, the trousers are actually named "The Perfect Pants." I tried them on and the pants redefined "slim fit" in a way that made me uncomfortable exiting the dressing room. Verdict: perfect for some, perhaps, but not me. And that's great. While I'm not their target, they are successfully serving some target audience better than the alternatives. That is what segmentation reveals to us: the differing preferences of groups of customers. Therefore, multiple successful offerings can exist in a given category by best serving the needs of specific segments. As we progress through defining our competitive frame of reference and our most compelling benefits, it must be through the lens of our target customers—that prioritized group of buyers who we believe will respond more favorably than others and thus receive more attention and resources from our firm.

Frame of Reference

The frame of reference (FOR) is the set of other options: the competition, and generally synonymous with the category in which you compete. If your target didn't buy your offering to satisfy their need, what else would they choose? You are Lufthansa and you compete against? . . . European airlines. Simple enough, so why do we take time to discuss this?

For decades I would create positioning statements for my brands without ever thinking about this part. It felt like an unneeded appendage. I felt this way until a new vice president joined our brand team. For context, at the time I was leading a portion of the American breakfast protein brand Jimmy Dean. It's a billion-dollar brand that makes both fresh (raw) breakfast sausage and a variety of frozen, precooked, convenient breakfast options that can be quickly prepared. I worked on the breakfast sandwiches business, and business was good. Our sandwiches were delicious and ready in about a minute. In the frozen sandwich breakfast category, there were few competitors and they were easily bested on taste. The positioning: For breakfast lovers (target), Jimmy Dean is the frozen breakfast sandwich (frame of reference) that tastes the best (differentiating benefit) because it's made with the original Jimmy Dean sausage (reasons to believe). The positioning was reinforced in advertising, and the brand had dominant market share, maybe 85% of frozen breakfast sandwiches. When the new VP asked about the business, I was happy to tell him about our success and high share of the category. So, not much room for growth, but in a great leadership position. While I waited for my accolades, he surprisingly replied, "What's your share of 'at home breakfast?'" The answer was some fraction of a percent. This led to a reframing of the category. We shifted to "convenient breakfast" as a frame of reference with a new target that was eating cereal and frozen waffles. Now the brand had a tiny share of the market with room to grow. And it did. This frame-of-reference adjustment caused the team to shift the benefit to be better than that competitive set, pursue new innovation opportunities, and grow the business hundreds of millions of dollars. The frame of reference can be an underleveraged path to potential growth.

In our Lufthansa example, we could take a step back from the obvious category answer of European airlines and ask: What need do we solve, and what other options exist? If someone wanted to travel from Berlin to Paris, how else might they get there? Taking the train or driving seem like obvious choices. If we're not growing against other European airline competitors, perhaps by expanding the frame of reference we find new growth. That leads to the next question: If Lufthansa is currently touting "most comfortable airline" as the main benefit, will that work in a new frame of reference? Likely not. The frame of reference not only clearly defines your path to growth but also establishes the set of competitors from which you must positively differentiate. Understand the other options so you can strategically position against the other top choices of your target.

This topic arose recently in a class for executives. A firm that specialized in ESG investing, managing investments for institutions or individual clients that direct money into socially responsible enterprises. As the optimal main benefit in the positioning was discussed, the frame of reference loomed large. If they were to position the brand as a classic investment management company broadly, then the ESG tilt to the strategy could become a differentiating benefit. If they position as an ESG investment management company, that "socially responsible" benefit becomes table stakes, and they need a further differentiator.

This leads to the last point on frame of reference. When a customer knows your frame of reference, they grant you immediate associations. If I told you there was a new luxury car company that is launching a sedan, could you tell me anything about your immediate expectations for this vehicle? Of course, you know the price will likely be high, the interior luxurious, the sound system premium, the handling and acceleration above average. Your frame of reference is a shortcut for customers to the shared characteristics of that category. So, the unloved frame of reference has value in multiple ways and deserves our attention. It conveys a baseline of information, establishes a clear competitive set among which we will differentiate, and establishes a path to growth.

Differentiating Benefit

In most categories, there are competing brands with varying levels of actual competence across the common attributes of that category. And there are customers who have perceptions of the competencies of these brands across the common attributes of the category. Reality and perception are frequently correlated, but not always. What we can say for certain is that within a category, a given segment of customers will have criteria for their choice as well as positive and negative associations with the various brand options among which to choose (whether actively cognitively processed or not). Positioning strategy is the act of reinforcing the most important, authentic, and distinct associations of your brand so that your target segment perceives your competence and easily accesses this compelling reason for choice.

Now it gets tough. Perhaps there are many reasons someone would choose our offering. The brand could have many benefits. As Steve Jobs once said, "It's a very complicated world, a very noisy world, and we're not going to get a chance to get people to remember much about us . . . . And so we have to be really clear about what we want them to know about us." It turns out that people just aren't going to devote much energy to remembering all those wonderful things about us. Even if we're Apple. And so it forces us to prioritize.

Aside from the obvious benefit of clarifying your advertising message, knowing your central benefit helps inform many other choices. Are we the most convenient coffee shop or the most comfortable? One territory leads you into lightning-fast service, resources devoted to developing an online ordering app, and handheld food options that can be consumed on the go. The other path requires comfortable furnishings, attentive staff, and beautiful decor. Different positionings lead to different choices across the business.

"I want to be all of it!" Okay, just ask yourself if by splintering your resources across multiple benefits, you'll ever be better than the firm that focuses on one. Can the coffee shop that desires to be the most comfortable and most convenient ever win on both against competition that single-mindedly pursues one path? It might be possible in a market with few competitors, unfocused competitors, or with an enormous resource advantage versus all competition. But, in most instances, as witnessed with Magic Leap, firms are forced to prioritize. Therefore, we circle back to who's our most valuable target and what do we need to do best so they choose us over the competition?

It's also important at this point to highlight that you may have several tiers of positioning. Many companies have complex portfolios of offerings that live beneath an umbrella brand. This overarching brand will have the largest audience and typically a more encompassing and less specific benefit: "IBM modernizes businesses." Moving down into a category like IBM's cloud storage versus IBM's consulting practice, the firm would develop more specific positionings for these audiences. Finally, at the lowest level you may find the need to create a specific positioning for IBM's AI consulting practice and that specific audience. These can and do all simultaneously exist successfully. The hallmark of a great portfolio positioning strategy is that it is synergistic with the positioning on varying levels supporting the other tiers. We can imagine that if Apple did launch a car, as has been rumored, the positioning for that vehicle would be specific against vehicle competition but would also align with the other products Apple offers.

I'll spend some time later in the chapter giving you some ideas on how to find this area, but let me leave you with the criteria for a good central benefit. It's MAD: m̲eaningful, a̲uthentic, and d̲ifferent.

- Meaningful: It's a benefit that your target customer prioritizes when making a choice.
- Authentic: It's real and—this is important—it's believable coming from your brand. Your four-person consulting firm might actually be the smartest in the entire world. But it's not believable.
- Different: The most difficult of them all. It needs to be a benefit that a competitor is not already strongly associated with. In a perfect world, you have a benefit that the competition does not and cannot provide. But when that is impossible, we still have a path. A tenet of this positioning concept is that we are focused on owning the association with a benefit in the mind of our target. We want the strongest mental linkage.

The implication is that a brand that is technically at parity on a benefit with the competition can still create the strongest association with that benefit and own the positioning. Which soap brand moisturizes best? Dove. Which detergent brand gets clothes cleanest? Tide. What premium car brand is safest? Volvo? Does either Dove, Tide, or Volvo really hold functional superiority? To a certain extent it doesn't matter. Benefits don't exist until they exist in the mind of the customer. If you build the association of your brand and a benefit strongly, and protect it through consistent reinforcement, you own the territory. Even if other competitors technically have this competency, your target customer will remember your association first and strongest. It is possible for a brand to "take over" another brand's position, but the attacking brand would need a very compelling rationale backed by a substantial amount of messaging to unseat an existing perception in the minds of customers. It does happen. And when a brand loses its positioning "space" to a competitor, it is almost always because they have splintered focus and stopped consistent reinforcement.

Reasons to Believe

Speaking of compelling, how do we best gain this foothold and reinforce our authentic basis for owning this benefit? Our last piece—the reasons to believe (RTBs)—are simply proof points provided to the customer that reinforce ownership of a benefit territory. Why should I believe that you're the safest cloud storage solution? Because Gartner rated you the number-one cloud storage solution in safety. Why should I believe that Titleist is the best golf ball? Because 70% of professional golfers use a Titleist. We don't have to be as dogmatic in the longevity of these RTBs. You can have multiple points. You can replace them. Their role is simply to buttress your main benefit claim.

How Do We Get There? How to Practically Find Your Brand's Positioning

There are many paths to identifying your most important benefits. Don't forget, the power of these benefits is predicated on the target segment's priorities and the competitive frame of reference. So, we keep that in mind as we progress.

It might be helpful to start by thinking of your firm as a combination of assets that create different solutions or benefits for the customer. You have ingredients—reputation in the industry, patents, expertise, a bilingual staff, existing brand perceptions, physical locations—that together provide value. This value is recognized by your customers as it creates benefits for them that outweigh the cost of purchase of your offering. We are interested in identifying that which creates the most unique value so that it can be better designed, communicated, and delivered. In this portion of the chapter, we'll investigate several paths to identify positioning.

Testing

Why do customers value you? Ask them. This takes the form of broad research studies, customer surveys, social data mining, and even simple conversations with our customers. Human beings aren't always excellent at identifying their core reasons for choice and sometimes (unintentionally) create rationalized justifications that aren't actually true. But that doesn't prevent us from starting here on the path to understanding. Brands commonly craft multiple variations of their positioning to test with customers. Often firms will use qualitative research (small groups, open-ended discussions) to get ideas for the positioning, then craft multiple options to be tested more rigorously in a quantitative setting (larger numbers, generally less open-ended). This is frequently done in conjunction with an advertising agency or consulting firm and provides guidance on the most fruitful potential positioning path. It can be expensive and time consuming, and so there is another route for those with more limited resources like startups. Because of the capabilities afforded by digital, we can "test" positioning in the real world. The approach is easiest with a purely digital offering where one can click on a search result or an ad and come to the site directly for purchase.

We start by creating a list of potential target segments and a list of potential key benefits. Then we run ads (or even paid search results), each one featuring a different benefit that will be advertised across the different targets

Create a set of potential target segments and lead benefits

Test the benefits against each segment on digital ad platform

Potential Target Segments

Potential Targets	Potential Lead Benefit
Segment 1	Benefit 1
Segment 2	Benefit 2
Segment 3	Benefit 3
Segment 4	Benefit 4

Potential Benefits

	1	2	3	4
1	Low	Low	Med	Low
2	Low	Med	High	Med
3	Low	Low	Low	Low
4	Low	Med	Med	Low

FIGURE 10.2 Digital Message Testing

(Figure 10.2). We then measure purchase activity by message shown and segment targeted. If we can't track purchase, we can generally track interest through some leading indicator like a click. And with additional resources we can even hire a research firm to track back offline sales to simple online impressions. The best analogy for this approach is fishing. My goal is to catch fish, and I have a selection of baits (main benefits). So I go fishing with each bait, and I see what fish (target segment) is caught. This can quickly help firms understand their most compelling benefit and their most valuable target customer.

Benefit Laddering

A classic tool for positioning work is the benefit ladder (Figure 10.3). It is grounded in the idea that every offering is a collection of objective features,

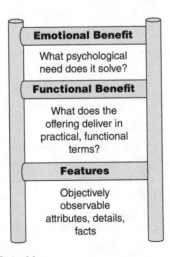

Emotional Benefit

What psychological need does it solve?

Functional Benefit

What does the offering deliver in practical, functional terms?

Features

Objectively observable attributes, details, facts

FIGURE 10.3 The Benefit Ladder

related functional benefits, and sometimes even emotional benefits. With laddering, we pull these apart. We start at the bottom with our features. What are just the facts? You have a hospital located in Seattle, Washington. The hospital offers immediate care at multiple satellite locations and is the largest intensive care unit in the region. It's ranked fifth nationally in cardiac care (first locally) and was the first hospital to do an aortic transplant. All lovely facts. So what? We move up to functional benefits. So, we have the best outcomes in heart surgeries in the region. So, we're able to treat people at our satellite locations with lowest wait times. And again, we can ask: So what? What emotional benefit does that mean we provide? So, when your loved one is in need of cardiac care, we provide the reassurance that you have made the right choice. So, we help bring loved ones home. Are you starting to think that the ladder will be different depending on the target we picked? You're absolutely right.

Building this out (Figure 10.4), you may find many things at each level—many features, many functional benefits, many emotional benefits. If you aren't seeing a full ladder, then you need to do more research. Gather different people from different areas for a brainstorming session, commission a study with customers, examine social media comments.

The next thing we need to do is identify the most important benefits using our criteria: MAD. Of all the things you've listed, which are most meaningful to your customer? Which are authentic *in their minds*? It's not uncommon to create a ladder and then look to customers for validation only to find out that they aren't following you all the way to the top. While nodding along with the

Meaningful to the customer's choice, Authentic/Believable, Different than competition		M	A	D
Emotional Benefit(s):	What specific psychological need do you solve?			
	Security? Peace of mind? Confidence? Happiness?			
Functional Benefit(s):	What are the functional outcomes of using this offering?			
	Healthy? Easier? Safer? Cleaner? More convenient?			
Features:	What are objectively observable aspects of your offering that act as the ingredients for what you provide?			
	Specially trained staff? Most user-friendly interface? Most variety? Latest tech?			

FIGURE 10.4   Benefit Laddering Worksheet

functional benefits, they might stop you when you say, "Johnson's Meat Pies make the world a more loving place." And, finally, we come to what is different from our competition. Here the checkmarks come less frequently. But dig in, go back into the features. What is different about your firm?

Brands sometimes find their advantage in a functional benefit. There is nothing wrong with that and in many categories can be incredibly successful. When examining more highly developed categories, the main benefit more frequently lives in the emotional territory. This is because as categories develop, the functional benefits are frequently copied by competition and become parity, forcing brands into an unclaimed emotional space.

As an illustration, Kellogg has a division that specializes in education for nonprofit executives and wanted to clarify their positioning. The goal was to better understand what elements of the program were most important to their prospective students in order to optimize external communications. They began by identifying the target and the competition. Then, leveraging insights from conversations with students, formal feedback collection, and social media comments, they entered the various elements in each of the major rungs. What follows is a simplified version.

Emotional Benefits
- Inspired/Energized
- Empowered/Confidence
- Connected
- Fulfilled

Functional Benefits
- Increased professional credibility
- Increased fundraising success
- Prepared to be successful in the role
- Knowledge of proven strategies and tactics

Features
- Top-tier participants
- Scholarships
- Wide variety of programs and modalities
- Nonprofit curriculum delivered by top-tier instructors

This listing leads us to the next step, identifying which elements were truly important: meaningful, authentic, and different.

Emotional Benefits
- Inspired/Energized
- **Empowered/Confidence in ability to effect change**

- Connected
- Fulfilled

Functional Benefits
- Increased professional credibility
- Increased fundraising success
- **Prepared to be successful in the role**
- Knowledge of proven strategies and tactics

Features
- Top-tier participants
- Scholarships
- Wide variety of programs and modalities
- **Nonprofit curriculum delivered by top-tier instructors**

So, the positioning statement could read: To nonprofit leaders (strategic target), Kellogg is the education provider (frame of reference) that best empowers you to effect positive change (differentiating benefit) because of the purpose-built curriculum delivered by world-class faculty (reasons to believe). While the overarching message of "empowered leaders" will be reinforced over time and act as the lead benefit, the team has also identified the supporting content pillars. Throughout the year, as the team plans for social media ads, emails, even the organization of content on the website, there is strategic guidance for what to communicate. Perhaps the January newsletter will be about "increased fundraising success." While not the main positioning, it has been identified as an important topic that reinforces the brand's overall positioning. Perhaps a section of the website will go deeper on the top-tier participants and the benefits of networking in this environment.

Many brands establish an annual "master brief" to guide ongoing social content throughout the year. At the top is the overarching or umbrella positioning for the brand, and underneath we have "content pillars" or key messaging areas that we've strategically chosen to reinforce over the year. As the need for content grows greater with channel expansion, brands often fail to fill these content needs strategically. A nice ancillary outcome of this exercise is that you have identified multiple benefits. Remember that content calendar you need to fill? As you cascade down from your main central benefit into sub-benefits and features, you have identified along the ladder the most important points that support your overarching positioning. These support pieces can help strategically prioritize a content plan. If we start with a clear knowledge of what's most important, we can make our efforts in this space much more impactful.

Purpose: When and How to Leverage a Higher-Order Social Purpose for Commercial Purposes

How high can you go on the ladder? Some brands are now laddering all the way up with purpose-driven advertising. They move past emotional benefits associated with their category to associate with human ideals and causes. Some modern brands are purpose driven from the start, and that purpose is woven through their entire offering. Some brands adopt a cause or higher-order benefit later. There is vigorous debate whether this is the ultimate achievement in brand communication or a misguided attempt to add meaning to mayonnaise. The answer is that laddering into higher-order human ideals is neither inherently bad or good, but rather a strategic choice that can be wise or foolish depending on the situation. I do have to pause and clarify that I am not opposed to any firm that wishes to do good for the world. Wonderful. And at times firms also pursue social good as a way to create value for their employees and potential employees. What we are discussing is whether that "good" should be the basis for their brand's external positioning to customers as a tool to drive purchase.

If we take a step back and think through the MAD framework, a social-purpose positioning could indeed work if customers found it meaningful as a reason for choosing the brand, it was seen as authentic, and it was differentiating versus the competition. Patagonia's stance on preserving nature is seen as a success in that it provides a differentiating reason for a customer to choose their goods (often at a higher price) than functionally identical competitive goods and is perceived as authentic. Red Rifle Coffee is another example, where the brand's politically conservative stance is embraced as a reason for choice in a crowded coffee market. Dove's Campaign for Real Beauty has provided a powerful umbrella positioning for two decades.

The mistake brands make is that they assume higher is always better. We find that emotional benefit and higher-order positioning works well in situations where the brand and category are mature. Customers are aware of the features and functional benefits, and the difference on these rungs between brands is small. With little choice for functional benefit differentiation, brands climb up the ladder to an ownable emotional space.

Some new brands or brands in less mature categories are leaping up the ladder as well. Frequently, they were founded on higher-order ideals and want that to be their main message. Being "good" doesn't have to mean talking about it. If your offering has substantial differentiation on the product features/functional benefit level, that's great! Don't force yourself up unnecessarily. Particularly with new brands, take the time to introduce yourself to your customers, explain who you are and what you do. Even Dove, a brand that has mastered this approach, will communicate at a more functional benefit level when advertising specific products. Portfolio brands will light up different benefits on the ladder for the different offerings depending on the specific situation of that product line.

If all the strategic elements align and playing at the top seems to make sense, be careful. Look hard at the authenticity aspect. Does this make sense for your brand and category? Before you talk, have you walked? The ease of access to information and the ability for people to share it quickly and broadly means that a "fake" purpose will be seen through quickly and likely cause more harm than good. And if it strategically makes sense, then execute it well. The stakes get higher as you move up the ladder, and while these communications can be powerfully good, they can also be powerfully bad. Lean into more customer feedback on your execution before you make it public.

AI-Enabled Personalization

Now back to this question of "Why do I need this when the machine will say the right thing to the right people?" The progression of computing power, data availability, and digital ad placement technology offers the opportunity to assemble custom messages for individual targets. While data privacy is a hot topic—with restrictions varying by country, platform, and category—in many situations marketers have enough data on a given customer to personalize a message.

Perhaps you sell office furniture. A potential customer googles "office furniture," visits your site, peruses the "modern collection," and downloads the "Guide to estimating furniture needs" pdf from your site. The next time this customer comes to your site, the homepage features modern furniture; they receive an email 8 days later with an article on the latest tips for optimizing furniture assortment, and 15 days later they see a video ad from your firm highlighting the new line of modern furniture. We can take the data from many sources—past purchases with our firm, past online behaviors, the current price of steel, the office vacancy rates, the customer's specific geolocation (and on and on)—to automate a message.

This personalization is enabled through a combination of consumer data collection and marketing technology automation. Based on the data attributes of a given customer, we can set up "rules" that personalize the delivery of content. And these rules can "build" the right content to match the attributes of that customer. With the addition of artificial intelligence, the machine can build and test different content to optimize against a given goal. I'll talk more about this topic later in Chapter 15, Developing an Impactful Communication Campaign.

Can we be done with strategy and just set up the machine to optimize messages? More than we used to. The technology does allow for matching the best message to a customer at a given time. But if we think back to why we have positioning in the first place, we still need the strategy. At the highest level, positioning strategy guides, not just messaging, but the overall strategic direction of our firm. Are we going to compete on low prices, high design, efficiency, service, or durability? The essence of strategy is prioritization.[4] We cannot be better than all competition on all metrics, and so we must be choiceful about where to allocate the firm's resources. And if we have strategically chosen to "win" on selected characteristics, then we should build memory associations on those attributes with our customers. That means our positioning strategy will guide even the personalized messages.

Think of the core positioning living at a higher level for long-term value. It directs the major decisions by the brand and informs the overarching messaging. Below that, we can tactically message as needed to optimize short-term sales. And here we will continue to find great value in creating auto-generated, personalized communications based on the data of the individual targeted.

Conclusion

Positioning is the strategic understanding of why you are chosen over the competition so that a firm can reinforce the associations that ground this differentiated reason for choice across all aspects of the offering. These associations will be driven by advertising, price, packaging, service, incentives, and the commerce experience that we deliver. So clarity of positioning, of "Why are we better?" drives strategic decisions across the portfolio.

The classic positioning statement starts with questioning for whom are we going to be best. This target prioritization then drives the remaining elements because it is through their lens that we can understand what is most meaningful, authentic, and differentiated. The frame of reference can be a powerful tool as a shortcut for consumers to understand your proposition, as a clear strategic foil for your main benefit, and as a path to find new growth. The act of understanding and prioritizing your benefits helps provide clarity on what we need to consistently reinforce over time to build memory structures with our customers. And it can also illuminate the supporting pillars that become strategic areas of supporting content.

When the concept of positioning was first developed, the marketing world was simpler. Higher barriers to entry in most markets meant fewer competitors. There were far fewer channels of distribution, far fewer options for our messaging in advertising, and far fewer touchpoints for experiences with our customers. The heightened complexity has made the positioning concept more valuable to marketers. As our options grow, our resources in time, attention, and effort cannot keep pace, and our need for focus and clear strategic direction will be paramount.

Author Biography

Kevin McTigue is a clinical associate professor of marketing at the Kellogg School of Management at Northwestern University. He teaches multiple classes for Kellogg's MBA and executive education programs. His career spans more than 25 years in teaching, consulting, brand management, and advertising. He is currently the academic director for Kellogg's Chief Digital Officer program and co-director of Kellogg's Advertising and Marketing Communication Strategy program. He co-authored *The Creative Brief Blueprint* and contributed to *Kellogg on Branding*. He conducts executive training and consulting for a variety of firms on the topics of marketing and advertising strategy.

PART 4

Creating Value with Brands

CHAPTER 11

Building
Strong Brands

Alexander Chernev

I n *Romeo and Juliet*, William Shakespeare famously wrote: "What's in a name? That which we call a rose by any other name would smell as sweet." While Shakespeare's insight may have been true centuries ago when he penned his masterpiece, today it is no longer the case: A name is not always just a name. As it becomes a brand, the name gains the power to influence our perceptions of the world around us, determine what we choose to buy, how we experience different products and services, and how happy we are with their performance. Because of their unique ability to influence behavior, brands have become a key driver of customer value. In this chapter, we will explore the role of brands as a marketing tool, the importance of creating a meaningful brand image, the ways in which brands create customer and company value, and the role of brand equity and brand power in brand valuation.[1]

The Brand as a Marketing Tool

Brands have a long history as a means of distinguishing the goods of one company from those of another. Some of the earliest known brands were used to mark the identity of a good's maker or owner. These simplest forms of branding were observed in the ancient civilizations of Egypt, Crete, Etruria, and Greece. During the Roman Empire, more distinctive forms of branding, including the use of word marks in addition to graphics, began to emerge. The importance of brands dramatically increased by the end of the nineteenth century when the proliferation of mass-produced, standardized products—a direct consequence of the Industrial Revolution—created the need for unique marks to help consumers distinguish between these products. As manufacturers began producing on a larger scale and gained wider distribution, they started engraving their mark into the goods to distinguish themselves from their competition.

Along with these changes, the nature of brands was transforming from simply marking the origin of the product to identifying its maker and serving as a symbol of product quality. Indeed, many brands started as product descriptors designed to identify their maker to help retailers manage their inventory. Over time, these products and services gained a reputation in the market, and customers not only sought them out but were willing to pay a premium for them. The name and the other identifying characteristics—such as the logo, motto, and packaging—acquired a meaning that went beyond simply labeling these products and services to imply characteristics and benefits that were not readily observable.

Nowadays, brands are ubiquitous. Their use extends beyond physical goods such as food products, cars, and pharmaceuticals. Brands are used to designate product ingredients that consumers never buy directly (Teflon, Gore-Tex, and Vibram). Brands can also be used to identify services (Netflix, Expedia, and Uber), companies (Unilever, Walmart, and Starbucks), and nonprofit organizations (NHL, The Nature Conservancy, and American Red Cross). Brands can also designate administrative units (countries, states, and cities), geographic locations (Champagne, Cognac, and Roquefort), and events (Olympic Games, Wimbledon, and Super Bowl). Brands can identify individuals (Lady Gaga, Madonna, and Michael Jordan), groups (music groups, sports teams, and social clubs), and ideas and causes (education, social justice, and health). The use of brands is not limited to consumer markets. Business-to-business enterprises have built strong brands that span industries including consulting (McKinsey & Company, Boston Consulting Group, and Accenture), commercial equipment manufacturing (Boeing, DuPont, and Caterpillar), and software solution services (SAP, Oracle, and Rakuten).

The ubiquity of brands in all aspects of business life stems from their ability to create market value. Not only do brands play a role in helping customers identify the company's offerings, but they can also create value above and beyond the value created by the product and service aspects of these offerings. In this context, brands can be defined as follows:

The brand is a marketing tool used to identify an offering, differentiate it from similar market offerings, and create distinct market value above and beyond that created by the other attributes of the offering.

The role of brands is often confused with that of products—partly because many managers confound product and brand management decisions in their daily activities. Yet, product management and brand management are two distinct activities that are unified by the common goal of creating market value. The difference between products and brands can be illustrated by the following example.

Consider a cereal company introducing a new offering. Let's say the company decides to target health-conscious families with young children with the value proposition of a tasty, healthy cereal that both parents and their children can enjoy. Once this strategy is in place, the next step involves creating the actual cereal that will be offered in the market, which is defined by seven tactical decisions: product, service, brand, price, incentives, communication, and distribution. Here, the product and brand decisions are two distinct attributes of the offering that follow the same overarching strategy.

When designing the product, a manager must develop an appropriate product strategy by identifying the key benefits that the product will create for target customers. In the cereal example, product benefits might involve factors such as taste and nutrition. To deliver these benefits, a manager makes a series of tactical product-based decisions that involve specific aspects of the cereal, such as its nutritional value (calories, sugar, fiber, sodium, protein, and vitamins) and taste (flavor, texture, crunchiness, and crispiness).

In addition to deciding on the properties of the cereal, a manager must decide how to brand the product. To this end, a manager must create a unique identity that is associated with the company's product to inform potential buyers that this specific product was created by a particular company rather than by one of its competitors. In addition, the manager might want to create an identity that not only differentiates its product from the competition's but also adds value to customers' experience with the product.

In the cereal example, the brand might aim to create the psychological benefit of building a relationship with customers so that it becomes an integral part of their breakfast ritual. To this end, the manager might create a character that will capture the personality of the brand, thus helping consumers easily recognize the company's cereal and at the same time connect with the brand on an emotional level. For example, Kellogg's Frosted Flakes uses Tony the Tiger as a brand character to uniquely identify this cereal in the grocery store and foster an emotional connection with the brand. Thus, the brand creates value that enhances the value created by the product. Indeed, when cereal manufactured by different companies looks and tastes alike, the brand becomes the key distinguishing factor. Furthermore, while enjoying the taste of the cereal, customers are unlikely to form an emotional bond with the product unless it is associated with an image that carries relevant meaning for these customers.

Product and brand decisions require different types of expertise. In the cereal example, product-focused decisions call for knowledge pertaining to human nutrition, food manufacturing technologies and processes, as well as consumer food preferences. In contrast, brand-focused decisions require in-depth understanding of the customer, including higher-level customer needs such as the need for self-expression, relationships, and belonging. The different competencies involved in product and brand management often lead to separating these two activities into discrete product and brand management functions and assigning these functions to different managers, who work together to develop successful market offerings.

Although brands are designed and managed by companies, their power stems from the image they create in people's minds. "Products are made in a factory, but brands are created in the mind," memorably noted Walter Landor, a brand pioneer whose firm created identities and logos for some of the world's largest corporations including Coca-Cola, Levi Strauss, Fujifilm, and 3M. Because brands are created in people's minds, they—unlike products—cannot readily be established in one country and exported to another. Instead, they need to be cultivated in each market to create a meaningful image in customers' minds.

The Brand as a Mental Image

The ultimate goal of a company's branding activities is to create a *brand image*—a mental image that exists in people's minds and reflects their thoughts, beliefs, and feelings about the company and its offerings. Thus, unlike the term *brand*—which is often used to designate specific attributes such as name, logo, and motto that identify the company and its offerings—the term *brand image* refers to the network of brand-specific associations that exist in people's minds. It reflects how customers view a particular brand through the lens of their own set of values, beliefs, and experiences. Simply put, the brand image reflects the way people perceive the brand.

Brand image can be visually represented as an association map delineating the key concepts linked to the brand name. Figure 11.1 illustrates a stream-lined brand association map representing a particular person's image of the Starbucks brand. Here, the nodes represent the different concepts related to the brand in this person's mind. The nodes closer to the brand name indicate thoughts that are directly associated with the brand, and the nodes that are farther away indicate the secondary associations that are less prominent in a customer's mind.

The type of associations brands evoke—as well as the breadth, strength, and attractiveness (positive vs. negative) of these associations—reflect the degree to which a given brand has successfully created a relevant, well-articulated, and positive image in a customer's mind. The stronger the brand, the greater the number of relevant benefits, usage occasions, experiences,

FIGURE 11.1 Starbucks Brand Association Map
Source: Alexander Chernev, *Strategic Brand Management,* 3rd ed. (Chicago, IL: Cerebellum Press, 2020).

concepts, products, and places associated with it—and the stronger and more positive these associations are.

Ideally (from a company's standpoint), the brand image that exists in the mind of each of its customers should be consistent with the image the company aims to project. In reality, however, this is not always the case. Because the brand image exists in a customer's mind and stems from this customer's individual needs, values, and knowledge accumulated over time, the same brand might evoke different brand images in different individuals. For example, some might associate the Starbucks brand with handcrafted espresso coffee drinks, while for others it might represent a part of their daily routine, and yet others might think of Starbucks as a place to meet with friends.

Given the idiosyncratic nature of customers' experiences, a company's ability to create a consistent image of its brand in customers' minds is often limited to identifying and communicating the key concepts that it would like customers to associate with the brand. Because the actual image formed in customers' minds varies based on customers' unique interactions with the brand, having a clearly articulated brand strategy can help the company overcome the diversity of customers' individual experiences and build a brand image that reflects the essence of the company's brand.

The brand image is intricately related to the value created by the brand, such that the value of a brand stems from the image that exists in the minds of its customers. In this context, the brand image reflects the meaning of the brand: what the brand is and what it is not. The brand value, on the other hand, reflects the benefits and costs that customers associate with this meaning. The brand image answers the question *What is Brand X?* In contrast, the brand value answers the question *What can Brand X do for me?* Thus, creating a meaningful brand image is crucial for a brand's ability to create market value.

How Brands Create Value

A brand's ability to create value can be related to the transparency of the benefits defining a company's offering. This is because not all aspects of a company's offering can be readily observed by customers. Some attributes are associated with greater levels of uncertainty and, as a result, their benefits are more difficult to evaluate than those of other attributes characterized by a greater level of transparency. Based on the level of uncertainty associated with their performance, an offering's attributes can be classified into one of three categories: *observable, experiential,* and *credence.*[2]

Observable attributes provide benefits that can be readily identified and evaluated. These attributes are associated with the least amount of uncertainty and are typically identifiable through inspection before purchase. For example, the size and shape of a toothpaste tube, the color of a car, and the type of cuisine offered by a restaurant are observable attributes.

Experiential attributes carry greater uncertainty and are revealed only through consumption. For example, the flavor of a toothpaste, the comfort of a car, and the taste of a meal in a restaurant are experiential attributes because their performance cannot be assessed by merely observing the offering.

Credence attributes have the greatest amount of uncertainty, and their actual performance is not truly revealed even after consumption. For example, the cavity prevention benefits of a toothpaste, the safety of a car, and the calorie count of a restaurant meal are credence attributes because even after experiencing the offerings, customers are unable to evaluate their performance.

The distinction between observable, experiential, and credence attributes is important because it determines the role a brand can play in creating customer value. The general principle here is that the greater the amount of uncertainty associated with an offering's benefits, the greater the role a brand can play in communicating these benefits. Indeed, communicating observable benefits is relatively straightforward and merely involves informing target customers about the properties of the offering's attributes. Likewise, communicating experiential attributes can readily be achieved by letting customers experience the offering using means such as trials and free samples. Communicating credence attributes, however, is more complicated and requires that customers trust the offering to deliver the promised attributes. Such trust can be achieved by building a reputable brand that can support the company's claims about the unobservable performance of its products and services.

There is an inverse relationship between the visibility of benefits and the importance of brands as a means of communicating these benefits: Less visible benefits require heavier reliance on brands to create market value. As a result, the greater the importance of unobservable benefits, the greater the role brands play in creating market value (Figure 11.2). Not only can a brand

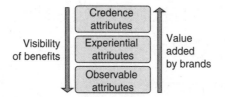

FIGURE 11.2   Benefit Visibility and Brand Impact
Source: Alexander Chernev, *Strategic Brand Management,* 3rd ed. (Chicago, IL: Cerebellum Press, 2020).

convey an offering's invisible benefits, it can also make these benefits more prominent in people's minds. In doing so, a brand's function goes beyond simply identifying a company's offering and differentiating it from the competition to create customer value by revealing this offering's performance on observable attributes. *Brands create value by making the invisible visible.*

Consider the success of evian. Following the opening of its first bottling facility in 1826, evian managed to become the top-selling premium spring water worldwide in an industry that at the time was perceived as a commodity. Evian achieved this by positioning its brand to address an unmet market need: Mothers were concerned about the purity of the tap water they were using to feed their infants. One of the reasons for their concern were the chemicals used to purify the tap water, which could be readily tasted when drinking it. Evian water, with its bland taste, was the perfect product to alleviate this concern because the lack of tap-water taste was viewed as a sign of purity. Evian made the purity and mineral content of water—attributes that at the time were not prominent in people's minds—important factors in the buyer decision process, and positioned its brand as the best at delivering on these two benefits. Thus, by making the invisible attributes of its offering prominent, evian was able to transform the way customers thought about drinking water and establish the superiority of its brand on these attributes.

Similar to evian, Michelin established its brand by emphasizing the importance of a previously obscure aspect of automotive tires—reliability. With its motto *Because So Much Is Riding on Your Tires*, Michelin brought to light the risk associated with buying tires that might be unreliable. In the same vein, DieHard emphasizes the longevity of its batteries, DeWalt underscores the durability of its professional tools, McDonald's focuses on the consistency of its meals, and Papa John's promotes the freshness of its pizza ingredients. Pharmaceutical companies often launch brands designed to solve problems that were invisible to customers until the company made these problems prominent. The branding strategies employed by these companies are effective because when customers cannot readily assess the benefits of the available offerings, they tend to rely on a brand's promise to deliver on the unobservable benefits and use the brand as a key factor in making their choice.

Brands as a Means of Creating Customer Value

The primary purpose of brands is to create value for their target customers and, by doing so, create value for the company managing the brand. Without customer value, there is no value to be captured by the company. Brands can create customer value on one or more of the three key dimensions: *functional, psychological,* and *monetary.*

Functional Value

Functional value reflects the benefits and costs directly related to an offering's practical utility such as performance, reliability, durability, compatibility, and convenience. Brands can create functional value in two ways: by identifying a company offering and by signaling the offering's functional performance.

Identifying the company offerings. Brands enable customers to identify a company's products and services and distinguish them from those of its competitors. For example, if Tide laundry detergent was not associated with a unique brand, customers would have difficulty locating it and would have to examine the ingredients of many detergents to ensure that the product they purchase is indeed the Tide detergent produced by Procter & Gamble. The identification function of brands is particularly important in the case of commoditized products that are similar in their appearance and performance.

Signaling performance. In addition to identifying the offering, brands can inform customers about the functional performance of the products and services associated with the brand. For example, the Tide brand signals cleaning power, the Crest brand signals effective cavity protection, and the DeWalt brand signals durability. Not only can brands inform customers about the performance of products and services, but they can also change the way customers experience these products and services. For example, the taste of beer, the scent of perfume, and even the effectiveness of a drug might be influenced by customers' knowledge of their brands.

Psychological Value

Psychological value reflects the mental benefits and costs of the offering, such as the emotional experience provided by the offering and its ability to signal a customer's social status and personality. Psychological value is often the key source of the market value created by brands. Indeed, because brands evoke specific associations in a customer's mind, they can convey a wider range of emotions and deeper meaning than the other attributes of the offering. Specifically, the psychological value created by brands stems from three types of benefits: emotional, self-expressive, and societal.

Emotional value. Brands can create emotional value by evoking an affective response from customers that is typically associated with positive emotions. For example, Allstate Insurance Company ("You're in Good Hands with Allstate") aims to convey peace of mind with its brand, and Hallmark ("When You Care Enough to Send the Very Best") evokes the feeling of love and affection.

Self-expressive value. Brands can create self-expressive value by enabling individuals to express their identity. For example, brands like Harley-Davidson, Diesel, and Tommy Bahama stand for different lifestyles, enabling consumers to express their unique personality by displaying these brands. In addition to allowing consumers to express their individuality, brands like Rolls-Royce, Louis Vuitton, and Cartier create psychological value by enabling their customers to highlight their wealth and socioeconomic status.

Societal value. Brands can create societal value by conveying a sense of moral gratification from contributing to society. For example, brands like TOMS, Patagonia, Product Red, UNICEF, Doctors Without Borders, and Habitat for Humanity that represent humanitarian causes create customer value by taking a stand on relevant social issues and implementing a variety of socially responsible programs.

Monetary Value

In addition to creating functional and psychological value, brands can also create monetary value. Monetary value reflects the financial benefits and costs of the offering, such as its price, fees, discounts, and rebates, as well as the various monetary costs associated with using, maintaining, and disposing of the offering. Specifically, brands can create two types of monetary benefits: signaling price and generating financial value.

Signaling price. Brands can signal the overall level of prices associated with the company's products and services. For example, the Walmart brand conveys the idea of low prices, fostering the belief that its offerings are priced lower than its competitors'. The price image conveyed by a brand is particularly important when buyers are unaware of the competitiveness of the price of a given offering and, in such cases, they often rely on the brand to infer the attractiveness of an offering's price.

Financial value. In addition to signaling an offering's monetary value, brands can also carry inherent monetary benefits, which are reflected in the higher price of branded offerings on the secondary market. For example, a

Louis Vuitton handbag commands a much higher resale price compared to a functionally equivalent unbranded handbag. In fact, the financial benefit of brands is one of the key factors in valuing alternative investments such as wine, watches, and automobiles.

Brands as a Means of Creating Customer Value: The Big Picture

The three dimensions of customer value—functional, psychological, and monetary—and the specific ways in which brands can create value on each of these dimensions are summarized in Figure 11.3. The value added by brands on each of these dimensions depends on a variety of factors such as the specific product category, customers' familiarity with the attributes of the offering, and the degree to which the offering's performance on different attributes is readily observable. The lower the customers' expertise and the less observable the offering's performance on attributes that are important to these customers, the greater the potential value created by the brand.

Not every brand can create value on all three dimensions. In fact, positioning the brand on some of the value dimensions might greatly diminish this brand's ability to create value on other dimensions. For example, a brand signaling a monetary benefit, such as low price, might not be credible in signaling high levels of product performance and conveying wealth and social status. In this context, the different types of customer value can serve

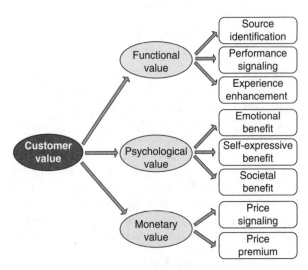

FIGURE 11.3   Brands as a Means of Creating Customer Value
Source: Alexander Chernev, *Strategic Brand Management,* 3rd ed. (Chicago, IL: Cerebellum Press, 2020).

as a guide to developing a brand's value proposition rather than be regarded as a requirement that a brand create value for customers on each of the three dimensions.

Brands as a Means of Creating Company Value

In addition to creating value for customers, brands can create value for the company. The ability of the brand to create company value is important because it enables the company not only to recoup the resources spent in designing and communicating the brand but also to create incremental value stemming from the brand. There are two main dimensions on which brands can create company value: *strategic* and *monetary*.

Strategic Value

The strategic value created by brands reflects the nonmonetary benefits that a company derives from associating its products and services with a given brand. Some of the key strategic benefits include bolstering customer demand, amplifying the impact of the other marketing tactics, ensuring greater collaborator support, and strengthening the company culture.

Bolstering customer demand. Because brands create customer value, they generate incremental demand for a company's offerings. For example, a customer who is not interested in an unbranded product might be interested in a branded version of the same product because this customer finds the brand meaningful and relevant. In addition to increasing the attractiveness of the company's offerings, brands might facilitate the usage of the company's offering, as customers are more likely to consume the branded offering more frequently. Offerings associated with an attractive brand are also more likely to encourage customer advocacy, which, in turn, is likely to further promote sales. For example, Zappos, Zara, and Apple have many customers who are passionate about the brand and help expand the demand for offerings associated with these brands.

Amplifying the impact of other marketing tactics. In addition to directly bolstering customer demand, brands can increase the effectiveness of the other attributes defining the company's offering. Thus, brands can enhance customer perceptions of product performance by making branded products appear more powerful, reliable, durable, safe, attractive, tasty, or visually appealing than their unbranded counterparts. For example, people tend to think that a drug is more effective if it is associated with a reputable pharmaceutical brand. Because brands create incremental customer value, companies tend to charge higher prices for branded products than for unbranded products. For example, Morton-branded salt commands a substantial price premium over the unbranded version, even though both contain the same ingredient. In addition to finding branded products more attractive and paying extra for them, customers are also more willing to search for the branded product across distribution channels and bypass more convenient retailers that do not carry their favorite brand—even when a functionally equivalent substitute is readily available. Customers are also likely to react more favorably to incentives and communication from a brand they patronize than those from identical unbranded products.

Ensuring greater collaborator support. Strong brands can create value for the company by securing greater support from its collaborators. For example, strong brands give manufacturers power over retailers, enabling them to negotiate more advantageous agreements, resulting in a better distribution network and greater promotional support such as on-hand inventory, product placement, and sales support. In the same vein, retailers with a strong brand can command greater support and better margins from manufacturers of products that are either unbranded or associated with weak brands.

Enhancing the corporate culture. Strong brands can help build, enhance, and sustain the company culture. This is because a brand can create a strong sense of identification among its employees, increase their morale, and bolster their teamwork. Furthermore, *brands can facilitate the recruitment and retention of skilled employees.* This is because employees often place a premium on working for companies whose brands resonate with their own needs, preferences, and value systems. Thus, companies with strong brands find it easier to attract and retain talented employees. In fact, employees are often ready to sacrifice part of their compensation and accept a lower salary to work for a company with a favorable brand.[3]

Monetary Value

Monetary value is directly linked to a company's desired financial performance and typically includes factors such as net income, profit margins, sales revenue, and return on investment. Monetary value is the most common type of value ultimately sought by for-profit companies. Brands can create monetary value for the company in several ways: by generating incremental revenues and profits, increasing company valuation, and creating a divestable company asset.

Generating incremental revenues and profits. A brand's ability to generate higher sales revenues and profits stems from customers' reaction to the brand, including their greater willingness to buy the branded offering as well as pay a premium for this offering compared to the unbranded version of the same offering. The incremental stream of revenues associated with the brand is the most important direct source of monetary value that benefits the company on an ongoing basis. In addition to the increase in revenues stemming from customers' affinity for the brand, a company might also be able to negotiate better financial terms with its collaborators, such as distributors and retailers, who are likely to benefit from the strength of the company's brand.

Increasing the valuation of the company. Brands' ability to generate incremental net income can, in turn, enhance the monetary value of the company, such that companies with strong brands receive higher market valuations. In fact, many companies have managed to build brands that are worth more than the value of their tangible assets. Apple, Coca-Cola, Disney, McDonald's, and Nike brands are each estimated to be worth tens of billions of dollars, making these brands one of their company's most valuable assets. The combined value of the top 100 brands is estimated to be in excess of a trillion dollars. We discuss the different approaches to assessing the value of a brand later in this chapter.

Creating a divestable company asset. In addition to contributing to a company's valuation, brands might generate additional value for the company if they are acquired by another entity. In particular, brands with names that are distinct from the parent company's brand might have significantly higher value when acquired by another company with better opportunities to unlock the true value of the brand. For example, over time Procter & Gamble divested many of the brands it helped to build and manage, including CoverGirl, Clairol, Duracell, Folgers, Jif, and Pringles, collecting tens of billions of dollars in the process, most of which were attributable to the power of these brands.

Brands as a Means of Creating Company Value: The Big Picture

In the world of rapidly commoditizing products and services, brands are becoming the new frontier of competitive differentiation and the key source of company value. The two dimensions of company value—strategic and monetary—and the specific ways in which brands can create value on each dimension are summarized in Figure 11.4. The monetary value created by the brand is often readily observable and, as a result, is frequently given priority in evaluating a brand's performance. The strategic value of the brand, although often invisible, can supplant the direct monetary value of the brand and, therefore, should be carefully nurtured to realize its full potential.

Understanding the ways in which brands create value for the company is important because it enables managers to better measure the effectiveness of their brand-building activities. Knowing the value a brand creates for the company also enables managers to frame brand-building costs as an investment

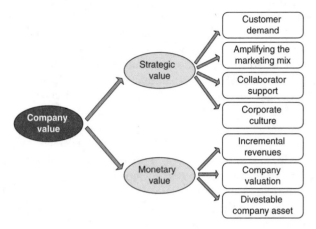

FIGURE 11.4   Brands as a Means of Creating Company Value
Source: Alexander Chernev, *Strategic Brand Management,* 3rd ed. (Chicago, IL: Cerebellum Press, 2020).

in a value-creation asset rather than merely as an ongoing marketing expense with no residual value. As the popular saying, commonly attributed to Peter Drucker, goes, "What gets measured, gets managed." Accordingly, the following section offers a more detailed discussion of assessing the company value created by brands, focusing on the concepts of brand equity and brand power.

Brand Valuation

A company can benefit from having an accurate estimate of the value of its brands for several reasons. Knowing the monetary value of a brand is important in mergers and acquisitions to determine the premium over the book value of the company that a buyer should pay. Knowing the monetary value of its brand(s) is also important to determine the value of the entire company for *stock valuation* purposes. Brand valuation is also important in *licensing* to determine the price premium that brand owners should receive from licensees for the right to use their brand. Having an accurate estimate of the value of the brand also matters in *litigation* cases involving damages to the brand to determine the appropriate magnitude of monetary compensation. Assessing the value of the brand is also important for evaluating the *effectiveness* of a company's brand-building activities as well as for deciding on the allocation of resources across brands in a company's portfolio.

To succeed in building strong brands, a company must have a clear understanding of how the brand creates market value, as well as the metrics and processes for assessing the value of the brand. The two aspects of brand value—*brand equity* and *brand power*—are outlined in more detail below.

Brand Equity as a Source of Market Value

Brand equity is the monetary value of the brand. It is the premium that is placed on a company's valuation because of brand ownership. The monetary value of a brand is reflected in the financial returns that the brand will generate over its lifetime. Understanding the concept of brand equity, managing its antecedents and consequences, and developing methodologies to measure brand equity are of utmost importance for ensuring a company's financial well-being.

The issue of brand valuation came into prominence in the 1980s when the wave of mergers and acquisitions, including the $25 billion buyout of RJR Nabisco, served as a natural catalyst for the increased interest in brand valuation and the development of more accurate brand valuation methodologies. Because the value of the brands owned by a company is not reflected in its books,[4] setting a fair price for brand assets that a firm has built over time is of utmost importance, especially given the fact that the value of a company's brands could exceed its tangible assets.

Despite the importance of brand equity, there is no single universally agreed-on methodology for its assessment; rather, there are several alternative methods, each emphasizing different aspects of brand equity. Three common approaches to measuring brand equity are the cost approach, the market approach, and the financial approach. All of these approaches view brands as separable and transferable company assets that have the ability to generate a stream of revenue. Where these approaches differ is in conceptualizing the sources of brand equity and the reliance on different methodologies to quantify the value of the brand.

The *cost approach* involves calculating brand equity based on the costs involved—marketing research, brand design, communication, management, and legal costs—to develop the brand. The cost method can be based on the historical costs of creating the brand by estimating all relevant expenditures involved in building the brand, or it can be based on the replacement cost— the monetary expense of rebuilding the brand at the time of valuation.

The cost approach is intuitive and is commonly used for evaluating a company's tangible assets. The challenge in applying this approach to assessing brand equity is that estimating the costs a company must incur to build an identical brand is extremely complicated, especially in the case of well-established brands that over the course of many years, and in some cases decades, have carved out a place in customer minds. Because of this limitation, the cost approach is more relevant for assessing the value of freshly minted brands for which the brand replacement costs are easier to identify—although even in this case accuracy is constrained because the cost approach might not take into account a brand's full potential to create market value.

The *market approach* measures brand equity as the difference between the sales revenues of a branded offering versus the sales revenues of an identical unbranded offering, adjusted for the costs of building the brand. For example, to assess the value of the Morton Salt brand, one would compare the sales revenues generated by the branded product with the sales revenues generated by its generic equivalent—regular salt—and then subtract the cost of building and managing the brand. In cases when a generic equivalent of the branded product is not readily available in the market, an alternative approach might involve using a test market to estimate the price difference between a single unit of a branded offering and (a prototype of) an identical unbranded offering, adjusted for sales volume and branding costs.

A key advantage of the market approach over the cost-based approach is that it requires fewer assumptions in assessing the value of a brand. At the same time, the market approach has several important drawbacks that limit its validity and relevance. One of these drawbacks is that this method focuses only on one metric of brand value (the price premium) and does not consider other aspects of value created by the brand, such as more favorable terms for a branded product from a company's collaborators as well as a brand's impact on a company's ability to recruit and retain skilled employees. Furthermore, this approach assumes that the company has fully utilized the value of its brand and, hence, does not account for the value created by potential product-line extensions, brand extensions, and licensing opportunities. The market approach also does not include the differences in the cost structure associated with branded and unbranded products because the difference in prices could also be attributed to differences in production costs rather than the price premium commanded by the brand. Another important limitation is that the market approach is not readily applicable to companies using an umbrella-branding strategy, in which a single brand is used across different product lines in diverse product categories.

The *financial approach* assesses brand equity as the net present value of a brand's future earnings. This approach typically involves three key steps: estimating the company's future cash flow, estimating the contribution of the brand to this cash flow, and adjusting this cash flow using a risk factor that reflects the volatility of the earnings attributed to the brand. By considering a wider range of factors, the financial approach addresses some of the shortcomings of the cost-based and market-based approaches. At the same time, the financial approach is also subject to several important limitations. The first limitation is the difficulty in accurately estimating the future cash flow derived from the branded offerings. This difficulty stems, in part, from the fact that a brand's ability to generate future cash flow is contingent on a variety of extraneous factors that are difficult to predict. For example, a brand's reputation can be damaged by a product failure or a catastrophic event such as what occurred in the Tylenol poisonings, the Ford–Firestone tire recall, and the BP Gulf of Mexico oil spill.

The cash flow generated by a brand can also be influenced by a change in the market in which it operates. To illustrate, the switch to digital technology greatly reduced the size of the existing market for Kodak and Xerox, significantly diminishing the market value of these brands. Furthermore, it is difficult to separate the cash flow attributable to the brand from the cash flow attributable to nonbrand factors like production facilities, patents and know-how, product performance, supplier and distribution networks, and management skills. Another important limitation of the financial approach is the difficulty of accurately estimating the life span of a brand, which is a prerequisite for defining the duration of the future cash flow attributable to the brand. The financial approach also does not take into account the brand value that has not been fully realized in the market, such as the value stemming from future brand extensions and licensing agreements.

The shortcomings of the different valuation methods underscore the importance of developing alternative valuation methods that employ testable assumptions and use diverse methods to measure brand value. Such approaches must take into account the strategic value of brands, including the potential for extending the brand beyond its current target markets and product categories, as well as the brand's power to influence the behavior of different market entities.

Brand Power as a Source of Market Value

Unlike brand equity, which reflects the monetary value of the brand to the company, brand power reflects the brand's ability to influence the behavior of the relevant market entities—target customers, company collaborators, and company employees. Thus, brand power reflects the difference in the ways customers, collaborators, and company employees respond to the brand. For example, if knowledge that an offering is associated with a particular brand does not change consumers' response, the brand is lacking in power and the company's offering is effectively a commodity.

Brand power is the differential impact of brand knowledge on customers' response to a company's marketing efforts.[5] A brand has greater power when customers react more favorably to an offering because they are aware of the brand. Brand power is not always positive; for certain customers, the value of the brand might be negative, making customers less likely to purchase an offering when it is associated with a particular brand. For example, some customers display a strong loyalty to the Harley-Davidson brand and would purchase only a Harley-Davidson motorcycle, whereas for others the Harley-Davidson brand might be a detractor because it conveys unfavorable associations.

Brand power is directly related to brand equity, such that the brand-induced change in customers' behavior generates monetary value for the company, which is reflected in the company's brand equity. The key determinant of brand power is the brand image, which reflects all beliefs, values, emotions, and behaviors customers associate with the brand. Thus, to build a powerful brand, a company must focus its activities on creating a meaningful brand image in customers' minds that can influence their behavior in a way that creates value for the company (Figure 11.5).

In addition to influencing customer behavior, brand power benefits the company by influencing the behavior of its collaborators and employees. Thus, brand power benefits the company by increasing the likelihood that target customers will purchase the branded offering, will use it frequently, and will be more likely to endorse this offering. Greater brand power also influences collaborators' behavior by increasing their willingness to work with the company. In addition, brand power helps the company attract a skilled workforce while enhancing employee loyalty and productivity.

Greater brand power does not automatically lead to greater brand equity. For example, the brand equity of Nissan is estimated to be higher than the brand equity of Porsche even though Porsche is a stronger brand, as reflected in its greater price premium compared to Nissan. Likewise, even though Armani and Moët & Chandon have greater brand power than Gap and McDonald's, the brand equity of the latter is estimated to be higher.[6]

Because brand equity is a function of brand power as well as a company's ability to utilize this power in a given market, brand equity is not always a perfect indicator of brand power. Instead, brand equity reflects the degree to which the company is able to utilize the power of the brand. Brand power, in turn, is determined by the company's strategy and tactics as well as the impact of the various market forces: customer needs; competitor and collaborator actions; and the economic, technological, sociocultural, regulatory, and physical context in which the company operates.

Given that brand power and brand equity are not perfectly correlated, it is possible to identify instances in which a brand's power exceeds its monetary value, as well as instances in which a brand's monetary valuation is overstated relative to the brand's power. A brand is undervalued when its brand equity does not account for the full market potential of the power of this brand. In contrast, a brand is overvalued when its equity overstates the underlying brand power. From a marketing perspective, brands whose brand equity is undervalued, meaning that their brand power is not fully monetized by the company, present brand-building opportunities. From an investment perspective,

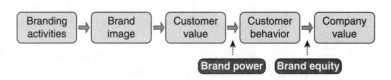

FIGURE 11.5   Brand Power and Brand Equity
Source: Alexander Chernev, *Strategic Brand Management,* 3rd ed. (Chicago, IL: Cerebellum Press, 2020).

undervalued brands present acquisition opportunities for companies that can unleash the hidden power of these brands.

Conclusion

Branding is the process of endowing a company's offerings with a unique identity to differentiate them from the competition and create value above and beyond the value delivered by the other aspects of the offering. A brand's success is defined by the viability of its strategy and the effectiveness of its tactics in creating market value. The complexity of the branding decisions involved in creating market value requires that a company's brand-building activities be guided by a clear understanding of the ways in which the brand will create value for its customers as well as the company. As companies struggle to distinguish their products and services through functional performance, they are increasingly relying on brands as a means of creating market value. In the world of rapidly commoditizing products and services, brands have become the new frontier of competitive differentiation.

Author Biography

Alexander Chernev is a professor of marketing at the Kellogg School of Management at Northwestern University. He holds a PhD in psychology from Sofia University and a PhD in marketing from Duke University. Dr. Chernev has been ranked among the top ten most prolific scholars in the leading marketing journals and serves as an area editor and on the editorial boards of many leading research journals. He teaches marketing strategy, brand management, and behavioral science and has received numerous teaching awards, including the Top Professor Award from the Executive MBA Program, which he has received fourteen times. Dr. Chernev has written numerous textbooks on the topics of marketing strategy, brand management, and behavioral science, and has worked with Fortune 500 companies to reinvent their business models, build strong brands, and gain competitive advantage.

CHAPTER 12

Creating a Meaningful Brand Image

Neal J. Roese

Brands are a powerful way to differentiate a company's products and services in a way that creates market value. Indeed, brands are increasingly an indispensable recipe for growth and profitability. The top 10 global brands are valued in excess of a trillion dollars, and many successful new businesses are built on a strong brand platform designed independently of product or service.

At its root, branding aims to create a psychological outcome, the brand image. The brand image is something that lives inside the mind of the target customer: It is what a customer subjectively believes about the brand. Specifically, the brand image is an aggregate of customers' beliefs, assumptions, experiences, and expectations about the brand. Collectively, the brand image in any given marketplace is the aggregate beliefs across all those who constitute the target market.

Understanding what the brand image is, how best to quantify it as a key performance indicator, and how best to build it is now essential for many business leaders. This chapter provides a brief overview of the power and value of strategizing through the lens of brand image, a fundamental psychological conception.

Integrate the Brand Image into Your Strategic Thinking

For any business leader, defining the business strategy entails a specification of the value-creation process. Brands create value for customers in part by

189

enhancing the psychological facets of consumption, such as emotions and self-expression. To harness the potential of the brand for profitability, it is essential for leaders to understand how the brand can bring profitability, why it is essential to build a brand image that is meaningful to customers, and how to connect the brand image to the delivery of psychological value.

Leverage the Brand Image for Profitability

Brands propel revenue. Indeed, in a commoditized world in which many products are increasingly converging on the same level of functional excellence, brands are a key means of differentiation. Over the years, the business value of brands has been verified empirically many times. For example, a McKinsey study revealed that the world's 40 strongest brands yielded almost twice the total return on investment to shareholders over 20 years as compared to a benchmark index.[1]

A recent economics experiment is particularly revealing. The researchers partnered with an Indonesian bank to launch credit card offerings that varied randomly in their branding yet carried identical financial benefits.[2] Thus, this "true experiment" permitted a clean separation between the psychological and functional benefits of a new product. Specifically, the difference between the two branding treatment conditions centered on the presence or absence of "platinum" labeling. The result of the experiment was that the mere impact of brand was a 7% sales lift over the week of testing, an economically significant magnitude in that market.

Of note, this was the barest-bones version of a "brand," consisting only of name and visual design, leaving aside all those additional facets that could potentially feed into a more complex brand image. As such, this experiment constitutes an "existence proof" of the effect of rudimentary branding. Overall, the brand revenue lift is a function of investment in the complexity, meaning, and emotional resonance of the brand image. Great branding—such as that practiced by global leaders like Apple, Disney, and Mercedes—brings considerably greater revenue lift.

Brands are particularly effective tools for building margin as opposed to volume. Consider the example of a power strip, a rather pedestrian piece of everyday household equipment. The device allows you to extend the reach of power connections and to unify inputs at a specific point in the home. Sometimes, however, a power strip is not just a power strip but also a means of self-expression. Let's take the example of a power strip with two electrical outlets and two USB outlets. At the time of writing, there is such a power strip branded by General Electric and priced at $19. This price point is standard across the category for this product specification.

But there is another power strip available today that is priced at $155. This power strip is branded by Shinola, a premium lifestyle brand founded in 2011.

What would seem to be a simple, utilitarian product is tricked out in the latter case with stylistic elements that bring psychological value to the customer in the form of aesthetic self-expression in interior design. The Shinola brand is built on a design language centering on heavy, high-durability, mid-century American industrial design. Compared to the General Electric product, the Shinola product demands that the company provide additional investment in stylistic design. And certainly there is the tradeoff of diminished volume; after all, how many people will pay eight times as much for an identical object? Yet, the margin benefit makes this brand-based play worthwhile. But what is it that makes one brand more profitable than another? The answer, to which we turn next, centers on the creation of a meaningful and resonant brand image. In short, customers will pay more for things they love.

Ensure That the Brand Image Is Meaningful to Customers

The brand image resides in the minds of target customers. In other words, the brand image is a structure within human memory containing interconnected knowledge of and feelings about the brand. How does this psychological aspect matter to the financial outcomes of the business enterprise? Businesses must generate revenue, and the place of brand image within the overall business model is the immediate precursor to revenue. The brand image drives revenue in the sense that customers buy what they believe will provide the benefits they desire. The clearer and more meaningful the brand image, the greater the opportunity for profitability.

A firm's overall business objective, typically profit, guides the marketing strategy, which then guides the marketing tactics such as product design, pricing, and advertising. Brand image is the result of a successful set of tactical executions. As we will see in a subsequent section, it is essential to coordinate the marketing tactics to create a coherent brand image.

The brand image embodies functional aspects of the offering such as performance, reliability, and durability, but it is the psychological aspects involving emotional connection that potentially drive profitability to the greatest extent. A great brand image is one in which the customer's understanding of the psychological side of the value proposition is crystal clear. And customers are willing to pay more for products that are meaningful to them.

The example of Fender is instructive. Fender is a classic American brand within the general category of music (e.g., instruments, amplification, production, etc.). Fender was founded in 1946 on the basis of innovation in the electric guitar, which in those days was a novel form of musical instrument.[3] The Fender Stratocaster was a breakthrough product that, beginning in the 1950s, occupied the imagination of several generations of "wannabe" musicians dazzled by the prowess of popular music entertainers. Fender's primary product innovation centered on music amplification by way of transforming stringed-instrument vibration into electrical signals that could be modified in innumerable stylistic ways, carving new sonic identities for country, folk, jazz, and rock music. The Fender brand image today contains elements of youthfulness, Americana, nostalgia, premium quality, classic rock stars, emerging new stars, and a "can-do" mindset of musicianship. Ask a musician today what they think of Fender, and they almost certainly will have an opinion!

How was the Fender brand image created? The answer is both simple and mysterious. It is simple in that coordination across tactical executions (product design, pricing, communication, distribution, etc.) yielded a coherent brand image. For example, product design reflected a mid-century industrial aesthetic based on molded plastics and flamboyant colors, indirectly referencing product design in automobiles like Cadillac and home furnishings by Herman Miller. The Fender brand is mysterious in that, as the best brands do, it finds ways to connect to cultural developments that add nuance and resonance to the brand image.

Take, for example, the product name "Stratocaster." When launched in the 1950s, this sub-brand name leveraged the cultural meaning attached to the words "stratosphere"—indicating superb and reflecting the high-tech emergence of commercial jet travel—and "broadcasting"—indicating the ability to communicate to a mass audience at a distance and leveraging the high-tech emergence of television. In the 1960s, the Fender brand leaned into cultural developments in popular music, particularly the explosive expansion of the youth music-buying market attracted by varied musicians including The Beach Boys, Bob Dylan, and Jimi Hendrix, all of whom featured prominently as endorsers in Fender advertising.

The continued interplay between branding and popular culture helped to create an enduring and meaningful brand image for Fender. Fender is not simply a set of products for musicians; it is a set of ideas that embody an emotional connection between company and customer. The takeaway for leaders is the imperative to plan a brand image that is uniquely meaningful to target customers. One way to clarify how the brand is meaningful is to design the strategic focus around psychological value, an idea to which we turn next.

Design the Brand Image around Psychological Value

Brands are a way to create and communicate psychological value. Psychological value is defined as the intangible, emotional, and/or identity-based benefits of the offering. A brand brings psychological value when the customer feels good about consuming the brand, sees a personal relationship—perhaps akin to a relationship with a loved one—with the brand, or thinks the brand shares facets of their own identity, preferences, and aspirations. These psychological benefits stand above and beyond the purely functional benefits afforded by a product. A BMW owner, for example, appreciates the status-signaling aspect in addition to the performance characteristics associated with the brand.

Psychological benefits may center on any or all of three key sources of value: emotional, self-expressive, and societal. Emotional value centers on the simple feeling of pleasure brought about by acquisition or consumption. Pleasure may take many forms, from excitement to contemplative calm, from awe to animal passion, from momentary joy to sustained life satisfaction. Products can certainly stimulate immediate emotion (as when biting into chocolate creates a brief rush of pleasure). However, great brands move to a higher level of emotionality, implying a longer-lasting emotional state. Whereas the Magnum brand of chocolate evokes pleasure simply through the specific recipe that combines cocoa and sugar, the Fender brand creates excitement by way of its years of association with a deep roster of popular and often rebellious music artists who themselves played Fender instruments.

Self-expressive value centers on how the customer thinks of their identity in terms of the brand.[4] Sometimes this self-expression is outwardly focused, such that customers broadcast something about themselves through brand usage (e.g., driving a Mercedes along a crowded strip, carrying an Hermès bag to the theater). At other times this self-expression is inwardly focused and not intended for public consumption (e.g., using a trusted personal care brand like Cowshed in the privacy of one's own home).

Finally, societal value embraces benefits beyond oneself as an individual customer that connects to others and the wider culture. For example, the individual customer may not benefit functionally from Warby Parker brand's "buy a pair, give a pair" initiative but may well benefit from the psychological satisfaction of helping others who are less fortunate.

The Fender brand is instructive in the way the brand image constitutes multiple facets of psychological value. In terms of emotional value, there is the pure joy that comes from music creation, performance, and appreciation. For a budding musician, using a Fender instrument to create the first bursts of musicality is a profoundly joyous experience. In terms of self-expressive value, Fender helps both new and seasoned musicians to express their deepest inner selves through musical performance. In terms of societal value, the Fender brand subsumes the Fender Play Foundation, a public charity dedicated to increasing access to music education.

Self-expression is a particularly potent avenue for brands to deliver psychological value. Self-expression embraces two fundamental motivations underlying identity: the need for uniqueness and the need for belonging. All people crave both uniqueness and belonging, but the relative craving for each varies considerably over time and across the life span.[5] Moreover, uniqueness and belonging exist in a state of opposition. In other words, there is a trade-off between the two. Being more unique means fitting in less with a group, whereas fitting in with a group means being less unique.

Because these motives are in opposition, brands cannot succeed by simultaneously appealing to both motives. Brands excel at delivering self-expressive psychological benefits when they specialize in one or the other. For example, many fashion brands (especially niche brands) cater to highly individualized forms of self-expression. Rhone (in the men's performance clothing category), for example, is tightly targeted toward delivering uniqueness because relatively few individuals will be aware of its functional capabilities in the athletic space. By contrast, nearly all sports teams specialize in belonging—that is, connecting to a group identity. The Chicago Cubs, a professional baseball team with a passionate fan base, caters to those who want to cheer in unison while wearing identical Cubs-branded clothing.

The key takeaway for leaders is to design the brand strategy and tactics to create and communicate distinct and differentiated psychological value for customers. Delivering psychological value is essential for brands to bring profitability. In this section we have discussed ways to integrate the brand image as a basic, essential component of marketing strategy. Once a brand image has been designed and launched, it is essential to track it, a key topic that is the focus of the next section.

Track the Brand Image to Verify Success

Because the brand image directly fuels revenue growth, it is tempting to gauge branding success solely via financial outcome metrics. However, the brand is one of several tactical executions that feed into revenue; hence, effective management requires monitoring quantitative indications of the brand image to disambiguate the relative contribution of one versus another tactic. If sales soften, it pays to know where the problem is.

Quantify Brand Image along with Awareness and Attitude

There are three key psychological performance indicators: awareness, brand image, and attitude. These three metrics answer three distinct questions: whether, which, and how much. Awareness is the presence or absence of brand-related information in customer memory. Fundamentally, awareness embodies attention and memory as the underlying psychological processes. Awareness answers the question of "whether" the brand's identity has been stored in customer memory.

Brand image is defined, as we have seen, as a set of mental associations between concepts in customer memory. Fundamentally, image embodies the organization of concepts. Image answers the question of "which" aspects of the company's intended positioning have indeed lodged successfully in customer memory. A brand may have been positioned on status, but if customers associate the brand with fun, then the wrong image has been formed—at least in terms of the brand strategy.

Finally, attitude reflects the overall liking the customer has for the brand. Fundamentally, attitude embodies evaluation and preference formation. Attitude is the preferred term among psychologists, but in practice many other terms are used that reflect this same basic meaning, such as affinity, sentiment, satisfaction, net promoter, and so on. Attitude answers the "how much" question in terms of quantifying the degree of liking versus disliking. One may be mildly appreciative of one brand while wildly passionate about another, and this variation in attitude is consequential for purchase, usage, and loyalty.

All three performance indicators—awareness, brand image, and attitude—reflect orthogonal psychological facets of brand health. Orthogonal means that knowing the state of one metric tells you nothing about another. For any brand health dashboard, awareness, brand image, and attitude are bedrock components upon which more nuanced metrics may be added. It is noteworthy that awareness is a more meaningful indicator for newer as opposed to more mature brands. As brands become successful or even reach the status of market leader, awareness hits a ceiling and then evinces only minimal variability. By contrast, brand image and attitude are highly informative performance indicators at all stages of the brand's lifetime.

Measure the Brand Image with Customer Testing

How is the brand image measured? Essentially, brand image is about concepts and characteristics, whatever they are, that are so memorable that they come immediately to mind to customers. Often termed "top-of-mind," whatever becomes memorable is usually something that is meaningful, important, or frequently encountered. Characteristics can be pretty much anything, including product attributes (e.g., reliable), functional outcomes (e.g., clean dishes), and psychological benefits (e.g., status). The successful positioning of a brand centers on the articulation of a very small set of characteristics—or perhaps even just one—that the brand wishes to be known for.

United Airlines for many years used the advertising phrase "Fly the friendly skies." Underlying this messaging was the strategic positioning of "friendly." In other words, the brand wanted customers to associate United with friendly, such that the first thing that comes to mind upon thinking of United Airlines is "friendly." The psychological approach to quantification of the brand image is survey based: The method is to prompt the customer to respond with characteristics that come immediately to mind after hearing the brand name. The mention of "friendly" is an "either–or" that can be aggregated across respondents with a simple frequency tabulation. The result can be summarized as the proportion of respondents who say "friendly" spontaneously after hearing "United Airlines." If a company desires multiple characteristics to be associated with the brand, then this brand image quantification can yield a list of characteristics ranked by frequency of occurrence across survey respondents. A strong brand image is one in which those characteristics designated to be part of the positioning appear with greater frequency than any other characteristics named by respondents.

Of key value to the business leader wanting to monitor psychological performance indicators is that awareness, brand image, and attitude may be expressed as percentages, enabling intuitively easy benchmarking. The frequency of characteristics, for example, can be expressed as the percentage of customers in the target market who after being prompted by the brand name respond by naming the one or more key characteristic(s) specified in the brand positioning. In quantifying brand image by way of frequency, its distinction from the other two psychological metrics, awareness and attitude, becomes more apparent. Awareness is quantified by the proportion of respondents who can name the brand after being prompted by the category (unaided awareness) or who say that they recognize the brand after being shown it directly (aided awareness). Attitude is quantified along a liking-versus-disliking scale.

Awareness is readily conveyed as a percentage. Attitude may also be conveyed as a percentage if the subset of individuals whose brand ratings are moderately or strongly positive (vs. weakly positive, neutral, or negative) is taken as a proportion of all possible responses (i.e., a "top-two box score"). These differences in quantification method reflect the conceptual differences among "whether," "which," and "how much" questions and answers. Newer methods, beyond old-fashioned surveys, are available to track brand metrics, a topic to which we turn next.

Quantify the Brand Image in Real Time

In today's business environment, a brand's digital health dashboard must include, at a bare minimum, quantification of awareness, brand image, and attitude. The longstanding practice of quantifying brand image using customer survey methodology is now being supplanted by digital, real-time quantification. Specifically, automatic analysis of online customer data can provide up-to-the-minute performance indicators in the same way that sales and distribution data now provide real-time snapshots of business dynamics. We may conceptualize online customer data in terms of three basic categories: search data, social data, and purchase data.

Search data result from customers' online searches for product and service information. Social data results from customers' text-based comments posted to social media. Purchase data result from records of past purchases within the relevant category. Brand image may be estimated reliably only from social data,[6] but not from search or purchase data. By contrast, both awareness and attitude may be extracted from all three: search, social, and purchase data.

Awareness is relatively simple, so the mere mention of a brand name during a search is a good proxy for awareness, as are the frequency of mentions in social media posts and past purchase data. Similarly, attitude may be roughly estimated from search data, based on the underlying assumption that people tend to search for things that they like or want, although there are rare exceptions to this assumption. Attitude may also be inferred from social data by way of an increasingly powerful technique called sentiment analysis. Finally, attitude may be inferred from purchase data because people typically buy things that they desire, but again there will be exceptions. Because the brand image is a more complex conceptualization of the link between brand and characteristics, it is less accurately estimated from search data. People may search for a brand or some characteristic such as a product feature or goal, but rarely both at the same time, making insight into brand image difficult. Similarly, brand image is difficult to infer from purchase data, for the reason that there is no source of information regarding concepts and characteristics relevant to the brand in purchase history.

To summarize, the opportunities for real-time quantification of brand performance indicators continue to widen. Three kinds of customer-relevant online data may inform performance indicators: search, social, and purchase data. Both awareness and attitude may be extracted from all three data sources, but brand image may only be inferred from social data and not search or purchase data. In the final sections, we turn to the question of managerial best practices for building a coherent brand image.

Ensure Consistency in Touchpoints to Build a Coherent Brand Image

In an ideal world, the brand image is a direct reflection of the brand strategy. That is, the firm decides what the brand stands for and executes its actions based on this positioning, with the result that customers associate the brand with precisely those same things. Reality, unfortunately, is rarely so tidy.

The difficulty for firms is that the brand image is influenced by a great many inputs beyond those within the firm's control. To be specific, what is within the firm's control regarding brand are the tactical decisions on product, service, price, incentives, distribution, and communication. Of these, product design, service design, and communication are obviously pivotal for brand image, but shrewd managers understand that all marketing tactics contribute to the brand image, sometimes hugely but other times subtly. In this section, we consider how leaders can build strong brands by ensuring consistency across marketing tactics, interactions with customers, and opportunities in cultural shifts.

Coordinate Tactics to Sharpen the Brand Image

Each and every tactical execution contributes to the brand image. Let's begin with product and service design. Product design is increasingly seen as an opportunity for branding, as when a coherent design aesthetic is deployed over multiple offerings. Automobile brands such as Porsche and Tesla, for example, design their portfolio of automobiles such that there is a recognizable "brand DNA" that is consistently evident in each new model design. In the power tools category, the DeWalt brand uses the color yellow along with a specific form factor to create an integrated "family resemblance" across its vast range of hardware products. And emblematic of best practice in branded product design is Apple's simple, clean aesthetic that permeates all of its offerings.

A key tenet of "design thinking" is the integration of product design with brand design, such that new product development supports the brand, and the brand gives direction to new product development, creating a virtuous circle. Indeed, customers derive inherent value from seeing a family resemblance in branded assortments.[7] Furthermore, a cohesive aesthetic design for a brand portfolio lends itself to comprehensive intellectual property protection under trade dress law.[8]

Service design feeds into brand image just as does product design. For example, Polaris is a branded airline service tier operated by United Airlines. Polaris embraces a blend of service components (pre-flight lounge), hardware (custom-designed seating), and co-brand partners (e.g., Saks Fifth Avenue) that together contribute to its brand image of premium air travel. Clearly, decisions regarding both product and service have the power to deepen or weaken the brand image. When Polaris launched, the partnership with the Saks Fifth Avenue, a more established premium brand, was instrumental in building customer associations of "premium" with Polaris.

Price and incentives feed into the brand image. Price may often be set by rule of thumb or by quantitative estimation of demand. Yet because price influences the brand image, smart managers recognize the power of pricing as yet another brand-building tool. All else being equal, a higher price signals greater quality and a lower price signals weaker quality. Thus, price information feeds into customers' assumptions about functional aspects of quality, capability, and durability, as well as into psychological aspects such as status and prestige.

One may even specify the price image as a subset of the brand image, consisting of the mental associations and shorthand assumptions regarding price that are connected to a product, a category, or a multi-category assortment.[9] Price image may not always be accurate: Customers sometimes assume a brand involves higher or lower prices than is actually the case. For example, much to the chagrin of Whole Foods, for many years customers overestimated the average cost of its assortment of offerings. This effect hinges on the inability of any one customer to recall precisely all of the prices within a large assortment. Instead, customers rely on mental shortcuts to infer an aggregated price point.[10]

By a similar logic, incentives also feed into brand image. JC Penney is known for offering frequent price promotions, which help to create a brand image centering on affordability but also lower quality. By contrast, premium brands such as Canada Goose deliberately refrain from price promotions because they detract from associations of high quality. Thus, decisions regarding both price and incentives have the power to deepen or weaken the brand image.

Distribution likewise feeds into the brand image. Where you buy a brand says a lot about the brand. Of note, retailers carry their own brand image. The difference in image between Walmart and Nordstrom (i.e., lower vs. higher price and quality) may potentially become associated with each and every individual brand carried within these respective retailers. A budget brand does better to associate with Walmart than Nordstrom; a premium brand does better to associate with Nordstrom than Walmart. Indeed, a key objective for a new brand is to find a retailer that "fits" with its intended brand image, thus unlocking opportunities to build and deepen its brand image by borrowing from the retailer's image.

The opportunity to create branded stand-alone retail is attractive in large part because the brand image may be more tightly controlled, as in Apple's deployment of branded stores in which the interior design reflects the Apple product design aesthetic of simple and clean. This insight has been executed effectively by automobile brands for decades. The look and feel of the Toyota versus Mercedes showroom, for example, go a long way toward inculcating the desired associations in customers' minds. Automobile firms with multibrand portfolios may benefit from creating stand-alone branded retail locations, as Hyundai has done with its premium Genesis brand.

Brand startups that began under a direct-to-consumer business model, such as Allbirds and Warby Parker, have now created branded brick-and-mortar stores, enabling them to further enhance their brand image. The direct-to-consumer approach was seen by Walmart as an opportunity for further brand-building that could leverage its competency in retail execution, a key reason behind Walmart's acquisition of Bonobos. The growth opportunity for business leaders lies in omnichannel, which is the creation of centrally managed platforms that offer multiple points of distribution for branded offerings that share a consistent visual and emotional brand tonality.

Finally, communication feeds into the brand image. Although communication campaigns may have various objectives, from raising awareness of a new product launch to a new price promotion, it must be emphasized that all communication necessarily has an influence on the brand image. From simple slogans to elaborate visual imagery, the information contained in advertising has the power to deepen and enhance the brand image.

A good rule of thumb for marketers is to plan explicitly when and under what circumstances pure brand-building communications will be deployed. Sometimes the timing is based on expediency: A lull in new product launches constitutes a window of opportunity for brand-building ads. An example is the legendary BMW Films campaign in which short-form (less than 15 minutes) big-budget action films created by and starring A-list Hollywood talent were distributed to potential BMW buyers.[11] Unlike the more routine advertising support for new product launches, the BMW Films campaign was an initiative centering purely on building brand image. The objective was to inject more adventure, romance, and excitement into the BMW brand to attract younger potential buyers.

Another case of "good timing" was Apple's objective to support new product extensions from home computing to consumer electronics (especially the iPod, its wildly successfully portable music player). In order to set the stage for this launch, Apple fielded the purely brand-building "Think Different" ad campaign. Think Different consisted of video and print media that featured imagery of iconoclastic creative minds: Amelia Earhart, Albert Einstein, Mahatma Ghandi, Martha Graham, Pablo Picasso, and others. Each of these famous historical figures has their own unique reputation and notoriety. In short, each has a brand image. And each respective celebrity brand image could potentially become associated with the Apple brand image, thus creating an aggregate impression of innovation and game-changing creativity. To use some traditional marketing parlance, the Apple brand image was "laddered up" to the more abstract level of game-changing creativity, an image that paved the way for success in new product categories beyond mere home computing.

Communication feeds into the brand image regardless of whether the advertising emphasizes brand building. Every ad is an opportunity to build the brand image.

Invite Customer Input

Customers contribute enormously to the brand image, and leaders must work with customers as co-creators to build a strong brand image. At the most basic level, seeing a branded offering being consumed by a customer is sufficient to create an association between the brand and that sort of customer. Seeing an affluent young adult holding a Starbucks coffee cup contributes to the Starbucks brand image of affluence. Seeing a vigorous young adult wearing Lululemon apparel contributes to the Lululemon brand image of vigor.

Ideally, leaders define their brand strategy around a particular sort of target customer, among whom sales and usage have been successfully stimulated. However, the advent of social media constitutes a monumental leap in the power of customers to project their individual voices to the wider culture. Customers drive the brand image as much as the company does. Customers may broadcast product reviews, share usage stories with friends, and post images of the brands and products that they love. Indeed, social media-based brand communities have sprung up rapidly and contributed to the growth of newly created brands, sometimes with astounding speed. Smart leaders look for ways to connect with and leverage such communities. For example, Emily Weiss, founder of the Glossier brand of cosmetics and personal care products, first amassed an active online community with her blog called *Into the Gloss*, and only later converted it into a business venture.

Brands obviously benefit from customer feedback, enabling them to recognize and react to nascent crises before they reach the boiling point. Such was the case when the Capri Sun brand of fruit juice experienced minor mold growth in some packages. Online critique was immediate. But so was the receptivity of the brand team under parent company Kraft-Heinz, which enacted both a short-term solution (reaching out directly to affected customers) and long-term solution (an engineering fix that precluded mold growth).

Nevertheless, the threat of brands being hijacked on social media by customers with different views of the brand than the company has cannot be underestimated. Fred Perry is an upscale British fashion brand with roots in tennis, yet the appropriation of its signature polo shirt as the uniform of the Proud Boys has tarnished its brand image with unwanted associations. The Proud Boys are notorious for their participation in the U.S. insurrection of January 6, 2021. The rapidity with which negative associations may form around a brand after it has been hijacked creates a new imperative for brand managers to monitor the cultural environment in real time. How best to defend the brand across a wide range of threats was explored in Kellogg professor Tim Calkins' book *Defending Your Brand*.[12]

Activate the Brand Image by Harnessing Societal Shifts

How do you elevate the brand to the next level of revenue growth? More to the point, how do you activate the brand image so that it is even more meaningful to customers? The answer is to connect the brand to cultural moments—that is, to link mental associations about the brand to significant trends in society.

Great brands got to where they are by recognizing cultural moments and connecting their brand authentically to unfolding events.

The Fender brand, which focused on country-and-western musicians in the 1950s, pivoted in the 1960s to targeting young, middle-class "musicians-to-be" who had become fascinated by rock-and-roll. Fender leaned into this cultural shift with celebrity endorsements by the hottest young performers of the era. The Fender brand image soon became inextricably intertwined with the youthful, rebellious attitude of rock music.

Harley-Davidson enjoyed a similar trajectory of cultural relevance. A major supplier of military vehicles to the U.S. government during World War II, the brand saw new life when post-war surplus motorcycles were appropriated by returning American service personnel as objects of inexpensive customization and, hence, self-expression. In the 1950s, "biker culture" exploded into popular culture as a means of rebellious self-expression. Harley-Davidson cemented its brand image by connecting to a counterculture, iconoclastic aesthetic. Harley-Davidson became the brand for those who refuse to play by mainstream rules.

Nike built its brand image by connecting to the societal shift toward physical fitness in the 1980s. Prior to this time, jogging and cycling were the leisure activities of a very few. The rise of home video exercise instruction (featuring stars such as Jane Fonda and Richard Simmons, among others) raised the profile of fitness, and by the 1990s fitness had become mainstream. Nike's mantra, "If you have a body, you're an athlete," exemplifies how Nike leaned into the cultural shift toward fitness.

In forging an internal company culture poised to lean into cultural movements, it is essential for managers to hire employees with highly tuned "social radars" that enable them to anticipate new trends. The brand team needs pop culture junkies. The good news is that it has never been easier to monitor new trends, which may be observed digitally by anyone with a laptop and a nose for the new.

Conclusion

Brands are a key means of differentiation and a powerful mechanism for value creation. The brand image is a psychological entity, a collection of information stored in the minds of target customers. Collectively, the brand image of an offering in a marketplace comprises the aggregated perceptions in the memories of all current and potential consumers. This chapter summarizes the key ideas and objectives for managing the brand image, with a specific focus on what the brand image is, how best to quantify it as a key performance indicator, and how best to build it. In an increasingly competitive business landscape, the brand is an indispensable tool for growth. Smart leadership depends on a deep understanding of the brand image.

Author Biography

Neal J. Roese is professor of marketing at the Kellogg School of Management. He holds a PhD from the University of Western Ontario (Canada). His scholarly research focuses on the psychological processes underlying choice, including how people think about decision options, make predictions about the future, and revise understandings of the past. At Kellogg, he teaches branding to MBA and executive audiences. In addition to his work as a legal consultant, his insights have received wide media coverage with recent appearances in media outlets including CBS, NPR, the *New York Times*, the *Guardian*, the *Wall Street Journal, Inc.*, *Fast Company*, *Forbes*, and the *Harvard Business Review*.

CHAPTER 13

Brand Resilience: Surviving a Brand Crisis

Jonathan Copulsky

R esilience refers to the ability of a material, a person, or an organization to recover or bounce back quickly from difficulties. In today's hyper-connected and high-speed world, brands face more threats than ever before. *Resilient brands* are brands that have cultivated the ability to survive, persevere, and thrive in the face of these threats. This chapter offers guidance in the form of a seven-step framework for brand stewards and the organizations they serve for anticipating and responding to threats that might otherwise sabotage and undermine the brand value they have worked so hard to build.

Brands as Signals of Quality

On January 1, 1876, thanks to an industrious employee waiting in line overnight, the Bass Brewery logo and brand name became the very first trademark to be registered under the UK's newly enacted Trade Mark Registration Act. Although Bass and its Pale Ale brand are now part of the global brewing powerhouse Anheuser-Busch InBev, its distinct logo and branding endure.[1]

Over the years, other iconic global brands have emerged, including business-to-consumer powerhouses such as Apple, Disney, and McDonald's and business-to-business giants such as Caterpillar, Boeing, and Salesforce. These brands enjoy wide recognition, premium prices relative to competitors in their categories, and high levels of customer loyalty and advocacy. Iconic brands attract customers like flowers attract bees, not only for their core offerings but also for new offerings that extend their reach into new categories, new customer segments, and new geographies. They also serve as magnets for talent, appealing to employees who relish their association with an iconic brand. Their employees serve as human billboards, wearing hoodies, carrying backpacks, and consuming coffee from mugs—all branded with the logos of their employers.

It is not surprising, consequently, that organizations measuring brand value—such as Kantar, Interbrand, and Brand Finance—attribute a significant share of leading public companies' market valuations to their brand value. While considered an intangible that never appears in financial statements, the financial impact of an iconic brand is very real and very significant. Apple tops the Kantar BrandZ Top 100 Most Valuable Global Brands at $947 billion, which represents a 55% year-on-year increase. In 2022, the total value of the 2022 Kantar BrandZ Top 100 Most Valuable Global Brands grew by 23% to reach almost $8.7 trillion, which is remarkable "considering the backdrop of high inflation and an unpredictable global economy."[2]

For Bass and its nineteenth-century contemporaries, the primary role played by brands was to communicate the *quality* of a company's products or services. In this context, quality means the ability to get the job done with freedom from defects, deficiencies, side effects, and significant variations. A quality razor delivers a smooth shave and a safe one. A quality car comfortably transports its passengers from place to place with a minimal number of unscheduled repairs. A quality meal is one that is enjoyable to eat and will not make one ill. When the primary role of the brand is to communicate quality, the underlying message is the promise that the customer will achieve what they set out to achieve when they made the decision to purchase the product, with no unintended consequences and no regrets.

But the need for brands to perform the role of quality communicator has diminished over time. Government regulators, like the U.S. Food and Drug Administration, mandate minimum quality levels and monitor compliance. Third-party evaluators and customer reviews provide advice and guidance to customers seeking to navigate the myriad of available options, helping customers avoid lesser-quality products and focus on the higher-quality ones. Meanwhile, the overall quality of goods and services has risen as new manufacturing technologies and new monitoring capabilities have increased. In addition, a heightened focus on the customer experience has led to higher-quality experiences in purchasing and using these higher-quality products and services.

The Shift from Communicating Quality to Signaling Trust

If the need for brands to communicate quality has diminished, then what has replaced it? Why do we need brands anymore? What is the role of brands in a world with far greater levels of transparency and higher overall quality levels than back in 1876 when that industrious Bass employee waited in line overnight so Bass could be the first UK company to register its brand and logo?

The answer is that *we choose brands because we trust them.* While we trust that they deliver quality, we also trust everything they stand for.

The brands that we choose use the right ingredients, purchased from the right suppliers and produced by the right employees, in the right manner. Freed from the burden of demonstrating quality, brands convey a much richer set of messages, which may include:

- We are sustainable.
- We use fair labor practices.
- We do not pay bribes to corrupt officials.
- We only use organic ingredients.
- We treat our employees fairly.
- We safeguard your private information and keep it private.
- We configure our offerings based on your needs and preferences.
- We reinforce and amplify your values and aspirations.

So, when we choose a brand today, it is as much about declaring who we are and what we value as it is about the product. We proudly choose brands and proudly display those choices. We have moved from mere consumption of a brand to a relationship with a brand. Our willingness to build these relationships with brands is what makes the most successful brands ubiquitous and therefore valuable.[3]

Think of this shift in how people regard brands as equivalent to Abraham Maslow's five-tier hierarchy of needs. Maslow's pyramid describes how human motivations start at the bottom with satisfying physiological needs that are vital to survival (e.g., food, water). As these low-level needs are satisfied, humans are more motivated by security and safety needs, social needs, esteem needs, and self-actualization needs.[4] Analogously, brands start with quality as the bottom tier; alignment with values and aspirations is at the top.[5]

Trust in a brand also means that we are willing to recommend a brand. This is the ultimate compliment that we can pay to a brand: making someone else aware of our trust and letting them know that it is okay for them to trust the brand as well.

Technology powerhouse Salesforce expresses it this way: "The Salesforce brand is . . . who we are as a company, why we exist, how we work, and how we treat one another. Likewise, our brand voice should capture our culture and our values, trust, customer success, innovation, and equality. Trust is our #1 value. Our voice is always truthful and genuine, avoiding exaggeration or misdirection."

Marc Benioff, Salesforce's founder, expands upon this sentiment, "A brand is a company's most important asset. . . . By consistently delivering an attitude that is future-focused and pioneering, we have created a personality. We act the way people expect us to, which has made them feel connected to us. It goes beyond logic. It's an emotional attachment, and that's an asset that cannot be stolen by any competitor."[6]

The Mounting Pressures on Brand Trust

The rising importance of brand trust means that any breach of our trust in a brand can be fatal to the relationship. If our brand behaves in a manner that suggests our trust is misplaced, we terminate that relationship quickly and decisively. Unrepaired and sustained breaches are particularly harmful.

Any number of factors can cause consumers to lose trust in a brand. For example, the COVID-19 pandemic caused more transactions to move online and created greater stress on the companies supporting these digital transactions. In a survey of U.S. consumers conducted in May 2021 after more than one year of pandemic-induced lockdowns, 50% of respondents reported that they had lost trust in brands. Moreover, 58% associated this loss of trust with poor customer service, while 48% indicated that misuse of personal information and 45% said that incessant advertising caused them to lose trust in a brand during the pandemic.[7]

But research from the American Customer Satisfaction Index suggests that blaming the COVID-19 pandemic entirely for this decrease in trust would be misplaced. "While COVID-19 has certainly played a role, the fall in customer satisfaction began before the advent of the pandemic. From 2010 to 2019, about 70% of the companies tracked by ACSI had declining or flat customer satisfaction scores. Since then, American customers have become even more dissatisfied. As of the fourth quarter 2021, almost 80% of the companies have now failed to increase the satisfaction of their customers since 2010."[8]

Mishandling of customer information may be one contributing factor unrelated to COVID-19. During the holiday season of 2013, cybercriminals were able to steal 40 million credit and debit records and 70 million customer records from leading retailer Target. Target settled for $18.5 million the following year, but, more important, experienced hundreds of millions of dollars in declining sales, customer traffic, and market value.[9] Since the Target data breach, hundreds of other data breaches have been reported.

A separate, but related, contributing factor is the misuse of customer data, leading to the reported concerns about incessant advertising. The deluge of digital advertising has overwhelmed us, leading to a slew of regulations regarding the use of third-party cookies and associated disclosures, such as the General Data Protection Regulation in Europe and the California Consumer Privacy Act. According to McKinsey research, 1 in 10 Internet users around the world (and 3 in 10 U.S. users) deploy ad-blocking software that can prevent companies from tracking online activity. In addition, 87% of survey respondents said they would not do business with a company if they had concerns about its security practices, and 71% said they would stop doing business with a company if it gave away sensitive data without permission.[10]

The other major change has been the emergence of ESG (environmental, social, and governance) issues as a factor influencing consumers' perception of and trust in brands. Each year, the global public relations firm Edelman publishes its research, encompassing more than 36,000 respondents in 28 countries, on trust between consumers and various institutions, including businesses, governments, NGOs, and media. The headline for its 2022 report is "Societal Leadership Is Now a Core Function of Business." Research findings include:[11]

- Respondents believe business is not doing enough to address societal problems, including climate change (52%), economic inequality (49%), workforce reskilling (46%), and trustworthy information (42%).
- Nearly 6 in 10 say their default tendency is to distrust something until they see evidence that it is trustworthy.
- People want more business engagement, not less. For example, on climate change, 52% say business is not doing enough, while only 9% say it is overstepping.

Complicating the issue of creating and sustaining brand trust is the reality that customers can lose trust in a brand for reasons beyond the brand's control: a disgruntled customer with a large social media following, a cybercriminal who circumvents carefully developed data privacy safeguards, a troll farm determined to undermine a brand whose CEO has been an advocate for LGBTQ equality. So, at the same time that brands are trying to play offense in building strong brands that radiate trust, they need to play defense against both known enemies working hard to destroy brand trust and unknown assailants using the strategies and tactics of guerrilla warfare and insurgencies.

Creating Resilient Brands

In 2011, I published a book entitled *Brand Resilience*. Brand resilience describes the need for brands to quickly spot potential threats to the brand (and specifically to the trust that it worked so hard to build) and bounce back or recover from these threats stronger than ever. At the time, I was particularly concerned about the velocity at which brand-damaging events could happen (due to the rapid growth of social media) and the need to preempt incidents of brand sabotage (versus just improving rapid-response capabilities). Hence, the subtitle *Managing Risk and Recovery in a High-Speed World*.

Since then, the term *brand resilience* seems to have gained currency and entered the vocabulary of marketing strategists. Kin + Carta created a "Brand Resilience Index,"[12] M Booth wrote about "The Five Tiers of Brand Resilience,"[13] a Landor executive recently penned a thought piece about brand resilience and COVID-19,[14] and the International Trademark Association sponsored the Brand Resilience Conference: Practitioner Roadmap for Guiding Change.[15] *Brand safety*, a related term, has also entered the vocabulary of marketers, but its use is more limited and refers to a set of measures that aim to protect the image and reputation of brands from the negative or damaging influence of questionable or inappropriate content when advertising online.

As I was drafting the book and developing a way to frame advice to marketers on how to respond to brand risks, a colleague suggested that responding to brand risks was equivalent to fighting insurgents. Inspired by this suggestion, I found myself reading the 2006 edition of the *U.S. Army/Marine Corps Counterinsurgency Field Manual* (FM 3-24), a document written to provide guidance to Soldiers and Marines serving in the field.[16] The University of Chicago published a version of FM 3-24 with additional material and explained that "When the U.S. military invaded Iraq, it lacked a common understanding of the problems inherent in counterinsurgency campaigns. It had neither studied them, nor developed doctrine and tactics to deal with them. It is fair to say that in 2003, most Army officers knew more about the U.S. Civil War than they did about counterinsurgency. The *U.S. Army/Marine Corps Counterinsurgency Field Manual* was written to fill that void."[17]

The premise of *Brand Resilience* is that marketers can learn from the insights developed from combating insurgencies and that the strategies and tactics highlighted in FM 3-24 can be adapted and applied to organizations facing brand risks.

Five big takeaways for brand stewards were inspired by my reading of FM 3-24:

1. At first, you may not recognize that your brand is under attack. FM 3-24 notes that a common feature of insurgencies is that the organization being targeted generally needs time to recognize that an insurgency is

taking place and that insurgents take advantage of that time lag to build strength and gather support.

2. Your natural tendencies to respond in a conventional manner to attacks on your brand may backfire. FM 3-24 gives the example of using massive firepower to overwhelm insurgents, resulting in the loss of the hearts and minds of surrounding civilian populations.

3. When it comes to building a resilient brand, the winners are the ones who learn and adapt more quickly. FM 3-24 indicates that in a counterinsurgency, the side that learns faster and adapts more rapidly—the better learning organization—usually wins.

4. The most effective operations for counterinsurgents are not aimed directly at brand saboteurs. FM 3-24 emphasizes the importance of garnering public support.

5. A tactic that works this week might not work next week. FM 3-24 notes that constantly innovating new counterinsurgency tactics and practices is essential as insurgents develop new and more deadly threats.

With that as background, the suggested actions from FM 3-24 for combating insurgents were distilled down into seven steps for marketers and brand stewards (Figure 13.1):

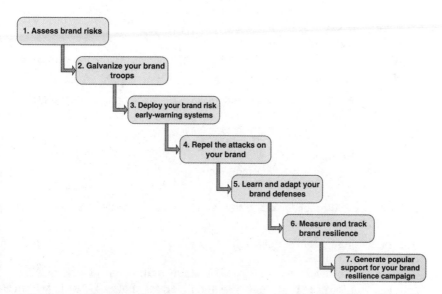

FIGURE 13.1 The Seven-Step Program for Managing Brand Risk and Recovery and Building Brand Resilience

Source: Adapted from J. R. Copulsky, *Brand Resilience: Managing Risk and Recovery in a High-Speed World* (Palgrave Macmillan, 2011).

1. Assess brand risks
2. Galvanize your brand troops
3. Deploy your brand risk early-warning systems
4. Repel the attacks on your brand
5. Learn and adapt your brand defenses
6. Measure and track brand resilience
7. Generate popular support for your brand resilience campaign

The remainder of this chapter reviews each of these actions in greater detail.

Assess Brand Risks

Without intelligence, counterinsurgents are like blind boxers wasting energy flailing at unseen opponents and perhaps causing unintended harm. —FM 3-24

The term *brand risk* describes anything that directly threatens brand value. Brand risks threaten brand value by rupturing the trust that customers have in the brand. Examples of brand risks include:

- Disgruntled employees posting on social media about how poorly they feel you treat them
- Third-party websites that include scathing reviews of your new products
- Executive team members behaving boorishly and caught on camera
- Less than well thought out changes to product packaging or formulations that generate significant negative customer feedback
- Repeated deep-discounting programs that make customers question whether they should ever pay full price for your products
- Unethical competitors anonymously spreading disinformation about your brand
- Unhappy customers creating music videos about your service and posting on YouTube
- Product quality and supply chain issues

Table 13.1 provides examples of threats to brands. In looking at these examples, you will see that the list includes threats that come from within (e.g., employees leaking sensitive information) and externally (e.g., customers posting negative comments on social media).

Over the past 10 years, most organizations have gotten better at identifying and assessing the risks that their brands face, but work may still remain on

TABLE 13.1   Internal and External Threats to Brands

The enemy within . . .	. . . and beyond your borders
Employees	Customer rage
• Leaks of valuable or embarrassing information • Egregious customer mistreatment • Unprofessional or brand-inconsistent behavior • Excessively rigid interpretation of policies and rules	• Return/exchange policies • Perceived mistreatment or poor service • Product quality and safety issues
Senior executives	Reviewers
• Conduct unbecoming (inappropriate relationships with subordinates or third parties, inappropriate or insensitive remarks, inappropriate or illegal financial transactions, inappropriate use of corporate assets, blatantly excessive compensation and perquisites, and tone-deaf behavior)	• Product and service quality and safety concerns • Product and service functionality concerns • Product and service pricing concerns
Unforeseen consequences of operational decisions	Gadflies and ideologues
• Brand licensing • Handling and use of confidential information • Introducing new products or extending the brand • Outsourcing and selecting suppliers and partners (environment and sustainability issues, labor practices, product safety, affiliations)	• Environmental and other ESG concerns • Excessive greed • Health concerns • Labor conditions • Product safety • Undue influence on government officials and regulators
Product pricing and discounts	Competitors
	• Price or value attacks • Product or service quality attacks

Adapted from J.R. Copulsky, *Brand Resilience: Managing Risk and Recovery in a High-Speed World* (Palgrave Macmillan, 2011).

making this a systematic and sustainable practice. This will only happen when organizations recognize that assessing brand risks is not only a job for marketing but for all parts of the organization that directly and indirectly touch the customer, including engineering, finance, IT, legal, and manufacturing.

Assessing brand risks begins with cataloging all of the participants in your extended ecosystem, considering the risks that may be associated with each, and identifying potential risks triggers. A simple example:

Source	Suppliers
Potential risk	Inability to manufacture and deliver products on a timely basis, resulting in disappointed customers who vent on social media
Trigger	Supplier plant shutdowns due to noncompliance with governmental safety standards

This is not a "one and done" exercise. Your ecosystem can change as you forge new agreements or enter new markets. The potential risks may change due to changes in strategies and operations (e.g., fraud associated with new types of payments systems). Triggers may be activated with greater frequency in the "new normal" that seems to be emerging. As companies begin to collect more consumer data, use more digital channels, and outsource more operations, new types of brand risks become possible. Transformational events such as sales of operating units, mergers, and restructurings increase the opportunity for risks to the brand if not carefully managed.

Brand risks are the unavoidable consequence of doing business. Assessment and monitoring of brand risks need to be integrated with your organization's overall strategy for creating a risk-intelligent enterprise. As with other types of risks, the enterprise needs to determine acceptable versus unacceptable levels of risk taking. Often brand risks begin with operational decisions (e.g., outsourcing, customer data collection, pricing), not marketing decisions.

Self-Assessment: Assess Brand Risks

- Have you done a systematic assessment of sources of brand risks, types of brand risks, and brand risk triggers?
- Do you refresh this assessment regularly?
- Have you shared this assessment broadly within your organization?

Galvanize Your Brand Troops

Effective . . . [counterinsurgency] operations require competence and judgement . . . at all levels. . . . Senior leaders set the proper direction and climate with thorough training and clear guidance; then they trust their subordinates to do the right thing. —FM 3-24

Reducing the damage from brand risks begins with building awareness of the threat and its consequences and teaching employees to assume personal responsibility for preempting, detecting, and reducing the possibility of their occurrence. Your employees are your brand troops. The three critical ingredients for effectively engaging your brand troops are:

1. A clear mission
2. A purposeful outreach and education program
3. A strategy for employee ownership of the mission

Think of the first of these three action steps as informing and inspiring your employees. A well-crafted mission provides clarity to employees to permit decentralized execution when it is supported by mutual trust and mutual understanding that subordinates will then do the right thing. Employees need to understand what the brand represents, and they need crystal clarity about what activities create value for the brand and what types of activities destroy brand value.

Outreach begins with sharing the mission and core values with employees on a regular basis. Johnson & Johnson (J&J) has long been recognized for its credo (crafted in 1943), which starts out with "We believe our first responsibility is to the patients, doctors, and nurses, to mothers and fathers and all others who use our products and services."[18] From there it proceeds to describe its responsibilities to its employees, communities, and stockholders. Every J&J employee is exposed to the credo repeatedly throughout their time with the company.

Salesforce employs a similar, but slightly different, approach. Salesforce Brand Central instructs visitors to "find out what sets us apart by learning about the Salesforce brand" and includes sections on brand voice, visual identity, the brand promise, and a bit of brand history.[19] While its tone is more playful than J&J's, it is equally forceful as it describes what the Salesforce brand means. Every Salesforce meeting and event reinforces the brand story with employees.

Outreach needs to be complemented with persuading employees that they are the first and most important line of defense when it comes to protecting brand value. Have you sent the unambiguous message to employees—Only You Can Protect Our Brand—and asked them to step up to this challenge?

Ideally, this process of educating employees starts with the recruiting process as you test the alignment between the company's brand and the prospective employee's values. It continues during employee onboarding and is renewed periodically as employees are promoted. It becomes particularly important during periods of significant change, ranging from a divestiture or an acquisition to a major new product launch or a merger.

The third critical step to energize your employees is making sure that they feel comfortable sharing knowledge of potential brand risks and have the ability to appropriately communicate these risks to others. The military uses the term *situational awareness* to describe the process of recognizing a threat at an early stage and taking measures to avoid it. Being observant of one's surroundings and identifying potential threats and dangerous situations is more of an attitude or mindset than it is a hard skill.[20]

Self-Assessment: Galvanize Your Brand Troops
- Do you spend as much time on educating employees about your brand as you do on the more operational aspects of your business?
- What materials can employees use to educate themselves?
- Have you taught your employees how to recognize activities that could potentially create brand risks?
- Are your employees willing to share what they learn about brand risks, and have you provided them with the platform for doing so?
- Have you allowed employees to learn from what their colleagues have observed and reported?
- Have you captured these collective learnings and incorporated them into your brand resiliency programs?

Deploy Your Brand Risk Early-Warning Systems

Establish . . . [an intelligence] network . . . to serve as "eyes and ears" on the street and provide an early warning system for tracking insurgent activity. —FM 3-24

Years ago, the United States Geological Survey (USGS) experimented with using tweets, in conjunction with physical monitoring devices, to detect and assess earthquakes. Apparently, people tweet in the midst of an earthquake, and the geotags built into Twitter allowed the USGS to pinpoint the location of earthquakes with greater precision than relying purely on physical monitoring devices. It is an example of how organizations can use a diverse set of tools to capture and evaluate the signals that are increasingly being generated in the digital world. Similarly, by listening to digital conversations, observing digital behaviors, and stitching together disparate pieces of information, organizations can anticipate and predict potential brand-damaging incidents before they happen and put mitigation plans in place.

Back in 2011, companies were in the early stages of experimenting with social listening tools, and innovative brands like Gatorade garnered frequent press mentions for their creative approaches to monitoring the brand in real time across social media. Today, social listening tools with out-of-the-box capabilities are available from most enterprise marketing cloud-solution providers. Other tools are available to cull through millions of news sources, blogs, and websites to understand what people are saying about specific products or topics beyond comments on social media.

So, it is easier than ever to find the tools to build your early-warning systems and alert you to potential brand risks. The trick is to ensure that there are clear roles and responsibilities when it comes to taking the intelligence that you have gathered and turning that intelligence into actions.

Self-Assessment: Deploy Your Brand Risk Early-Warning Systems

- Have you acquired the sensing tools and technologies to help detect brand risks in the early stages?
- Do you have a process to go from detection to action?
- Are responsibilities for acting clearly spelled out, and do the responsible parties understand their roles?

Repel the Attacks on Your Brand

There may be times when an overwhelming effort is necessary to destroy or intimidate an opponent and reassure the populace . . . however, counterinsurgents should calculate carefully the type and amount of force to be applied and who wields it for any operation. —FM 3-24

Despite your best efforts, attacks on your brand will occur, and you need to be ready to repel them.

In 1982, seven people on Chicago's West Side died mysteriously. Within days, two off-duty firefighters connected the deaths to the use of Tylenol. They informed their superiors, and the news of the connection between Tylenol and the deaths quickly became common knowledge. What, in fact, had happened is that a person or persons unknown had replaced Tylenol Extra-Strength capsules with cyanide-laced capsules, resealed the packages, and deposited them on the shelves of pharmacies and food stores.

Tylenol's manufacturer, McNeil Consumer Products Company, and its parent company, Johnson & Johnson, formed a strategy team charged with protecting consumers first, and saving the product second. They started out by asking consumers not to consume any type of Tylenol. They halted Tylenol advertising and production and withdrew all Tylenol capsules from Chicago-area stores. Subsequently, they ordered a nationwide withdrawal of all capsules, resulting in the destruction of more than 31 million capsules at a cost of more than $100 million.

In conjunction with these actions, J&J set up toll-free numbers for consumers and the media, organized press conferences, and sent its chair to appear on major news and talk shows. It also introduced tamper-evident packaging for Tylenol. J&J's proactive communication helped it bounce back to pre-crisis sales levels within months of the incident.

The elements of J&J's response included repentance, or asking for forgiveness; remediation, or giving compensation to the victims of a crisis; and rectification, or taking actions to prevent the recurrence of a crisis in the future. While these elements still make a great deal of sense, the world has changed tremendously since 1982. Brands have moments, not days, to react, and the opportunities for brands to control the narrative have gotten more difficult as social media has exploded. As a result, brands need to develop and rehearse responses to brand-damaging incidents long before the actual incidents occur.

Think of this as the equivalent of "active shooter drills." If Step 1 is assessing brand risks and triggers, Step 2 is creating situational awareness among your employees, and Step 3 is developing your early-warning systems, then Step 4 is responding to an actual attack on your brand. But to do this in the time required, you also need to develop potential responses appropriate to the situation, establish the protocols for activating your response, and rehearse your response so that everyone understands their individual roles and how the various roles need to collaborate with one another.

Overreacting with overwhelming force can be as dangerous as failing to act at all. Responses need to be calibrated to the threat itself, as well as to how other stakeholders will respond to the threat itself and the nature of your response. Directly attacking a customer who speaks up on social media may wind up backfiring.

Self-Assessment: Repel the Attacks on Your Brand

- Have you developed your potential responses to the brand risks that you identified in Step 1?
- Have you established the protocols for determining when you will activate your responses?
- Have you rehearsed your responses so that all of the respondents understand their roles and how their roles complement one another?

Learn and Adapt Your Brand Defenses

[In counterinsurgency] the side that learns faster and adapts more rapidly . . . usually wins. Counterinsurgencies have been called learning competitions. —FM 3-24

Designing your responses to brand risks is an iterative process. Each time we respond to a brand risk, we discover what works as expected and what does not. Our job is to embed these discoveries into our next response with the goal of perfecting our responses to known threats, recognizing that new types of brand risks will continue to emerge. We can also learn by observing how other brands have been attacked and how their organizations have responded.

Sometimes this requires connecting the dots in unconventional ways. After the World Trade Centers were destroyed on September 11, 2001, observers noted the unusual means that the attackers employed (i.e., passenger airplanes). But as the report from the 9/11 Commission states, while the use of passenger vehicles to attack landmark buildings was novel, the concept of weaponizing vehicles to attack sites was not and had previously been observed in attacks on Marine barracks in Lebanon and the USS *Cole*, anchored in Yemen territorial waters.

As Rahm Emanuel, the former mayor of Chicago and chief of staff to President Obama, commented, "You never want a serious crisis to go to waste. And what I mean by that [is] it's an opportunity to do things you think you could not do before."

Learning and adapting require taking a hard-nosed look at what really happened. Examples of scrutinizing incidents after the fact to determine what to do differently abound in the military and other governmental agencies. The National Transportation Safety Board (NTSB) has, since 1967, investigated every civil aviation accident in the United States. NTSB's goal is to determine the probable cause of the accident and to extract lessons learned that will prevent similar accidents in the future. As a result of its work, the number of fatal accidents as a percentage of flight hours and miles flown has declined precipitously, despite significant increases in both flight hours and miles. The National Highway Traffic Safety Administration performs a similar function for highway accidents and has had similar results.

Imagine a similar process at work in your organization relative to its handling of brand risks:

- Log the incident.
- Describe what happened.
- Assign an investigative team.
- Focus on determining cause and developing preventive measures rather than assigning blame.

- Formulate the recommendations.
- Assign implementation responsibilities.
- Track implementation progress.
- Review impact of remediation programs.

Self-Assessment: Learn and Adapt Your Brand Defenses

- Do you have a process in place to review how your organization has performed in its response to brand-damaging incidents?
- Is the process focused on determining cause and developing preventive measures?
- Are the results of this review process shared broadly across your organization?
- Do you track the impact of the remediation programs that you have put in place?

Measure and Track Brand Resilience

Data and metrics can inform a commander's response . . . however . . . subjective and intuitive assessment must not be replaced by an exclusive focus on data or metrics. Commanders must exercise their professional judgment in determining the proper balance. —FM 3-24

The right measurement and tracking capabilities are crucial to understanding whether your efforts to manage brand risks are effective. In working with organizations, I have observed the following three levels of maturity relative to measuring and tracking brand resilience.

- Level 1 (emerging) focuses on the importance of brand as a tool for winning and retaining customers. Investments in brand building and brand favorability are also tracked. Organizations frequently use a version of Net Promoter Score (NPS). In lieu of or in addition to NPS, organizations may do periodic surveys to assess aided and unaided awareness, consideration, favorability, use, loyalty, and advocacy.
- Level 2 (developing) builds on Level 1 metrics and tracking, including investments and voice of customer (VOC) scores. Brand risks are identified and tracked, along with impact measurement.
- Level 3 (leading) includes Level 1 and Level 2 metrics and tracking, along with a more explicit focus on brand value, both at the aggregate level and at the value-driver level (i.e., tracking the factors that appear to be highly

correlated with brand value). Employee perceptions of brand and brand performance as well as external perceptions are measured and tracked. Brand risk tracking and remediation programs are built into an overall enterprise risk-management process, and brand value and brand risks are regularly part of the board agenda.

One way to get a sense of how an organization thinks about its brand is to look at what it says in its external communications, such as its annual report or SEC-mandated 10K report. Salesforce, for example, says with no equivocation that "our continued success depends on our ability to maintain and enhance our brands"[21] and mentions the Salesforce brand extensively throughout its annual report.

Self-Assessment: Measure and Track Brand Resilience

- What metrics do you use to track your brand?
- Do you measure brand value and measure the factors that drive brand value?
- Do you measure employee and ecosystem partner perceptions of your brand, as well as customer perceptions?
- Do you track the impact of brand risks as part of an overall enterprise risk-management program?

Generate Popular Support for Your Brand Resilience Campaign

Insurgents and counterinsurgents seek to mobilize popular support for their cause. Both try to sustain that struggle while discouraging support for their adversaries. —FM 3-24

Our final step is enlisting various stakeholders to help us build brand resilience. We already talked about employee engagement in Step 2. The other stakeholders include your customers, influencers, analysts, alumni, and ecosystem partners (on both the demand and supply side).

If you need an example of how a counterinsurgency effort failed due to its inability to generate popular support, watch the 1966 Italian film *The Battle of Algiers*. The film is a fictional narrative based on France's efforts to neutralize Algerian insurgents in the late 1950s through assassinations, summary executions, torture, intimidation, and other violent tactics. While their efforts are initially successful, the French never gain the support of the masses; rather, the masses begin to actively support the insurgents. The movie ends with a series of demonstrations and riots that set the stage for Algerian independence.

By contrast, a great example of an organization that engaged a critical stakeholder group is the United States Forest Service (USFS). In 1944, the USFS launched a still-running inspired campaign featuring Smokey the Bear and the slogan "Only You Can Prevent Wildfires." The campaign astutely engaged ordinary citizens in reducing the threat of wildfires and included advertising, educational materials, merchandise, out-of-home ads, newsletters, and eventually a vibrant digital presence.

Procter & Gamble's Pampers offers another example of outstanding stakeholder engagement. In 2010, Pampers changed its manufacturing process to produce 20% thinner diapers with no loss of absorbency. Unfortunately, customer reactions were not universally positive. Some parents believed that the newly reengineered diapers were causing their babies to break out with diaper rash. They complained. P&G responded with a combination of direct customer outreach and postings to various websites and social media sites. But customers were not completely satisfied and launched a Facebook campaign, lodged complaints with the U.S. Consumer Product Safety Commission and Health Canada, and filed lawsuits. While Pampers was ultimately vindicated by regulators, a critical element in its response was reaching out to and educating trusted "mommy bloggers" who were able to carry the message to their millions of followers.

A key part of building popular support for your brand resilience efforts, consequently, should be to identify the individuals and organizations that influence public opinion and actively work with them on an ongoing basis, not just when a crisis hits. In conjunction with identifying these individuals and organizations, you need to proactively educate them, inform them, and equip them to amplify your messages and advocate on your behalf.

Self-Assessment: Generate Popular Support for Your Brand Resilience Campaign

- Are you aware of the stakeholders who are most important to influencing public opinion about your brand?
- Have you established lines of communication with these influential stakeholders?
- Are you communicating regularly with these influential stakeholders and enabling them to communicate with you?
- Have you established protocols and practices for leveraging these influential stakeholders in the event of a brand-damaging event?

Conclusion

We began this chapter by describing how the role of brands has shifted from communicating quality to signaling trust. This new role has become more important as customer expectations have risen and digital technologies have increased the likelihood of brand-damaging events and the speed at which these brand-damaging events occur.

Organizations need to prepare and plan for brand risk and recovery in a high-speed world. We recommend a seven-step program that starts with an objective assessment of brand risks and includes engaging employees, creating early-warning systems, preparing and rehearsing responses to brand risks, learning and adapting brand defenses, measuring and tracking brand resilience, and building popular support for your brand resilience campaigns.

There is no reason to believe that the risks to brands will decrease in this time of false information, alternative facts, and willful disregard for the truth. While rapid response capabilities are essential to brand resilience, they need to be complemented by careful preparation and planning and by harvesting learnings from each and every brand-damaging event.

Author Biography

Jonathan Copulsky is senior lecturer of marketing and academic director, Business Marketing Strategy at the Kellogg School of Management at Northwestern University. He is the author of *Brand Resilience* (Palgrave Macmillan, 2011) and the co-author of *The Technology Fallacy* (MIT Press, 2019) and *The Transformation Myth* (MIT Press, 2021). Prior to joining the Northwestern faculty, he was a senior partner, chief marketing officer, and global insights leader at Deloitte and chief marketing and sales officer at CCH Incorporated, a NYSE-listed professional publisher.

PART 5

Crafting a Successful Communication Campaign

CHAPTER 14

Managing Advertising: From Strategic Planning to Creative Review

Derek D. Rucker

Advertising is a powerful means to establish, maintain, and grow one's brand. Great advertising can, among other functions, bring value to a brand by helping to attract new users, stealing users from competitors, and increasing the premium a brand can charge. Indeed, throughout this chapter, I will share real-world examples in which great advertising meaningfully contributed to brand success. However, not all advertising is great, and some brand managers have lamented the failure of a costly campaign. Brands have even spent money on advertising that ultimately upset consumers or even dampened sales.

Why does some advertising succeed where other advertising fails? Successful advertising, in its most realized form, can be likened to a fine Swiss watch: An intricate series of mechanisms working in unison result in an accurate and precise forward movement. In the same way, successful brands carefully coordinate their advertising and communication efforts to move the needle of their businesses forward. Just as a loosened screw, an incorrect winding mechanism, or a bit of dirt or water damage can stop the movement of a watch, an advertising campaign can derail if problems are not detected and resolved before it is launched. Advertising that cannot aid business objectives is no better than a timepiece that cannot keep time. How can brand managers shift the curve of their advertising efforts so they operate like a Swiss watch as opposed to a broken and useless timepiece?

The objective of this chapter is to help practitioners take a strategic approach to planning and evaluating advertising. In this regard, this chapter is relevant to brand managers, consultants, entrepreneurs, and anyone who might be involved in developing a strategy for an advertising campaign. To accomplish its objective, this chapter focuses on three bedrock layers of advertising strategy. First, it offers a brief primer on critical stages in advertising. Second, it focuses on the strategic planning of advertising via the creative brief. Third, it provides guidance on how to both evaluate and give feedback on creative work. The ultimate aim is to provide the reader with an understanding of how to maintain and care for their advertising so that it provides a reliable means of serving business objectives.

Critical Stages of Advertising

Advertising is a complex process, and entire books have been devoted to its intricacies.[1,2] However, one useful means to understand advertising is through three distinct stages that illuminate the process of advertising campaigns: (1) strategic planning, (2) tactical execution, and (3) analytical measurement (see Figure 14.1). More intermediate steps can be added, but this categorization reveals the critical stages that require decisions, evaluation, and opportunities for discussion and learning. Before delving into these stages, it is useful to note that the term *advertising* is used here to refer generally to any form

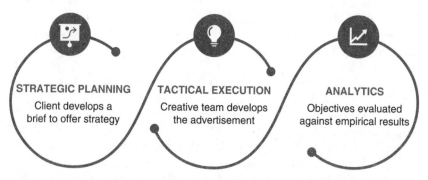

STRATEGIC PLANNING	TACTICAL EXECUTION	ANALYTICS
Client develops a brief to offer strategy	Creative team develops the advertisement	Objectives evaluated against empirical results

FIGURE 14.1 Three Distinct Stages of Advertising Campaigns

of brand communication or messaging toward a target. This definition differs from classic definitions, which sometimes define advertising as any form of paid media. I view advertising more broadly because any communication, whether it is in a paid channel (e.g., a YouTube ad) or an unpaid channel (e.g., a brand's website), can benefit from the principles of strategy shared in this chapter.

The first stage of advertising consists of strategic planning. This stage involves decisions related to defining one's objectives, segmentation, and targeting; obtaining insight; developing a position; selecting media channels; and setting measurement approaches. As will be elaborated, a powerful means to synthesize the planning function is through the development of a creative brief. The strategic planning process itself can encompass multiple parties such as—but not limited to—brand teams, innovation teams, market research teams, and agency partners. However, core to the first stage is that the emphasis is not on the development of the actual advertising to be presented but on an underlying strategy to guide the tactical development. For example, in attempting to attract a young target to its deodorants, Old Spice obtained insights on how younger consumers thought about the brand and the consumers' needs. The company realized that young consumers had a need for confidence, to which the brand advertisements could be responsive. It had a strategy in place before any creative work began.[3]

The second stage of advertising is the tactical execution—that is, the development of the advertising. This stage involves taking the high-level strategy and putting it into a tangible form. One aspect of this stage is the creative work: the development of the advertisement. This process often involves a creative partner that will bring the strategy to life. This creative partner could be a third-party agency or internal creative team. For example, Old Spice wanted to communicate to consumers the idea that its scent would help them feel confident. How should this strategy be transformed into an advertisement? The agency, Wieden+Kennedy, brought the strategy to life by using spokespeople who walked and talked with confidence and gave credit to Old Spice as central to their transformation. Another aspect of the tactical execution is detailing the media plan, which entails discussing the media channels through which advertisements will be delivered, how often advertisements will be presented, and how long the campaign will run in the market. The media plan often involves a media planner, which could again be a third party or an internal team.

The final stage of advertising is analytical measurement or measurement for parsimony. Measurement involves efforts to understand whether an advertising campaign has produced the desired effect. For example, in the case of Old Spice, the brand saw sales of their scent move from being the poorest-performing scent in its product line to the number-one-performing scent. Of note, while measurement comes after the development of the tactical execution, it is possible to engage in measurement prior to the launch of a campaign in the market. For example, a brand might want to see whether early-stage creative efforts get across the intended message to consumers. Indeed, brand teams might see the creative work as a storyboard pitch or an animatic and be asked to offer feedback. Proper measurement is a complex process that involves questions related to understanding what to measure, when to measure, and how to measure.

With an understanding of the stages of advertising in mind, the remainder of this chapter focuses on two critical issues. First, I discuss, via the lens of the creative brief, the critical blocking and tackling required to establish a sound strategic plan. Second, I discuss how to offer feedback on the tactical execution to get the most out of partnerships with the creative team. I intentionally choose to emphasize these skills as they represent core skills that any brand team should employ. I fully recognize that developing creative work and sound measurement are equally important, and I have discussed these aspects elsewhere.[4]

The Creative Brief: A Strategic Blueprint for Success

Perhaps the single best tool for strategic planning is the creative brief. The creative brief is a document meant to inform the creative team of the strategy behind an advertising campaign. However, in actuality, the creative brief is more than a document for the creative team: It provides a framework for the brand team to think through their strategy. Creative brief writing confronts a brand team with critical questions and forces them to articulate their strategy and/or realize the lack of strategy. The creative brief structure I use when teaching at Kellogg consists of six domains that help to prompt and organize critical thinking (see Figure 14.2). The focus here is to offer the reader a primer that provides an understanding of each part of the brief; a discussion of strong creative brief writing (on which I have written extensively elsewhere),[5,6] and initial tips to avoid common mistakes.

Objective

The creative brief starts with an objective. Put simply, what is it that the advertising seeks to accomplish? The question may seem simple, but I have seen many poor objectives over the years. So let's discuss how to develop a strong objective.

First, a strong objective should take the form of a communication objective as opposed to a business objective. Business objectives often focus on sales,

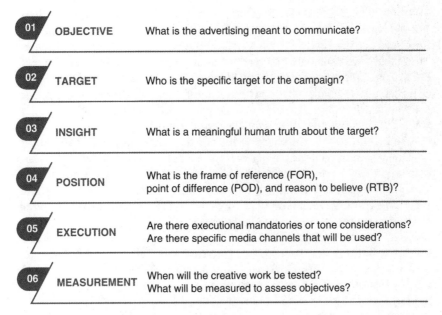

01	OBJECTIVE	What is the advertising meant to communicate?
02	TARGET	Who is the specific target for the campaign?
03	INSIGHT	What is a meaningful human truth about the target?
04	POSITION	What is the frame of reference (FOR), point of difference (POD), and reason to believe (RTB)?
05	EXECUTION	Are there executional mandatories or tone considerations? Are there specific media channels that will be used?
06	MEASUREMENT	When will the creative work be tested? What will be measured to assess objectives?

FIGURE 14.2   Structure of the Creative Brief

market share, and/or number of users. Business objectives can be important because they can justify the resources spent on advertising. The problem is that business objectives alone are often bad at informing strategy. Although a business objective to "increase sales" is a desired outcome, it provides little guidance for the advertising strategy. Thus, a creative brief should emphasize the communication objective, which explains the role of advertising in a clear fashion. For example, take a brand that has the business objective of increasing sales by 5% in the next fiscal year. Advertising could facilitate this objective in a number of ways. A brand could raise awareness of its presence in the marketplace. A brand could use a new technological feature to persuade consumers that the brand's product is the best option in the market. A brand could advertise to create a more emotional connection to consumers. Put simply, a brand can increase sales through a number of different means. Clear communication objectives explain the role of advertising to help accomplish the business objective. In some cases, brands want to have their business objective on the brief to remind themselves that advertising has monetary benefits. Business objectives can appear on a brief, but the key is that they should be accompanied by a clear communication objective.

Second, a strong objective should be falsifiable. That is, we want to have a clear benchmark to gauge whether a campaign was successful or unsuccessful. How do we make objectives falsifiable? The answer lies in putting parameters around our communication objective. We can be specific with regard to both the type of change we want to see and the accompanying time frame. For example, imagine we are launching a new product and want to increase awareness of the product for a specific target. Rather than write "Increase awareness," we can write "Increase awareness of our product offering from 0% to 20% within three months of launch." Notice that the latter statement is much clearer about what constitutes failure and success than the former statement. Clear objectives can still be parsimonious; the second objective, while offering more detail, was still a single sentence.

To illustrate the value of specifying falsifiable communication objectives, consider three hypothetical objectives for a candy bar company: (1) "Make a print ad," (2) "Increase sales," and (3) "Make a splash!" What do you think of these objectives? Based on the previous paragraphs, you are probably thinking, "Those are horrible objectives," which is good—because they are! First, none of them are communication objectives. The first is not even a business objective; it simply describes the task to be done. The second is a business objective, but it is very vague. Does "increase sales" mean having one more consumer purchase a product? The third is more of a desired outcome, but it gives no direction as to how to get there. Moreover, what does "make a splash" mean? It is so abstract that it is not falsifiable.

Can we make a better objective for our candy bar campaign? Absolutely. For example, a much better objective would be: "Raise agreement that our candy bar satisfies hunger from 15% to 40% in six months." Now we have a communication objective. And the creative team has more direction as to what message has to be delivered for the work to be considered a success. Moreover, if we wanted to reference our business objective, we could easily have it read: "Raise agreement that our candy bar satisfies hunger from 15% to 40% to facilitate a 10% sales increase in six months."

Target

The second element of the creative brief is the target. Targeting has been a staple principle in marketing. The core premise is that few, if any, products are designed for a homogenous consumer. Consumers exhibit rich variation in their preferences. As an example, consider the ice cream category. First, not all consumers like ice cream, although I know that might be hard to believe! What is more important is that even if people like ice cream, they vary as to whether they prefer dairy, soy, almond, or a wide assortment of bases. And people vary in their preferences for vanilla, chocolate, strawberry, and coffee. Indeed, a dairy-based ice cream that does not offer a cherry flavor would make it questionable to focus advertising dollars on people who are looking for a soy-based ice cream that is cherry flavored.

Determining a target is often the output of a segmentation and targeting analysis. Segmentation refers to the process of understanding the different groups of targets that exist. Segmentation can be thought of as carving up the world to understand the different groups that might potentially consume (and not consume) one's offerings. For example, in the ice cream category, it could be important to understand that some groups prefer their ice cream simple in form (e.g., plain coffee ice cream), whereas others prefer their ice cream loaded with ingredients (e.g., coffee ice cream with Heath Bar, fudge, and almonds). Once a brand understands the segments, it must choose a target to go after. This portion of the brief provides a high-level description of the target, which might include both sociodemographic (e.g., age, income, education) and psychographic (e.g., interests, activities, and motivations) data.

Of note, brands commit a number of common mistakes when it comes to targeting. First, some brands fail to either segment or to choose a specific target. They essentially choose the "everyperson" target—that is, they want to target everyone and eschew the notion of differences between consumers and customers. The problem with this approach, as our ice cream example illustrates, is that segments exist; most, if not all categories, have heterogeneity among consumers. Similarly, within the beer category, it would seem questionable to target those who do not like alcohol, deplorable to target expectant mothers, and morally reprehensible to target children. Rather, the aim is to find a target of sufficient size that is profitable and meaningful to our brand.

A second error in targeting is considering only the "popular" target. That is, in some categories, targets exist that are particularly attractive because of their size or amount of consumption. The problem is that multiple brands often go after the popular target, which means fierce competition exists. Often the category leaders have succeeded in obtaining this target, and they defend it aggressively. Smaller brands might find greater success in targeting a less served target. Indeed, Yellow Tail wine is an example of a brand that grew by focusing its advertising efforts toward a more underserved target. In particular, rather than target those familiar with wine, who accounted for higher wine profits, Yellow Tail targeted novice wine drinkers, who represented a new and less tapped segment. The brand even went as far as to use its website to educate consumers about what wines they might like based on taste preferences. The observation here is not that the popular target cannot be pursued, but that merit exists in giving thought to other targets before committing to the popular target.

Insight

The insight portion of a brief, for many, is arguably the most difficult. Insights reflect, and require, knowledge of the consumer or customer. The way I think about consumer insight is that it reflects a *meaningful human truth*. Let me deconstruct this definition. First, an insight is *meaningful* in that it has value that informs a brand how it should advertise. Insights are springboards for taking action. The most powerful insights create value because they unlock new and different ways to advertise. Second, insights are *human*; that is, they are situated around the consumers' needs. An insight is not about what a brand can do; what a brand can do is related to a brand's position, which I will address momentarily. Third, insights are *truthful*. Insights often start as hypotheses—that is, a belief about how people think or what they care about. Such an approach is fine, but hypotheses should be vetted and tested. In some cases, we can be wrong about our hypotheses, and it is a dangerous thing to operate on beliefs that are false!

To illustrate an example of an insight, the Snickers candy bar brand leveraged the insight that people do not act like themselves when they are hungry. Remember, an insight is a meaningful human truth. Snickers' observation was meaningful on two fronts. First, because no other brand in the candy bar category was talking about this issue, it had immense value to the brand as a unique consumer talking point. Second, it was meaningful in that the need state had considerable weight in the mind of the consumer. It was not just a unique talking point for the brand; it was important to the consumer as well. Snickers' observation was also focused on the consumer, which met the criterion of being human focused. Finally, Snickers' observation was truthful; that is, talking with people verified that many indeed had the experience of not being themselves when hungry. All of this led to Snickers' "You're Not You When You're Hungry" campaign, which received awards for its creativity and its effectiveness and was associated with a sizeable increase in brand sales.

In terms of pitfalls regarding insight, they are too numerous to discuss in detail here. However, I will share two. One common mistake is that people sometimes put facts in the insight section. Facts are pieces of information and can be helpful, but they are not the same as insights. For illustrative purposes, consider the fact that people consume less yogurt in the United States than in Europe. This information tells us something about consumer habits, and it might be truthful, but it is not inherently meaningful. That is, it does not tell us how to communicate with the consumer. An insight goes beyond facts and offers something that reveals a novel consumer value or belief that can guide the communication strategy.

A second common mistake is that brands sometimes use insight to emphasize the value they bring to the consumer. For example, an entrepreneur once told me that one of his mistakes was increasing the number of colors offered for an electronic product he sold. From his perspective, he thought it was great that the brand could offer consumers a variety of colors. However, consumers did not respond to the increased color assortment, and his innovation did not meaningfully grow sales. See the problem? His emphasis was on something new the brand could offer, but he did not research whether this was an important benefit for consumers. And, as it turns out, consumers did not care about having more colors.

Position

The position of a brand, also referred to as positioning, involves how we intend to represent the brand to the consumer. Positioning helps inform the message that will be communicated to the consumer. For years, Kellogg has taught positioning through the idea of a positioning statement. A common template for a positioning statement contains four pieces of information: (1) target, (2) frame of reference (FOR), (3) point of difference (POD), and (4) reason to believe (RTB). When a positioning statement appears on a creative brief, the target might be removed, since the target is already acknowledged. However, in general discussions around positioning, the inclusion of the target is a reminder that the communication is tailored to a particular group. The idea of the target has already been discussed, but the other three elements merit elaboration.

Frame of reference refers to category membership or how people think about using the product. As such, it also informs what other products compete against the brand. For example, before a brand explains why consumers should dine at its new restaurant, it is important that consumers recognize it is a restaurant. Moreover, the restaurant needs to associate itself with the subcategory of restaurants it belongs to. Large differences exist between fast, casual restaurants and gourmet restaurants. A brand must establish itself as belonging to the specific category to which it seeks to belong. The frame of reference part of a positioning statement makes sure that category membership is part of the conversation and also helps direct the creative effort in terms of making sure the tactical execution conveys, or at least does not confuse, category membership.

Point of difference refers to how a brand differentiates itself from others within a category. For example, among coffee shops, Starbucks has been known to highlight its Frappuccino, a delightful and decadent frozen drink. Selecting a point of difference should be tethered to the insight. If we understand what the target values, then we want to present a benefit that is responsive to their needs or problems. Indeed, one way to think of the link between insight and positioning is via problem–solution thinking. Strong positioning is understanding a problem for which the brand is the solution. As reviewed earlier, Snickers understood the problem of not being yourself when you are hungry, and the brand was the solution. A corollary of this point is that if a brand cannot solve an identified problem, then this is not the right insight, and possibly target, for the brand. Brands do not want to advertise benefits that they cannot deliver. The purpose of advertising is not to trick consumers into buying things that will not solve their problems; the purpose of advertising is to communicate benefits that our product can offer to solve a problem.

Finally, the *reason to believe* can be thought of as the evidence or the proof point for the point of difference. Essentially, a reason to believe helps consumers understand why they can believe the product provides the represented benefit. For example, Nike has long touted the quality and performance of its products, using a variety of spokespeople from Michael Jordan to Serena Williams. Although the spokespeople might serve a variety of purposes, in the case of Nike they serve as evidence of the quality of the products. If the products are good enough to be used by the world's best athletes, it supports the idea they are of superior quality and performance. As an alternative example, Jif peanut butter positioned itself as having better taste and supported this claim via an attribute of the product: It had more fresh-roasted peanuts in every jar than competitors.

Perhaps the most common error evident in positioning statements is that they are incomplete. For example, marketers might focus on the benefit without giving proper consideration to the frame of reference or the reason to believe. However, both the frame of reference and reason to believe provide information of value to the creative team, and thus I recommend their inclusion. Another common error observed is that people try to put too many benefits into one positioning statement. While a product might have multiple benefits, a danger exists in attempting to communicate too many benefits at once, which might be overwhelming to consumers and lead to poor retention of any of the benefits. In many cases, emphasizing one benefit is often of more value to the consumer—and to the brand.

Execution

Execution refers to the more tactical elements of the creative work. Although the creative brief is a strategic document to facilitate creative work, some tactical elements can be included—in particular, tactical elements regarding tonality, mandatories, and channels.

Tonality refers to the tenor of a message. For example, some brands might be more serious and solemn in how they represent themselves, whereas others might be more lighthearted. Tonality gives the creative team direction to what the brand is comfortable with regarding how the message is expressed. As an example, Dove has often focused on a more heartfelt delivery that stirs emotions in consumers. In contrast, Red Bull is known for pithy and playful humor in its ads. Note that tonality does not tell the creative team how to create the ad; rather, it gives some initial guidance on what the brand is comfortable with.

Mandatories are requirements of what must be featured and/or excluded in the ads. For example, Nestlé Tollhouse might require that an advertisement end with a visual of its logo. Nike might require its iconic swoosh to be shown somewhere in the advertisement. Related to mandatories are what are sometimes termed brand assets. Brand assets need not be included, but they give the creative team a sense of elements they might leverage. For example, the retailer Target might mention that it is associated with the color red. Of note, even when including mandatories, deference should be given to allow the creative team to determine how to best integrate them. For example, even if a mandatory is to show the brand logo, this does not mean that creative needs to be micromanaged with further details (i.e., what second of the ad to show the logo, how long it should be presented, etc.).

Channels refer to the media in which the advertising will air. Understanding channels is valuable because it can help the creative team understand the canvas it is working with. Asking for a Super Bowl execution versus a print execution in a trade publication are two different tasks that vary vastly in scope. Some brands prefer to discuss media channels after the initial creative work is developed. The idea is that the brand wants to give the creative team the flexibility to develop an idea and then to assess which channels might be useful. In such cases, it might be helpful to at least have a discussion of the ad budget. Having a creative team come back with an omnichannel campaign when the brand only has the budget for a campaign on Facebook could lead to the wrong type of work being generated.

The execution portion of the creative brief, as with all portions, should be concise. To be clear, the idea is not to unpack your entire media plan but to provide an overview. And if you need more than one line for your mandatories, well, you are probably asking for too much! Indeed, a key mistake in brief writing is to use the execution section to essentially design the creative output yourself. We have creative partners because tactical execution is a skill set unto itself; most brand managers cannot do the creative themselves. The execution section offers high-level guidance and should avoid massive micromanagement.

Measurement

The final section of the creative brief is measurement. Core questions around measurement involve what we will measure and when. One aspect of measurement is whether the brand will do any testing of ad concepts prior to launching a campaign in the market. For example, we might test early concepts with focus groups or expose a panel of consumers to the actual advertisement prior to launch. Having these measurement plans in our creative brief helps with setting a realistic timeline.

Another aspect of measurement concerns how we will test whether our advertising had the desired effect. For example, if our goal was to "Raise agreement that our candy bar satisfies hunger from 15% to 40% in six months," how will we know how far we have moved toward this goal? Will we conduct pre- and post-campaign surveys? Will we conduct interviews in markets where the campaign ran compared to markets where the campaign did not? Will we look at search behavior related to our brand? Will we analyze consumer sentiment to understand consumer satisfaction? Measurement is, of course, its own topic, but having a portion of the creative brief dedicated to it helps us understand and prioritize measurement in advance.

Perhaps the biggest problem in measurement is solved by having it appear in the brief. Namely, when measurement is not set in advance, people often find themselves unable to measure what they need to. For example, if we did not measure initial awareness and advertised in all our markets, then it's not possible to do either a pre- or post-campaign survey or a matched market test. Imagine that we sell commercial trucks to businesses. We might gauge awareness of the advertising campaign by asking the sales team to ask customers whether they have seen the recent ad campaign. However, if we do not set up this approach in advance, then we may have missed the opportunity for measurement because the sales team has already sold the vehicle and does not have the data from the customer. By setting up measurement opportunities in advance, we can avoid these problems.

To close on the creative brief, it allows us to communicate our strategy to a creative team so the team can develop the creative work. Put simply, it is a strategic document that provides a concise summary. The best creative briefs are, well, brief. I train people to write single-page creative briefs. This approach does not mean that a brand team cannot have a deeper and more elaborated strategy elsewhere. If you want to have a deck that shows the rigor and detail of the segmentation and target analysis, this is absolutely fine; in fact, it might be a great idea. However, when it comes to the creative brief, it should be a precise and concise summary of the strategy.

Creative Review: Structuring and Providing Feedback

Once a creative brief has been delivered, the creative team will generate a tactical output or execution. This tactical execution might take the form of a storyboard pitch, an animatic, or even a completed advertisement. At this point, it often falls on the brand team to provide feedback on the creative work. For more than a decade, Kellogg has focused on empowering client-side brand managers to give structured and meaningful feedback. A first means to structure feedback is via the creative brief. As we just discussed, the creative brief is a culmination of the brand strategy. We can use the creative brief as a roadmap to structure our feedback. For example, does the creative work represent the insight about the identified target? Are the executional mandatories present? In fact, another reason to invest in writing the creative brief, besides helping us have a sound strategy, is that it offers talking points with the creative team. Indeed, when giving feedback, we refer to creative work that follows the creative brief as "on brief" and creative content that departs from the brief as "off brief."

In addition to the creative brief, we use two other tools to offer structure and organize feedback. The first tool is captured in the acronym ADPLAN, which asks a series of questions that help further evaluate the strength and weaknesses of the execution. The second tool is something we refer to as "four zone feedback," which is a means to deliver feedback in a way that both prioritizes information and facilitates interactions between an agency and a client.

The ADPLAN Framework

The ADPLAN framework was first introduced by Brian Sternthal and me.[7] The framework is designed to capture common elements of advertising that help ads succeed or cause them to fail. The framework depicted in Figure 14.3 essentially focuses on six critical elements to appraise and consider when evaluating creative work. Moreover, the framework is rooted in academic research in fields such as psychology and marketing. As this framework is discussed in detail elsewhere, my focus here is to provide a brief overview.[8,9]

The first dimension of ADPLAN is *attention*. The idea of attention is two-fold. Advertisements benefit from both capturing a target's attention as well as maintaining that attention. A consumer who presses the skip button on

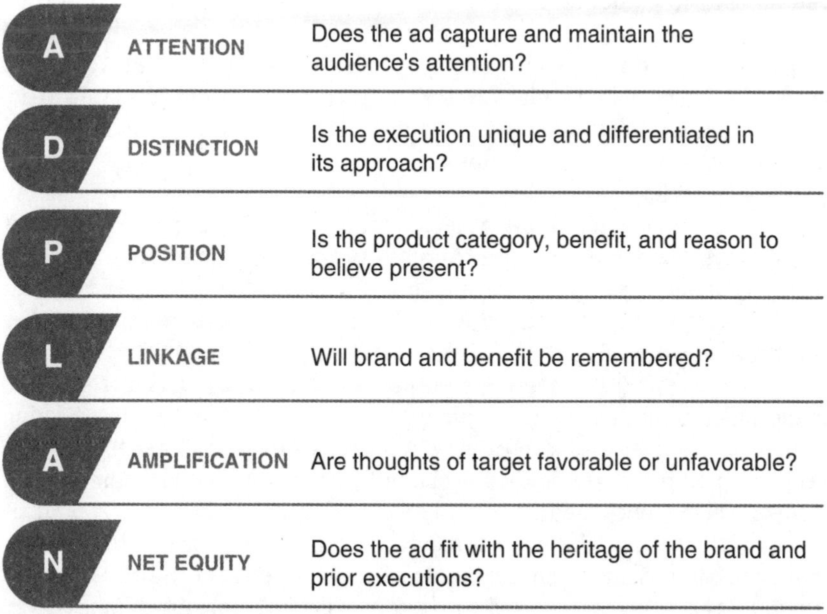

A	ATTENTION	Does the ad capture and maintain the audience's attention?
D	DISTINCTION	Is the execution unique and differentiated in its approach?
P	POSITION	Is the product category, benefit, and reason to believe present?
L	LINKAGE	Will brand and benefit be remembered?
A	AMPLIFICATION	Are thoughts of target favorable or unfavorable?
N	NET EQUITY	Does the ad fit with the heritage of the brand and prior executions?

FIGURE 14.3   The ADPLAN Framework

a YouTube ad, changes the channel when a television ad appears, or mutes the volume when a radio ad comes on is unlikely to be persuaded by the content that follows. If an ad succeeds in capturing attention but the consumer disengages before the key benefit is shared or the brand is revealed, the ad once again might prove ineffective. Indeed, one of the reasons brands work with advertising agencies or creative teams is that such partners are skilled in designing ads that break through and capture attention.

Distinction refers to whether an ad is differentiated from other advertisements. For example, Apple created an entire campaign around dancing silhouettes to promote the emotional feeling of using an iPod. This campaign was like nothing else in the market, which allowed it to stand out. Strong distinction can help with attention because a departure from the routine might foster interest in the consumer. In addition, when a brand establishes itself through a strong creative approach, people quickly come to recognize and identify the brand. For example, Old Spice hired actor Isaiah Mustafa to bring its brand to life. He essentially became "The Old Spice Guy," which meant that as soon as he appeared on consumers' television or computer screens people knew the content to follow was for Old Spice. As such, strong distinction can help with identifying and remembering the brand.

Positioning refers to how the brand is represented in the advertisement. Essentially, this is a reminder to assess whether the advertisement represents the correct frame of reference, conveys the desired point of difference, and presents the reason to believe. In addition, while the ADPLAN framework can be used to guide the creative work for one's own brand, it can also be used when assessing the creative work of the competition. Even though you will be unlikely to be given the competition's creative brief, ADPLAN can be used to deconstruct and understand what the competition is attempting to do. Indeed, an exercise I frequently give to my students is to analyze competitors' advertising to extract their positioning.

Linkage refers to whether the brand and benefit will be remembered. An advertisement could be attention grabbing and distinct, but people might fail to remember what it was for. As an illustration, one marketer ran a new online promotion campaign for a chain of convenience stores. The ad featured the promoted product, Coca-Cola, in the center, with the name of the convenience store relegated to a small square at the bottom. The advertisement was presented as a pop-up in online radio channels (e.g., Pandora). The brand failed to attract many people to the promotion. When the marketing team investigated the issue more closely, it turned out to be a linkage problem. People remembered seeing Coca-Cola, but they had no recollection of what store was being advertised.

Irrespective of whether an advertisement breaks through or communicates its position, consumers can respond positively or negatively. *Amplification* is the term used to capture what the consumer takes away from the message. Positive amplification refers to positive responses to an advertisement, whereas negative amplification refers to negative responses. To illustrate, Volkswagen ran a Super Bowl ad that featured a kid dressed up as Darth Vader trying to use his force powers to move objects. It ended with the child pointing at a Volkswagen Passat, which caused the engine to roar; the kid was astonished while the father, brandishing an automatic starter, smiled. People loved the advertisement and, based on various positive comments, the ad elicited positive amplification. In contrast, Nationwide Insurance once ran an advertisement that featured a kid talking about how he would never grow up and enjoy life because he died in an accident. Although the advertisement attempted to convey a message about protecting children, people found the execution in bad taste. Negative comments were posted online, and the brand eventually apologized—this example illustrates, regardless of the brand's intended message, the result was negative amplification.

Net equity is the final piece of the ADPLAN framework. Net equity essentially asks whether the execution is consistent with, builds upon, or undermines established associations with the brand. For example, Gatorade has long positioned itself as a healthy and wholesome brand. The brand is unlikely to intentionally use a spokesperson with a bad image, which would undermine its equity. Similarly, BMW has positioned itself as the "ultimate driving machine" and is unlikely to run advertisements that depict the brand and product offering as mundane or ordinary. Thus, the question of net equity pushes us to ask whether the execution is consistent with how the brand represents itself.

Some additional notes on the ADPLAN framework are in order. To start, the framework is not meant to be exhaustive with regard to all elements that might render an advertisement more or less successful. For example, one might evaluate creative work by asking whether it could lead to sharing among consumers; brands might prefer creative work that leads consumers to organically share the ad over creative work that does not. Rather than exhaustive, the ADPLAN tool is meant to be a parsimonious means to deliver feedback around key aspects of communication that can influence its effectiveness. Indeed, separate from ADPLAN, the creative brief is another critical framework for offering feedback. Thus, ADPLAN is best viewed as one valuable tool in providing feedback.

ADPLAN is also not a checklist whereby a piece of creative work must address all elements. Rather, it is a framework designed to generate and facilitate discussion. Creative work that has a deficit on one dimension of ADPLAN does not inherently mean that it should not go to market. Instead, it calls for discussion on how the deficit can be addressed. For example, if one raises a concern about linkage in a video execution, this concern might be assuaged by following up a video execution with a personal sales call that reinforces the brand and message featured in the execution. Or consumers who have logged on to a website and seen an advertisement might be subsequently sent an email to remind them of the brand featured in the advertisement. In this regard, the ADPLAN tool is applicable to the entire campaign, not just a single advertisement. A simple digital display might not be super attention grabbing or convey much of the brand positioning on its own, but if it reminds people of a rich and elaborate video ad, that might be all it has to do.

Finally, in some cases, disagreement exists between people as to how an advertisement performs on a dimension of the ADPLAN framework. Disagreement does not mean that both parties are correct or that the framework has failed. ADPLAN is a framework that facilitates discussion; however, each part of the framework can be measured empirically. As such, when disagreements arise on how an advertisement performs on a given dimension, these can be resolved empirically. As one example, those curious about whether an advertisement captures attention can look at what percentage of consumers skip the ad on YouTube. Or, if there is uncertainty as to whether an advertisement that makes fun of a popular celebrity will generate positive or negative amplification, one could expose consumers to the ad and ask them to evaluate it and to share their thoughts. While there are multiple means to measure each element of the ADPLAN framework, the point is that when in doubt the answer can be resolved empirically.

Four Zone Feedback

Whereas the creative brief and the ADPLAN framework provide areas on which to give feedback, how that feedback is delivered can be equally important. When we are giving feedback to a creative team, we have a few goals. First, we want to make sure that the creative work is true to the brief and represents the brand appropriately. However, there's more to giving feedback than this goal. We also want to make sure that we give feedback in a manner that builds, as opposed to burns, our relationship with the creative team. We want to give feedback that prioritizes the next steps and excites the creative team to integrate that feedback. However, all too often I have heard creatives complain that the brand does not appreciate their efforts. And I have heard clients state that after they gave feedback the creative team got rid of elements they liked and produced less exciting work.

It turns out that how we give feedback matters a lot. At Kellogg we use a tool we refer to as *four zone feedback*. This tool involves taking notes and offering comments on four elements: things I love, things I like, questions, and red flags (see Figure 14.4). These zones are essentially a means to organize comments that pertain to the creative brief and the ADPLAN framework. When I'm discussing creative work, I will often draw a horizontal line crossed with a vertical line to create four zones on my paper; I then take notes in each quadrant as I process the creative work. Let us take a look at each zone.

The first zone captures the things we love. In most creative work, we will only encounter one or two of these in a given campaign. Perhaps the execution

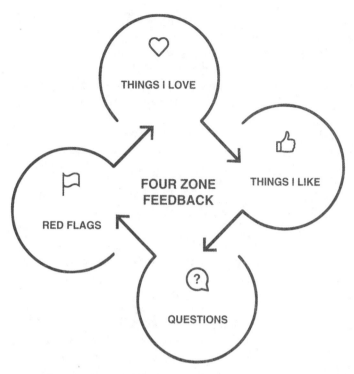

FIGURE 14.4   The Four Zone Feedback Framework

is amazing in how it grabs our attention; we should share that with the creative team! Or perhaps the team absolutely nailed the insight; again, we should share our excitement. Of course, if you do not have something you love, that is okay; this zone is not an exercise in building egos. Maybe the new Facebook campaign features solid work; it is fine to move on to the things you like—our second zone.

The "things I like" zone allows us to take time to acknowledge aspects of the work that meet expectations. We usually have more to say in this zone compared to things we love, but the enthusiasm is more modest. We are essentially helping the creative team understand that things worked without overrepresenting how powerful or important they are. Some people say sharing the things we love and things we like is just being nice. While it is true that sharing what you love and like about the work is, indeed, being nice, it has a strategic purpose regarding the quality of the creative work. If we raise questions or red flags, as we will discuss momentarily, the creative team may make changes. Telling the creative team what we like is a means to convey what is working for us and should be kept.

The next zone focuses on questions. Here we are sharing candid questions about the creative work. In some cases, these might be questions with no evaluative judgment. For example, we might ask why the creative team chose a particular phrase in the voice-over, or we might wonder why they used a particular color scheme. Essentially, we are curious, and a little curiosity is fine. In other cases, however, questions are essentially a harbinger of concerns we have. Bringing such questions to the table is an art. The key is to treat these concerns as questions as opposed to accusatory statements. Let me illustrate. Imagine we have just seen a commercial in which our brand does not appear until the very end. We might have a very valid linkage concern about whether people will make the connection to our brand. The mistake people make is to pose this concern as an accusatory statement such as, "There is late identification of the brand; consumers won't remember us!" Instead, as the zone title suggests, turn that concern into a question: "Do you think with the late identification consumers will remember us?" The simple act of turning the statement into a question changes this query from potentially adversarial to collaborative.

The last zone consists of red flags, which are essentially nonstarters for us. For example, if an ad depicts the brand in a negative light, it is our job to protect our brand. Basically, red flags go beyond questions because, rather than being a question, we see a real problem and need it to be resolved. Red flags might be creative work that engenders undesired associations—for example, an advertisement presenting content that we find offensive. Or, if a brand undermines our net equity, it may also be a nonstarter. In addition, red flags can be raised for legal reasons. For example, an ad featuring a benefit our product does not offer would raise a red flag, as we are not in the business of false advertising. Note that not all creative work engenders red flags; in fact, in my experience most does not. However, the red flag zone exists to hold us accountable and make sure we voice our concerns. Once we note a red flag, we better make sure we share it! Of course, even when we share a red flag, the discussion should not be combative. We do not need to say, "Great job, Pat; this ad is offensive," but we can say, "I can see people regarding the comment in the ad as offensive; I would like to see that addressed."

You may have seen this coming, but the way we deliver feedback is in the order in which each zone was reviewed. We start with the things we love. Then, we move on to things we like. These two zones allow us to share the creative team's excitement and lets the team bask a bit in its efforts when it comes to what really worked or met expectations. By starting the conversation on a positive note, we have reminded everyone in the room that we have a common goal: to do great work. This approach creates a collaborative environment as opposed to a combative environment. With that safe space established, we can then get into the questions. Finally, if any red flags are present, we can raise those in a candid fashion. Let me be clear: If red flags exist, they need to be discussed; however, it is often more productive to put those on the table after we have started from a place of acknowledgment of, and respect for, the efforts of the creative team. In fact, after we have discussed the red flags, we can end by going back to the things we love to reinforce the effort that went into the creative work.

Finally, in giving feedback on creative work, it is important to remember that part of our job is to let the creative team do its job. Outside of stating the mandatories in our creative brief, we should refrain from telling the creative team how to fix problems we have identified. So, if we have questions we should listen to their answers and, if we are not satisfied, we should ask for a remedy. However, a big difference exists between alerting the creative team to a linkage concern and asking them to fix it versus telling them to show the brand for the entire advertisement. Thus, our job in giving feedback is to reinforce what is working, raise questions, and voice concerns, but we should allow the creative team to make revisions as they see fit.

Conclusion

As a multibillion-dollar industry, advertising is a source of considerable expenditure for brands. This chapter has focused on enhancing advertising effectiveness via proper creative brief writing and feedback. It has offered the reader initial tools to build, maintain, and/or repair their advertising strategy to help it run like a Swiss watch. Although considerable discipline, effort, and time is required, the output of such investments is a synchronized process that reliably moves the brand needle forward.

Author Biography

Derek D. Rucker is the Sandy & Morton Goldman Professor of Entrepreneurial Studies in Marketing at the Kellogg School of Management at Northwestern University. He holds a PhD in Psychology from The Ohio State University. His research focuses broadly on social rank, compensatory consumption, persuasion, and consumer behavior. His work asks, and seeks answers to, what makes for effective advertising and what motives underlie consumer consumption. To answer these questions, Dr. Rucker draws on his rich training in social psychology. His work has appeared in leading journals, including the *Journal of Personality and Social Psychology, Psychological Science,* the *Journal of Consumer Research,* the *Journal of Marketing Research,* and the *Journal of Consumer Psychology.*

CHAPTER 15

Developing an Impactful Communication Campaign

Kevin McTigue

"Should we be on TikTok?" Of all the questions asked about media channels to help grow a product, it feels like the most common one might be the generic "Should we be on X?"

Over the past 20 years, you could swap out TikTok for Facebook, Periscope, YouTube, Clubhouse, Instagram, Meerkat, Amazon Alexa, Snapchat, Twitch, Vine . . . and, recently, metaverse sites like Decentraland. Every couple of months the landscape shifts a bit, with new players emerging and audiences moving. This ever-changing world of channels can make it difficult on marketers. Some say exciting; some say crazy. It doesn't feel all that long ago that our media plans were simpler artifacts: a solid combination of television, print, radio, and some out-of-home perhaps. But every year it grows more complex. And so the question always comes: "Should we be on X?"

We want the answer to be easy. We want to pull down a sheet of benchmarks that say "for your offering in this category, these are the top 10 channels and you should expect Y% return on your investment." Sometimes we can find benchmarks, but with media habits changing so frequently, they can become outdated quickly. So that leaves marketers frustrated when looking for the answer to "Should we be on X?"

So let's back up. What do we want from our communication campaign? We can start by assuming that we have identified a goal that can be achieved by messaging. We would like to grow awareness or change perceptions about our offering by conveying information. And we would like that to be achieved at the most efficient cost possible. At the simplest level, what must be true for this to happen? There are four key factors that marketers must consider:

- *Who:* To be most efficient, our message must reach all the people who can be influenced by the content and waste nothing on those who will not be influenced by the content.
- *When:* We must reach this efficient target audience at the times when they are most likely to be compelled by our message.
- *Where:* We must also reach the audience in the places or channels where they are most receptive.
- *What:* And finally, the content of the message itself must be compelling enough to achieve the goals of the campaign when delivered.

Who: Targeting in Communications

The importance of selecting target customers is increased when you get into communications. Not everyone you could possibly reach shares the same propensity to react positively to your message. Therefore, you use targeting to efficiently spend your budget. There is the obvious first cut of people who have never and will never buy your category. Here a dollar spent is a dollar wasted. There is the second cut of people who may be category purchasers but have a low chance of responding to your message. They have reasons to stay with their current choice, an inability or unwillingness to pay your premium, or a set of needs better served by the competition. And, finally, there are audiences you could reach that would have purchased your product anyway without messaging. All are inefficient uses of money and time resources that could be directed toward more profitable potential customers.

As you continue to pare down the potential audience, you now reach the tiers of firms or consumers that would respond positively. Even within this group, savvy marketers are choiceful. There may be some segments of potential customers that are more likely to stay customers for a longer period of time. Or segments that require less budget to acquire. Or spend more with you per year. When you add in the concept of customer lifetime value (the net present value of all future profit—acquisition costs), marketers can sharpen their efforts to optimize their spend.

But sometimes "waste" makes sense. Even with all of the targeting tools at your disposal, there are circumstances where going broader is smarter. There is a handful of very large brands in widely used categories for which the incremental cost of narrowing down the target is not efficient. Or the data needed to narrow the targets are unobtainable. Therefore, we see ads for things like mobile phone companies, pharmaceutical drugs (in the United States), auto makers, insurance providers, and chain restaurants advertising broadly. There is a cost and a data requirement associated with specificity in targeting, and sometimes logic simply pushes the decision to go broad.

The marketing director of a large chain restaurant that spends over $250 million in advertising in the United States recently said about targeting, "We can afford to reach everyone, but the problem is that in speaking to everyone we are speaking to no one." It raises the other point of targeting in communications beyond just cost efficiency. What do you say to "everyone"? Think about trying to convince your partner to agree on a restaurant for tonight. You know what they like so you can mention the vegan options, craft cocktails, or celebratory atmosphere. Now, think about trying to convince a room full of strangers. What do you yell on the megaphone to the crowd? They aren't all vegans or interested in craft cocktails and have different ideas of what the perfect restaurant atmosphere is. Segmentation is essentially dividing up that room of strangers into groups of people who have similar needs and interests. Then you can not only prioritize your budget but also speak specifically to that group's needs. When you yell through the megaphone to the whole group of strangers, you're forced to generalize your message, to take the lowest common denominator: "You should eat at this restaurant! The food is . . . good!"

That's what this restaurant chain was facing. In yelling to the crowd, it couldn't be specific enough to be impactful. Even when budget efficiency is not an issue (which is debatable), you still encounter the problem that it's incredibly difficult to craft a persuasive message without a clear idea of who is receiving that message. Having a clear idea of the intended audience drives efficiency of spend and effectiveness of message. And having a clear idea of your intended audience is the path to answering the next questions.

When, Where, and What: Multi-Channel Planning

"So should we be on TikTok?"

There is one person who can tell you: your customer. Until the great splintering of media channels in the mid-2000s, choices were limited. You would have an "omnichannel" plan that consisted of TV, print, radio, out-of-home, and some digital banner ads. You had a message and funneled that message through the available channels to meet your goals for reach (the number of people messaged) and frequency (the number of times they encounter our message).[1]

As digital matured, channels proliferated and marketers began to get access to more information. This evolution caused several major changes in how you approach the process of communications planning and buying. The fundamental change was that you used to buy advertising on channels that overindexed with the profile of your target audience. For instance, you would buy an ad on television programs, magazines, and websites where the audience profile of the viewers (e.g., women 25–54) matched the profile of your target (e.g., women 25–54).

The Rise of Data

Digital data collection allowed us to move past "women 25–54" and get into specifics like past customers, people currently reading an article about vacationing in Brazil, mobile phone customers who have an expiring contract in the next 45 days, and German financial analysts who are interested in steel commodity trading. This wealth of data enabled the shift of advertising from "the places they are likely to be" to "buying your specific audience wherever they might be." And now, buying audiences at specific times within their purchase decision process.

Data sources for communications are commonly referred to as first-, second-, and third-party data. The terminology is more important today than ever as data privacy laws are enacted, Apple moves to increase limits on advertiser data use, and major platforms globally are restricting some of the more common data tracking tools, like cookies, used over the past decade.

First-party data are generally classified as data that your firm collects firsthand. It could be your own customer data. It could be emails or traffic data from your site or owned properties. As long as you followed the rules in collecting the data (appropriate opt-ins, etc.), then this data is the kind that can continue to be used even as the restrictions tighten. It's your data and it's the most valuable. Firms across the world and across industries are rapidly ramping up efforts to collect, store, and manage this data.[2]

Second-party data, quite simply, are someone else's first-party data. If you are a car dealership and you partner with a car repair shop that shares customer data, the data it shares with you is second party. The most common second-party data you'll encounter are from the large ad networks like Google, Facebook, or Amazon. All of the data Google has on its users is second party (to you), and Google will let you use this second-party data as part of its media-buying process. And you can imagine that the logged-in users of these large networks leave behind an enormous digital trail of their interests and behaviors that are valued by advertisers.

Third-party data are frequently the most specific and the most expensive. Large data aggregators buy first-party data from multiple sources to create an expansive offering of customer data that advertisers can purchase. Would you like to advertise to all the thoracic surgeons in New York? Would you like to advertise to current drivers of Audi automobiles whose lease is up in the next four months?

Advertisers use a combination of first-, second-, and third-party data to create the segments that they desire. Data privacy laws require multiple steps in the process to remove personally identifiable information for any one customer. But there are multiple data connectivity platforms that help marketers stitch together first-, second-, and third-party data in allowable ways.

Here's an example. Let's say Japan's All Nippon Airways (ANA) wants to target frequent travelers to Europe for a new campaign. They could start with first-party data from their own frequent flier program, the ANA Mileage Club. Then they could partner with the Google Ad Network to source users who have exhibited online behaviors that signal interest in European travel: second party. Finally, ANA could purchase the third-party data from an aggregator that has credit card information about people who have bought flights to Europe from Japan. Combining these three would create a robust audience of those most likely to respond to ANA's campaign.

This data influx, paired with the right advertising tools and ad technology, allows you to move from targeting *places* where your customers are likely to be to targeting *customers* wherever they are. This enables a smarter approach to messaging. Using the digital data trail, you can frequently assess taln where a customer is in the overall process of purchasing and craft messages accordingly.

To plot this out, you could use something like the old purchase funnel. How many are aware of you? How many consider you? How many buy you? How many buy you again? There is still some value in this approach. A better approach is to look at the process from the customer's side. How do they move through the buying decision and usage journey? Looking at this process through the customer's lens is called customer journey modeling. To be more specific, in this instance you are using journey pathing to understand how to best connect your message with your customers to drive value.

Practical Journey Mapping to Inform When, Where, and What

Here we offer a practical customer journey mapping framework that can be built and used quickly to help inform strategic decisions; it can be evolved into an automated platform and then into an algorithmically driven system.

Customer journey maps gained popularity as groundwork for complex digital initiatives, but can be time-consuming, rich with complexities, and intermittently useful. Over time a need has arisen to take the idea of the process and make it more practically usable more often. So, the following framework was designed and it's been used across firms around the world, from local dentists and nonprofits to large CPG firms and international car companies.

It starts with the target customer, the *who*. If there is more than one relevant target or collaborator in the process (B2B, pharma), you can create more journeys. But the lens needs to be on a singular segment, so you don't water down the journey by stretching it thinly across too broad a population.

Then think through the phases or stages the target goes through, the *when*. This will vary by target and industry, but all stages start with the same phase: "pre-need." "Pre-need" is the time before customers begin the purchase process. They aren't active in the category and will spare very little thought for you. Most journey models, however, are missing this stage. The *when* phase is incredibly important because it's used to align the *where* and *what*.

Most of the time potential customers are not actively involved in your category. There are some categories with frequent purchases, but even in consumer-packaged goods (CPG) the buy rate might be three times a year. So, most of the time you are reaching out to your audience they don't need you and are not actively seeking information to help make a decision in your category. This insight can significantly shift the messaging strategy for this phase.

After pre-need, the next phase is always triggers (see Figure 15.1). Triggers are the events that occur in the customer's life that start them on the active buying path. It's when they enter the category actively. Sometimes the triggers are obvious, like national holidays: Singles Day in China, Diwali in India, Christmas in many parts of the world. Some are personal events: graduating from school, having a baby, getting married, a firm going public. Some are situational: car breaks down, a contract expires, machine age hits 10 years.

Savvy marketers know the key triggers that cause their customers to enter their category. The most obvious triggers are usually crowded with

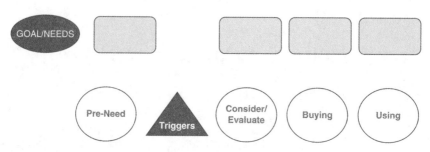

FIGURE 15.1 Practical Journey Map with Phases and Goals

competitors bidding up Google search terms. So, keep looking. What are the less obvious reasons someone would enter your category, and how do you show up to meet them first?

After the first stages, the path varies by industry. A law firm, a music subscription service, or a hospital system can all have varied phases that follow. What makes something a unique phase in the journey is that the customer's primary need is very specific and bound within that phase.

In this example, assume a three-part journey following the trigger: an evaluation phase, a buying phase, and a usage phase. Think about what the different primary goals/needs might be by phase. In **pre-need**, consumers want to stay current in their industry, succeed in their job, and so on. In the **consider/evaluate** phase, the needs are generally to establish a set of criteria and to rank their options based on that criteria. In **buying**, the customer would like to purchase a preferred option at a certain price and without risk or inconvenience. **Using** might involve optimizing machine uptime in B2B, seeing symptoms subside in pharma, or making a cake the family loves in CPG. This journey is not simply about one-time acquisition, so the using phase also needs to be examined to understand how to optimize your interaction with customers through messaging or experience. After the final phase, it's assumed that the user circles back to the beginning in pre-need but with the benefit of all the experience gleaned in this journey.

The next step layers in the current attitudes or beliefs of your target (Figure 15.2).

This becomes particularly important as you do your best to understand what the most pertinent perceptions are about your brand or category that can help or hurt you. Perceptions are sometimes divided into "drivers" and "barriers." Drivers are positive associations that move the customer farther down the path to choosing your offering and having a positive experience. These positive perceptions can exist in varying degrees of prevalence. So there might be a driver that is present in the minds of your customers but is not strongly held or doesn't come easily to mind. Your efforts, therefore, are to increase the mental prominence of this positive attitude: to reinforce the driver.

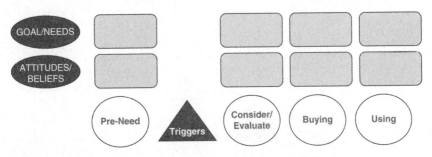

FIGURE 15.2   Practical Journey Map with Attitudes and Beliefs

Barriers are best defined by a quote from Daniel Kahneman in the book *Thinking, Fast and Slow*: "Instead of asking how can I get him or her to do it, it starts with a question of why isn't she doing it already?"[3] In this phase, what might be keeping her from thinking of you as the best choice? Are there misperceptions about the strengths of your offering versus the competition? Just as the needs evolve from phase to phase, so do the attitudes and beliefs. As the customer acquires more information, their perceptions change. Think of your last major purchase. At the beginning you probably knew a little, and as you explored and learned more your perceptions of the different offerings probably evolved.

Finally, customer behaviors and touchpoints are added (Figure 15.3): *Where* are they going? *What* are they doing? As you plan your communications, acknowledge that the customers have different behaviors. Particularly in pre-need, they are not going to be researching options. Your ideal end state in this area of the journey map would be a prioritized list of the most frequented channels or touchpoints. Are they following thought leaders on Twitter? Are they passively listening to the same podcasts? Are they searching YouTube for product demonstrations? And these might not all be "media" channels. Speaking with peers or visiting with friends might seem inconsequential, as you're not "sponsoring" their peers and friends, but there is value in understanding the full ecosystem of influence. It may open your eyes to influential sources of information.

How does one do this? Option 1 is hiring a firm to do research and fill everything out. That's expensive and time consuming. Expensive and time consuming sometimes mean that the tool will have limited application because people are reluctant to dedicate the necessary resources. Most organizations have some research done over the past five years that is applicable. In addition, most categories have some secondary research, published research that's available online. Finally, the people in your organization have at least some idea of what's going on in some of these areas and can offer insights.

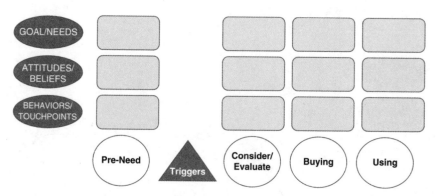

FIGURE 15.3 Practical Journey Map with Behaviors and Touchpoints

One way to glean these insights is to invite six to eight people from the organization that either have important information or whose participation would help ensure advocacy and usage of the completed journey later. Assign each person a piece of research to present at the workshop so that no one has to re-read everything. Then map out on a whiteboard what is known or believed to be true for the various areas. Sometimes teams even bring in clients to get the insights firsthand. What you'll typically find is that you can fill in many of the blanks, and that this "80% right" version can offer enormous value. You might also find holes where you know nothing. This is where it might be most useful to bring in an internal or external research team and task them with specific questions based on the holes in your journey.

Leveraging what has been learned about your customers, you have built this framework from their perspective, letting their needs and behaviors drive the model. To achieve real value from this, you now need to add in the goals and key performance indicators (KPIs) of the business (see Figure15.4).

What is viewed as a successful outcome at each stage? How will that be measured? When done fairly well, you have identified the business goal for any communication effort focused on a customer in a particular phase. When done precisely well, you can start to see the impact that a change to an earlier phase will have on a later phase. Does increasing positive perceptions in pre-need from 25% to 35% result in a deal-close rate increase of 15% to 20%? That level of specificity informs a more holistic view of the entire process.

You now have isolated the distinct phases through which your customer progresses and identified the most important need they have at each phase. When paired with some basic digital targeting, you can address your

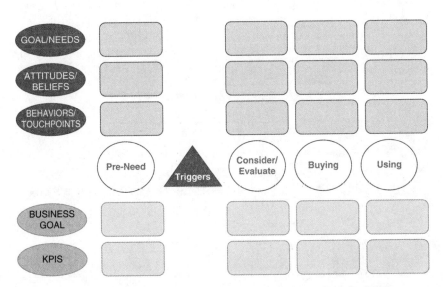

FIGURE 15.4 Complete Practical Journey Map with Business Goals and KPIs

customer *when* they are at specific points to be more effective. Because you know their need and their most important perceptions at any phase, along with our primary goal as a business, you know *what* to say at each phase to be most effective. And finally, you know *where* to meet them with your messaging because you have prioritized a palette of touchpoints or channels. This approach allows us to move from the channel-focused communications planning of the past to a more customer-centric approach (Figure 15.5).

This is a low-fidelity, 80%-right journey model that immediately informs better, more customer-centric decision making. Questions like "should we be on X?" are answered beyond just yes or no. You can add in exactly what we should be saying on X.

Companies also use this as a way to prioritize activities. If you are doing well in phases 2 and 4 but have a real pain point in phase 3, focus your efforts there. And you're well set up to do so. You have a clear business goal, a focused audience, know the most relevant perceptual drivers to reinforce or barriers to overcome, and know where to intersect the customer most efficiently.

In my experience across industries and geographies, this model has never been completed without discovering new opportunities. What is perhaps most surprising about the value created is that, most of the time, the

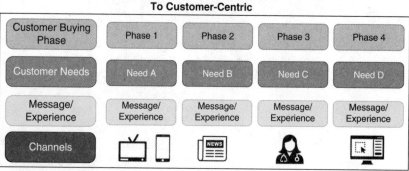

FIGURE 15.5 The Evolution of Multi-Channel Marketing

information assembled is not new. It is simply organizing the information in a new way, from the customer's perspective, that helps us see what we could not before.

Next-Generation Journeys

Data capabilities are opening new doors to allow this relatively simple approach to be both personalized and scaled. A wide range of firms offer technology to automate marketing actions matched to customer behaviors.

Let's say you visit my website for specialty teas. The first thing you'll see is a cookie notification that requests permission to track you. Now, I don't yet know you, but I can reach you again online through that data. Now, I'd like to know who you are. I'm going to serve a pop-up window that offers to trade you 10% off your first order for your email, your first-party customer data. You enter the email and browse the site. You go to the matcha tea section, browse for about a minute, and then leave the site. In three days you see an ad for my matcha tea on Instagram. Somehow you ignore that, but four days later you see an ad for free shipping on matcha. Nothing yet? Okay, two days after that you get an email for a weekend sale of 20% off all matcha products on the site. You click through to a specific matcha tea promo page, and finally I get you to purchase.

Behind the scenes, there is a customer data platform and a marketing automation platform working in tandem. Based on pre-set rules, the marketing automation platform automatically generates tactics based on the actions logged by the customer data platform about you. This is automated, journey-based marketing. At the most basic level, it serves up pre-set marketing actions based on associated customer actions. Even at this most basic level, it can be pretty amazing. Even if you didn't give me your email, I could serve you ads for matcha or reconfigure my site to be matcha-focused the next time you visit. If you do give me the email, you become a known user, and I can check to see your past order history, send you emails, more broadly target you across ad networks, and even alert someone on my sales team.

That might not make sense for matcha tea, but if you are a B2B company with high-touch sales, just think through the ramifications. Customer A visits the site and looks at a new financial product that they don't currently buy. The system generates an email to the assigned salesperson alerting them to your interest. At the next lunch, the salesperson isn't boring them with unneeded information but happens to have rich information on just the thing that Customer A is interested in.

With machine learning we can take this further. Everything said so far requires no machine learning, just a series of "if this happens, then do this" coding instructions. With machine learning, I could serve a portion of matcha page visitors different messages and offers. By looking at the data profile of each of my visitors and the response rates to the differing offers/messages, the machine learns which data profiles respond best to what stimuli so that through experimentation, the machine refines my tactics to optimize the most profitable return rate.

This AI-based "next-best pathing" isn't coming soon; it's been around for a while. The limiting factors have been the need for a robust amount of good data, which historically required significant capabilities outside firms' current resources. What's happening right now is that companies are collecting the data, and more vendors are making the technology more accessible to more kinds of firms.

What's Next

The biggest question looming is how to balance firms' obvious desire for data with consumers' need for privacy. It's not hard to imagine this going too far, from helpful to annoying to creepy. So the question will not be "What *can* we do?" but "What *should* we do?" There is not an answer in the market now. Individual firms are meeting with their media agencies and AI specialists to have early conversations about the ethical implications and develop a set of guiding principles. The answer will likely be found in transparency. Media costs are subsidized by advertising, and many consumers have accepted this trade-off, if grudgingly. Recent data collection efforts are generally opaque, and consumers are rightly suspicious. But there is a path forward. We as marketers could promise less interruption and advertising that is aligned with consumer preferences (things they are actually interested in). In return, we ask for a transparent sharing of customer information. Marketers win and customers win.

Conclusion

Should you be on X? That question is going to continue to get more complicated, and chasing tactics will drain your resources. Chase your customer. Know who you are chasing. Let their needs, perceptions, and behaviors drive your choices. Using a simple framework like that illustrated in this chapter can immediately allow for better decisions that match content to channel to business objectives. And the idea of this can be automated and then algorithmically optimized. But just as we use the customer's lens to understand *when*, *where*, and *what*, it will be increasingly important to look through their lens so that we can be ethical and effective as we tackle the *how* question.

Author Biography

Kevin McTigue is clinical associate professor of marketing at the Kellogg School of Management at Northwestern University. He teaches multiple classes for Kellogg's MBA and executive education programs. His career spans more than 25 years in teaching, consulting, brand management, and advertising. He is currently the academic director for Kellogg's Chief Digital Officer program and co-director of Kellogg's Advertising and Marketing Communication Strategy program. He co-authored *The Creative Brief Blueprint* and contributed to *Kellogg on Branding*. He conducts executive training and consulting for a variety of firms on the topics of marketing and advertising strategy.

CHAPTER 16

Marketing in the Metaverse

Mohan Sawhney

The metaverse began to generate a lot of excitement in 2021. The hype surrounding it reached a crescendo with Facebook's November 2021 name change to Meta. Announcing the change, CEO Mark Zuckerberg proclaimed, "Our overarching goal . . . is to help bring the metaverse to life."[1] Not to be outdone, Microsoft announced plans to buy Activision Blizzard for $69 billion in early 2022—a move the company said will accelerate its growth in gaming across "mobile, PC, console, and cloud and will provide building blocks for the metaverse."[2] While gaming will continue to be a major entry point to the metaverse, conjuring the now-familiar images of gamers using augmented reality (AR) and virtual reality (VR) headsets, the metaverse is much more than a next-generation gaming platform. For marketers, the metaverse presents a wide array of opportunities, from immersive commerce to brand building and promoting thought leadership.

This potential was highlighted by Zuckerberg, who envisioned "a billion people in the metaverse doing hundreds of dollars of commerce, each buying digital goods, digital content, different things to express themselves, so whether that's clothing for their avatar or different digital goods for their virtual home or things to decorate their virtual conference room, utilities to be able to be more productive in virtual and augmented reality and across the metaverse overall."[3] Despite this optimistic vision, the metaverse is still in its infancy and there is a lot of uncertainty about its evolution. Moreover, unlike the internet, the metaverse will not appeal to everyone, with its requirements of headsets and a steep learning curve for new users. But there will be enough opportunity to market in the metaverse to put it on the radar of companies today—particularly those that aspire to be innovative, cutting edge, and trendsetting.

Every marketer needs to understand what the metaverse is and how it can be used to drive demand, build brands, and engage customers. Whether you work for a business-to-consumer (B2C) or a business-to-business (B2B) company, a legacy company, or a high-tech startup, the metaverse is an important digital platform—potentially as significant as the development of the World Wide Web and mobile commerce. Although B2C companies have been early adopters of marketing in the metaverse, B2B marketers can also harness the power of the metaverse for customer engagement, product demonstrations, creation of digital twins of manufacturing facilities, collaborative work, and many other uses. It's an open field of potential, but is not without its risks and challenges.

How marketers choose to play in the metaverse will depend on many factors, from their culture to their competitive stance—proactive and aggressive or reactive and conservative. To determine if and how to proceed, marketing executives need to take a step back and deepen their understanding of the metaverse, so that they can see beyond the hype and identify real opportunities for driving revenues and building brands.

The purpose of this chapter is to introduce marketers to the fundamentals of the metaverse and its implications for marketing. We begin with a definition of the metaverse and its components. Next, we discuss how the metaverse can be used as a platform for executing marketing initiatives. Specifically, we look at B2B and B2C marketing use cases for the metaverse. We use a "three-horizon" framework to help marketers align their metaverse marketing initiatives with their business strategy. In the final section, we examine the metaverse marketing strategy for Nike, a pioneering marketer that has been experimenting with several initiatives in the metaverse.

Lest we get carried away by "shiny object syndrome," it is important to remind ourselves that the fundamentals of marketing will not change despite the innovations that the metaverse will make possible. Marketing has and always will be about engaging customers, driving demand, building brands, enhancing reputation, and exploring new markets. The metaverse is simply the latest platform for marketing—albeit a sophisticated and complex one, with opportunities as well as risks.

What Is the Metaverse?

Although the term *metaverse* is much talked about, there is still a great deal of confusion about its precise definition. The metaverse can best be thought of as a three-dimensional digital environment that uses AR, VR, blockchain, and social media to create immersive user experiences that mimic and extend the real world. Unlike the internet as we know it, where the focus is on *information and content,* the metaverse focuses on *activities and experiences.* Until now, we have interacted with content on the internet using HTML, websites, mobile browsers, and apps. In the metaverse, we will participate in this interactive, digital environment. As McKinsey observed, "We believe that the metaverse is best characterized as an evolution of today's internet—it is something we are immersed in instead of something we look at."[4]

Metaverse, as a term, was coined in Neal Stephenson's 1992 dystopian sci-fi novel *Snow Crash,* in which characters use digital avatars (representations of themselves) to explore a fully digital world. As the metaverse evolved, it allowed individuals to have a second life—or a second, digital version of a physical life. This was made possible through technology and using VR and AR headsets. In this universal virtual world, people can spend time interacting with friends and associates as well as play, attend concerts, purchase virtual property, and shop for digital and physical objects for themselves or their digital avatars. Anything we do in the real world, we can potentially also do in the immersive 3D environment of the metaverse.

A summary of the metaverse in terms of its key characteristics is shown in Figure 16.1.

While some may think of the metaverse only as a digital representation of the physical world, it is much more than that. It extends the physical world into a new dimension. For example, in 2021, Ariana Grande appeared on the *Fortnite* metaverse stage in a live concert that *Tech Crunch* called "impressively smooth and visually inventive."[5] Not only could millions view it simultaneously, but each person could also dance on the stage (via an avatar, of course) with Grande, which they could never do in real life. The popularity of this type of entertainment experience has exploded. In 2022, rapper Travis Scott appeared in a concert hosted by *Fortnite,* which attracted a record 12 million people.[6] What was most exciting, aside from the massive reach of the event, was that every participant could have a front-row seat.

What looks like fun and games, however, is made possible by the confluence of significant technological advancements. Examining what brings the metaverse together shows just how cutting edge this virtual world really is and where it could be headed.

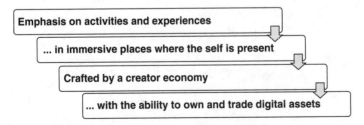

FIGURE 16.1 Key Characteristics of the Metaverse

The Seven Layers of the Metaverse

The inner and outer workings of the metaverse are best understood as layers. There are, in fact, seven layers of the metaverse, as depicted by Jon Radoff and shown in Figure 16.2.[7]

The core of the metaverse model begins with an underlying infrastructure composed of 5G and fast networks, high bandwidth, cloud hosting, data analysis, and other computer-intensive components. The next layer is the human interface, which includes wearables such as VR and AR headsets, smart glasses, and other interface devices. Next, there is the decentralization layer, which contains computing services and microservices—from edge computing to AI agents and blockchain, the latter being critical to the usage of nonfungible tokens (NFTs) that allow for the creation and ownership of metaverse assets, including digital land.

The spatial computing layer is composed of the programming power required to create next-generation, 3D environments. This includes technologies such as Unreal Engine and Unity Engine, which are platforms for creating videogames and, more recently, the metaverse. Next is the creator economy, where metaverse developers create content and assets. (This is the metaverse equivalent of app developers for the mobile world.) On top of that is the discovery layer, which allows users to navigate the metaverse via stores, agents, and other middlemen that connect participants to experiences. The parallel here is the creation of the internet, which led to the rise of search engines such as Yahoo and Google.

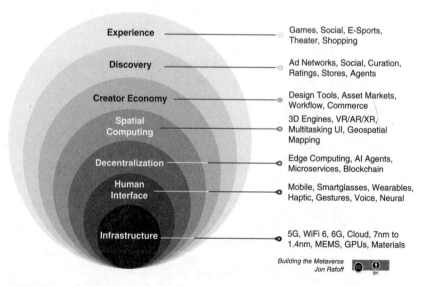

FIGURE 16.2   Seven Layers of the Metaverse

The final layer, closest to the end user, is the experience layer; this is what participants see and engage with. Experiences can include gaming, playing sports, attending events, and shopping, to name a few. The experience layer is also where marketers connect with customers, as well as meet with current and potential customers and others who will experience their brand and products in new ways.

A notable example is Nike's NIKELAND, created on the *Roblox* video game platform. As one of the first major brands to stake a claim in the metaverse, Nike has rolled out a digital space in which players can use special Nike products to outfit their avatar.[8] As we explore later in the chapter, Nike's foray into the metaverse presents an interesting case study of a marketing strategy meant to not only build a brand but also enhance a pioneering brand's reputation.

This brief tour of the metaverse's layers gives some perspective of the magnitude of what it takes to create this kind of environment. To appreciate the development of the metaverse more fully, we can look back on the development of the digital path that has taken us to this point.

Three Decades of Marketing in a Digital World

To look forward into the digital future of marketing, it pays to look back at the evolution of marketing and commerce on the internet over the three decades from 1993 to 2022. The evolution of digital marketing can be broadly divided into three eras. The first era was the creation of dot-coms and e-commerce, dating back to the founding of companies such as Amazon and Yahoo (both established in 1994). This first era (roughly 1994 through 2007) was all about figuring out how to search and how to sell online. In 2006, researchers published a paper that posited: "At the end of its first decade, it is clear that a solid foundation for e-commerce has been established. What will e-commerce look like by end of the next decade?"[9]

That answer came with the launch of the iPhone in early 2007, which ushered in the second digital era—one characterized by a new generation of smartphone platforms that enabled mobile commerce. Suddenly, a phone wasn't just for calling; it was a device for customer engagement that led to the creation of companies such as Uber and Lyft that use mobile apps, not websites, for commerce.

In 2021, we entered the third era, defined by the evolution of the metaverse, which offers a brave new world for digital commerce and marketing. However, the concept of the metaverse is not entirely new, as we will see in the next section.

Precedents of the Metaverse

In some ways, the metaverse is the second coming of a 1999 social platform Second Life, which enabled people to use digital representations of themselves to socialize and connect with others and even to shop and build property to enhance their digital lives. However, Second Life stagnated at about 1 million users in 2008. Later, the social and economic aspects of the game were reimagined, and users gained a better experience. As of the end of 2021, Second Life had about 200,000 daily active users.

Another metaverse-like platform was Minecraft, a wildly popular platform owned by Microsoft that boasted 141 million active players in 2021. Like the newer metaverse platforms, Minecraft was decentralized, customizable, and immersive—without requiring expensive hardware and digital media such as AR and VR. However, both Second Life and Minecraft were glitch filled, prone to hacking, and spawned nefarious activities from fraud to intellectual property violations, and more—some of the same flaws and risks that exist in the metaverse as well.

As we move from these precursors into the full-on metaverse, there have been, and will continue to be, growing pains. Some bad and disappointing experiences are inevitable, particularly as old thinking is brought into a new medium. It's the same thing that happened during the early days of the internet, when websites were filled with display ads like billboards because that's what we were used to. Only later, with time and experience, did we start to create native, new thinking such as YouTube, Instagram, and TikTok. And that's what we're seeing now among the new metaverse platforms and players: imagining a wide range of innovative user experiences.

Metaverse Platforms and Players

A big misconception about the metaverse is that it is just one environment. Actually, there are hundreds of metaverse platforms. Multiple platforms raise the challenge of interoperability. Ideally, all metaverse platforms would be connected and interoperable, allowing for a seamless transition from one "world" to the next, just as citizens of the European Union can move seamlessly across national borders in the physical world. And, ideally, our metaverse avatars should be able to move from one platform to another while preserving their identity. Users should be able to take their assets and collectibles to any place and participate in activities such as live auctions and concerts on different platforms. Unfortunately, this is not possible today because metaverse platforms are being created as "walled gardens." Consequently, marketers need to be careful in deciding which metaverse platforms to bet on. A wrong choice of platform can result in "stranded assets" such as virtual real estate that becomes worthless if the metaverse platform fails to attract enough users. The following is a brief list of the leading platforms and players jostling for mind space in the metaverse.

Horizon Worlds   In December 2021, Meta (Facebook) opened Horizon Worlds, its virtual reality world, to anyone 18 or older in the United States and Canada. Horizon Worlds offers many possibilities. For example, the Horizon Workroom app offers virtual meeting rooms and video call integration for up to 50 people at a time. Despite the massive investment that Meta is making in its metaverse platform, critics have called the Horizon Worlds experience "strange," saying it mimics a virtual office rather than a digital playground. *TheGamer* panned it as a "broken metaverse" that was "less of a virtual utopia, and more of a glitchy, incomplete cluster of experiences."[10]

Decentraland   Developed on the Ethereum blockchain, Decentraland was the most popular metaverse in 2021. Backed by more than 20 investors (including Digital Currency Group, Kenetic Capital, and Coin Fund), it built partnerships with brands such as Samsung, Atari, and Polygon, as well as the South Korean government. Decentraland allows users to purchase virtual land where they can monetize their assets and content. Decentraland has more than 90,000 parcels, which include individual parcels, estates (multiple parcels), districts (parcels with similar themes), and plazas (owned by the community). It also offers three types of tokens: MANA, the native currency; WEAR, for wearables and articles; and LAND, for owning a virtual plot of land.

The Sandbox   The Sandbox permits users to tour virtual space, purchase virtual land, and interact with other players. It was backed by a $93 million funding round by Softbank, one of the biggest investors in the world. It also partners with brands such as Adidas, Atari, the rapper Snoop Dog, and NFT company CryptoKitties. Like Decentraland, The Sandbox was developed on the Ethereum blockchain. However, The Sandbox has four types of tokens: SAND, the native currency; ASSETS, content created by users; GAMES, created by users; and LAND, the virtual land. The Sandbox has more than 166,000 plots of land that have been grouped into estates (owned by one person) and districts (owned by two or more people). The Sandbox managers have followed a clear strategy for the future: to bring the platform to mobile devices before the end of 2022 and launch it on consoles such as PlayStation and Xbox. The Sandbox company also wants to create in-game jobs that would allow users to work, as they do in the physical world. With more investors, partnerships, and a clear roadmap for the future, The Sandbox appears to be gaining on Decentraland.

Roblox   Developed and released in 2006 by Roblox Corporation, *Roblox* is an online gaming platform. The video game platform emulates aspects of a social media network. For many years, the platform was relatively small, but its growth accelerated after 2015. *Roblox* was free to play, but in-game purchases were available through a virtual currency called Robux. By 2020, it had 164 million monthly active users; most U.S. users were younger than 16. *Roblox* users can create their own games with Roblox Studios, which can then be played by other users. *Roblox* also allows users to buy, sell, and create virtual items to decorate their avatars. Although an older platform, it has a large user base. Along with Epic Games, creator of *Fortnite*, *Roblox* has built an impressive virtual world in which millions of people socialize, spend digital money, and play digital games.

Metaverse Use Cases: B2C

The metaverse's promise of immersive digital experiences makes it applicable for a rich variety of activities. As noted earlier, most are associated with B2C and activities such as gaming, digital commerce, live concerts, and more. At the time of writing this chapter, it is unclear which use cases have the most potential and would attract early adopters. But a few promising use cases have emerged.

E-Commerce Shopping and commerce have played a key role in the metaverse, with people buying and selling things in the virtual world just as they do in the physical world. Anything from shoes to candles to food to clothes (all digital, of course) can be bought and sold in the metaverse. Creators and sellers can have an exclusive launch party, attended by people anywhere who enter the digital world. Users can have a seamless channel-to-channel experience, cardless payments, and hyperpersonalization, among other benefits. The metaverse also has shown promise in merging physical and virtual experiences. For example, when sneakers are sold in the physical space, the virtual version can be unlocked as well. Conversely, a digital currency or NFT could be traded for physical goods.

Gaming Games like *Roblox* and *Fortnite* already include many elements of the metaverse. Hundreds of millions of people have played these games, which have created billions of play sessions. Now, people in the metaverse can engage at a yet-unseen level, not just with a few but with all the games available. The combination of technology, NFTs, e-commerce, and engagement is resulting in increased virality and better monetization of games. The metaverse can also promote the growth of play-to-earn games, where people can play to earn third-party revenue. Gaming has been expected to disrupt the system, bringing gamers into crypto investing (which is not without its risks). The big technology companies aren't the only ones interested in gaming. For example, VR startup Aldin Dynamics, based in Iceland, has been building a virtual world based on the game *Waltz of the Wizards.*

Education/Learning   The metaverse's value in learning come from enabling immersive learning experiences. Technologies like VR and AR allow users to explore and experience high-quality and immersive content, not simply read about it. For example, students could use their avatars and VR headsets to experience museums, participate in shared environments, engage with instructors, and collaborate with other students. Service professionals could learn how to repair complex equipment through realistic simulations. Medical students could perform virtual surgeries. Several educational virtual experiences have already been created, such as Britain at War; Fossil Museum (an immersive exhibit); and Nautilus (about the Great Barrier Reef), which includes a 180-degree viewing observatory.

Real Estate   Using cryptocurrency, people buy and sell properties in the virtual world, as they do in the real world. Even though real estate dealings in the metaverse are considered highly speculative, some experts believe the metaverse could expand to host its own fully functioning economy. Digital real estate already has been selling for millions of dollars. In Decentraland, a plot of virtual land sold for $2.4 million worth of crypto, and one sold for $4.2 million at The Sandbox. The popularity of digital land has been spurring other companies to create digital worlds and digital properties. As one observer noted, "Just as in physical communities, people flock to interesting places in the metaverse. And popularity naturally drives up the value of virtual land—exactly as it would in Paris or Beverly Hills."[11] For example, SuperWorld allows a player to collect, buy, and sell plots of virtual land. It has unique plots, including Mount Rushmore, the Eiffel Tower, and the Taj Mahal, valued at a total of $64 billion.

Retail   E-stores, malls, and other shopping venues are being created in the metaverse. However, the retail experience in the metaverse is much more than simply replicating the physical world. It is much more immersive, designed to be above and beyond anything ever possible in the real world. This is not just another flavor of e-commerce: It is being reimagined as *immersive commerce*. Consider the experience of buying a car. Rather than simply buying from a showroom, the metaverse allows people to take an immersive, adrenaline-fueled test drive on the virtual racetrack of their choice and then have the car delivered in the real world. Similarly, the beauty product buying experience could be revolutionized by allowing a buyer, with the flip of a switch, to access a beauty adviser in the metaverse and ask for a personalized recommendation of products. Brands such as L'Oréal have already built a line of virtual cosmetics—virtual versions of skincare and haircare products—as well as virtual perfumes for purchase in the metaverse.

Such possibilities are prompting store designers and marketers to rethink and reimagine what a store could be in the metaverse. The goal is to create hyperpersonalized and immersive experiences that far exceed anything that exists in the physical world. Status symbols such as virtual cars, virtual jewelry, virtual houses, and other virtual belongings could become every bit as important and prestigious as their real-world counterparts in the physical world.

Brands in the Metaverse

Fashion brands have quickly jumped on the metaverse trend and the burgeoning passion for the virtual world. These brands are quickly realizing the potential of the metaverse and the promise of increased engagement and immersion from fans and customers.

- Gucci started selling a virtual fashion collection on the ZEPETO platform. It also launched a version of *Gucci Garden* on the *Roblox* platform in December 2020. Players could choose and customize their avatars and purchase exclusive digital items from Gucci. For example, a Gucci Dionysus bag on *Roblox* sold for 350,000 Robux (roughly $4,115), a higher price than in the real world, where the same bag costs $3,450.
- Vans created a skateboard-themed virtual world on *Roblox* in September 2021. In Vans World, players could purchase skateboards and shoes, go skateboarding with friends, and win exclusive Vans gear.
- Ralph Lauren opened a virtual world called Winter Escape on *Roblox* for Christmas 2021. Fans could visit the Polo store, skate with friends, and decorate the Christmas tree. A few months earlier, in August 2021, the brand launched a 50-piece virtual clothing series in partnership with ZEPETO and added attractions such as the Ralph Lauren coffee shop and the Ralph Lauren flagship store.
- Balenciaga, the Spanish fashion brand, decided to leverage the power of *Fortnite* and designed clothing for four characters in the game. Players could pay for the costumes using the *Fortnite* currency, V-Bucks. Players who made these purchases could submit photos of their avatars for placement on the game's town square billboards. In the real world, people could shop the Balenciaga + *Fortnite* collection in the store's New York location on Madison Avenue.
- JPMorgan Chase was among the banks getting in on the metaverse with a virtual bank branch. It focused on three verticals: enabling game platform providers to access bank-grade products, enabling game and content creators to commercialize their offerings easily, and scaling the metaverse industry across multiple currencies and payment methods with custom solutions. JPMorgan Chase also opened a virtual lounge in Decentraland to navigate issues such as account validation, transaction status, and fraud prevention.

E-Sports   Sports in the metaverse are immersive and creative, with people joining leagues, interacting, buying products, taking photos, chatting with sports stars, and even meeting up in a virtual bar to socialize with other fans. With these activities, the metaverse has promised to revolutionize and lift fan engagement to an unprecedented level. In the virtual sports arena, fans create their own sports avatars, purchase sports equipment and souvenirs, socialize, watch events with others, train, work, party, and participate in gaming. Physical and geographical boundaries melt away. American football fans, for example, could create sports avatars and watch with their friends (located far away), and socialize with other fans. They could watch from a variety of vantage points, zoom in on any play, and even run with the players on a virtual field with multi-view camera technology. Fans could also purchase a seat in a virtual VIP box without the restrictions of availability that plague the physical world. They could browse virtual stores for physical and digital offerings. The sports industry is taking this seriously: Organizations such as the International Cricket Council are already partnering with advocates of the metaverse.

Virtual Travel   Far off, exotic places—some even prohibitive to reach in the physical world—suddenly become accessible in the metaverse, providing virtual travelers with rich, immersive experiences. For example, touring Egyptian Heritage sites virtually and going to dangerous places are now possible and in much simpler (and cheaper) ways than in the real world. This need not be a solo journey; rather, fellow travelers can explore sites from the Great Pyramids to the Tombs of the Pharaohs. In addition, virtual travelers can even take in sights that no longer exist in the real world, such as the Colossus of Rhodes and the Lighthouse of Alexandria.[12]

Metaverse Use Cases: B2B

While much of the metaverse discussion focuses on B2C use cases, the metaverse may hold even more promise for B2B marketers. B2B products and services tend to be complex and customers' buying processes tend to require more high-touch interaction between buyers and sellers. The metaverse allows B2B marketers to create immersive, high-touch experiences to facilitate customer buying journeys without limitations of geography or time. As *Inc.* magazine observed, "B2B brands, once bound by the parameters of expensive business travel and trade shows, can now connect with business decision-makers virtually via the metaverse. . . . The metaverse also provides a pipeline to the rising younger cohort of business decision-makers who grew up gaming and prefer to explore and convert in digital channels."[13]

From a customer engagement standpoint, companies can create very sophisticated product demonstrations, from medical diagnostic machines to aircraft engines. For example, for a highly technical, complex product that has countless parts and components, the metaverse would enable demonstrations that take users *inside* the workings of the product, machine, or advanced technology.

The metaverse could also provide new opportunities to meet with clients to provide education and customer support. Consider a customer with a problem with a machine or a component. In the metaverse, holographically projected support personnel could take the customer inside the machine and show them the solution. And for sales, it's easy to imagine scenarios in which the metaverse could be an invaluable tool, thanks to immersive demonstrations and virtual connections.

B2B use cases also extend to internal operations, from the next generation of virtual workspaces to expanded virtual training with immersive experiences. Consider law enforcement training on handling a hostage crisis or medical simulations involving patients with life-threatening illnesses or injuries. Such simulations can replicate the high-stakes, unpredictable nature of these scenarios as they would occur in the real world.

Another example is simulating workflows, such as in automotive design and engineering. German automaker BMW used NVIDIA's Omniverse platform to create a digital twin of its factory floor. It is important to note that this is not an approximation but a true-to-reality representation, which could facilitate training, time and motion studies, ergonomics, and production efficiencies. Richard Kerris, vice president of Omniverse at NVIDIA, said that BMW can simulate virtually having 300 cars running on a conveyor, while allowing users to identify the safest paths for employees around the factory.[14] Moreover, BMW can market this simulation in the metaverse to its dealerships around the world.

A list of the most promising B2C and B2C use cases for the metaverse is shown in Figure 16.3.

B2B COMPANIES	**B2C COMPANIES**
Product design and engineering	Digital commerce
Product demonstrations	Virtual goods and NFTs
Virtual conferences	Immersive games
Virtual trade shows and customer events	Live sporting events and concerts
Client meetings and communication	Live fashion shows
Customer service and support	Customer engagement, experiences, and entertainment
Virtual workspaces	Advertisements and digital campaigns
Immersive training	
Gamified activities at work	

FIGURE 16.3   Metaverse Use Cases: B2B versus B2C

Risks and Challenges of the Metaverse

The metaverse is full of promise, but it is also fraught with peril. Marketers need to be aware of the risks and challenges of the metaverse, such as the NFT ecosystem's weak infrastructure and the sheer number of scams, hackers, and nefarious developers and investors. For example, digital art has seen rampant fraud and theft, to the degree that fraud alert systems had to be deployed in NFT marketplaces. Another illegal activity is "wash trading," in which an asset's volume and value are artificially inflated by buying and selling to oneself or among an organized group. NFTs have also been used to raise money for questionable projects in which anonymous founders simply took in millions of dollars and then disappeared with all the money. The scale and volume of theft and fraud have led many critics to call the NFT ecosystem broken. Unauthorized reproductions and trademark violations have been increasing, and it remains unclear how trademark law will be enforced in the metaverse. The rise of digital currencies has created a corresponding acceleration in the metaverse of harmful graphic, 3D, and auditory content. Regulators have yet to establish robust mechanisms to prevent fraud and abuse in metaverse platforms.

The metaverse also presents safety problems that mirror those in the real world. These include unwanted contact, racial abuse, data privacy, and violent content. In the metaverse, an individual can get access to someone's virtual space and get up close in a very intrusive way. Avatars could be hacked by cybercriminals who could access extremely sensitive and private data, and users could unwittingly end up interacting with these people instead of with known and trusted friends.

Given the risks and challenges, as well as the need to discern between hype and reality, marketers must weigh the pros and cons of becoming involved in the metaverse. There have been companies (such as the brands highlighted earlier) that have been among the first movers in the metaverse. Many other firms are taking a wait-and-see approach.

One way to approach the metaverse is with a portfolio involving multiple probes and diverse initiatives. Just as with traditional marketing, deciding on a strategy comes down to a key question: What is the job to be done by marketers and marketing? To answer this question, it is useful to organize marketing initiatives into three horizons, each with differing time frames, goals, and methods. This three-horizon framework can then be used to organize metaverse marketing initiatives into a coherent portfolio.

Three Horizons of Marketing

- **Horizon 1** is about generating demand. The objective of marketing initiatives in this horizon is to generate marketing qualified leads (MQLs) and to convert leads into revenues. Marketing deliverables in this horizon focus on effective demand-generation campaigns within a time frame of 12 months. In terms of business impact, marketing effectiveness in Horizon 1 is measured by revenues and market share.

- **Horizon 2** is about building assets. The goal here is to build brand equity and customer relationships. Deliverables center on effective value propositions and brand positioning. The time horizon is medium term, generally one to three years. The benefit to the business is perceptual impact.

- **Horizon 3** focuses on shaping new markets. The goal here is more ambitious: the creation of new markets and ecosystems. Thought leadership is key, with visionary scenarios and experiences as the key marketing deliverables. This is the longest-term horizon, spanning as much as 5 to 10 years. The goal for the business is to influence impact.

The three-horizon framework is summarized in Figure 16.4.

As we look across the first two horizons, we can see that Horizon 1 focuses on *revenue outcomes* whereas Horizon 2 focuses on *brand outcomes*. These are two separate endeavors, and it is important not to mix them up. After all, it is possible to build a brand without directly generating revenues in the short run. In fact, as we will see, that is exactly what Nike is doing with NIKELAND. This metaverse experience is best thought of as an experiential theme park. This is *not* a Horizon 1 initiative. Rather, NIKELAND seeks to create user experiences that are all about building the brand. On the other hand, creating a digital storefront or selling virtual merchandise are Horizon 1 initiatives, whose aim is to generate revenues.

Case Study: Nike in the Metaverse

Nike has led a major shift in digital transformation by diving into the metaverse. Although Nike had already made several forays into the metaverse and in related digital products, in early 2022 Nike's digital team charted a course to expand more aggressively in the metaverse. This has meant placing the right bets at the right time in a very dynamic and confusing space.

The Nike leadership saw the metaverse as an opportunity to stay true to the brand's reputation for pioneering design and innovative marketing. Nike's digital team created several experimental metaverse marketing initiatives, including an in-game collaboration with *Fortnite*, blockchain-based digital sneakers, and a virtual 3D showroom in *Roblox*. It also acquired RTFKT, which makes next-generation collectibles that merge culture and gaming—a move that Nike CEO John Donahoe called "another step that

Dimension	Horizon 1: Generate Demand	Horizon 2: Build Brands	Horizon 3: Shape New Markets
Marketing Goal	Drive revenues and market share	Build brand equity and customer relationships	Create new markets and ecosystems
Marketing Deliverables	Effective demand generation campaigns	Effective value propositions and brand positioning	Visionary scenarios, experiences, and ecosystems
Business Impact	Revenue impact	Perceptual impact	Influence impact
Time Horizon	Short-term (<12 months)	Medium-term (1–3 years)	Long-term (5–10 years)
Scope	Outbound marketing–Sales as key interface	Inbound and outbound marketing– engineering and sales	Entire ecosystem– partners, customers, suppliers, influencers
Primary Tools	Events, webinars, DM, SEM, SEO, enterprise sales, partner management	Advertising, PR, broad customer connection, content marketing, engagement marketing, CRM	Executive speeches, PR/AR, evangelism, white papers
Success Metrics	Marketing qualified leads (MQLs), revenues, market share	Awareness, perceptions, consideration, loyalty	Perceived thought leadership in emerging categories and markets

FIGURE 16.4   The Three Horizons of Marketing

accelerates Nike's digital transformation."[15] Nike's metaverse initiatives were designed to put Nike on a strategic and cohesive path, balancing pioneering efforts with caution.

In May 2019, Nike launched a digital sneaker in the videogame *Fortnite*. This was revealed to the public with two new characters in the game wearing Nike shoes from the Nike Jordan brand. While it's not clear if Nike shares profits on the "skins" sold, the partnership has continued with the release of more Nike outfits in the game. Eventually, this led the parent company of *Fortnite*, Epic Games, to forge a deal with the National Football League to bring jerseys into the game.

Nike also ventured into developing blockchain-compatible sneakers known as CryptoKicks. By selling shoes in the digital market, the company can attach digital assets to a physical product, verifying the owner and adding them to a digital locker. Nike also signed a deal with the videogame *Roblox* to reach younger audiences. Players can outfit their characters with Nike clothing and participate in games such as dodgeball in a venue where the floor is lava. At the end of 2021, Nike filed for trademarks for the company to make and sell virtual Nike clothing and sneakers in the metaverse, punctuated by the RTFKT acquisition.

Nike's metaverse initiatives can be mapped onto the three-horizon framework for marketing by analyzing how each of the initiatives contributes to the goals of generating revenues (Horizon 1), building brands (Horizon 2), and shaping new markets (Horizon 3). This mapping is shown in Figure 16.5, which illustrates that Nike has a good mix of initiatives across the three horizons of marketing.

Nike's digital team hoped that its "probe and learn" approach through a range of metaverse initiatives would help the company gain firsthand understanding of the promise and potential of the metaverse for its brand, revenues, customer relationships, new product development, and thought leadership. As a brand with a reputation for pioneering and innovative marketing, Nike had no choice but to stake a claim in the metaverse. Not doing so would put it behind the competition and potentially undermine its brand image. Therefore, Nike set itself apart as an early mover. Yet, it did not adopt as aggressive a stance as its competitor Adidas, which made cash investments by purchasing the Bored Ape Yacht Club NFT #8774 for $156,000[16] and buying a plot of virtual land inside The Sandbox, which it plans to fill with exclusive content and experiences.

Metaverse Initiatives	Horizon 1		Horizon 2	Horizon 3
	Generate Revenues	Expand Audience	Build Brand Equity	Shape New Markets
CryptoKicks	✓	✓	✓	✓
RTFKT	❓	✓	✓	✓
NIKELAND (Roblox)	✕	✓	✓	✕
Fortnite Digital Sneaker	❓	✓	✓	✕

FIGURE 16.5 Mapping Nike's Metaverse Initiatives to the Three Horizon Framework

Making Moves in the Metaverse

As marketers consider their own moves in the metaverse, they could conceivably follow Nike's path. Being an innovator, however, carries both benefits and potential risks. To illustrate, let's use the analogy of buying virtual land in the metaverse. It is possible to be among the first to make such an investment and reap the reward of significant appreciation. The flip side, though, is to buy land on the wrong platform and end up with a worthless asset. The same can be said for being a pioneer in the metaverse with a branding initiative. To achieve brand-building goals, marketers need to make the right moves on the right platforms. And they need to be careful to protect their brands from bad actors in the metaverse.

In summary, marketers need to approach the metaverse with a mixture of enthusiasm and caution. It is important for marketers to step back and ask what they really want to accomplish through their metaverse marketing initiatives and how aggressively they want to lead their industry or category. If a company's brand is positioned as an innovator, then the company needs to be a metaverse pioneer, as is the case with Nike. But for a more conservative brand, such as Toyota, the attitude would more likely be to wait and see until pioneering brands have shown what works and what doesn't and until the most promising use cases and platforms are better defined. For a slow and steady company, there is wisdom in letting others go first and being a follower.

This need not be an all-or-nothing proposition. Marketing in the metaverse can be a series of probes and pilots to gain experience and learn lessons from smaller investments. For example, a company such as Unilever might choose one of its many brands—such as its Axe line of personal care, aimed at young hipsters—and push it forward in the metaverse. Its Dove skincare line, however, has a very different brand reputation that might not be well suited for the metaverse. Marketing in the metaverse is not one size fits all, either within a company or across an industry. Companies and brands need to be true to who they are. The onus will be on marketers to understand the metaverse and to organize their metaverse marketing initiatives in a way that meshes with their business strategy and their company's culture.

Key Questions for Marketers

- What opportunities does the metaverse present for our company's growth, innovation, and brands?
- What alliances and partnerships should we leverage to pursue these opportunities?
- What controls or processes do we need to explore the opportunities and risks associated with the metaverse?
- Should we create a technology committee to evaluate these opportunities and risks?

- What policies or processes do we need to put in place with respect to digital assets and digital currencies?
- What are the risks and benefits of being an early adopter rather than a fast follower?
- What are our peers doing with respect to leveraging or investing in the metaverse?

Conclusion

The metaverse is the next generation of the internet experience, characterized by immersive, three-dimensional environments that can host a wide range of customer activities and experiences. In principle, the metaverse can be a powerful platform for marketers to engage with customers to drive revenues, build brands, and create thought leadership for their companies. However, the metaverse is a complex, confusing, and challenging space. Marketers must proceed with caution in placing their bets on metaverse platforms and initiatives. Marketers also must avoid the shiny object syndrome by linking their metaverse initiatives to their strategies for growth and brand building. Hopefully, this chapter will serve as a guide for marketers as they navigate the dynamic and uncertain landscape of the metaverse.

Author Biography

Mohan Sawhney is the associate dean for Digital Innovation and McCormick Foundation Professor at the Kellogg School of Management at Northwestern University. He is a globally recognized scholar, consultant, and speaker in innovation, product strategy, modern marketing, and AI strategy. He has co-authored seven management books, dozens of academic articles, 30 case studies, and two strategy simulations, and has created eight online executive education courses. He consults widely for leading technology companies and technology startup firms. Professor Sawhney holds a PhD in marketing from the Wharton School, an MBA from IIM Calcutta, and a B. Tech. from IIT Delhi. He received the Distinguished Alumni award from IIM Calcutta in 2016 and the Global Alumni Recognition Award from IIT Delhi in 2022.

PART 6

Designing Effective Distribution Channels

CHAPTER 17

Strategic Channel Management

Julie Hennessy and Jim Lecinski

This chapter provides an introduction to the important and dynamic field of marketing channels. Channels of distribution play a crucial role in value creation for both firms and customers. While target selection and positioning are initial centerpieces of a marketing strategy, market execution must also be thoughtfully, strategically grounded. Therefore, it is critical to think carefully about each piece of execution—product and service design, branding approaches, revenue capture, and the best way for your product to reach your customer.

In this chapter on strategic channel management, we will introduce you to the foundational concepts of the discipline. We will define exactly what we mean by channels of distribution, and explore how the addition of channel partners often increases the size and value of a market for a product. We will explore how two models, the survey of *customer service output demands* and the *channel map*, help marketers match the needs of their target customers with the channel structures they design for a business.

Next, we'll get to know two of the most frequently encountered channel partners as we explore the world of retailers and the roles played by wholesalers and distributors. We will gain a perspective on how retailers add value by providing a showcase for customer contact with brands. We will also explore the less visible and less understood worlds of wholesalers and distributors, and the strategies they employ to be much more than "middlemen."

Finally, we'll touch on two areas that have been particularly topical of late. We'll shine a light on the world of "direct to consumer" business strategies, where brand manufacturers choose to interface directly, without intermediaries, with their end customers. We'll explore the advantages, and limitations, of this approach. And finally, we'll take a detailed look at the interesting world of marketplaces, arenas designed to allow multiple vendors and multiple customers to come together, view, and transact, often in a virtual way.

There is a lot here to learn. Let's get started.

What Is a Channel and How Does It Create Value?

What do we mean by a *distribution channel*? The Merriam Webster Dictionary cites 12 different meanings for the word "channel"—12 different ways to define this word, if we are using it as a noun. So, there are plenty of reasons that you might be confused about exactly what we mean. There are definitions referring to channels of a river, channels as a means of communication, and channels as a pathway of electrical current. But what all these definitions have in common is the sense that channels are about connection.

Kellogg Professors Louis Stern and Anne Coughlan defined a channel as a set of interdependent organizations involved in the process of making a product or service available for consumption or use to a final consumer. This definition retains the sense of a channel as a means of connection, a conduit, or a pathway. The channel is a set of organizations that serve to connect a product manufacturer to its final purchaser or user.

Channels are necessary because the set of products or services that individual producers choose to make is often not the same as the set of products or services that customers would ideally like to view, compare, and select from. To that end, distribution channels serve to make available to the customer the right product, at the right place, at the right time. The channel adjusts assortment from what producers choose to make to what customers want to pick from. The channel moves products to places, physical and virtual, where customers want to research, buy, and use. And, the channel makes products available within the time frame that customers need.

Professors Stern and Coughlan also say that in this way, the channel can be thought of as a chain of activity that facilitates exchange and has its goal to maximize profit for the business overall. Chains of activity exist inside and outside of a firm. Within a firm, we might have activity to purchase raw materials, manufacturing activity, sales activity, and post-sale service activity. But these activities all reside within the legal boundaries of the firm.

When we talk about a channel of distribution, we are typically talking about activities conducted by separate legal entities—often a firm and other firms—in the service of connecting a manufacturer with its end users. These separate entities are called each other's channel partners—organizations that are both legally independent and achieve their goals when they work together as a system. At least in theory, these cooperating entities work together to make a business bigger, more profitable, and more competitively defendable than it would be without the shared effort. Of course, the practice is more complicated than the theory, but that is the interesting part.

Introducing the Channel Map

Take a look around you, wherever you're sitting, and find something that you've recently purchased. Maybe you've bought a new mobile phone, perhaps a new pair of shoes, or maybe that cup of coffee sitting on the desk next to you as you read. Think for a minute about the journey that product may have gone through in order to get from the point of production into your hands.

Perhaps you bought it directly from the manufacturer on their website. Or perhaps you bought it at a retail store in your neighborhood, maybe a Walmart or a local family shop you like. If you bought it from a small store, it probably sourced the product from a distributor, who in turn bought it from a manufacturer. And after you purchased, maybe you had this store deliver the product directly to your doorstep through a post-purchase "last-mile" deliverer.

These are all possible channel routes, or "routes to market," as they are often called. The route to market is the path a product follows from the point of production to the point of consumption. Your challenge as a business manager is to design the optimal route, the best pathway from point of production to point of consumption. Now, of course, there are many choices for this "go-to market" strategy, the blueprint used to deliver your firm's offerings to end consumers. The key will be to design a route to market in a way that conforms to your target customer's preferred mode and method of buying and receiving brand communications.

Let's take a deeper look into the go-to market choices that one global brand has made. The Stihl Company is a German manufacturer of chainsaws and other pieces of hand-held power equipment, including trimmers and blowers. The firm was founded in 1926 by Andreas Stihl, an important innovator in the early development of chainsaw manufacturing and production. Today, the company is still privately held and owned by one of the descendants of Andreas Stihl, with headquarters located near Stuttgart in

Germany. Stihl is one of the world's best-selling brands of chainsaws. It has annual revenue of about €4 billion, and its products are sold in 41 different countries.

If you want to buy a Stihl chainsaw in the United States, you'll need to know exactly how to find one. It may surprise you that you can't purchase most Stihl chainsaws at one of those giant big box hardware stores; nor can you buy them directly on Stihl's U.S. website. No, you will likely have to go in person to an authorized Stihl dealer store, usually a local hardware store or landscape supply store. There and only there will you find a dedicated section of the store devoted entirely to Stihl power products. Only there will you find store staff who are fully trained and educated in all of the latest Stihl products and models, so that they can answer any and every one of your questions. They can demonstrate the product for you, they can set it up for you after purchase, and they can even train you on how to safely use a Stihl chainsaw.

Now, if we were to visually depict the choices that the Stihl brand has made on how to bring its chainsaws from their factory, the point of production in Germany, to you at the point of consumption, we could draw and depict that as what we call a channel map (see Figure 17.1).

Channel maps are drawn from left to right. On the far left is the producer. Sometimes, this producer is called "the brand" or "the vendor" or "the supplier" or "the manufacturer." Typically, it's the producer that acts as "the channel captain." This channel captain takes a lead role in the decision making for and ownership of the channel for the product or service.

On the far right-hand side of our channel map is our end customer—the person, company, or entity who will ultimately buy and use our chainsaw. In between sits any intermediary entity like a distributor, wholesaler, reseller, or retailer. Intermediaries like wholesalers typically buy from manufacturers and then in turn sell to other channel intermediaries like a retail store. They typically don't sell to end customers and users. We'll learn much more about how these intermediaries operate and why you might want to consider including them in your channel ecosystem later in this chapter.

Of course, there are many different possible channel structures and, thus, many possible different channel maps. But the channel map is a tool you will use to illustrate your current channel and to lay out and evaluate possible new, improved route alternatives that you might be considering.

FIGURE 17.1   Channel Map

To describe the position or role of each participant in your channel, we'll use a river analogy—that is, we'll talk about a channel map in terms of a stream. Channel participants on the far left are said to be upstream, with the river flowing left to right. The end customer on the far right is considered to be downstream. Sitting in the middle between you and your downstream partners are intermediaries, whom we describe as sitting midstream.

With this analogy in mind, you should be able to draw a channel map for that product you were thinking about at the beginning of this chapter—that new smartphone, pair of shoes, or cup of coffee. You may be able to depict the specific route that this product took, how it got from the point of production at the factory all the way to your hands. Or, you may find that some of the route is a mystery to you, since some channel partners are more obvious to end consumers than others. We'll talk about these steps in the channel, both the ones you know and the ones you don't, in just a little while.

The Functions of a Channel

Let's think for a minute about why all these channel members exist. What do they do? And why would you need them? A strong and well-aligned channel system is an asset that's not easily replicated by other firms. To meet the needs of customers, the channel captain and channel partners together must perform the nine channel functions.

These channel functions include: carrying and holding your inventory; generating demand through sales activities; distributing the products to their ultimate end point of purchase; engaging in after-purchase service and support; providing information, training, and advice; and possibly even extending credit or financing to the other channel members. As the channel captain, it is your job to design a channel so that all of this work gets done (see Figure 17.2). Let's take a deeper look into each of the nine channel functions.

FIGURE 17.2 The Channel Ecosystem: Nine Key Functions

Physical Possession: This refers to the channel activities pertaining to the storage of goods, including the transportation between channel members. Surprisingly, even digital and service businesses face issues of physical possession. In the online billing business, firms have physical possession costs tied to the hosting of databases, and costs to maintain the data involved in these transactions.

Ownership: Often, physical possession and ownership costs move together, but not always: A channel partner can hold title to goods without having physical possession or can have physical possession without technically owning the goods. Frequently, firms refer to an "inventory holding cost," representing expenses tied both to physical possession and to ownership. Insurance costs, maintenance costs, and storage costs could all fall into these buckets.

Promotion: What are channel partners telling end buyers about the advantages of your product versus others? This could be physical selling, it could be media advertising, or it could be publicity. These are the activities that seek to increase the awareness and raise the attractiveness of your product.

Financing: Financing costs are inherent in any sale that moves from one level in the channel to another. Many buyers, but especially B2B buyers, care a whole lot about financing. Are you requiring payments in 30 days, 60 days, or 90 days? Are there discounts for early payments?

Negotiation: The negotiation function is often tied closely to the financing function. Who decides what the terms of sale will be? Are you doing that? Or is a distributor or intermediary doing that?

Risk: Risk and long-term credit contracts between a distributor and the end user may specify some price guarantees over time for future delivery of products at a certain price. These contracts specify who holds risk should the market price of the merchandise change as it passes through the channel. This function is of crucial importance in commodity markets where the value of goods fluctuates both widely and quickly.

Ordering: Who will take the orders and bear the cost of taking the orders? Who owns the data about customers and their orders? Is that data shared across the channel or guarded jealously? Increasingly, the data about customer identity and purchase behavior is an important asset worth fighting over.

Payment: Who takes payment, holds cash, and absorbs risk when customers or other channel partners do not pay?

Information sharing: Information and expertise are crucial assets in most businesses. Who is the product expert responsible for answering the questions of the end customer before and after purchase? Who is the customer expert with intimate knowledge of customers, their problems, and why they buy what they buy? In many businesses, the party with the info has an enormous advantage.

There is a lot of work to be done in a channel. The job of a channel captain—negotiating a system of who will do what, when they will do it, and how they will be compensated—is not easy. Keeping members of the channel believing that they are fairly compensated for the roles they play and work they do is even harder. Ideally, each channel partner's level of compensation in the channel ecosystem should reflect its degree of participation: how much work they do, and how much value they're creating in your channel map. This is known by marketers as the *equity principle*.

You may have heard that famous phrase, "We've eliminated the middle-man to pass the savings on to you." As you can now see, it's often not as easy as that. Sure, you can certainly eliminate any middleman or any intermediary, but not the functions that they were performing. As the channel captain, you always have the option to either add, remove, or substitute a channel member in your channel map. However, the crucial functions that your customers require still must be performed.

When you remove a member from the channel, someone else must absorb the work they were doing. This could be the channel captain, someone in the chain, or even the end customer. This is what marketers refer to as "the iron law of distribution." It doesn't matter who performs the function, but someone has to do it.

If you eliminate that middleman, maybe hoping to capture some margin or pass along the savings, that is great. But don't forget that you need to fig-ure out who absorbs the functions that the middleman was performing. And, you'll need to adjust the compensation within the channel to reflect these changes. These are the things you must keep in mind in designing an optimal channel system.

Not impossible, certainly. But as you now see, it's not an easy job.

Understanding Service Output Demands

You've learned a lot already. You know about drawing channel maps and the functions of a channel. But to make decisions about the optimal channel struc-ture, to build a channel map that will result in real competitive advantage, we need one more thing. It turns out, we really can't discuss what functions will be important in a channel until we define what customer we're trying to make that channel design perfect for.

Let's start with a little example. Have you ever bought something from a vending machine? What did you buy? How did you feel about your experi-ence? We're all used to vending machines for a bottle of Coke or some Oreos, but how about for headphones or chargers?

If you ask most people where they buy their tech supplies, I'm sure a vending machine would not be their first answer. But I bet some of you have seen these in an airport. And I'm guessing that most of you can think of an occasion when you'd be glad to see this. What situation, or "need state," comes to mind?

Maybe you're in an airport with two hours between flights, and you want to join a meeting at work. You want to connect on your smartphone, but you don't want to share the contents of the call with everyone else at the gate over your speaker. Problem is, you left your earbuds at home. Or maybe you're about to get on an 11-hour international flight, and you realize you don't have the power cord for your laptop—and you've got a big presentation that needs to be created on the plane and done by the time you land. We've all been there.

To decide how to optimize a channel map, we need to have a target customer in mind. This target may be defined as a certain type of person, a certain type of need state, or both. But we must have a clear picture of a business target before we can have a useful conversation about optimizing a business channel.

Specifically, we are interested in what we call the *service demands* of the target. Just as there were a set of nine functions of the channel to consider, we have a set of six customer service demands that are important to think about.

Let us share with you a useful way to organize this customer information: It's called the Service Output Segmentation Matrix, shown in Figure 17.3. Across the top, you'll see a set of potential customer service demands listed. These include things like bulk breaking, spatial convenience, and delivery speed. Along the side, brand managers list different potential target segments they are considering. Sometimes I use this chart to show how different targets have different needs, a sort of compare and contrast. Other times, I use just one line to describe a single target on which I want to focus.

Let's go back to our example of an airport vending machine and your needs as a customer on a business trip. In this context, we'll look at the six service demands and rate your needs as a customer as high, medium, or low.

SERVICE OUTPUT DEMAND						
Segment Name/ Descriptor	Bulk Breaking	Spatial Convenience	Delivery/ Waiting Time	Assortment/ Variety	Customer Service	Information Sharing
1.						
2.						
3.						
4.						
5.						

FIGURE 17.3 The Service Output Segmentation Matrix

We'll start with bulk breaking. Your need for bulk breaking is high. I'm betting you probably aren't looking for a volume discount on a case of earbuds in that situation. You just want to buy a single one of whatever it was you forgot to pack, whether it's earbuds or a charger.

Spatial convenience? Well, here your needs are super high. You need something right here, right now. In fact, you want to stay within earshot of your gate for when they call for boarding. You'll even pay extra to get it at this vending machine instead of backtracking and heading out of the gate area into the main concourse.

Delivery and waiting time? You've got to be kidding. You're not waiting. The meeting starts in five minutes; you need it now. So, in this situation, with your timing needs, even Amazon same-day shipping is far too long.

Assortment and variety? Well, we know that normally you're a comparison shopper; you would carefully consider a few different product options and debate between a few different competing retailers for where to buy the item. But in this situation, you're just happy that they have one that works for you in the vending machine, right then and right there.

Customer service? Again not here, not from this vending machine in this situation. If this cord will work, get me through this call, get me through this trip—hey, I'm good. It's probably going to go into the bottom of my laptop bag as a spare after that.

Information sharing? No. There's no blue-shirted Best Buy salesperson at the vending machine to educate me and talk me through the different options in that moment. But I don't need or miss them.

Is this vending machine how Best Buy will do most of its business? Of course not. Most of their business will run either through their physical stores or their website. But in this case, it's an additional option for travelers in a specific need state: the busy, non-price-sensitive customer in the gate area with an urgent need. It's a perfect match between that customer's service demands and the channel structure. It works for the business, it works for the customer, and that's the goal.

The Channel Partners

Now that we understand the function of the channel, the work that channel partners do, and how this has to dovetail with the needs of our specific target segments, let's take a deep dive into the worlds of some of our most frequent channel partners. We'll start with the retailers. More than any other, this is the channel partner that many of us feel like we know well. We'll talk about the major categories of retailers, and we'll work on mapping each of these categories to the service output demands that they satisfy best.

While retailers are both highly visible and useful to consumers, sometimes there is work to be done in the channel that neither the vendor nor the retailer is equipped to do effectively or efficiently. In this case, we often utilize other less visible intermediaries like distributors and wholesalers. We'll take a look at the value that these intermediaries provide. And finally, we'll take a brief look at some of the post-sale intermediaries focused on delivery that are becoming more frequent parts of the channel.

Retailers and What They Do

Let's start our deep dive into the world of retailing with a definition. What do we mean by a retailer? For our purposes, let's note that a retailer is usually an independent business. While there are times that a vendor like Apple owns its own stores, retailers typically are separate legal entities from the brands they represent. Retailers source products either from a vendor like Weber Grills or from a wholesaler, and then sell the products to an end buyer either online or offline. Generally, we think of these end users as individual consumers.

There are certainly exceptions. Home Depot sells to contractors along with individual homeowners. Costco was originally set up to meet the needs of small business club members. But while there are exceptions, to understand the core of retailing, you should generally think of retailers as separate legal entities that purchase from vendors or their wholesalers and sell to end users.

In understanding the global retail landscape, it's useful to think about the basic types of retail formats that exist. So, let's look at the 10 major retail formats. While the individual retailers often differ from one country to another, I think you'll find these classifications familiar across most markets. The 10 retail formats are: food, drug, mass, club, convenience, dollar, hypermarket, specialty, big box, and department.

Many of these will be familiar to you. There is the food format, like Kroger's or Loblaws in Canada. There are drug stores, like Walgreens or Boots, in the UK. Examples of mass merchandisers are Walmart or Target. There are club stores like Costco and Sam's Club. Convenience stores are often, but not always, connected to gasoline, like 7-Eleven and Lawson in Japan. Dollar stores often put dollar in their name as in Dollar Tree, Dollar General, or Family Dollar. The hypermarket format is a sort of hybrid, a marriage of a discount department store and a grocery store, like the Walmart Supercenter and Meijer in the United States and Big Bazaar stores in India. Specialty stores are category specialists like Sephora in beauty and Lululemon for athleisure wear. Big box stores specialize, too, but in a larger format: Dick's Sporting Goods is an example of a big box, or even Wayfair, a sort of virtual big box in home furnishings. And finally, an early and lately not-so-healthy format, the department store like Macy's or Harrods.

While there's something neat and clean about these 10 bucket classifications, it's worth noting that real life doesn't fit completely into boxes. There's some hybridization going on here: Just like brick-and-mortar players have opened e-commerce operations, pure online players are opening physical stores. There's also some blurring of the edges of these classifications.

As a brand owner considering what format of retailer to partner with, it's important to think again about our target. That handy service demands matrix we built can be a big help here. Does our target need bulk breaking, or are they willing to buy in large quantities? Do they need help and advice, or is self-serve just fine? You'll see a little cheat sheet we built for you that matches the format with the services they provide best. With just a glance, you'll see that if your target wants to buy in small quantities, the club stores will not be your friend. And if immediate access is important, you're probably going to be a fan of convenience stores.

You'll also notice at the left of the chart some commentary on the cost focus of each of these operations. Specialty and department stores maximize profit through margin, and grocery stores and dollar stores maximize profit through a focus on the volume of sales.

Across the buckets, what do these retailers actually do? Well, let's start with the most obvious. They make their product available nearer, virtually or physically, to the consumer or end user than where the manufacturer would probably want to produce the product. A company like P&G might manufacture Tide or Pampers at four or five plants across the country. But consumers want to be able to buy these products within five minutes of their house or order it for delivery tomorrow. Furthermore, P&G also wants to ship great big shrink-wrapped pallets of product. But if you want to buy less than that, even at Costco, you need a retailer. You also want an assortment that's different from what any single manufacturer chooses to make and sell, all assembled together in one place. Light bulb manufacturers never make cheese and mascara, but we expect to be able to buy all of these products together at the grocery store. Finally, retailers provide customer service. They explain and demonstrate how products work, they help consumers sort through options, they accept returns. Retailers also complete the process of turning a prospect into a customer, answering questions and closing the deal.

It's interesting that while we think of companies like General Mills, P&G, Unilever, and Miller/Coors as expert consumer marketers, they actually have very little direct contact with end-user consumers. These companies sell more than 95% of their goods through retailers. And in terms of direct knowledge of consumers—what, why, and how they buy, and even what they looked at and didn't buy—retailers often have the deepest access to this information, especially the online retailers.

Clearly retailers get a lot of value from their vendors. But if you ask the vendors, they will comment that they are definitely paying for that value provided. And in country after country, the retail landscape has consolidated. Let me give you an example. Forty years ago, the top grocery store in California was Safeway. In Boise, Idaho, it was Albertsons; in Chicago, it was Jewel; and it was Star Market in Boston. Today, those brands are all part of the Albertsons Companies, with a presence in 34 states. They compete with national grocery players, something that didn't really exist before, like Whole Foods, Trader Joe's, and Walmart's presence in grocery.

Across format after format, stores have built national and multinational footprints, and these bigger retailer players have more power to negotiate with vendors. Contracts are negotiated between vendors and their retail partners that detail myriad aspects of the relationship. Depending on the relative power of the vendor brand versus the retailer, either side may be able to dictate terms. When a brand like Apple works with a retailer like Target, they define exactly how the retailer will price, display product, merchandise, and promote. They also reserve the right to give Target access to some of their products and not others. Apple even competes with Target directly by running its own stores, both physical and online. On the other hand, when Target negotiates with weaker brands, especially those that are not category leaders with strong consumer loyalty, Target holds the power in the relationship and calls the shots.

How Retail Buyers Think

Just as it was important to have deep insight about your end user, it also helps to understand how your buyer thinks and operates. It turns out that retail buyers, sometimes called "merchants," have a challenging job. Each buyer has a specific scope to their responsibilities. For example, at Lowe's there's a buyer managing the "shower" category and another focused on kitchen faucets. If you are a vendor like Kohler, these buyers are very important people in your world.

To win as a brand, it's important to make your retailer partners successful. So, let's take a look at the KPIs (key performance indicators) that your buyer and your buyer's boss are watching.

Clearly, retail buyers care about the dollar (or euro or yen) volume of your products that they sell. They track the average number of items carried and typical price points. But there is a sea of retail terms that you are likely to encounter as well. Let's provide a glossary of the terms you are likely to hear in a discussion with a buyer.

There's quite a bit of language with which to become familiar.

Let's start at the top. *Off-invoice promotions* are monies that are available to decrease the effective price a retailer pays compared to the full invoice sticker price for your items. Usually these off-invoice incentives are provided for some sort of retailer performance, but sometimes they're so ubiquitous that large retailers rarely pay the full invoice price for anything.

Billbacks are similar but calculated after a performance period. In a sense, they give a retailer the right to "bill back" the vendor if they achieve some sort of rolling month, quarter, or annual volume goal. Think of this as akin to some sort of rolling cashback offer that you might have on a credit card, depending on what you spent.

Free goods are just that. These are most frequently given for a new product when the brand is seeking to get authorization and distribution of a new item. They offer the first case or cases free if they are ordered by a specific date, often tied to the start of advertising for the item.

Also tied to advertising are *co-op ad allowances*. Here, a vendor is paying for some of the retailer's cost of advertising the vendor's items. With display allowances, vendors pay for additional or preferential placement in a store. For example, products move on average about three times as fast on an end aisle display compared to regular shelf placement. Therefore, if you want your product on an end aisle, your retailer may want to charge you for that. Online retailers do the same sort of thing, charging for preferred placement of your item in response to a consumer search.

Sales drives are periods of particular importance for brands. For instance, beer distributors will set up incentives for volume pushes just before big events like the Super Bowl or the World Cup. Inventory financing is a way to encourage vendors to take on and hold inventory of your product and pay for it later. This decreases the retailer's risk of tying up capital in inventory.

Back to new products, *slotting allowances* were originally conceived as money paid by a brand to cover the cost of a vendor setting up a slot for a new product in their warehouse. However, as retailers have become more powerful, they've been able to charge slotting tolls far in excess of these actual costs. Like free goods and inventory financing, slotting covers some of the risk for a retailer on newer and unproven items.

Finally, if you hear the term *street money*, that's just a general "all other" bucket of funds. At the end of a meeting with your buyer, don't be surprised if you hear an open-ended question like, "Anything else you got for me today?" Or "Anything else to sweeten the deal?" After all, it doesn't cost your buyer anything to ask.

If all of this sounds to you like a lot to negotiate, you're right. And if it sounds expensive, you're right about that, too. Unless you have a very, very strong brand that your retailer feels they absolutely need to survive, your full invoice price to the retailer turns out to be just a starting point for the negotiations. For many brands, the budget that they have for "trade marketing"—dollars spent on channel partner incentives—is even larger than their budget for consumer advertising, dollars spent to try to create demand with end consumers.

There's a terminology for this. Trade incentives are called *push efforts*, since they are money spent to help "push" the product through the channel by incenting the trade. Consumer demand-building spending activities are called *pull efforts*, since they create demand and encourage consumers to "pull" product through the channel.

A brand like Apple has built such strong consumer equity that it will pay almost nothing in push for retailer performance. That's because it's more important for Walmart to have Apple products than it is for Apple to be in Walmart. This pull/push trade-off is a big strategic issue for brands. The stronger and more uniquely positioned the brand, the less they have to pay in push incentives, even to large and powerful retailers. This, in turn, leaves more of their spending to devote to quality product development and communication, which in turn make the brand even stronger. On the other hand, a brand that is less distinctive has to spend a lot of its available resources on trade push incentives, reducing the money available to improve the product and communication. For a weaker brand, this can become a vicious circle, as the brand becomes more and more beholden to their channel partners to stay afloat.

The Less Visible Channel Partners: Wholesalers and Distributors

While retailers are the most visible and best known of all manufacturers' channel partners, they are certainly not the only ones. So next, let's take a look at some of the less visible and less obvious intermediaries. We start by talking about those partners that sit pre-sale or upstream between your loading dock and your retailer. Later, we turn to the post-sale or downstream intermediaries who go to work after the sale has been made.

As an introduction to these players, let's take a look at an example from the food business. Right now, no segment of the food business is growing faster than plant-based meat substitutes. While companies like Morningstar Farms have been in this category for over a decade, newcomers Beyond Meats and Impossible Foods have recently set this area on fire by engineering products that more closely mirror the taste, texture, and even juiciness of real meat.

After success in the burger area, Beyond Meat and Impossible Foods are expanding to other meat categories like ground meat and sausages. They are distributing their products in grocery stores but also through restaurants. Restaurants are an important channel for these companies since they provide individual consumers with an easy, low-risk way to try products themselves before buying them for the whole family.

Let's take a closer look at the Impossible Foods distribution system for the foodservice channel. For the purposes of this discussion, our retailers will be restaurants, and we'll think about how Impossible Foods meets the needs of both chain and individual outlets. Indeed, most big food companies have both a consumer or B2C arm and a foodservice or B2B arm. Products selling on the foodservice side don't come in two- or four-burger packages; they come in 100- or 200-burger packs. That's much bigger than you would see even at a club store like Costco.

To add to the challenge, there's a landscape of literally tens of thousands of restaurants to serve. If you can forgive the pun, it would be simply impossible for the Impossible Food sales force to call on every one of those restaurants, one at a time. So, to do the impossible, they work with an intermediary, a big food broker called Sysco. Impossible Foods gets its products listed in the Sysco catalog. Sysco supplies the vast majority of independent restaurants in the United States and Canada. If you have been to a restaurant in your neighborhood, most likely it is a customer of Sysco's.

One of my favorite restaurants near the Northwestern campus in Evanston is called Cross-Rhodes. They get a delivery from Sysco several times a week. Sysco brings napkins, forks, cleaning supplies, buns, and yes, Impossible burgers right to the back door of Cross-Rhodes. If we were to draw a channel map for this, Sysco would be a pre-sale or pre-retail intermediary, sitting between Impossible Foods and its restaurant customers as a wholesaler.

However, let's change the scenario for a second and consider a situation where you don't have time to stop in at Cross-Rhodes. So, instead you decide to have them deliver a burger to your home, your hotel, or campus. In this case, Cross-Rhodes will use a different intermediary in addition to Sysco. Looking back at our channel map, you'll also notice another intermediary, post-sale or post-retail, which gets involved after the cash register rings.

You may be familiar with some of these post-sale sale intermediaries, like DoorDash, Uber Eats, Seamless, and Grubhub. They are all in the business of what we call "last-mile distribution." More and more of these players are popping up all the time, and we talk about them later. But for now, let's get to know the world of pre-sale partners, wholesalers, and distributors.

Again, let's start with some definitions. While the terms are often used interchangeably, a wholesaler is legally a separate partner from the manufacturer that sits between the producer and their retail partners. While there are some exceptions, wholesalers typically sell to other businesses but not to consumers or end users. They are a link in the chain, but are not the end of the chain. Wholesalers typically sell the physical inputs that go into a retail business. For a restaurant like Cross-Rhodes, that could be everything from shelving and lighting fixtures to refrigerator cases, to the burgers, ketchup, and buns that we were talking about before. But a wholesaler might also provide services—things like inventory management software or store design consulting or even accounting and cleaning services.

So, you might be wondering, what's the difference between a wholesaler and a distributor? Well, we'll answer your question, but we're also going to tell you that, some of the time, our answer doesn't turn out to be right. As we mentioned before, wholesalers tend to sit between a producer and their retail (in this case, restaurant) clients. Distributors are similar but tend to sit between a producer and their industrial clients. But we have to be honest with you, sometimes these terms are used interchangeably.

Let's identify some examples of world-class wholesalers and distributors. A great wholesaler example is McKesson. We're betting that most of you haven't heard of McKesson. Remember how we talked about the intermediaries being sort of invisible to end users? Although many of you haven't heard of McKesson, it ranks in the top 10 of *Fortune* magazine's Fortune 500 firms and is the world's largest drug distributor. Multiple times a week, a McKesson truck shows up at each Walgreens store, full of plastic totes of Tylenol, Mucinex, and all of the prescription drugs that Walgreens is likely to need.

McKesson buys in enormous quantities from J&J, AstraZeneca, and Pfizer. They break those huge bulk purchases into small quantities that individual drug stores want. Think about it, drugstores are expected to carry hundreds or even thousands of over-the-counter or prescription items—or have access to them within 24 hours. And yet the space in the store to hold inventory is very small. So, it's McKesson's job to make sure Walgreens can get you any prescription your doctor may write, in any dosage size, either immediately or within hours. After all, your life may depend on this reliable supply. McKesson does other things for Walgreens, like providing software systems that monitor dangerous drug interactions so that a pharmacist is alerted when one of a customer's meds might interact with another, even if the two drugs were prescribed by different doctors. This protects patients' safety and also protects the retailer, Walgreens, from lawsuits. McKesson can command a margin for this unique value they provide.

On the distributor side, we see similar patterns, but serving industrial customers. One of the many things that wholesalers and distributors have in common is that they usually take title (or ownership) to the goods that they sell. Inventory is held in their warehouses until they resell it to an industrial user for their plant or factory. In a sense, the McKesson of the industrial world is W. W. Grainger, another Fortune 500 player. If we take a look, we'll see Grainger performing every one of the channel functions we discussed for channel partners. They educate customers, they promote vendors' products, and they finance purchases for customers. They help customers manage and track their inventory. They even help industrial customers improve and innovate by facilitating learning across noncompeting industrial customers.

These added-value services are absolutely crucial for wholesalers and distributors. It's important that the intermediary bring something to the party that neither the producer nor the retailer can do for themselves. Otherwise, an intermediary is nothing but a middleman, ripe for disintermediation. We're sure you've heard firms claim to "Eliminate the middleman and pass the savings on to you." If a channel intermediary produces no added value, this disintermediation becomes possible.

On the other hand, when intermediaries like McKesson and Grainger fulfill unique functions for the channel, they add more value to the whole of the business than they extract in margin and become crucial to the total business profit pool. That, of course, is their goal.

So, as a brand owner, when do you want a pre-sale intermediary? Well, when they do something that is worth the 5% to 25% margin they are likely to take: when they have contacts, relationships, and expertise that you need; when they combine your products with other products that your customers will want to buy together; when they save you or your customers time and effort; or when they speed your entry into a new market. Good wholesalers and distributors may be low profile, but they do all of these important things.

The New Channel Partners: Last-Mile Distributors

Finally, we take a look at the post-sale channel partners. These players provide their services after a product has gotten into retail, after the consumer is aware of the product, and after the consumer buys the product. Post-sale distributors are particularly in the news now since technology-enabling and context changes like the pandemic have made them particularly relevant. Instacart, Shipt, Postmates, DoorDash, and Uber Eats quickly went from niche to mainstream as the pandemic lockdowns encouraged consumers to stay at home and order delivery. But many consumers have found that they enjoy the convenience and time savings that comes from these services and have stayed on board as the restrictions eased.

This is not just a North American phenomenon. In China, Meituan (formerly Meituan Dian Ping) has built a massive food delivery business with a bigger goal ahead to be the omnipresent "Amazon of services." In Delhi, India, a company called Pidge is offering same-day, on-demand delivery services for both food and office supplies, claiming to be the fastest courier service solution in the market. These are businesses that create a bridge from the point of sale to the point of final use or consumption.

Companies from local pizza places and florists to appliance and furniture stores have been performing delivery, installation, and setup services for decades. But, historically, these were performed by employees of the retailers themselves. What is newer is the growth of these across-retailer, tech-enabled, last-mile-focused businesses. These businesses function in different ways. With some, delivery is paid for entirely by the end consumer. With others, most of the margin covering delivery comes from the retailer.

With the explosion in demand for these services brought on by the pandemic, there's been a lot of discussion about just where that piece of the margin will come from. In cases where the end user is willing to pay for the convenience of delivery, there's more margin to go around and room for the delivery partner to add value without the retailer being hurt. However, increasingly massive players like Amazon have trained consumers to expect delivery for free.

When a consumer wants delivery and expects it for free, this puts retailers (or restaurants) in an interesting margin situation. If they refuse to offer the service, a consumer may go to a competitor. If they pay for the delivery out of their own margin, that might be the difference between making money and not. So, the question of who pays for these newly expected delivery services has become a bit of an existential issue for these low-margin players. This will truly be an interesting area to watch in the years ahead.

Trending Channel Structures: Direct-to-Consumer Models and Marketplaces

With a good sense of the nature and contributions of the most frequent channel partners in your mind, we can talk about two significant trends in channel structure. We start with a look at what's driving the shift toward direct-to-consumer (DTC) or direct-to-consumer routes to market. From large, established brands to a myriad of new startups, firms are jealously protecting their relationships with the customer and rethinking decisions about whether to share that route to the end user with intermediaries. We take a look at why this is happening and the world of DTC.

Then, we look at firms that take this close customer connection to another level—connecting with both the downstream end users and the upstream suppliers as customers. This is called the *marketplace model*, where firms in the middle function as virtual matchmakers, helping potential vendors find customers and customers find vendors that meet their unique needs.

The Direct-to-Consumer Route

We've talked a lot about the help that intermediaries, from wholesalers to distributors to retailers, can provide, bringing their market knowledge, proximity, relationships, and skills to grow the entire profit pool. This certainly is often the case. However, in the past decade there has been a sea change in the opposite direction, with firms increasingly deciding it's worth the work to be the sole owner of that connection to the end user. So now, we examine this trend toward direct-to-consumer routes to market.

At a basic level, channel partners help a lot. They fill their warehouses, catalogs, and websites with our products. They hold inventory and shift assortment from what we want to design and make as manufacturers to the selection that our end users want to see and compare. But we also explored more advanced ways that intermediaries can help, with sophisticated service additions that justify margin and protect against disintermediation. Well, it turns out there's a challenge here. The more important the intermediaries make themselves, the more dependent vendors become on them. And at a certain point, this dependency actually causes some concern.

There's a trade-off—a yin and yang, so to speak—between help and control. As a firm, I might carefully employ consumer insights to design a perfect product. But, if my channel partners display it in the wrong way, or message in a way that's inconsistent with my positioning, or price it in a way that destroys value, then they can do a lot of damage. So, I might decide that the only way to get a job done right is to do it myself. Certainly, it's a lot of work, a ton of investment, but I can reap what I sow, to quote scripture. And lately this has been going on, in biblical proportions.

A look at the business press will reveal a lovefest with DTC models. It's been the inspiration for the birth of literally thousands of startups. But it's not just the startups. The DTC trend is also being embraced by large, established, formerly heavy intermediary-using players.

A great example of this is the mega brand and master marketer Nike. In the early days, Nike was built on a set of one-to-one relationships with a very focused target market. Phil Knight and Bill Bowerman were obsessed with the performance needs of serious competitive runners. And Jeff Johnson, their first employee, literally drove his Volkswagen van from track meet to track meet, selling shoes to the track meet competitors. He used a set of paper index cards to detail each athlete's contact information, preferences, and shoe size. Think of this as a prehistoric version of the dataset that Amazon has about each of us today. Like startups today, Nike built awareness and a brand reputation with a highly involved target market as a starting place. But as Nike grew, it used a network of wholesalers and retailers to scale.

At this point in the story, both the specialty running shoe stores and the sporting goods big boxes played a central role. Nike carefully curated a brand reputation as the enabler of serious athletes with some of sports' winningest as spokespeople, but channel partners made the brand available and ubiquitous to everyday athletes and wannabes alike.

However, Nike is pivoting its strategy. While Nike still sells over two-thirds of its volume through the channel, much of its internal focus is now on selling direct. Nike's multiple apps work to build engagement with consumers at different stages of the customer journey, from feeding the intrigue of sneaker fandom and facilitating the experience of participating in sports to shopping and purchasing product.

Nike has opened its own owner-operated stores in several formats—from big city museums for the brand, to stores right-sized for neighborhoods, to outlet stores. These compete directly with retailers like Foot Locker and Dick's Sporting Goods. In e-commerce, Nike tried but decided against distribution through Amazon, instead focusing on its own Nike.com site to better control the experience and collect consumer data.

While non-Nike-owned retailers still account for the majority of revenue, Nike increasingly tries to serve its best, most valuable customers directly. Their newest and most hype-worthy products are sold only in their direct channels. Better still, they know these customers better, with end-to-end information about their interests, their purchases, and even their day-to-day participation in sports. They view this information base and relationship intimacy as a key competitive advantage.

We talk more in the next chapter about how to integrate these various formats and channels into an "omnichannel" customer experience.

The Online Marketplace Platforms and Amazon

Although the trend toward direct-to-consumer business models is fascinating, one cannot discuss the world of channels today without taking a good look at the marketplace model, and Amazon in particular. For almost every company, there are "Amazon impacts." Either we buy from them as a supplier, or we sell through them as a channel to market, or we fear them as a competitor, or we hear the expectations they have set reflected in the demands of our customers: "Amazon offers next-day delivery; why can't you do that?" Let's start by defining what we mean by an online marketplace.

What we are talking about in marketplaces is a form of e-commerce, so we are primarily focused on digital paths to market. A marketplace is a platform that connects buyers and sellers within a single system where they may purchase, sell, rent, swap, or negotiate for products and services. These platforms can be B2C, B2B, B2G, or all of these. Think about it: Amazon sells Clorox wipes to single households but also carburetor parts to repair shops. Platforms can be horizontal, selling a wide range of general merchandise, or vertical, serving a specific category like hotels.

There are two key features that define an online marketplace platform. The first is that they are multi-vendor. This means that there are many different sellers trading on the same platform. This is different from the **Hyatt.com** website that just sells rooms from Hyatt's own properties. Second, an online marketplace platform allows you to buy or complete your transaction without leaving the platform and going to another site.

Now, there's a subclassification of models that we should discuss—in a sense, two flavors of marketplaces. There are those that act as marketplace only, where the marketplace itself doesn't have its own horse in the race. These marketplaces are simply an arena inviting third-party sellers and buyers to come in and facilitating their meeting one another. Etsy and eBay fit into this classification. But there are also marketplaces that, in a way, play both sides of the fence, and that's what Amazon does. In this case, the platform both hosts other retailers and acts as a retailer itself. Amazon both owns the stadium and has a team on the field.

There are lots of marketplaces all around the world. We're showing you a whole bunch here. We'll bet that you know some of these, and not the others. Some are vertical, and some are horizontal; some are global, and some are regional. You'll see several of the Alibaba platforms here like Ali Express, Tmall, and Taobao. They are huge and quickly growing. PayPay Mall and Rakuten are from Japan, Zalando is in the fashion business in the EU, Mercadolibre is in Latin America, Flipkart is in India. And right in the center there's Amazon.

If you're a brand manager or channel manager for a business, what interests you about a marketplace? Well, several things, really. The first is just that there is a lot of traffic there, and there's something to say for being where people already are. It's really the equivalent of a mega mall. The second is speed to market. There's more to it than this; many decisions are about exactly "how" you might partner with Amazon, although, actually, a vendor can set itself up to sell on Amazon in a couple of hours. Marketplaces including Amazon, offer a mix of options on that control versus help continuum. Depending on your choices, Amazon can do almost everything for you. If you pay Amazon to do it, they will advertise your products, handle packing, fulfillment, and returns, and even figure out the optimal pricing. Or if you prefer, you can be more hands-on and maintain more control—again, that trade-off of help versus control we were talking about earlier.

While there are certainly things about marketplaces that interest vendors, there are also concerns. As is true with any intermediary, when you work with Amazon, you lose some control over the customer experience. Placing your product on Amazon is not like Apple putting its products in its own stores, where they can curate everything from the way a product is displayed, to the way an Apple genius interacts with you, to exactly how you will pay for and receive your product. On Amazon, there's some homogeneity about how all the different products are displayed, how reviews are shown, and how you pay.

In addition, if your product does well, Amazon may even create its own private label, an Amazon Basics version of your product. And it will make sure consumers see theirs first. Finally, Amazon and its vendors often fight over the customer and purchase data. Does this belong to the marketplace? Amazon thinks so. Or to the vendor? This "who owns the customer data" issue is very important and differs from marketplace to marketplace. So, in dealing with any mega-marketplace, from Amazon to Alibaba, it's important to be careful. The devil is in the details.

Conclusion

In this chapter, you were introduced to the concept of the marketing channel and the roles that channel captains and partners play in the creation of value both for firms and for customers. You now have a sense of the functions of the channel and how to think about the service needs of target customers. You've learned to draw a channel map and to evaluate how different route-to-market alternatives might meet the needs of your target.

You've also gained some insight into retailers and the roles they play, as well as wholesalers, distributors, and post-sale intermediaries. You've learned about the value these players can add, but also about the trade-offs firms face between maximizing their own control versus getting help from others.

And, finally, you've considered some news in the market, some recently prevalent changes in distribution strategies that firms are choosing. You understand some of the rationale behind firms' decisions to "do it themselves" and emphasize direct-to-consumer models—controlling the interactions with the consumer and collecting rich data. You've also glimpsed the globally growing role of marketplaces, arenas where buyers and sellers come together online.

Channels of distribution is a dynamic field, complex and always changing. But this is a good start toward understanding the foundations of channel decisions today.

Author Biographies

Julie Hennessy is clinical professor of marketing at the Kellogg School of Management at Northwestern University. She teaches Marketing Management, Marketing Strategy for Growth and Defense, and Marketing Consulting Lab. She is also actively involved in executive education, with recent work with McDonald's, Coca-Cola, Crate & Barrel, Textron, UPS, Wayfair, Uber, John Deere, Nike, Athletico, Medtronic, and AbbVie. Professor Hennessy twice received Kellogg's prestigious Lavengood Professor of the Year award and has also been a frequent recipient of Student Impact and the Core Marketing professor awards. She has written numerous business cases that are used in top business schools around the world.

Jim Lecinski is clinical associate professor of marketing at the Kellogg School of Management at Northwestern University. He teaches popular courses on Marketing Strategy and Omnichannel Marketing. His teaching has been recognized with the Sidney J. Levy Teaching Award and the L.G. Lavengood Outstanding Professor of the Year Award. Jim is a recognized expert, in-demand consultant, and keynote speaker with over 30 years of marketing industry experience, including a notable 12-year career at Google, where he was vice president of Customer Solutions for the Americas. Professor Lecinski's seminal book *Winning the Zero Moment of Truth* has been read by over 300,000 marketers worldwide and was featured in the *New York Times*. His second book, *The AI Marketing Canvas*, was published by Stanford University Press and has been named a top AI book and a top business book of 2022.

CHAPTER 18

Go-to-Market Omnichannel Design

Jim Lecinski

This chapter examines how the marketing manager can effectively knit together a collection of the channels described in the previous chapter to deliver customers with a superior, integrated experience called an "omnichannel."

First, we define exactly what we mean by omnichannel. The omnichannel is a relatively new concept in marketing, coming to the fore only within the last decade. Because of its newness and because the word omnichannel is often imbued with multiple meanings, we begin with a clear articulation of the concept.

Armed with this foundational understanding of omnichannel, we will consider an example of a brand delivering an omnichannel experience, the financial services company H&R Block, and dissect the two main elements required to deliver such an experience. Each element will in turn be further examined. Taken together, these two elements offer a roadmap for the marketing manager wishing to create and operate an omnichannel brand experience, which will be illustrated with a second example of an omnichannel brand, the automotive company Subaru.

Many brands whose channels are not currently knit together may wish to embark on an omnichannel transformation. Doing so successfully is neither easy nor quick and is often fraught with missteps, setbacks, and even failures. Thus, in the last section of this chapter we consider some of the managerial implications and imperatives surrounding an omnichannel transformation.

What Is an Omnichannel?

Marketing leaders and channel managers are increasingly focused on creating and developing a customer experience that's come to be called an "omnichannel" approach. Omnichannel is a two-sided concept with meanings for both marketers and for buyers. For buyers (and retailers), omnichannel is an expectation about their shopping and buying experience. Forrester defines an omnichannel experience as "one that is a seamless cohesive and contextual experience between physical and digital touchpoints across the entire customer journey."[1] Increasingly, buyers all around the world, whether B2B or B2C, expect to be able to discover, research, communicate, and buy when they want, where they want, and how they want. Disconnected, disparate, and isolated buying and communication channels are frustrating. For marketers, an omnichannel is a go-to-market growth strategy encompassing and connecting marketing, advertising, sales, and customer service. The marketer has twin goals in pursuing an omnichannel strategy: to improve customer satisfaction in the shopping and buying experience, and to create a competitive advantage that results in financial gain.

In other words, omnichannel is a way of meeting customers' expectations and behaviors. Simply stated, today's buyers expect omnichannel. In its "State of the Connected Customer" survey, Salesforce, the global technology platform company, found that 74% of customers used multiple channels to complete a transaction, and 76% prefer different channels depending on the context. It should be noted that omnichannel differs from multichannel in that it endeavors to synchronize all the various channel members and channel interactions so that buyers do not experience any "disconnected" moments during their customer journey. In contrast, with a multichannel approach, a marketer makes its product or service available via several different channels but acts largely independently: One channel is unaware of what customers may have experienced in another channel. For example, if a customer visits a brand's website, phones its customer service call center the next day, and visits a retailer the following day, are these cross-channel interactions known and acted on in order to optimize the customer experience and the financial outcome for the brand?

What an Omnichannel Experience Looks Like: H&R Block

For the marketing channel managers, the question then becomes how to design and operate a system that delivers an omnichannel experience to buyers. It's clear that this is a nontrivial challenge. Even a modest-sized business with several thousand customers, a dozen touchpoints across the customer journey, and several channels is quickly faced with tens of thousands of possible options when it comes to delivering the "right message to the right person at the right time, in the right way, with the right product and the right offer/price." While some might consider designing such a system to be a Herculean task, it can be done. Let's examine one brand that is delivering an omnichannel experience: H&R Block.

Founded in 1955, H&R Block is a global financial services company specializing in payroll, business consulting services, and tax preparation for small businesses and individuals. Of these service lines, Block is perhaps best-known for tax preparation. In some 70,000 worldwide locations, including in its offices in the United States, Canada, and Australia, Block will help you complete your income tax forms to meet your annual required government obligations. In total, Block's annual revenue is approximately $3 billion USD.

For most of its history, Block has been a "unichannel" business, working with its clients in only one way: face-to-face in its offices. Clients (and potential clients) would call the nearest Block office, schedule an appointment, and then appear in person with all the relevant documents, receipts, and papers in hand and discuss these with a Block tax expert. After the meeting, the tax expert would then begin preparing the client's tax filing. Typically, they might phone the client a few days later with some questions. And when the government filing documents were complete, the client would return to the office to sign them (hopefully all before the mandatory filing date!).

Then, in 1993, Block acquired the packaged tax software TaxCut as do-it-yourself taxpayers moved rapidly from paper and pencil to computer-assisted tax preparation. At this time, TaxCut came in the form of CD-ROM software for home computers. Initially, this was a completely separate channel from the in-person channel; the two channels were in no way connected. A tax expert in a local Block office had no awareness of or ability to help a customer using the CD-ROM-packaged software. Thus, Block was pursuing a "multichannel strategy."

Slowly, however, Block began connecting or synchronizing its two separate channels. By 2000, TaxCut was offering customers what it billed as "the next best thing" to a Block tax professional with the "Professional Review" feature in TaxAct. Users could fully complete their tax return within TaxAct and then send their return electronically to an H&R Block tax advisor, who would review the return and answer any questions before the taxpayer filed. While this was a first step from multichannel toward omnichannel, for the most part the two channels remained largely separate.[2]

By the following year, Block added a feature to TaxCut called "Ask A Tax Advisor." This feature provided tax advice via phone, chat, or e-mail from H&R Block's nationwide network of tax professionals by routing customers to their nearest local tax professional. In 2001, for the first time, Block offered the ability to route inquiries to a nearby professional. It was Block's acquisition of an online tax program called TaxNet, which enabled taxpayers to complete and e-file their returns quickly and conveniently, that began Block's deliberate move toward omnichannel.

Fast-forward to today and Block now offers a full omnichannel experience to its customers. By 2017, when new CEO Jeff Jones joined Block, he referred to it as "a classic legacy, omnichannel company and there is incredible goodness in being that. We have relevance to today's and tomorrow's consumers."[3] Indeed, this is because customers can now engage with Block when they want, where they want, and how they want. As Block's website states, "Get tax help however you need it. We're available online and in person to help you get every credit and deduction you deserve. Get your taxes done by a tax pro in an office, via video, or by phone. Or do your own with expert, on-demand help."

Block's omnichannel transformation continues to evolve and develop. As chief marketing and experience officer Jill Cress noted, "Today's modern marketing organizations require a new way of understanding and connecting with our customers and using data at every step of the customer acquisition and retention process."[4]

The Elements of an Omnichannel Experience

It follows from the H&R Block example that to deliver an omnichannel experience, marketers must develop, implement, and perfect two elements: a synchronized front-end user experience and the back-end technology system to power and deliver the experience. Together the front end and the back end compose what David Edelman and Mark Abraham call *intelligent experience engines* that assemble high-quality customer experiences using AI powered by customer data.

We are now at the point where competitive advantage will be based on the ability to capture, analyze, and utilize personalized customer data at scale and on how a company uses AI to understand, shape, customize, and optimize the customer journey. This is not just an exercise in journey mapping or technology planning. It is about developing the front-end flow to the customer and the back-end fuel to drive intelligent experience engines.[5]

The Front-End User Experience

Channel managers must intentionally design a user experience that enables customers to interact with a brand when, where, and how they want.

This requires brands to provide experiences along two dimensions. The first dimension is digital versus physical, and the second dimension comprises experiences owned and operated by the brand versus experiences owned and operated by downstream channel members such as retailers. This results in four possible front-end experiences that channel managers must establish. To visualize this, it's useful again to think about a channel map. But this time, the channel map will reveal several, not just one, routes to market. Drawing a two-by-two matrix can be useful. Across the top, we'll map first-party and third-party options. Vertically, we'll map both online and brick-and-mortar paths.

Let's think about each of these four boxes and what they would mean. We'll use Allbirds shoes as an example. For Allbirds, we'd start in the online first-party box with **allbirds.com**. This is where the bulk of their business comes from. But then move down on the map, and there are new Allbirds physical stores, which the company owns. They are opening them in trendy neighborhoods in cities all over, from Chicago to New York to Seattle. Just recently, though, they've also started experimenting with selling a few of their styles in Nordstrom stores. This would go in the bottom right box since it's both third party and brick and mortar. Finally, if Allbirds start appearing on **Nordstrom.com** or **Amazon.com**, that would go in the top right box. Additionally there is a newer, developing type of channel partner that is neither owned and operated by the brand nor a third-party retailer in the traditional sense. Here, we are referring to online buying platforms from the major tech platforms such as Google Shopping, Pinterest Shopping, Twitter Shopping, and Instagram Shopping.

Taken together, we can illustrate all these front-end customer-facing elements in an omnichannel map, or "omnichannel blueprint" (see Figure 18.1). The front end of this "2×2+1" channel map, together with the partner commerce platform on the back end, make up what you need to deliver an

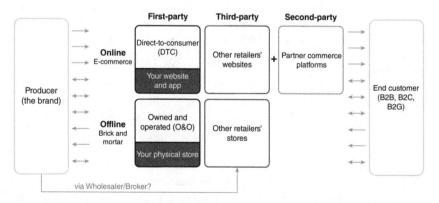

FIGURE 18.1   The Omnichannel Blueprint

omnichannel experience to customers: a "plan" + a "platform." When these five buying and communication channels are synchronized, customers are able to flow back and forth across and among them and experience a seamless real-time experience that characterizes an omnichannel. This multi-path mapping helps firms visualize their options. Frequently, they add metrics—percentage of sales, margin earned, and, potentially, rate of growth—to the four route-to-market boxes. These metrics make this map a really useful strategic tool, helping a firm understand their business, where it's coming from, and where it's going.

The Omnichannel Blueprint for Samsonite and Away Luggage

Consider the global luggage manufacturer Samsonite. Samsonite is the world's largest travel luggage company with approximately $3.5 billion annual global sales and 50% gross margin. It is the category leader in brand awareness and purchase consideration.

If you were to need a new rolling suitcase for an upcoming trip, your path-to-purchase journey might perhaps start with a Google search for "Samsonite luggage." There you see that CNN has rated the Samsonite Omni PC hardside rolling suitcase its top pick for best affordable carry-on. From there you might visit the Samsonite brand website to learn more about the Omni PC carry-on. You notice that you can actually purchase the suitcase right there on Samsonite's website. But first you might head over to Amazon to check the price and read the reviews: 4.5 stars and #1 Best-Seller!

However, before buying you might wish to see and handle the suitcase in person, so you visit your nearest department store or local independent luggage store. Perhaps you live near a Samsonite store and go there. You also might see that a Bed Bath & Beyond store near you has several available for purchase. In person, you like this suitcase quite a bit, and since you are a member of this store's loyalty rewards program (and you need the suitcase for a trip this weekend), you purchase it right then and there in the store and bring it home.

What can we observe from this experience? Samsonite has made its Omni PC available for research, consideration, and purchase when, where, and how a potential buyer might want it via both the company's own first-party and third-party retailer channels, both online and offline. This is an omnichannel front end.

Notice that "traditional brands" like Samsonite are increasingly adding first-party channels to their omnichannel blueprints. This has the benefit of giving consumers additional ways to shop and buy, while at the same time giving Samsonite more control over the experience (messaging, pricing, and the like) than it has when selling through third-party retailers. Additionally, it provides Samsonite with first-party data; it now directly knows who its buyers are and can use that data to personalize and customize future communications and interactions. In addition, first-party channels result in typically improved margins because Samsonite now does not have to share margins with downstream channel members such as wholesalers and retailers, although as described in the previous chapter, Samsonite now incurs the costs of delivering all nine functions of the channel by itself.

As of 2021, Samsonite reported that approximately 66% of its U.S. sales came from third-party retailers, just under 25% from its own retail stores, and slightly more than 10% from its own online business, with this channel growing the fastest. Nike, for example, as it has implemented the omnichannel blueprint and focused on more direct first-party selling, has stated that it has seen a 40-basis-point improvement in gross margin following just a +3% shift in channel mix from retail to direct-to-consumer sales.[6]

Now let us consider the omnichannel blueprint for a direct-to-consumer (DTC) brand. One of the more prominent DTC luggage brands is Away Luggage, founded in 2015 by Jen Rubio and Stephanie Korey. *Vogue* magazine called Away's suitcase "the perfect carry-on." For perspective, Away has roughly 10% of the revenue of Samsonite.[7] As a unichannel business (DTC only), Away began to explore other channels to help drive growth for the company. DTC businesses often seem to top out at around $300 million in revenue and then must seriously consider becoming omnichannel. The omnichannel blueprint suggests that Away has six strategic options:

1. Grow their current unichannel DTC business.
2. Open their own physical brick-and-mortar stores.
3. Begin selling through traditional large retailers in their physical stores.
4. Begin selling through the websites of traditional large retailers.
5. Begin selling to wholesalers that supply smaller local luggage retailers.
6. Begin selling via social shopping platforms like Facebook Shopping or Google shopping.

As a luggage shopper, you would ideally want to be able to find Away when you want, where you want, and how you want, just as with Samsonite. Notice, however, that all of these six options will offer lower margins than selling DTC, as each channel partner added to Away's channel map will require compensation for the work being performing (recall the equity principle discussed in Chapter 17). Of the options, opening stores that are "owned and operated" by a DTC brand generally has the least negative impact on margins. This is why you see so many DTCs now opening their own showcase brick-and-mortar stores first, before secondarily selling wholesale to other retailers. This in part explains why Casper, one of the first DTC brands, is now distributed in 28 retail chains, and why approximately half of all Warby Parker sales are now through its owned and operated stores.

The Back-End Tech Platform

Now let us examine the back end of an effective omnichannel system. Recall that we refer to this as your "platform." Having a data-driven back-end platform is essential to stitch together the five channels in your front end, the plan that I previously referred to as your omnichannel blueprint. Absent a data-driven way to connect these channels, the result would be simply an interesting multichannel go-to-market in which each channel was well intentioned about coordinating and delivering a real-time, personalized, contextual experience but inevitably would fall short of doing so given each channel member's independence and the high degree of complexity at hand.

Therefore, the channel manager must employ more than mere business rules, contracts, norms, or conventions to fully synchronize these five channels. While it may be tempting to try using these simple heuristic methods to deliver the omnichannel experience, it will quickly become apparent that the sheer number of possible permutations and combinations in each customer's journey multiplied by the total number of customers (and potential customers) interacting with your brand makes this impossible. The channel manager must employ advanced technology—automation and machine learning—in order to achieve channel synchronization.

Most modern marketing operations already employ several technology systems. These have collectively become known as "martech." There has been an explosion of marketing technologies over the past decade, and, as of early 2022, there were some 10,000 different marketing technology solutions across 49 different categories.[8] According to "The State of Martech 2022" report, "The drive to deliver better digital customer experiences and streamline digital business operations accelerated the demand for martech," which grew 24% over the past two years. So marketing teams have no shortage of marketing technology, from email delivery systems and dashboard reporting systems to marketing automation systems, to programmatic media buying platforms and customer relationship management systems (CRM).

So why do you need yet another system to implement data-driven omnichannel experiences? In order to connect and integrate all these disparate places in your organization where data sits, you need a new system called a *customer data platform* (CDP). Digital Marketing Depot describes it this way:

> *A Customer Data Platform is a ready to use system designed for non-IT use to streamline the flow of customer data throughout the martech*

stack and create a single view of the customer. A CDP consolidates and normalizes disparate sets of data collected across multiple touchpoints into a profile representing the customer, helping your sales, marketing, and service professional team deliver the ideal omnichannel customer experience.

Rather than housing customer data in a traditional customer relationship management (CRM) application, which can be more challenging to access, organizations have started to employ CDPs to make data more accessible to a range of omnichannel applications that drive multiple digital business transformation initiatives.

In effect, the CDP becomes the hub around which customer engagements—occurring in real time over email, phone, social media platforms, or mobile applications—are all tracked.[9]

While it is possible (although generally not recommended) to fully build a CDP from scratch in-house, most marketing organizations access a CDP through a variety of third-party vendors, which include some large tech firms like Adobe, Oracle, Microsoft, and Amazon, as well as smaller firms that specialize in CDPs such as ActionIQ, TreasureData, and Segment.

The good news is that a CDP implementation can start to show impact and value—that is, begin delivering an omnichannel customer experience—in as little as one quarter (although, of course, it will take much longer to fully implement and realize the maximum value of a CDP).

How a CDP Works

While the specifics will vary from CDP vendor to CDP vendor, in general all CDPs consist of the following four steps.

Step 1: Data Collection and Connection

Given that the purpose of a CDP is to synchronize the customer experience, it's natural that the first task of a CDP is to ingest customer data from a wide variety of sources. These sources might include sales transactions from your enterprise resource planning (ERP) system, call center data from your call center software, website data from your site analytics tool, email data, and advertising campaign data.

Data from these sources are imported into your CDP using an application programming interface (API). APIs are a way of connecting two computer systems or programs. Specifically, CDPs use a web API that connects computer systems connected to the internet. Your CDP vendor will help you import your data into their CDP. It's important to note that once this API connection is made, future data and data updates that happen within any of these connected systems will be reflected in your CDP. For instance, future purchases that a customer makes from your website will then subsequently also be known in your CDP.

CDPs also have the ability to import static datasets, such as .csv files. Marketers may, for example, have either historical or nonrecurring datasets in this format. These are imported into your CDP as a one-time batch upload. Additionally, where allowed by law or regulation, CDPs also have the ability to import data from third-party sources such as credit bureaus, data companies, and third-party loyalty or frequent shopper programs. At this point your CDP is configured to receive data from a variety of sources.

Step 2: Data Unification

In order to determine the best subsequent experience for each customer and make recommendations to them at the best time via the best channel in the best way, your CDP next begins the task of stitching together all of the data imported from the various disparate data sources to create an integrated view of each customer.

This process results in a "unified customer profile," whereby we can start to understand that it was the same person who called our call center, registered for our whitepaper on our website, subscribed to our email list (and opened or didn't open the last email we sent), visited our store, and/or interacted with one of our key channel partners such as a retailer.

Different CDPs handle this process in different ways, but in general they use both deterministic and probabilistic approaches to match the millions of ingested interactions, touchpoints, and activity and assign them to a customer profile—usually giving each one a record number as its identifier. In other words, in some cases a customer is definitely identifiable, perhaps because as part of a purchase the customer provided their name, address, mobile number, and email, and those identifiers exactly (or nearly) match previous interactions with that same name, address, mobile number, and/or email. In other instances, those identifiers may not exactly match but can be inferred as likely to be the same customer record—say, if a customer used a different name but the same address and mobile number on two different purchases. Here, the CDP will make an inference and match the interaction to the record.

It should also be noted that some CDPs also allow for a third-party profile unification company to handle this task. There are several major players who specialize in profile unification. Marketers should evaluate whether to use the native function within their CDP or to plug in that service from an outside specialist firm.

Step 3: Data Analysis and Prediction

At this point, with unified customer profiles in hand, the CDP can proceed to analyze these customers. They can be segmented into groups such as high-value customers, customers who are likely to repeat or not repeat, and so on. CDPs employ a form of artificial intelligence known as machine learning to make these predictions about customers, and, further, predict what the best subsequent interaction should be (what is the best product to suggest and when, how, and via what channel?). Machine learning uses examples ("training data") to find patterns and then make predictions, in a sense "forward thinking" and "learning" or improving over time without explicit programming instructions.

This is a crucial step because it's here where your CDP starts to determine how to provide each customer with the optimal next best interaction with your brand. Should it be an email or a text? Should it be a free shipping offer or a 10% off coupon? Should it encourage the customer to visit your store or website? The CDP allows you to determine personalization at scale across channels—a true omnichannel experience.

Step 4: Customer Activation

The final step a CDP performs is activating these personalization omnichannel recommendations. Here, the CDP executes marketing campaigns. CDPs can activate the predictions it has made to then customize a visitor's website experience, send personalized emails, show custom Google and Facebook ads—even trigger a personalized in-store experience with a sales associate. Now you start to see how a CDP is truly delivering an omnichannel experience at scale. Remember, if your data is siloed, you can't create a consistent experience for your customers. Without that central data hub, you can't provide the omnichannel experience customers expect, with up-to-date interactions regardless of which channel the customer communicates (and purchases) through.[10]

Following the customer activation, their response (or nonresponse) will be fed back into your CDP as input for the next time through this four-step cycle. That is, if a customer makes a purchase, that interaction will become a piece of reinforcing training data in your CDP's prediction model for the next time it makes a prediction. Alternatively, if the resultant interaction failed to result in a sale, that, too, will be fed into the CDP as training data, helping its machine-learning model to "learn" and make better predictions in the future. With sufficient interactions and time, it's clear that your CDP can become a powerful tool for delivering an omnichannel customer experience.

Schematically these steps then look like what is shown in Figure 18.2.

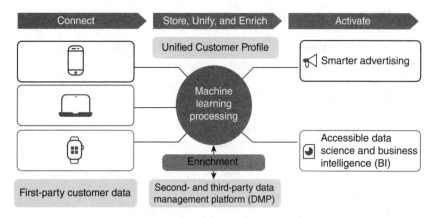

FIGURE 18.2 Essential Elements of a Customer Data Platform

Subaru: Combining the Front End and Back End for an Omnichannel Experience

What does this total experience look like? Let's look at an example from Subaru. Subaru is a global vehicle manufacturer with approximately $30 billion in annual sales. It is known for producing "go anywhere" mid-sized passenger vehicles powered by its "Symmetrical All-Wheel Drive" system.

Car buying is a daunting and often frustrating process for many buyers, given the infrequency of purchase and the relatively high price compared to everyday items bought more frequently. Shoppers can seek information and interaction directly from the Subaru brand via its website and also via Subaru's presence at local auto shows and driving experience events, where they invite potential buyers to test drive a Subaru and competing models, often at an empty stadium parking lot. At present buyers do not purchase directly from Subaru, but the company does facilitate locating a nearby vehicle at dealers and finding financing offers.

At the same time, local Subaru dealers provide messaging, offers, and information to potential buyers. Dealers offer the ability to physically experience a Subaru in person. Typically this involves talking with a salesperson and then taking a short test drive. Increasingly, dealers connect with potential customers via messaging within its website, email, chat, text, and/or phone. The dealer will sell, deliver, and service the vehicle.

Meanwhile, potential Subaru buyers are also working with other intermediaries like car research and review sites. These sites also list available Subaru inventory nearby and allow the shopper to communicate and negotiate with a Subaru dealer fully within their platform. Many of these car research and review sites also facilitate financing. You can't quite yet fully buy a car within these platforms, but nearly so!

It's also worth remembering that in many car-buying consumer journeys, shoppers simultaneously are doing all of the above with multiple brands and/or multiple dealers. Given how complex this process is, car shoppers increasingly expect a synchronized omnichannel journey that provides them with the right information and offer via the right channel at the right time.

Knowing this, Subaru embarked on an omnichannel journey that presented the shopper with a front end based on the omnichannel blueprint and a back end powered by a CDP. Subaru selected TreasureData as its CDP partner and within six months had consolidated over 1 billion data records.[11] Ogawa Hideki, chief engineer of digital innovation at Subaru, noted that the company derives a distinct advantage because it can segment based on its own data. This makes its web advertising more efficient and allows better targeting of new shoppers. Says Hideki, "Using machine learning, we've improved our forecast reliability by as much as 30% for 'likely' buyers. That information greatly improves sales efficiency, helping dealers better allocate always-limited staffing resources."

Of course, all this real-time personalized messaging also helps improve the shopping experience for the customer. Subaru is a strong example of a brand that has implemented the front end and back end, the plan and the platform required to deliver a true omnichannel experience

Managerial Considerations When Leading an Omnichannel Transformation Implementation

Up to now we have discussed how two elements, a plan and a platform, are required in order to enable an omnichannel customer experience. However, it should be noted that while the plan and the platform are absolutely *necessary*, they are not however wholly *sufficient*. To achieve a successful omnichannel transformation, channel managers must lead the change process. Doing so also requires the presence of six additional critical elements: talent, leadership, communication, execution, processes, and controls.

Talent. Moving from a uni- or multichannel route to market to an omnichannel experience generally requires the inclusion of new skills. In particular, implementation of a CDP, although often described as "off the shelf," frequently requires a fair amount of customization. This work can range from identifying internal and external datasets, to securing the authorization to connect those datasets to the CDP, to actually making the API connections. These are skills beyond the experience of many marketers, so adding team members with data management experience is typically imperative. Further, once the data are imported into the CDP, the rules for segmentation and campaign management must be declared. CDP vendors may provide help in this area, but it's generally advisable to have data analyst expertise on the team that can lead this effort.

Leadership. While the case for omnichannel transformation may be self-evident to the channel manager, it is not always clear and convincing to other stakeholders. This means that the channel manager must make the case for change within the firm and to key external partners. Executive management, including the chief financial officer and likely the board as well as franchisees and other external channel partners, will need to be briefed on the reason for transformation, the expected challenge, costs, and benefits. Here, the channel manager must go beyond the details of implementing and operating an omnichannel system in order to paint a compelling vision for the future. What gains are to be had as a result of a transformation? What risks or downsides are likely by not undertaking a transformation? Channel managers would be well advised to carefully articulate and have clear answers for these "big picture" themes in order to secure support and buy-in before embarking on an omnichannel transformation. A leadership model like John Kotter's famous eight-step change plan from his book *Leading Change*[12] will be invaluable to the channel manager.

Communication. As noted in the leadership point above, the ability to communicate cross-functionally is a critical element of any successful transformation. An omnichannel will involve far more than just the marketing team. Just to name a few of the cross-functional groups involved, channel managers must partner with the sales, customer service, store, e-commerce, finance, and fulfillment teams internally, and likely others. A best practice is to establish a cross-functional work group that meets on a standing basis, typically weekly, in order to agree to and communicate a common set of desired outcomes, priorities, and projects. In addition, channel managers should expect to use digital communication technologies like shared online documents, cloud file storage, and real-time messaging/chat in order to increase the flow of communication surrounding the omnichannel transformation initiative.

Execution. Channel managers interested in implementing an omnichannel approach would be well served by executing the transformation using a "test, learn, expand" model. Rather than try to transform the entire enterprise—all brands in all geographies for all customers all at once, a process that may take months or years to complete—instead select a manageable first initiative such as transforming one product line in one geography from a disconnected, frustrating customer experience into a synchronized omnichannel experience.

Choose a scalable CDP that can handle all of your product lines and data when you are ready. But start with a "sprint"—a one-quarter (13-week) effort to get a pilot up and running. Then immediately following that experience of going live, plan to pause and let it run for another quarter, observing what is working and what is not, and adjusting accordingly. Then, following a proper project management "after-operation assessment," determine how to expand the pilot, building on these initial learnings.

Process. World-class project management processes are essential to an omnichannel transformation. Commonly, a project-management process involves setting the project scope and objectives as well as budget, determining the schedule, identifying the necessary resources, and defining individual roles and responsibilities. There are now many web-based project management tools that facilitate processes and workflow. Some of these tools are free and some involve paid subscriptions (typically per user per month). Likely your company already has a project management tool like Airtable, Basecamp, or MeisterTask that includes a kanban board feature. If not, channel managers would be wise to secure such a tool to manage the process.

Controls. The channel manager must determine and set a group of key performance indicators (KPIs), metrics that control future actions. If KPIs are being met, then the omnichannel transformation is proceeding smoothly and should continue. If the KPIs are not being met, then adjustments need to be made to the plan and/or the platform in order to achieve the desired results. The KPI targets and current performance should be depicted in a visual representation known as an omnichannel dashboard. The channel manager owns the omnichannel dashboard and is responsible for its creation, for weekly or daily result updates, and for disseminating the dashboard to key stakeholders. Of course, an omnichannel dashboard may be created from scratch using common spreadsheet software; however, there are many excellent dashboard packages that the channel manager might consider that visually show the most recent results, often using the color convention of green (on track to target), yellow (cause for concern), and red (significantly behind the target).

Conclusion

In this chapter, we examined the concept of an omnichannel customer experience. We noted that, increasingly, buyers—both business buyers and consumers—are frustrated with disconnected and different experiences when they communicate, shop, and buy from a brand. Although you may have made your brand *available* in many different channels, as described in the previous chapter, if these channels are operating completely independently (or worse, at odds with one another), then you are presenting your customers with only a multichannel experience.

We illustrated a connected or synchronized omnichannel experience using several brand examples. Then we showed you that in order to create and operate an omnichannel system, the channel manager must design a front-end user experience (your "plan") and implement the back-end technology (the "platform"). The plan is your omnichannel blueprint, the "2×2+1" channel map; the platform is a customer data platform (CDP).

And finally, we examined some of the important managerial considerations to be aware of when leading an omnichannel transformation. These considerations include the right talent, leadership, communication, execution, processes, and controls.

Remember that your customer wants the subsequent best message about the next best product and offer at the next best time coming to them via the next best communication vehicle—whether their last interaction with your brand was online or offline, with your brand directly, or with one of your downstream channel partners. While delivering this synchronized experience is a challenge, brands that undertake an omnichannel transformation stand to gain a real competitive advantage.

Author Biography

Jim Lecinski is clinical associate professor of marketing at the Kellogg School of Management at Northwestern University. He teaches popular courses on Marketing Strategy and Omnichannel Marketing. His teaching has been recognized with the Sidney J. Levy Teaching Award and the L.G. Lavengood Outstanding Professor of the Year Award. Jim is a recognized expert, in-demand consultant, and keynote speaker with over 30 years of marketing industry experience, including a notable 12-year career at Google, where he was vice president of Customer Solutions for the Americas. Jim's seminal book *Winning the Zero Moment of Truth* has been read by over 300,000 marketers worldwide and was featured in the *New York Times*. His second book, *The AI Marketing Canvas*, was published by Stanford University Press and has been named a top AI book and a top business book of 2022.

CHAPTER 19

Sales as Storytelling

Craig Wortmann

Sales is a critical business function just like any other studied in business school: marketing, finance, leadership, operations, strategy. Sales has its own body of knowledge, its own set of skills, and requires tremendous discipline to become great at it. In addition, sales knowledge, skill, and discipline stand on the foundation of research into persuasion and influence drawn from neuroscience, social science, and psychology. We view sales as *helping people make progress in their lives.* Everything we do springs from that mindset.

Sales and Marketing

As a sister function of marketing, sales has a lot to learn from marketing and vice versa. While these functions are distinct, there is some important common ground. And one place where the Venn diagrams of sales and marketing overlap almost completely is storytelling. Marketers and salespeople are inherently storytellers, and both professions need to get much better at telling *the right story at the right time for the right reasons.* Therein lies the opportunity and the reason we decided to include this chapter in a book on marketing.

Marketing is best thought of as *one-to-many,* using multiple channels to build awareness and brand and attract the right customers. Marketing tells stories about the company, its value proposition, its solutions, and its customers—all of which are conveyed through many channels to reach as many of the right customers as possible.

Sales, on the other hand, is *one-to-one,* and so are the stories that salespeople tell, whether in a room or on a zoom. They're personal, and they're meant to be relevant to each listener and the progress they are trying to make. Although different in approach, sales and marketing are acts of persuasion. This chapter focuses on storytelling largely from the sales point of view, with the objective to bridge understanding and encourage more collaboration with marketing.

Before we dive into storytelling, we first need to acknowledge what so many of us get wrong. Too many people in our professions mistake facts and data for persuasion. Attempts at persuasion that just throw datasets and charts and bullet-pointed lists of facts at people, using intellectual arguments in hopes of winning their hearts and minds, are doomed to fail.

The main problem with that approach is that most people are what I call "bulletproof"—largely immune to the barrage of bits and bullets lobbed at them in hopes of influencing a decision, such as in making a sale. When facts and data come their way, most people simply put up a shield comprised of all the opinions and points of view they already carry around. Facts alone are poor persuaders.

The way we approach selling is far different. It unleashes the power of storytelling to make a connection first, which then allows people to see the possibilities for improving their own lives or businesses in some tangible way. One of my favorite quotes on this subject is from Hollywood screenwriting coach Robert McKee, in an interview with *Harvard Business Review*: "The other way to persuade people—and ultimately a much more powerful way—is by uniting an idea with an emotion. The best way to do that is by telling a compelling story. In a story, you not only weave a lot of information into the telling but you also arouse your listener's emotions and energy."[1] McKee's comment should come as no surprise since storytelling has been around from the dawn of civilization, first as oral tradition and then written down. Humans have intuitively understood the impact and importance of stories.

In recent years, there has been greater emphasis on storytelling in everything from corporate branding to creating a movement. The emotional power of storytelling has also been uncovered by an ever-increasing body of scientific research, such as identifying parts of the brain involved in telling and hearing stories and determining how the brain processes these narratives to understand complex concepts and ideas.[2] Frequently quoted research also shows that storytelling is exponentially more effective at making things memorable for the listener than merely reciting facts. Some claim it's 20 times more effective[3]; a seminal study from 1969 showed storytelling to be six to seven times more effective.[4] Whatever the number, the point is obvious: Stories help people remember information and experiences because of the emotions involved. Hence, whether someone is selling a product, service, or technology, the research indicates a story will be much, much more effective than any fact or datapoint alone.

What we now know from decades of research is that if you are trying to persuade someone to do something, your most powerful tool is story. Given the well-recognized power of stories to persuade, it only makes sense that business professionals in general—and sales and marketing professionals in particular—should be equipped with this tool as they go to market.

Since 2000, when I helped launch a company focused on stories, I have been on a mission to help everyone from MBA students to business leaders be better at capturing, distilling, labeling, curating, and telling their stories. For example, in training sessions, I frequently pose this question: "Could you come up to the front of the room right now and tell me 100 different stories?" Admittedly, the high number is meant to add a little shock value, but it really isn't far off the mark for the kind of repertoire an experienced salesperson should build.

I think back to when I got my job at IBM and how crucial storytelling was. I was a scared young kid working at a government job in Washington, DC, and IBM took a risk bringing me in to work with them in Chicago. Arriving in Chicago, I knew nothing about sales, business, or technology, but what happened next changed my life.

IBM placed me in a year-long sales school where I first had to learn business, then technology and computers, and finally sales. This was one of the hardest yet most amazing years for me because I emerged from this program a very different person. The biggest gift IBM gave me was a new mindset: "I can do this" and "I can get better at this." And that became part of my story, which I use to connect with sales teams today.

In a training session I held recently for a sales team from one of the world's top tech companies, I asked them to tell one story after another—for example: the company's origin story, what it is like to work with such an amazing company, why they joined the firm (their "origin" story), how their team took care of customers, their last five customer successes, their last five customer failures, how they compete against the tough competition they face every day, and why they are excited to be part of the sales team. The point wasn't the content of these stories, but rather experiencing the raw power contained in these stories—the kind that these sellers and every other sales professional should have in their metaphorical quiver. And yet, sadly, sales pitches continue to be driven by 95-page PowerPoint presentations packed with data on features and benefits—not stories uniting ideas with emotions.

Yet, I remain convinced that when we begin to understand and experience the power of stories, we will change our approach. We'll move away from merely trying to persuade with facts and tap the raw persuasive power of stories.

If we are to be powerful and effective sellers and marketers, the question we each must answer is:

Do you carry a quiver on your back that contains hundreds of stories, such that in any room or on any zoom or for any campaign on any channel you can always tell the right story at the right time for the right reasons?

The rest of this chapter is devoted to enabling you to respond, *"Yes!"*

Why Story?

"This toothpaste is 5X better than its nearest rival."

It's the kind of statement that sales and marketing teams too often rely on in hopes of influencing customers with data. This is in spite of the fact that time and again it's been shown that facts alone do little to convince people of the merits or benefits of a particular product, service, or concept.

As Annette Simmons, author of *The Story Factor,* states provocatively, "Facts are neutral until human beings add their own meaning to those facts. The meaning they add to facts depends on their current story. People stick with their story even when presented with facts that don't fit. They simply interpret or discount the facts to fit their story. This is why facts are not terribly useful in influencing others."[5]

Every time I share this quote with others—from students to researchers, entrepreneurs to medical doctors—I encounter pushback. People have a hard time accepting that facts are not the most powerful of all persuasion tools. But a second look at the quote reveals an important nuance. It's not that the facts are wrong or disputed. Rather, they are neutral; they lack a positive or negative emotional charge. The charge only happens when you add a story to bring the facts to life. Not to change the facts or alter them in any way, but to illustrate them.

Two powerful examples I use with students prove the point. The first is a 2007 study by three Carnegie Mellon researchers who approached undergraduate students with the premise of wanting to study how they use technology. After taking a survey about their technology use, students were paid $5 for their trouble. In their envelopes, along with the money, some students found a donation pledge for the charity Save the Children, with facts about food shortages in Malawi, lack of rain in Zambia, and dislocation of millions of people in Angola. Others received a pledge form and a story about a young girl, Rokia, who lives in Mali. Those who received the facts alone donated $1.14 on average to Save the Children, while those who read the story about Rokia gave $2.38.[6]

The survey, as you might guess, was only a ruse. Researchers did not care about technology use among undergraduate students. Rather, they were trying to measure the impact of facts versus stories. And the result was clear: Stories had twice the impact of facts alone.

A second example is a storytelling experiment by Rob Walker and Joshua Glenn from 2009, entitled "Significant Objects." The project involved selling thrift store items on eBay with descriptions that included short stories written by more than 200 writers. The objects were purchased for $1.25 each on average and sold for nearly $8,000 in total; a 2,700% markup. For example, a $1.49 paperweight sold for $197.50 because the story that went along with it resonated with the buyer, making it much more valuable. Then there was the tiny jar of mayonnaise—about an ounce or so—that was given out as a sample. In other words, the original price was free. But once a story was attached to it ("Guy comes on the train, Sunday morning . . ."), it sold for $51. (The proceeds, as with all the auctioned items, went to charity.)[7] In this case, we might say that the story created *all* the value, since no one would mistake a tiny jar of mayo as being worth $51. But someone found it to be that compelling because of the story's sheer emotional power.

The stories we tell as salespeople and marketers can move people to see the real value in what we're offering by showing how a product, service, or solution will help them make progress in their lives. With one significant difference: While the Significant Object project involved made-up stories, we are in business and, thus, our stories must be true stories. We are not inflating, manipulating, or changing the facts. Rather, we're using the power of emotion to create a connection and make those facts more relevant and memorable.

One of my favorite examples of the power of stories comes from something I witnessed a couple of years ago. The seller in this instance was a young entrepreneur named Daniel Rotman, who was pitching a cat litter business to a venture capital firm where I serve as an operating partner. As with any initial VC pitch, Daniel had about 20 minutes to convey the uniqueness and viability of his business idea in hopes of gaining our interest in taking a deeper look at a possible investment. When I heard about this phone interview, I just had to sit in on it. What could I learn from a pitch about cat litter?

The call between Daniel and the e-commerce expert at our VC firm kept getting pushed back due to scheduling conflicts. Finally, it was held in the evening at the end of a long day for all of us. This was hardly an ideal time or setup for Daniel to make his pitch. Making matters worse, the e-commerce expert was driving through a rainstorm, while I was at home. But with our apologies, we told Daniel he had our full attention.

At this point, imagine that you were in Daniel's position. What would you do to make the most of those 20 minutes, knowing that they could be an important chapter in the future of your nascent company? Most of the time, entrepreneurs shower the VC with facts in hopes of convincing them that theirs is a great business. "Here are our features and our specs and our pro-forma revenue line. And look, it goes up and to the right!" Instead, Daniel took the opposite tack.

After a pause, he told us, "Three years ago, my cat died. And I was devastated. He was a two-year-old, seemingly healthy cat, and one day he was here, and the next day he was gone." With that opening line, he had our full attention. We were immediately drawn into his story.

After his pet died, Daniel told us, he wandered around in a funk. And then he got angry. "I had to know why this had happened," Daniel continued.

We listened intently as Daniel explained how he channeled that emotion into action. "I talked with lots of veterinarians, and you know what? I learned a lot about cats. I learned that they are stoic animals, which means that they wear their emotions on the inside. I don't know if you two are dog lovers or cat lovers or even pet owners, but if you have a dog and you get home from work, you know exactly what you are getting because dogs wear their emotions on the outside. Cats are very different, and what that means is that your cat can have a very debilitating disease and you will never know it. You'll never know it unless you take your cat to the vet-recommended quarterly checkup that costs an average of $287 a visit. I didn't do that . . . and I regret it."

At this point, Daniel pivoted his story to explain how this series of events caused him to start his company. He resolved to address this difficulty of early detection of illness in cats by inventing a new cat litter. He called it "PrettyLitter" because it's based on a white silica that exists in only four mines in China—and he owned the exclusive rights to one of those mines. White silica is important, he explained, because silica is four times lighter than clay, which means the litter can be shipped. (Cat litter the world over is made from clay, which makes it very heavy to ship.)

"But now I can disrupt that business model and this industry because I can create a subscription business for cat litter." Daniel said, "Furthermore, I've treated the white silica with an enzyme, such that if your cat has any of seven disease states, when it pees on the cat litter the litter turns red. So now you know."

After taking us on that short but compelling journey of how and why he started PrettyLitter, Daniel finished his engrossing story by simply asking: "What questions do you have?" We were hooked.

Even today, PrettyLitter is marketed and sold with the power of stories about pets and their owners, who want to detect health issues early and avoid unnecessary veterinarian bills. And every time I share this story, I hear the same thing from the cat owners in the audience: "Where can I get this product?" As for Daniel, in 2021 he went on to sell PrettyLitter to Mars Inc. for a valuation of $500 million to $1 billion.[8]

As this example compellingly shows, whether you're selling a product or selling a company, you need to reach for the right story at the right time for the right reasons. You can't make them up on the spot. You need to generate and curate these stories out of real-life experiences—yours, your company's, and those of your customers. To do that, you need to learn a little about the mechanics of storytelling.

The Two Arcs of Storytelling

Stories, from a literary perspective, have what's known as a narrative arc, meaning how the story unfolds from beginning, to middle, to end. The narrative arc drives the plot and the character development. By the end of the story, the reader has been transported along an arc that follows the rise—or fall—of a character and the change in that character's life.

For our purposes, we'll look at two distinct arcs that help us tell our sales and marketing stories: The *business arc* and the *emotional arc*. Let's examine them one at a time. The business arc refers to the "job" a story is doing. Entrepreneurship often uses the phrase "job to be done" when referring to the purpose and function of a new company or its solutions. What's the job to be done by this startup (ideally, one that's not being done now)? In the case of PrettyLitter, the job to be done is ensuring that your cat is healthy.

We can ask the same question of our stories: What job is this story doing? When I think of Daniel telling his company's origin story, the job to be done was to attract investor interest in his company by showing the passion and commitment that led him to invent a new cat litter product and establish a company. In one tight story, he answered two questions we sales and marketing professionals must always be prepared to answer: "Why you?" and "Why now?"

So how does a story accomplish that job? That's where the business arc and the emotional arc come into play. My friend and fellow Kellogg professor David Schonthal and I have collaborated on defining these arcs as a way to structure stories. When we work with business audiences to help them construct their stories, we frame them in terms of the five Cs:

1. Character: Who is this story about?
2. Context: What is the setup?
3. Conflict: What is the challenge or problem to be solved?
4. Climax: What was the moment of breakthrough?
5. Closure: What do we do from here?

To see the five Cs in action, we can re-examine the PrettyLitter story. Clearly, the character is Daniel, since he's sharing a personal journey that became the origin story of the company. (In a different story, the character could be a customer, and the story could be about that customer's experience with a product that changed their life in some way.)

The context, or setup, in Daniel's story is that three years ago his cat died. The conflict was his anger and need to find out what caused his cat's death, which led him to seek out veterinarians and engage in research. The climax was his invention of a new type of cat litter as a diagnostic tool to promote feline health. Closure was asking us what questions we had to further explore how we might do business together.

The five Cs of Daniel's story clearly served the job to be done: Obtaining venture capital interest by presenting a compelling business case. We can also see that his storytelling did that far more effectively than any slideshow presentation backed with bullets and data points. But notice, too, that Daniel was able to simply weave the facts into and around the story. As we can see, the business arc is not a decision of facts versus stories. It's a technique that brings the facts to life by adding context, shape, color, and emotion.

Next, we look at the emotional arc—the ups and downs, trials and tribulations experienced by the character. The emotion is what makes a story relatable (as we listen, we feel those same emotions) and memorable. In Daniel's story, the arc starts at a very low point, with the death of a beloved pet and Daniel's grief that turned to anger and propelled him into action. By the end, the excitement and sense of purpose from formulating PrettyLitter and securing a supply of silica bring the emotional arc to a high point.

Bringing the two arcs together, we have a short but impactful story. The business arc lays out the elements of the story and what happened, one event following another. The emotional arc rises and falls along that linear timeline, through the highs and lows in succession.

You don't have to be a great writer to do this, and you do not need memoir-worthy stories. You just need to know what stories to tell and when to tell them. As illustrated, the facts are still important, but it's all about how you use them. When facts are wrapped up in emotion through story, they are far more potent in how they make people feel about and connect with a product, a solution, or a company.

Here is the common ground where marketing and sales can work effectively together. It's like an actor in the scene of your favorite movie. If you think about it, you know the actor is reciting words that were written down in a script—words that someone else wrote. But the minute the director says, "Action!" the actor embodies that story. As the viewer, you lose the conscious realization that this is an actor because you are lost in the emotion. In the same way, getting those stories down is what marketers and salespeople have to do together.

Not everyone buys into this thinking. The objection I hear occasionally is that, in what I am describing, stories appear to be curated or designed in a way that seems robotic. This kind of pushback, however, reveals misconceptions about the story process. It is not manipulating or going into the wind-up of "Have I got a story to tell you!" It requires listening to the customer, understanding with empathy where they are coming from and what progress they are trying to make, and then reaching into your quiver and sharing a story about someone else's experience and how they made progress, changed a circumstance, eliminated an obstacle, or opened a door to a new opportunity.

Viewed this way, the salesperson telling a story is no different from a counselor who shares the experience of someone who struggled with a similar problem or faced the same challenge and found a way forward. In fact, I believe that all professionals do better when they leverage the power of stories to help people see themselves, their circumstances, and what can change their lives for the better.

A New Asset Class

Given how important they are, stories are an asset class. Too often, though, organizations don't treat them as investments. Rather, we treat them more like anecdotes or conversation starters. Instead, we invest loads of money in other assets that help us run our sales and marketing organizations, like our customer relationship management (CRM) systems and our demand-side platforms (DSPs). While these are powerful systems that help organize and guide our behaviors, there is another asset to consider—one that guides the behaviors of our customers. You guessed it: That asset is stories.

In our work with some of the largest sales forces in the most successful companies in the world, we frequently hear this lament from the leadership teams: Why do our salespeople just talk at our customers using 95-page Power-Point decks? And our answer is that salespeople are taught "product, not people." Product is communicated by facts, whereas people communicate by stories.

Having an inventory of stories to tell, and selecting the right one to share depending on the customer interaction the salesperson is engaged in at a particular moment, is what having a quiver full of stories is all about. That means stories must be uncovered, learned, and categorized so a salesperson can describe an opportunity, challenge, or pain point that someone else faced. In telling that story, a current or prospective customer can see themselves in it and can see the path to progress.

The Story Matrix™

Our name for this quiver of stories is the Story Matrix™. The purpose of the Story Matrix™ is to give salespeople and marketers ready access to stories so that they can be more consistent and intentional about weaving those stories into their communications.

To understand the Story Matrix™ concept, think of the brain as a storage room. We are constantly accumulating more information and knowledge and cramming it into the storage room. What a mess! When it's unorganized, we can't find anything, especially when we need it most. The Story Matrix™ acts like shelving, containers, and labels for your information and knowledge—all packaged in your stories. With the Story Matrix™, you have an organizing implement at your fingertips that makes your most powerful tool of influence—your stories—accessible and usable.

The Story Matrix™ is a simple spreadsheet designed to allow easy access to the *right story at the right time for the right reasons*. Like any spreadsheet, it has rows and columns. The rows are the jobs to be done and the columns are the types of stories we should be telling about those jobs to be done.

The Columns

Let's first tackle the columns of your Story Matrix™. These are the types of stories all professionals should be telling in life and in business: Success stories, failure stories, fun stories, and legends. Why four different types? Because each type of story has a different impact on your audience.

Success: These are the types of stories we all love. We tell and retell them. They are easy to remember and often are promoted in our marketing materials and recounted at our sales meetings. They feel good, but they also serve a very important role in helping potential customers relate to the progress you and your company will help them make. Success stories show the way—a problem solved, an obstacle overcome. If someone else achieved success with a particular product or solution, then others can too.

Failure: Yuck. Who likes to tell stories about failure? And yet, these stories play an incredibly important role. For one thing, they can help customers avoid the traps that others have fallen into. Failure stories let us see inside a failure to understand exactly what went wrong. When sharing a failure story with a current or prospective customer, the salesperson can convey why something did not work and why a new product or solution might be a better answer. Personal failure stories also demonstrate humility and illustrate that we are all human and that we are coachable.

Fun: We need to bring humor back into its rightful position. Everybody could use a little fun and a laugh. It should be appropriate, of course, and never demean or belittle anyone. Fun stories are powerful ways to lighten the mood and lower the intensity. Unlike failure stories that are often packed with lessons learned, fun stories simply show that we don't need to take ourselves too seriously.

Legends: This final type of story is distinct from the other three. We all grew up on legend stories that are essentially teaching stories from history, culture, and spirituality and are designed to impart wisdom, character, and values. Businesses also have their own form of legend stories. Just as Daniel did, we must always be prepared to tell people why we are here, what we stand for, why the company exists, and the values that animate our company and our people. These are our legend stories, and they build strong connections to the "why" of what we do.

As sales and marketing teams collect stories, they must group them into these four categories, thereby ensuring that they have access to the different types of impact that each delivers.

The Rows

Now let's tackle the rows of your Story Matrix™, which organize your quiver based on jobs to be done. One job to be done in sales is to always introduce yourself and your company in a compelling way; that's why you need stories that populate that row. For instance, Daniel's origin story of PrettyLitter would live in a row that might be called "Why us? Why now?"

One job to be done in marketing is articulating the value proposition and explaining how your company or product or solution or team is differentiated. In Daniel's case a story about discovering that white silica has better traits than clay (less dust, less smell) and is four times lighter than clay lives in a row called "Value Proposition/Differentiators." Let's call that story "Lighter Than Clay."

Another job salespeople must do is to highlight the returns their solution will deliver to customers. But again, be very careful here. This job is often tackled with facts and data and charts showing the return on investment. While this is fine, how might we wrap that information in a story about a similar customer who was trying to make the same sort of progress? That's a story to tell around the facts. Let's call that story "Let's Go 5X Faster" and place it in the "Return on Investment" row.

And on this goes. As salespeople and marketers who go out into the world doing what we do, we must be vigilant to collect the stories we experience. Of course, not every story is worth retelling, but many are. At the Kellogg Sales Institute, we see just how often people miss the opportunity to collect their best stories. They see them or hear them or read them, but don't write them down. And within minutes, those stories are gone. The Story Matrix serves as a repository to write down our best stories, so we always have access to them to grow our businesses and help customers have a different and better experience.

Finally, our brains need labels for things to make them memorable. The Story Matrix™ forces us not only to be aware of the stories that are all around us, but also to label our rows "jobs to be done" *and* to name our stories. That way, we can more easily put our fingers on just the right story.

Putting this all together, Figure 19.1 is an illustration of what Daniel's Story Matrix™ might look like.

Forward Together

The Story Matrix™ answers a fundamental question that we may not be accustomed to asking: How do I get access to the right story at the right time for the right reasons?" This question brings us back to the premise of this chapter: Marketing and sales need to collaborate to create a shared Story Matrix™. This repository of stories then becomes a treasure trove of assets that marketing can use for its one-to-many campaigns while sales uses them for one-to-one meetings and presentations. Since they both benefit from stories, who better to identify, capture, and label those stories than sales and marketing working collaboratively?

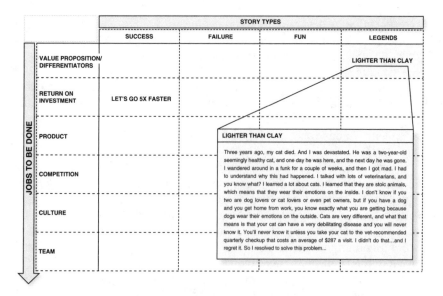

FIGURE 19.1 Daniel's PrettyLitter Story Matrix™

Where do we go from here? Here's what we recommend:

- Step 1: Assign a very small team from sales and marketing to sketch out a draft Story Matrix™ with the right "job to be done" rows.

- Step 2: For each row, assign two champions, one from sales and one from marketing. The champion's role is to search for stories to populate that row.

- Step 3: During weekly meetings, ask one person on the sales and marketing teams to capture, distill, and then write up a story and deliver it to the champion for that row.

- Step 4: Edit the story for clarity and impact using the 5Cs and place that story in the company Story Matrix™.

- Step 5: Have fun. Celebrate storytelling and give awards for the best story told at company meetings and weekly meetings, as well as in marketing campaigns and customer presentations.

In our work with organizations all over the world, we often find that beginning with these simple steps results in the building of a robust and powerful organizational Story Matrix™. And that's a tool that will benefit sales and marketing and the organization as a whole.

Conclusion

For both the marketing and sales teams, it is critical that they become better storytellers. As we have seen, stories are one of our most powerful tools of persuasion and the best way to help our customers discover the progress they are trying to make. We have no shortage of data, but we must work hard to capture, distill, label, and tell our best stories that bring that data to life. In other words, we must be always ready to tell the right story at the right time for the right reasons. This is the key to crafting a successful communication campaign.

Author Biography

Craig Wortmann is a clinical professor of marketing, CEO of Sales Engine Inc., and an operating partner with Pritzker Group Venture Capital. He is also the founder and academic director of the Kellogg Sales Institute, which defines sales as "helping people become both magnetic and unstoppable in their pursuit of progress . . . for themselves and for everyone they come across." Craig's teaching covers a wide range of topics based on his experiences as a professional salesperson, CEO, founder, entrepreneur, and investor. In all of his teaching—from interactive online courses to MBA and Executive MBA classrooms—Craig attempts to create immersive experiences that help people develop into dynamic leaders who drive predictably consistent high growth for their organizations.

PART 7

Data-Driven Marketing

CHAPTER 20

Leading with AI and Analytics

Eric T. Anderson and Florian Zettelmeyer

"How can we use AI and analytics to improve our marketing strategy and drive value?" Some form of this question routinely comes up in the analytics workshops run for leaders across industries. Even among marketing executives who are generally quite good at what they do, AI and analytics—we'll call it "AIA" here—remains a challenge for them, despite all the data they can access. In fact, in a survey of about 400 chief marketing officers, the leaders noted high barriers to using data, including lack of processes, tools, and talent for analytics.[1] That's a problem, given that as a marketing leader you need to draw on data-driven decision making to create, sustain, and grow advantage for your business in an ever more competitive market. That reality is not going to change.[2]

Moreover, while it may be tempting to see AIA as a problem owned by AI, analytics, or data science groups, that's simply not the case. *Every* business leader, including those in marketing, has to see AIA as a leadership problem, take ownership of it, and use AIA proactively as part of their approach to strategy and tactics. Doing that effectively starts with gaining a working knowledge of data science, or what we call a high data science intuition quotient (DSIQ). It's important not to confuse DSIQ with expertise in data science; rather, DSIQ is about harnessing your existing critical thinking skills to gain a feel for what good AIA looks like. Indeed, that's why the "I" in DSIQ stands for "intuition," not "intelligence"; the latter seems like more of an inherent, instinctive attribute in contrast to intuition, which you can learn.

The mission of business professors and consultants is to raise the DSIQ of professionals across all fields and functions by helping them understand AIA concepts, tools, and frameworks, then use them to identify good (and not-so-good) analytics, understand where to use AIA to add value, and lead AIA initiatives capably and confidently. Doing that will ensure that you shift from uninformed or misinformed decision making to *evidence-based* decisions—and help your broader organization do the same—whether you are a CMO, marketing VP, product manager, or any other marketing professional.

This chapter makes the case for raising your DSIQ as a marketer by sharing the "truth" behind a well-known analytics story, laying out the main reasons it's critical to gain a working knowledge of AIA (with specific examples), and sharing our AIA Framework, which takes you from business objectives to outcomes using AIA as a core value driver. Finally, it presents an in-depth marketing-focused example of using predictive and causal analytics to move from prediction to profit.

Moneyball: What Really Happened

The "Moneyball" story of a professional baseball team's high-impact use of analytics illuminates the relationship between leadership and AIA. Author Michael Lewis's bestselling book of the same name chronicled the Oakland Athletics' (A's) turnaround in the early 2000s,[3] motivating the use of the term *Moneyball* for the application of statistical analytics to sports strategy in place of intuition for activities like recruiting and trading players.

But it turns out that the way most people think of the baseball story is misguided: The use of analytics actually isn't the main driving force. So what is?

Before we answer, consider the Moneyball story's premise and plot. Billy Beane—played by Brad Pitt in the *Moneyball* movie—had been a struggling professional baseball player before moving to the A's scouting organization in 1990 and ascending to general manager, the top leadership role, seven years later. In that position, he oversaw recruiting of new players, with a focus on high school talent, as is the sport's norm. The focus of recruiting efforts at the time was on traditional skills such as hitting, fielding, and speed.

Beyond discerning high-potential talent, Beane faced the challenge of a recruiting budget about 70% less than that of the A's iconic American League rival, the New York Yankees. But Beane was willing to think differently and did so in 1999 by recruiting Paul DePodesta, a Harvard economics-degree-holder who'd previously worked with the Cleveland Indians (now called the Guardians). Together, Beane and DePodesta revolutionized the A's recruiting approach to focus less on traditional skills and more on subtler statistics related directly to scoring runs. Their analysis suggested that on-base-percentage (OBP, the proportion of times a batter reaches base) and slugging percentage (the number of total bases divided by the number of at-bats) were worth recruiting for—as much as or more than traditional metrics like batting average—and that players scoring high on these metrics could be secured less expensively because other teams weren't seeking out those statistics.

That bet paid off in a big way: The A's reached the playoffs every year from 2000 to 2003, and in 2006 the team made the American League Championship Series, the doorstep of the World Series, despite ranking 24th of all 30 Major League teams for payroll. Other teams copied Beane's approach, including the Boston Red Sox and Chicago Cubs, who soon won their first World Series titles in 86 and 108 years, respectively.

It's no surprise, then, that most people see analytics as the "star" of the Moneyball story, the force behind the now widespread use of statistics-based decision making in every major U.S. sport. Indeed, it's easy to place data and analytics center stage in the revolution that began with Beane and the A's at the millennium's turn. In general, people believe the shift to analytics was brought about by some combination of new data, innovative statistical methods or computational capabilities, and more skilled analytical talent.

Our take on the Moneyball story suggests otherwise. For example, with regard to data, voluminous statistics had been available since the late 1800s, over a century before Beane became the A's general manager.[4] Moreover, Beane and Podesta used analytical techniques based largely on regression, a statistical approach established long before and requiring only modest computing power such as that of a desktop computer. Finally, there was no evidence of more skilled analytical talent in the A's story, as the Society for American Baseball Research (SABR) had promoted application of analytics to the sport since the early 1970s, including recognition of the value of the OBP statistic that became central to Beane's success.

That leaves only one feasible solution to the mystery of what drove baseball's analytical moment: *leadership*. Billy Beane himself brought about the shift through his conviction regarding the power of analytics and leverage of an analytics-rooted management approach to turn around his struggling team. So, while the data, tools, and techniques Beane used weren't new, his style of leadership was. In fact, the revolution could have come years earlier, given that all the necessary pieces were in place. But it took the right leader to believe in and lead the analytics-fueled change. That's also the case in any business organization or industry.

Analytics and AI Are Every Leader's Problem—Here's Why

Billy Beane was the top executive at the Oakland A's. But we see AIA as every leader's problem because of their large influence on strategy, planning, culture, and all other kinds of decision making. But to really drive the point home, consider several mutually reinforcing reasons why AIA is a leadership issue, as presented in the following subsections.

AIA Requires Managerial Judgment

Leaders routinely make high-stakes decisions, and these are increasingly based on data. Even the most experienced executives may struggle in this domain. As an example, at a thought leadership retreat for a digital-marketing business serving the automotive industry and other sectors, the marketing VP said that a recent analytics initiative had "made the link" between digital ads and offline sales of cars—a long-elusive association due largely to the difficulty of securing comprehensive sales data from dealers. Their team had worked with IT to track ad views and clicks, then used cookie information from a post-sale survey to assess whether individuals had purchased an automobile after viewing an ad for it. The sales conversion chart seemed to highlight the ads' effectiveness, as shown in Figure 20.1.

It's no surprise the executives were excited to see the conversion rate soar from less than 1% to 14% when people saw both retailer and manufacturer ads. But as most of the retreat participants considered how to leverage this evidence of ad effectiveness, another VP pointed out that people who had seen no ads (the left-most column) were likely not searching for automobile information online, while those consumers served both retailer and manufacturer ads (right-most column) had probably searched for cars with specific keywords manufacturers and dealers had bid on, triggering the ads.

The second VP was right: Ultimately, all the chart showed was that someone who had expressed online interest in buying a car (and thus was served digital ads) was more likely to buy a car than someone who hadn't expressed such interest—hardly an earth-shattering insight. Indeed, the dataset the

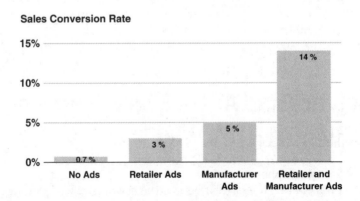

FIGURE 20.1 Digital Car Ad Sales Conversion Rate

marketing team had collected offered no route to knowing if ad exposure had *any* effect on purchase, because it failed to meet a key requirement for a true experiment: random assignment to conditions. But nearly all the high-level executives at the retreat failed to grasp that.

They are not alone. Similar examples of flawed or incomplete interpretation of analyses occur in nearly every group of managers we work with. It's human nature to want to believe seemingly convincing data. In fact, the data themselves are "real" and truthful but are often misinterpreted to mean something they don't. That's where sound managerial judgment, based on a high DSIQ, is critical.

The Illusion of Insight

Another reason AIA is a leadership problem is that data can create the illusion of insight. Today, nearly every marketing manager has a dashboard that provides numerous metrics on performance. It can be tempting to believe, then, that having more data leads to better decision making. The problem with that assumption is that many marketing leaders lack data science intuition and can easily be misled by these dashboards, resulting in suboptimal decisions.

Consider the example of a marketing executive in a large B2B software company. Senior management wants to compare the performance of a new, expensive CRM system the business is testing to one that has been in place since 2018. The new CRM system has been designed to help salespeople enhance their general selling effectiveness and increase conversions of prospective enterprise customers. To test the new CRM system's performance, the executive completed a one-month pilot in two regions, East and West, comparing the legacy and new systems on revenue per salesperson.

When the data came in, the manager was surprised to see no improvement in revenue per salesperson for the new system, as shown in Figure 20.2. Based on these results, the executive intended to recommend that senior management *not* invest in the new CRM system.

But it turns out that's the wrong decision. What the dashboard did not reveal was that the pilot test involved an opt-in decision for each salesperson. The regional manager in the West strongly endorsed the new CRM system, and 90% of salespeople in the region tried the system during the one-month trial. But the East's regional manager did not promote the new system, and only 10% of salespeople in that region adopted the system. Indeed, a closer look at the data showed that revenue in both regions increased with the CRM system (see Figure 20.3)! But blending the results from regions with very different opt-in rates led to the "finding" of no difference in system performance. This is a subtlety that is lost without a deep understanding of how the test was set—something most decision makers don't think of as "their" problem.

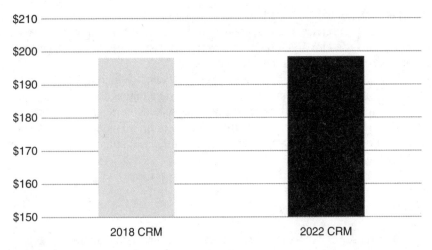

FIGURE 20.2 CRM Results: 2018 versus 2022

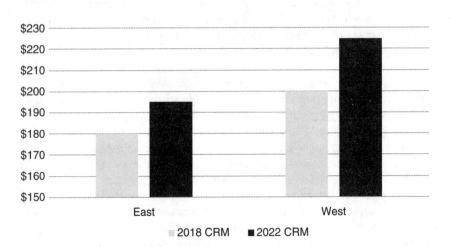

FIGURE 20.3 CRM Results by Region

That means that the initial results would have been an accurate representation of the new CRM system's performance only if the adoption rate had been identical between regions. This was far from the truth, resulting in a misguided investment recommendation. As in the digital advertising example presented earlier, the numbers were true but the conclusion was erroneous. Many marketing managers simply don't have the training or instincts to see past the numbers presented, especially when they are dealing with so much data in dashboards, presentations, and other sources. That's why you need a high DSIQ to facilitate your critical thinking and decision making related to AIA.

AIA Requires Structure, Process, and Incentive Shifts

To illustrate the tight relationship between AIA and structure, process, and incentives, we introduce Marge, a mid-60s retired nurse from Long Island. Along with enjoying crochet, crosswords, and bingo, Marge is an avid gambler, playing slots and video poker everywhere from Atlantic City to Chicago to Las Vegas, traveling with her husband and friends on multiple annual gambling trips.

Based on Marge's presence in casinos nationwide, gaming-business marketing teams consider her a "cross-market gambler." As the new millennium approached, industry stalwart Harrah's sought to target customers like Marge. It was part of the business's attempt at a much-needed comeback. At the time, Harrah's operated casinos in large markets like Las Vegas but also in an array of smaller market regions. The business faced increasingly stiff competition from rivals like Steve Wynn's Mirage Resort and Casino—which featured Siegfried and Roy's famous white tiger show—along with Luxor, the MGM Grand, and other casinos. As a result, Harrah's gambling revenue had faltered, and marketing and other leaders sought to drive up room revenue, which required a large investment.

In this high-stakes situation, Harrah's market research, including customer interviews, revealed that while the typical Vegas gambler restricted most of their play to that city, those patronizing Harrah's, like Marge, were more likely to be cross-market gamblers who played year-round across U.S. regions. Despite Harrah's strong geographic coverage, in 1998 they'd captured only 36% of all cross-market players' total spending.

To boost that share, Harrah's leadership sought to identify the cross-market segment more accurately, target the segment's most profitable customers, and offer the right incentives (free rooms, food, and the like) to attract the high-profit customers. These are three core activities of any marketing manager. Surely Harrah's marketing team could execute against these goals.

But there was a problem. At the time, Harrah's operated each casino as an autonomous business, including separate P&L and reward programs. That made property managers territorial about customers; moreover, rewards earned at a given property could be redeemed only at that property. Consequently, simply rolling out a new cross-market rewards program would have been a doomed initiative due to the lack of supporting structure and incentives.

Luckily, strategy and marketing leaders recognized that issue and worked to shift Harrah's focus from properties to *customers* as the key value driver. That required development of a whole new organizational structure: Property managers now reported to the COO rather than the CEO, to reflect that customers belonged not to each casino but to the broader company. Similarly, leaders worked with technology teams on a new behavior-tracking system underlying a "total rewards" program through which customers could use a single membership card across all Harrah's properties. They supported the program with predictive analytics to forecast customer value and create effective reward-program incentives.

The new structure, systems, and data generated critical, actionable insights. For instance, Harrah's now understood that customers who'd begun their gaming tenure with the business had a higher lifetime value than other gamblers, so it was worth offering them larger incentives early on, even before they'd spent much at Harrah's, to ensure their loyalty.

The new strategy proved a winning bet. By 2001, Harrah's had increased its share of cross-market spending from 36% to 42%, garnering hundreds of millions in new profits. Leadership has continued to improve the strategy to the present, using real-time, data-driven models to boost value—such as offering drinks and other incentives in the moment to high-value customers facing frustrating losses at the blackjack tables. Indeed, the gaming industry considers Harrah's a story of exemplary strategy.

Harrah's challenges are common well beyond gaming and entertainment, given the presence of siloed organizations and poorly integrated systems, processes, and data across sectors—as so many leaders would confirm. To win, Harrah's had to completely remake its structure and customer strategy to ensure they could deploy analytics effectively. A high DSIQ will help you invest in the right structure, systems, and data to support your business's strategic goals and initiatives.

Analytics Requires a Problem Focus and Upfront Planning

Marketing and other executives often overlook something critical: Analytics requires starting with a business problem and a clear plan.

That's easy to forget when you're floating in a sea of data related to sales, growth, other financials, customers, and conversion, among others. The temptation becomes to go looking for something, *anything*, in the data that may deliver insights. But for many marketing managers, these insights are the end of the process. They uncover new information about buyer behavior and then ask themselves: "What's next?" In many cases, the process moves from data to insight and then stops. Such approaches ultimately yield little to no business value.

So, What's the Problem?

Marketers need to start with a high-stakes business problem. Then they need to ask, "How can the data help me address this business problem and make better decisions?" Moreover, marketing leaders need to identify and frame the strategic problems that guide data analytics rather than seeing this as the domain of data scientists or IT specialists.

Owning this challenge fully means taking ownership of planning for analytics. Remember *Mad Men*, the award-winning TV series focused on fictional 1960s ad agency Sterling Cooper and creative executive Don Draper? It was easy to find the advertising campaigns featured on the show—for Samsonite, Kodak, Hilton, and other well-known brands—appealing, but where was the analytics-based evidence of their effectiveness? There wasn't any. Advertising is just one domain where analytics is implemented after the fact at best, or never at all. As the earlier digital advertising example illustrates, you may have massive amounts of data on exposure, clicks, and purchase but still lack real evidence that a given online campaign actually worked.

What's missing from the vast majority of business plans is an *AIA business plan* proposing data and models to test the performance of a new strategy or initiative. Such a plan must be crafted before the launch of a new idea, which renders the analytics more feasible and implementable. Today's highest-performing companies apply the same rigor to AIA planning as they do to executing their core business.

All of the ideas in this section make clear that AIA is a leadership problem, and every current and rising leader in marketing or any other area should aim to boost their DSIQ. That will maximize your performance with regard to understanding the validity of data-driven business cases, framing strategic problems and planning analytics, and using analytical insights to craft changes and initiatives related to structure, process, and incentives. As we mentioned earlier, you don't have to gain expertise in data science; rather, you need a working knowledge of this domain.

The AIA Framework for Marketers

Success with analytics requires a shared understanding of AIA and a structured process for developing and implementing initiatives. The problem is that even senior leaders in data science diverge in their definitions of AI, analytics, and their relationship. Given that there's no consensus view on AIA, we've used a business-oriented perspective built on decades of working with companies on AIA initiatives to create an AIA framework. It serves as a set of organizing principles and steps to work on AIA challenges and strategies in your organization, offering a process-driven approach and common language around this key domain.

Most businesses struggle to craft and implement AIA projects due to a lack of understanding of fundamentals and a systematic process for linking business priorities with AIA. Existing AIA frameworks are often misguided or incomplete. For example, some view analytics maturity as the driver of business value (not always true); others fail to make key distinctions among analytics approaches (which can lead to poor business decisions); and many fail to integrate AI and analytics effectively (an important connection).

The AIA Framework for Business Decisions is a way for you to create a shared vocabulary and process for AIA while customizing it to your organization's needs. Of importance, the foundation for this framework is the traditional business decision-making process that starts with a business objective, understanding of the problems related to that objective, and a set of business ideas leading to a decision, as depicted in Figure 20.4. Note that data and models figure into decision making, but much less than intuition does in most businesses today, hence the proportions of those components in the visual.

The goal of the AIA Framework for Business Decisions is to make the AIA layer—the "Data and Models" component—much thicker, with opportunities not only to use AIA to assess ideas but also to generate them by transforming data, through learning, into knowledge. Figure 20.5 depicts our AIA framework, nicknamed the "Lexus Grille" due to its resemblance to the distinctive fronts of cars from that automaker.

The framework provides a repeatable process connecting business outcomes with analytics-informed decisions, enabling you to systematically replace intuition with *evidence*. As Figure 20.5 illustrates, the framework includes three specific types of analytics:

1. *Exploratory Analytics:* Describing data, explaining the generation process for the data, and assessing variability within the data
2. *Predictive Analytics:* Using AIA models to anticipate future outcomes
3. *Causal Analytics:* Using AIA models to *influence* future outcomes

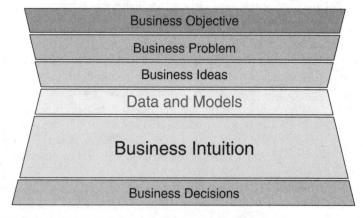

FIGURE 20.4   Traditional Business Decision-Making Process

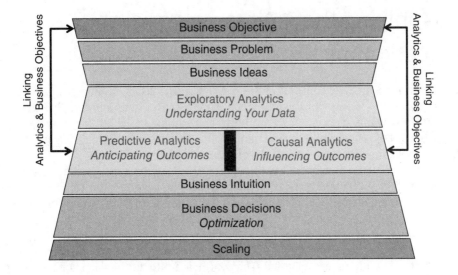

FIGURE 20.5 The AIA Framework for Business Decisions

Consider the subtle but important distinction between predictive and causal analytics by placing yourself in the shoes of a marketing leader for an online retailer like Harry's (shaving products) or Bombas (socks and other clothing) that wants to forecast demand (orders received) for the upcoming month. That requires a *predictive* model that anticipates future outcomes, assuming business as usual. But now suppose the CMO asks whether the firm can use a new marketing campaign to boost order volume by 5%. You've just entered the domain of *causal* analytics, or seeking to influence a future outcome. As this simple example suggests, predictive and causal analytics speak to different business questions; moreover, the resources each requires can differ significantly, so it's critical for leaders to understand the distinction here, which we'll illustrate further shortly.

The last parts of the framework involve making business decisions through scenario-driven optimization and scaling the related ideas or actions organization-wide. Rather than goals in and of themselves, think of predictive and causal analytics as inputs for optimization, thus linking analytics with the overarching business decision. For scaling, AI can play a critical role in automating learning and creating usable knowledge across the business. A word of caution is in order: Take care not to see the AIA-generated answer as the end-all solution; instead, integrate model-based recommendations with your business intuition to determine the best way forward.

Applying the AIA Framework in Marketing: Propensity Versus Uplift

To bring the general concepts of the AIA framework to life in marketing, let's consider the journey of a gaming company, Creative Gaming. Imagine the business wants users to purchase an in-app campaign called Zalon, which costs $14.99. For the past several months, the firm has run a Zalon advertising initiative that has led to about 10% of users buying the campaign.

An in-house data science team suggests that Creative Gaming can use the historical data to identify the types of prospects who have adopted Zalon so far. Their model identifies factors like gaming skill and propensity to click on ads that are associated with campaign purchase. The marketing team then uses this model to target advertising to a set of gamers seen as most likely to adopt.

After one week, the results of the targeted advertising campaign come in, and the executives are delighted. The conversion rate for this latest offer was 12%, more than double the base rate of 5% and 20% higher than the previous advertising initiative. Clearly, the targeted advertising was working!

In modern marketing departments, this type of analysis takes place daily. It's known as "propensity modeling," which is a key approach in predictive analytics. Note how the model used in this example seeks to identify the best prospects and then send ads to those gamers.

But Is This the Best Approach?

Your DSIQ comes into play when you recognize that maximizing ad effectiveness is not about predictive analytics but instead a causal analytics problem—and it requires a different analytics approach, namely "uplift modeling." Uplift modeling is different from propensity modeling in that instead of asking "Which consumer is most likely to buy?" we ask instead, "Which consumers' *purchase behavior* is most likely to be influenced by an ad?" For instance, if a customer is 95% likely to buy Zalon without ever seeing an ad, it may not make sense to target advertising to them. But, if a customer's chance of buying quadruples from 10% to 40% when they are shown an ad, it makes a strong case for targeting them. Uplift modeling, then, is a form of causal analytics. We ask how an action, in this case targeted advertising, will change buyer behavior.

So What Is the Best Model for a Firm to Use?

It turns out that uplift modeling maximizes profits for a firm. But it is not trivial to implement. For example, there are numerous challenges to measuring the incremental change in consumer behavior attributable to a specific campaign. Consequently, our message to marketing leaders is that they need to understand this distinction (uplift vs. propensity), assess challenges to implementation, and then guide their organization in the best direction. The AIA Framework helps leaders see the critical difference between predictive analytics (propensity models) and causal analytics (uplift models) and develop the right strategy for the business problems they want to solve.

Conclusion

There's a strong case to be made for the central message here: Analytics is a leadership problem, and as a marketing leader it's critical to raise your DSIQ, or data science intuition quotient. That's not at all about becoming a data science expert; rather, it is gaining a working knowledge of AIA to drive business value, using the ideas here and elsewhere.

Leaders who invest in this working knowledge of data science will become more effective in leading their teams through challenges large and small, identifying the types of projects where AIA delivers the greatest value, and collaborating on the execution of these initiatives. Together, these activities can transform your organization. Best of luck on your AIA journey, wherever it takes you.

Author Biographies

Eric T. Anderson is the Polk Bros. Professor of Retailing, professor of marketing, director of the Kellogg-McCormick MBAi program, and former chair of the Kellogg Marketing Department. He holds a PhD in Management Science from MIT. His articles have appeared in top scholarly journals in marketing and economics, as well as in the *Harvard Business Review* and *Sloan Management Review*. Academic research awards (Paul E. Green Award, Weitz-Winer-O'Dell Award) recognize his impact on the field of marketing. His book *Leading with AI and Analytics* (co-authored with Florian Zettelmeyer) was published by McGraw-Hill in December 2020. Eric has served as marketing department editor of *Management Science* since 2014 and has been a member of the Canadian Tire board of directors since 2016.

Florian Zettelmeyer is the Nancy L. Ertle Professor of Marketing and former chair of the Marketing Department at the Kellogg School of Management at Northwestern University. He also founded and directs the Program on Data Analytics at Kellogg. Professor Zettelmeyer specializes in evaluating the effects of analytics and AI on firms. He teaches the MBA elective "Customer

Analytics," a key analytics course at the Kellogg School of Management. He has received numerous teaching awards and has been voted "Outstanding Professor of the Year" by Kellogg MBA students. He is a research associate of the National Bureau of Economic Research (NBER). Professor Zettelmeyer co-directs Kellogg's "Leading with Big Data and Analytics" executive education course for senior leaders. Professor Zettelmeyer received a Vordiplom in business engineering from the University of Karlsruhe (Germany), an MSc in economics from the University of Warwick (UK), and a PhD in marketing from the Massachusetts Institute of Technology.

CHAPTER 21

Leveraging Technology to Manage the Customer Experience

Aparna A. Labroo

Technological changes over the past decade have given rise to new opportunities and new challenges for firms with respect to managing profitable growth through effective customer acquisition, retention, and development. In this chapter, we discuss some of these opportunities and challenges and the importance of targeted customer acquisition to boost subsequent customer retention and development, as well as how repeat customers can provide indispensable guidance on how a firm can prioritize its efforts and resources. We outline the ways business-to-consumer firms have embraced these opportunities and challenges and how using technology to enhance consumer experiences impacts firm growth and profitability. We also review case studies of the ways in which effective business-to-business firms are embracing the opportunities and challenges technology offers to manage customer experiences and relationships and grow their revenues exponentially. We highlight the similarities and differences in customer needs and relationship challenges unique to business-to-business firms and delineate frameworks for managing customer relationships in both business-to-business and business-to-consumer contexts.

Profitable Growth Through Customer Acquisition, Retention, and Development

Firms earn revenues when customers purchase their products and services. As a result, firms often focus on providing more products and services and garnering more customers. Growing one's share of customers in the marketplace, however, does not guarantee that a firm will become an increasingly profitable venture. A firm becomes profitable when it provides products and services that solve important problems its customers are facing, when it solves these problems better and faster than its competitors can, and when it solves these problems in a manner that employs its unique strengths that are not easily copied by competitors. For this reason, a crucial source of competitive advantage for the firm includes a deep understanding of customer experiences; what customers value and what they do not value; how, when, and why they consume the offerings; and what their pain points are. In the era of big data and artificial intelligence, a large volume, variety, and velocity of transaction and customer data are available to firms. These data can allow firms to predict the return on marketing investment of different marketing decisions such as customer targeting, pricing, distribution, or advertising.

The garnering of such insights is facilitated when first-time customers become repeat customers. When customers repeat purchases, a firm learns about these customers and has access to insights that its competitors may not have. By using these insights, the company can anticipate and develop new products that better serve the needs of its current customers and a cluster of similar customers, which competitors without similar insights cannot offer. Customer learning, therefore, can enable a firm to better direct its scarce resources of money and time into ventures that offer it the most returns, and, in a sustained manner, create a win–win situation for itself and its customers. When a firm provides increasingly exceptional products and services to its customers, these customers in turn seek additional products and services that serve more of their needs from that firm. By garnering a larger share of the customer wallet, the firm can increase switching costs for that customer. Firms that focus on increasing their "share of wallet" of a customer—that is, the proportion of a customer's overall needs served—rather than just "share of customers" become increasingly indispensable to their customers. The firm can also learn what the deal-breakers are that might prompt its customers to trade off the value they get from their current firm and start afresh with a competitor because the competitive offering provides more incremental value despite the switching costs.

Focusing on current customers' share of wallet instead of increasing share of customers in the marketplace can feel risky to managers, especially to startups and smaller firms for whom gaining new customers may be a key goal. Ironically, focusing on share of wallet can be a more effective pathway to also increasing share of customers in the marketplace, for both smaller and larger firms. Customer learning can help a firm prioritize where to direct its limited resources to attract new customers who are more likely to value its offerings over customers who may be harder to convince; moreover, advocacy from existing customers who share positive word of mouth regarding their experiences can reduce the acquisition cost of such customers, who in turn are more likely to become repeat customers. The most valued asset a firm can have, therefore, may be the ability to learn about its customers, and to turn that learning into relevant action faster than the competition can. Even small differences in customer retention can have sizeable downstream consequences in terms of a firm's future growth and profitability. Thus, the pathway to a larger market share may be through a strategy to gain a larger share of the customer wallet.[1]

For example, consider two firms, Firm A and Firm B. In Year 1, both begin with a base of 100,000 customers. Starting in Year 1, both also have an acquisition rate of 20%. That is, each firm's customer base grows yearly by 20%. The only difference is that Firm A has a customer retention rate of 85%. Firm B understands its customers better than Firm A and, therefore, has a customer retention rate of 90%. Assuming these customer retention and acquisition rates remain the same year after year, in Year 15 Firm A would have 197,993 customers, whereas Firm B would have nearly twice that number, or 379,349 customers. Thus, in less than two decades, assuming an identical acquisition rate and a constant retention rate of 85% versus 90%, Firm B would have nearly twice the number of customers that Firm A has. It is important to note that this number pertains to the number of customers, not to sales from these customers. The difference in customer sales between these two firms is likely to be even larger because return customers, compared to new ones, on average spend more and spend more often. Furthermore, the higher retention rate is likely to ultimately result in a higher acquisition rate for Firm B, because returning customers generate more positive word of mouth that in turn reduces the firm's customer acquisition cost and/or increases its customer acquisition rate.

Not surprising, firms with exceptional marketing teams pay close attention to acquiring the right customer as doing so can boost their customer retention rates. They also invest resources in trying to retain their existing customers, targeting similar customers, and developing their customer relationships to gain a larger share of the wallet of these repeat customers. We now turn our attention to describing why managing customer experiences and relationships can be the path to profitable business growth for B2C firms.

Managing Consumer Relationships and Experiences in the B2C Context

This section reviews a case study showing that managing customer experiences and relationships can be the path to profitable business growth compared to focusing on increasing customers for any firm, and especially a startup. We argue that to build effective customer relationships, firms must prioritize from the start which customers to acquire and, just as important, which ones to not acquire. Next, to help managers assess which customers to acquire and which segment to target, we present a decision tool they can use to calculate the lifetime value of a single customer that any segment might deliver. This calculation forces managers to think about the profitability of a customer into the future rather than as a sale transaction in the present moment. This valuation, along with other factors such as untapped segment size, segment growth rate, fit with the firm's capabilities, and attractiveness of the segment, can help managers to make strategic customer acquisition decisions. After providing a guide to managers on how to choose which customers to target based on the ease of acquiring and retaining them and the margins they provide, we then provide managers with guidelines regarding how to choose which experiences to mass-customize from a universe of opportunities that technology now offers to them for their target customers. The section concludes with a discussion of the customer journey and how managers can develop systems that connect meaningfully with their customers to enhance customer experiences.

Managing Customer Experiences and Relationships Is the Path to Business Growth

As discussed in the opening section of this chapter, effectively leveraging technology to build relationships and enhance experiences of users of its products and services—especially for resource-constrained startups—can lead a firm from marketplace irrelevance to marketplace dominance. For market leaders, processes that effectively leverage technology to build relationships and enhance experiences of users can provide continued competitive advantage and differentiation.

A case study that effectively highlights both these propositions is Netflix.[2,3,4,5,6,7] Founded as a subscription mail-order DVD company in 1997, it has redefined entertainment and now is the top digital streaming platform, with over 167 million subscribers. Through the preference data it has available on its users, Netflix knows even before its subscribers do that a program will entertain them. Where Netflix stands today is a far cry from when it beseeched Blockbuster in 2000 to buy it out for $50 million. Its turnaround came in 2003, after Netflix became profitable for the first time. With a profit of around $300 million and only 1.5% of the DVD market, Netflix looked at its current users to garner insight into who valued its service and why. It discovered both: It had a disproportionately large share of the indie film market compared to its primary competitor, Blockbuster, and a disproportionate share of its customers were seeking indie films. This discovery led Netflix to the insight that while receiving DVDs at home may be more convenient for subscribers and the lack of late fees may be desirable, these factors were *not* its differentiator with Blockbuster; it was unlikely that indie film viewers found Netflix more convenient than non-indie film viewers. Rather, the differentiator was variety and the range of DVDs that Netflix could offer, and Blockbuster could not. Because a brick-and-mortar business is constrained by limited shelf space, Blockbuster focused on popular film offerings that served mainstream subscribers. As a result, the tail of the market—those seeking offbeat films—would often not find the offerings they preferred. Netflix, released from shelf space constraints, could focus on serving these subscribers.

By focusing on the needs of these users for offbeat DVDs, Netflix was able to proactively use its preference data to develop the world's most exceptional recommendation system, enabling users to discover offbeat offerings they did not know about. Mining a treasure trove of subscriber data on what its customers watched—when, how often, on what medium, for how long, and at what time—allowed it to efficiently offer a wider range of offbeat offerings to its targeted cluster of indie film lovers. Knowing what these indie film lovers would recommend to other subscribers with whom they shared tastes and preferences allowed Netflix to develop clusters and networks of customers and make mass-customized recommendations, proactively offering subscribers recommendations from similar subscribers of what else to view. This approach led to a loyal base of customers but also rapidly attracted new users looking for indie films from a largely underserved segment.

With the evolution of technology, Netflix in time became a mainstream global entity and went on to broaden its target segment to include users seeking offbeat content and to redefine itself as an original content provider serving the immediate anytime, anywhere entertainment needs of subscribers. The deep customer insight garnered through analyzing decades of the sheer volume, velocity, and variety of intricate data on networks and clusters of subscriber preferences was the basis of this growth and transformation. Even today these data are a competitive advantage for Netflix to defend itself against new and intensifying competitive threats from Disney, Apple, Hulu, and others. Insights from these data enable Netflix to attain an original content success rate substantially higher than that of an average network program. Focusing on customer experiences and relationships with existing users, therefore, can provide a resource-constrained firm with the insight to make strategic trade-offs that help it prioritize resource allocations to activities that are likely to yield higher returns and is the foundation of successful firm growth and profits.

Strategic Customer Relationship Management Begins with Acquiring the Right Consumer

To be effective, firms should carefully consider and separate from the start which customers they wish to prioritize acquiring and others who are not their main target. The same dollar is better spent by a firm targeting customers who have a higher need for the firm's products or services and, therefore, are easier to acquire and retain, offer higher margins to the firm because they buy more frequently, buy more expensive options, and buy a range of options. In this context, it is important to recognize that consumer needs are heterogeneous and that different consumers value different product benefits. Whereas consumers may say they want everything in a product and for free, they recognize there is no perfect product for free and that they will need to trade off various product benefits to optimize what they truly want most. It is unlikely that any firm will have adequate resources of money, time, personnel, and so forth to provide all experiences to all customers and more effectively than the competition, especially the competition that chooses to focus on a particular need. Thus, firms must choose which customer needs to serve.

Customer data allow firms to group potential consumers into completely exhaustive and mutually exclusive clusters—that is, groups in which each potential consumer is in one group and only one group—based on the benefits they value most. Some clusters necessarily will be larger than other clusters in terms of how many consumers they contain, but this difference does not imply that a firm should target a larger (or more mainstream) cluster over a smaller one.

For instance, consider the market for prepared coffees. For some consumers, coffee is an add-on to other more substantial breakfast items. For other consumers, the coffee is the main experience and food is the add-on. Both sets of consumers are likely to say they value high-quality coffee at a reasonable price. What they mean by high quality and reasonable price, however, is likely to differ, with the former group being more price sensitive than the latter group. A firm such as Starbucks may be ill advised to focus on the former group, even though that group is likely to be larger and more mainstream, whereas a McDonald's may be able to serve that target more effectively. Both firms, therefore, would benefit from estimating how valuable each type of customer may be to them.

To Acquire the Right Customer, Calculate Their Lifetime Value

The value of a customer can be calculated using techniques like those managers use to compare the lifetime returns of other types of capital investment opportunities and choose among them. Just as a manager who wishes to maximize returns on an investment in any capital project might compare the opportunity cost of investing resources to pursue one project over another, a manager could adopt a similar mindset to consider the opportunity cost of investing resources to pursue one type of target consumer over another. Customer acquisition is akin to acquiring an asset, and different groups of consumers are differentially valuable assets for different firms.

A useful decision tool to estimate how valuable a customer of a certain type is to a firm is to assess the lifetime value of that customer to the firm. This enables managers to think about the profitability of a customer into the future and move beyond the mentality of a one-time immediate-sale transaction. The only substantive difference between methods used to calculate lifetime returns of a capital investment and lifetime returns from an acquired customer is that, unlike a capital investment, a customer is not guaranteed to remain with the company indefinitely; therefore, a yearly retention rate adjustment must be made to account for the probability that the customer will remain with the firm. This valuation, along with other factors such as untapped segment size, segment growth rate, fit with the firm's capabilities, and attractiveness of the segment, can then be used by managers to make strategic customer acquisition decisions.

The lifetime value of a customer is the sum of returns or margins the firm expects from that customer discounted to its present value and adjusted for the probability the customer remains a customer for the given period, less the cost to acquire that customer. For example, consider that this year it costs Starbucks $100 to acquire a customer (AC) who values coffee as an experience as opposed to an add-on. Starting the following year after acquiring this customer, Starbucks earns a margin (M) of $250 each year from the customer, which is the difference between the price and variable cost of providing any one product to that customer summed over the total number of products the customer buys. Let us assume further that the retention rate (R)—the probability a customer returns the next year—is 70%, and that the cost of capital (i)—or the current value of a future return—is 7%. Starbucks additionally estimates that this customer will stay with Starbucks for five years. The lifetime value of this customer for Starbucks would therefore be (−) acquisition cost + present value of [year 1 margin * probability the customer is retained year 1] + . . . + present value of [year 5 margin * probability the customer is retained through year 5] = $-AC_0 + M_1 * R/(1 + i) + M_2 * R^2/(1 + i)^2 + M_3 * R^3/(1 + i)^3 + M_4 * R^4/(1 + i)^4 + M_5 * R^5/(1 + i)^5 = \$316$.

Starbucks could also calculate the lifetime value of one customer who prioritizes price over experience. For Starbucks, the acquisition cost of such a customer is likely to be both higher than the acquisition cost of a customer who values experience and higher than what it might cost a firm such as McDonald's, which is set up to serve the price-sensitive customer. Furthermore, the margins are likely to be lower because prices Starbucks could charge these customers are likely to be lower and costs of serving such customers higher compared to the competitor who is set up to leverage operational efficiencies at the cost of customer experience. As a result, the retention rate of such customers is likely to be lower for Starbucks compared to customers who value experience and compared to the competition. Starbucks could do these calculations not just for itself but also for its main competitor.

These calculations are likely to reveal two things: first, that the experiential customer may provide a higher lifetime value to Starbucks than a value-oriented customer, and second, that the experiential customer may provide a lower lifetime value to McDonald's than a value-oriented customer. Accounting for segment size and the fact that most firms are unlikely to be able to exhaust the entire segment and acquire every person in the segment, Starbucks may find that it is more remunerative for it to enhance experiences over operational efficiency, while the reverse may be true for McDonald's. Thus, unless there is a strategic reason for Starbucks to focus on efficiency (e.g., inefficiency is undermining the customer experience), Starbucks may be better off building experiences that its own type of customers value.

Technology Enables Mass Customization, But Managers Still Must Choose Which Experiences to Scale

Technology is now enabling firms to become more customer centric than ever before. But along with opportunity to become more customer centric—serving individualized needs at a mass level—comes the challenge of choosing which of a universe of possible experiences to prioritize with limited firm resources. In such situations, managers are often tempted to copy what their more successful competitors are doing. Instead, managers may be better served by choosing among experiences to mass-customize those that its users value most and that are in line with building out the firm's differentiation or competitive advantage. Specifically, in any industry a firm is likely to be relatively more operationally efficient (e.g., McDonald's, Toyota, Samsung), more innovation driven (e.g., Wendy's, BMW, Apple), or more driven by the variety of experience (Burger King, Mercedes, Starbucks) than its competition. Managers should force themselves to recognize which one of these business models or disciplines provides them the highest competitive advantage against a specified set of competitors.

Keeping this differentiator in mind and what their customers value most (e.g., speed/convenience, innovation, variety), managers can choose which experiences to mass-customize. The path to success is different for each of these business models; target consumers of operationally efficient firms, for instance, may value customization that improves speed and consistency of service at an individual level, whereas target consumers of variety-driven firms may value the range of offerings they are provided at a customized level even if it comes at the cost of speed. This proposition should not be read to claim that firms should *only* invest in opportunities that build on their strengths but that they should excel where they have unique strengths while being adequate where competitors excel.

Starbucks is a customer-centric firm that differentiates itself based on providing varied customer experiences.[8] Through its app, it focuses on enhancing experiences of existing consumers. It enables them to buy their favorite customized beverages anywhere and at any time, with minimal waiting, even when they were not planning to make a purchase. A major functionality of the app, however, is that the technology proactively makes recommendations to create and satisfy an unplanned urge for a customer's favorite beverage and recommend associated products at an individualized level based on the customer's purchase history. Mobile order and pay make the process seamless for the customer, reducing the pain of payment by automating it and ensuring that the beverage is available as soon as the customer arrives to pick it up. The star rewards and drink rewards serve as an additional incentive to buy, and Merry Monday special promotions offer reward customers special offers to share or for themselves. These aspects make the Starbucks experience more enjoyable for their customers; they also improve operational efficiencies for Starbucks and allow the firm to serve these customers more seamlessly, further improving their experience. Customized cobranding with iTunes or the *New York Times* further delights the core customer and increases commitment of this customer to the Starbucks brand.

The McDonald's app functionally does almost all the things the Starbucks app does at an individualized level. On a superficial level, the two apps are indeed very similar. However, the strategic purpose of both apps and the kinds of experiences they prioritize are different. McDonald's still focuses on ensuring speed and consistency when it provides individuated recommendations to its consumers, offering promotions of popular items at times the store may be less full. Providing "deliciousness at your fingertips," the app emphasizes exclusive deals that prompt purchases of their bestsellers and easy ordering.

The Starbucks app instead prompts discovery and purchases of varied, even lower-selling items the customer may come to like based on their past purchases. The McDonald's app customizes experiences for the masses in a manner that is driven by making the firm even more operationally efficient because its target consumers value convenience, ease, and value, therefore driving unplanned sales toward bestsellers. In Europe, the Exxon app does something similar. Through mobile pay, Exxon focuses on the convenience and ease of its customers and allows them to fill up and be on their way as quickly and conveniently as possible; it also makes recommendations about where customers can fill up sooner and more quickly because this is the benefit their consumers value most. The goal of the Starbucks app instead is to make experiences even more discovery driven because that is what their target consumer prioritizes; therefore, it drives unplanned sales toward variety, new products, and high-margin unique purchases. The important takeaway here is that functionality differs; many apps may look similar, but brands must prioritize the delivery of those experiences their customers value most. Functionality should be driven by the needs of target consumers and the firm's competitive advantages in serving its consumers.

Thus far we have argued that (a) a focus on improving share of wallet of one's target customers can increase share of customers in the marketplace and may be the pathway to rapid and sustained business growth; (b) because firm resources are limited and customer needs are heterogeneous, firms have to choose from the start which customers to acquire and, therefore, which experiences to optimize; (c) the largest segments of customers may not be the most profitable for a firm and just as any manager compares returns on different capital investments, managers should compare the lifetime value that one customer in any segment delivers and from that calculate the firm's business opportunity; and (d) while technology is fundamental to enhancing customer experiences, firms have a universe of experiences they can deliver. Managers should mass-customize experiences that arise from and build on their key differentiators and serve their customers' most important needs.

We now turn our attention to how managers should execute customer experiences once they have chosen who their customers are and which experiences to mass-customize.

The Customer Journey: Executing on Customer Experience

A popular aid for organizing tactical decisions regarding when, how often, and what experiences to deliver to customers is the customer journey framework. The customer journey framework allows firms to design customer experiences and build digital capabilities that map the consumer's mindset at each phase of the decision process to the firm objectives that can be achieved most effectively given the consumer mindset in that decision phase.

The consumer decision process typically moves from a preliminary stage in which the consumer may have a latent need, or one is created, to a stage where the consumer becomes more aware of the need and actively begins seeking a solution to that need, to engaging in a consumption activity and fulfilling that need, to reflecting on that need post consumption. Consider, for instance, a consumer's need to travel. The consumer may begin "dreaming" about travel. This latent need may become overt after they view travel posts on Instagram or Facebook from friends, colleagues, or even strangers. As the consumer becomes more conscious of this need, they might enter the next phase of "research and planning." In this stage the need experienced by the consumer becomes more concrete, and the consumer begins to search for viable travel options—dates, locations, travel itineraries, and so forth. The consumer next makes a purchase by booking the travel. They then consume the product or service and experience a stay at their travel destination. The final and fifth stage is post-experience reflection when they might post about their experiences to others. For any firm, managing customer experience begins with phase one of this decision-making process and continues through phase five, with each phase offering opportunities for the firm to influence new customer acquisition and retention. Using technology to create customer experiences, it may be possible for firms to merge several of these decision-making phases—for example, by evoking a need in a consumer and moving them toward the consumption process more quickly.

In each of these decision phases, the consumer has a particular mindset and approach to information. In the dreaming phase a consumer may be looking more for entertainment and, therefore, be more open to emotional connections with the firm. As the consumer moves toward research and planning, and then purchase, the consumer may become more deliberative and look for rational reasons to educate themselves and then make the purchase. Once the consumer experiences the product or service and engages in post-purchase reflection, they may again become more emotional and be swayed by and more likely to share their emotional experiences with others.

A firm's goals in connecting with the consumer across these five decision phases moves from entertaining the consumer, to educating the consumer, to converting the consumer, to persuading the consumer of the value of the experience, to inspiring the consumer to inspire other consumers to try the firm's offering. Furthermore, different social media platforms, social media content, and other technologies connect more effectively with different mindsets of consumers and accomplish different firm goals. For instance, viral videos and Instagram may help a firm connect more effectively at an emotional level with consumers, promote dreaming, and create an initial awareness, interest, and desire to buy among consumers. Search engines may instead connect more with the rational consumer and facilitate research, planning, and purchase.

To create a digital plan, managers can build a matrix in which they map firm goals to consumer mindsets and in turn to the type of social media that best accomplish firm and consumer goals jointly. Consider, for instance, the Accor group, a global, asset-light (mostly franchised or managed properties) hotel conglomerate with over 500,000 rooms that spanned the economy, mid-level, and luxury segments across nearly 4,000 properties, 17 brands in 92 countries and 6 continents by 2015. At this time, Accor discovered that the entire hotel landscape had changed. Consumers were more digitally connected and had higher expectations than ever before. Accor's main collaborator—the travel agent—had now become competitors and taken the form of online travel agent (OTA), and aggregators such as **Booking.com** and **Hotels.com** were putting price pressure on the conglomerate. In addition, there was new competition in the form of two-sided platforms such as Airbnb serving consumers seeking authentic travel experiences. With a value proposition promising customers reliable consistency across properties within each brand, the challenge to create enriching travel experiences that offered consistency across the parent brand and within each brand globally, as well as an authentic local experience, was considerable. Accor designed these experiences by employing content strategies along the customer journey that mapped the firm's goals to the consumer mindset.[9]

The problem Accor faced was that they ended up paying huge fees to **Booking.com** and other similar OTAs or aggregators when consumers booked through these agencies. Consumers tended to book through these agencies because they were able to offer better preference matching to consumers across hotels in all locations; they also offered more trust and certainty regarding what the consumer would find once they arrived at the property by presenting reviews from other consumers. The challenge for Accor, therefore, was how to get travelers to book directly through Accor property websites. Knowing that its differentiator from other hotels was consistency and reliability of experience, Accor set out to mass-customize reliability. For those consumers who booked directly, Accor was able to determine the types of guest amenities they preferred. Accor also was able to offer locally authentic entertainment and other options to travelers, such as cooking classes or visits to a spice market depending on the property, while still ensuring consistency of the overall hotel experience. Finally, Accor was able to personally delight consumers, especially those consumers whom they could identify as regulars and those who were influential on social media, by designing special events for them such as a birthday gift or other freebies. These actions led these influential consumers to generate word of mouth about their experiences on social media, which in turn helped with new customer acquisition. Finally, to ensure consistency, Accor set up systems to monitor complaints online and offline for each of its properties on a real-time basis and monitor the speed at which these were addressed to ensure that consumers who came through

OTAs would leave satisfied and be more likely to write positive reviews, helping to manage customer churn.

Accor's digital plan included actions to drive traffic to the **accor.com** website, host interesting user-generated content to increase conversion of visitors to the website, put Accor at the top of review sites, anticipate guest online venues, and share posts from platforms such as TripAdvisor, Instagram, and Pinterest to further create direct connections with consumers who are in the dreaming, planning, or booking stages. Accor additionally created an app to host content and interact with user-generated content in real time, planned activities to surprise/delight influencers, and captured even more user-generated content while consumers were experiencing their stay. Post stay, Accor continued to connect with its consumers by managing content on Google, Accor, and TripAdvisor and by using insights from the user-generated content to further enhance consumer experiences that future users would be more likely to share.

This example highlights the strategic nature of the decisions Accor made to create specific experiences that served its target consumers' needs for a consistent experience that incorporated local attractions and authenticity that could generate positive word of mouth. The decisions were based on an understanding of the major challenge faced by Accor—that OTAs had eroded its value proposition of offering the ultimate in trust and consistency—which Accor excelled in addressing by focusing on its strengths. The plan also put Accor on a more level footing relative to platforms such as Airbnb that were all about individuated experiences; Accor could not have customized the guest experience to that extent. Thus, Accor successfully customized mass experiences to create stronger connections with its existing customers and used their word of mouth to attract similar customers, allowing it to take on the competition by OTAs that previously threatened to commoditize Accor.

Managing Customer Relationships and Experiences in the B2B Context

B2B managers may wonder how these learnings regarding customer experience and relationship management apply to their firms. In this context, it is important to remember that customers of B2B firms also are heterogeneous and have different needs.

Small customers are resource constrained and generally have less access to providers for their needs. At the same time, because of limited resources they cannot carry large inventories, which means that being out of a component needed to run their business can be extremely costly for them.

Thus, small-firm customers typically prioritize things such as invoice accuracy and transparency, better credit terms, and an omnichannel approach; they also appreciate the ability to connect with the provider anytime, anywhere, and in different ways so they can get their orders fulfilled in the quickest, most flexible, and most urgent manner and get immediate answers to simple questions (e.g., Where is my product?). In addition, they value advice on product choice based on value for the money and technical characteristics.

Large customers are less resource constrained and have more channel power. Providers to larger firms, therefore, must go beyond offerings that can become commoditized and result in price-driven competition. In this respect, larger customers may benefit from things that allow them to differentiate from their competitors: These can include, for example, dedicated account teams, applicative support and expertise, and direct connection to software and procurement systems that ensure activities run smoothly and only superficial day-to-day contact with the provider is needed. Factors such as joint innovation days from which the provider can derive insights to develop the next generation of products that provide cutting-edge advantage to large customers and build long-term relationships with customers can be valuable to differentiate the provider from its competition.

Technology can be employed to create experiences customers value the most and that deliver on these aspects. An example of a B2B firm that does exceptionally well in leveraging technology to serve thousands of small customers is AirGas[10]. AirGas supplies gas cylinders to all kinds of small firms, including contractors, mechanics, and welders. Their customers rely on the gas to cut, join, weld, melt, disinfect, heat, or cool surfaces and is therefore required by a large number and range of small firms.

Founded in 1982 by Peter McCausland with the acquisition of $3.5 million local industrial gas and welding distributor Connecticut Oxygen, AirGas raised $20 million through an IPO in 1986 and a secondary offering in 1987. By 2018, it had acquired 500 independent gas and welding distributors, had experienced a compound annual growth rate of 18% over 30 years, and had $5 billion in revenues and 16,000 employees.

The reason for this incredible success is that McCausland identified a huge unmet need of small firms ($1–$12,000 per year)—customers in this space rarely had sales reps call—and leveraged technology to create valued customer experiences and relationships. Although each customer might provide only a small amount of business, aggregating these amounts over 1.2 million customers meant the estimated market was over $2.5 billion a year. At the same time, these small firms could not be without parts because they could not afford to carry inventory. Thus, McCausland decided to focus on small accounts, designing customer experiences using technology and following the motto "think like a small business owner." To serve these small, neglected, geographically dispersed customers, AirGas needed to guarantee immediate product delivery.

Airgas set up an omnichannel that included a professional sales force and branch offices, each one with one or two employees and an average sales of around $10 million. As the internet developed, AirGas improved its online presence. It also allowed customers to connect via telephone. Rather than sit and wait for breakdowns for customers in remote areas and for their orders to come in, AirGas set up "Total Access," a proactive system that would estimate needs of different customers in advance of these needs arising and make additional product recommendations based on learnings from similar customers. This system resulted in 70% of the calls from the center being proactive outbound calls and allowed AirGas to achieve next-day service to 60% of the United States and 48-hour service to 95% while logging 20 million service transactions per month. In many ways, this model is not very different from the one used by Netflix. Understanding the customer need and building experiences that strengthen customer relationships is indispensable in both the B2C and B2B context.

One difference between the B2B and B2C contexts is that in the B2C context, relationships can go through a more distinct ignition phase, maintenance phase, and reactivation phase. The needs of customers can change based on whether the customer is a large or small firm but also based on what phase the relationship is in. For instance, for small firms in the early phase of the customer relationship, setting up credit terms may be a primary factor influencing the customer experience, but for large firms the primary factor may be to designate an account manager. In the maintenance phase, the primary factors influencing the customer experience for small firms may be on-time delivery and invoice accuracy, but for large firms the primary factors may be designing joint R&D days or electronic data interfaces. In the reignition phase, omnichannel may be a primary factor influencing the customer experience for small firms, but for large firms the primary factor may be to discover new partnership opportunities through joint R&D days. Effective customer experiences are designed with keeping the primary customer need in mind, as these are likely to yield the maximum return on the investment of capital and time.

Conclusion

This chapter reviewed the importance of setting up effective customer experience and relationship systems. It discussed steps necessary to build such systems—starting from defining goals, choosing targets, and employing the customer journey. Various case studies demonstrated how these systems can be set up to deliver the maximum return on investment to a manager. We also demonstrated similarities and differences in how B2C and B2B firms set up these systems. Overall, we highlighted opportunities for managers to leverage technology to grow share of wallet of existing consumers by understanding their needs rather than by an unfocused strategy of maximizing share of consumers in the marketplace.

Author Biography

Aparna A. Labroo is a consumer psychologist and professor of marketing at the Kellogg School of Management at Northwestern University. She has an MBA from the Indian Institute of Management (Ahmedabad) and her PhD is from Cornell. An exceptional educator and an expert on branding and marketing strategy, she teaches courses in the EMBA, Executive Education, and MBA programs, and is winner of the J. Keith Murnighan Outstanding Professor Award and the Chair's Core Course Teaching Award. Through her career, she has worked with over 5,000 executives, has served on advisory boards of startups and nonprofits, and has consulted in the pharmaceutical and nonprofit space. Her research on consumer decision making, including health decisions, financial decisions, prosocial behaviors, and creativity has been featured in the *New York Times, Time, MSN, Forbes*, the *Financial Times, BusinessWeek, Scientific American*, and other leading media outlets, and she has presented this worldwide. She is the recipient of the Society for Consumer Psychology Early Career Award and is or has served as editor-in-chief, associate editor, or on editorial boards of leading marketing and psychology journals.

CHAPTER 22

The Consumer INSIGHT Framework: A Hypothesis-Driven Approach to Data Analytics

Derek D. Rucker and Aparna A. Labroo

Porsche, established in 1931, continues to exude an iconic identity around high-performance sports cars. The Hershey Company, founded in 1894, maintains itself as a beloved and highly recognized confectioner. DuPont, established in 1802, remains a leader in science and engineering innovation more than 200 years later. None of the founders of these companies is alive, yet their brands continue to live on and enjoy a healthy life. Indeed, perhaps one of the strongest signs of great marketers is their capacity to build a brand identity, persona, and vision that long outlive their progenitors.

Achieving enduring brand success of this magnitude is difficult. Marketers must analyze factors related to consumer needs, competitive actions, and company strengths to formulate their marketing strategies and deliver relevant tactics. Marketers must also respond to changing marketplace conditions and rapidly evolving technologies. Indeed, as contemporary marketers strive to achieve the success of Porsche, Hershey, and DuPont, they find themselves in rocky territory. The rapid rise of technology has increased the urge among marketers to react instantaneously to the large volume, variety, and velocity of data at their fingertips, and a marketing manager's focus has become increasingly tactical.

In this chapter, we call for a shift in how marketers should think and practice. We suggest reining in unguided action in favor of hypothesis testing of cause–explanation–effect relationships. If followed to its fullest, our perspective offers a potentially transformative advance in how to think about, manage, and build one's brand.

The Need for a Hypothesis Generation Mindset

A core problem that has arisen in today's marketplace is that marketers have pressure to act with immediacy at the cost of formulating adequate hypotheses regarding the predominant cause of the problem they are trying to solve. This step, however, is crucial for managers who wish to direct their limited resources of money and time in a potent fashion. A central problem with the practice of marketing today is that it all too often adopts an *action-oriented approach* as opposed to a *process-oriented approach*. Put simply, marketers act first and explain later rather than observe and theorize first and then act with precision.

Faced with the need to act, one of marketing's fundamental bedrocks—strategy—can languish and even risk being forgotten. The problem is that such behavior is analogous to pressing down the accelerator to speed forward in an automobile without a working steering wheel. Yes, you will get somewhere fast, but that somewhere might not be a desired destination at all. Let us share an example to better illustrate what is meant by an action-oriented as opposed to a process-oriented approach.

We turn to consider a situation faced by Procter & Gamble and their Head & Shoulders shampoo in India. From 2014 to 2017, the brand faced decreasing market share despite media presence and distribution being stable. A tactical, reactionary solution, might have involved increasing media spends and improving distribution. Perhaps P&G might have directed resources to markets where competitors were gaining share. Big data could have spotlighted the markets where share was declining fastest and where competitors gained the most. However, while this approach would allow immediate action, this solution could also have been suboptimal or even incorrect. Many factors could have caused share decline. The product may not have been effective, competitors may have had a more effective product, or consumers may not have had a need for such a product. Directing resources to media and distribution, while actionable, would not have solved any of these problems.

Instead of immediately acting, the team at P&G tested and ultimately dismissed these hypotheses. They offered an alternative hypothesis: Consumers believed that any shampoo would prevent dandruff. Rather than direct resources to increase brand awareness or improve distribution, the team focused resources on solving the problem they had identified—that their consumers believed that any shampoo prevented dandruff. The brand ran advertisements that showcased embarrassing instances of having dandruff because other shampoos failed to prevent it. Rather than act with immediacy, the brand team took time to develop and test hypotheses to understand the underlying cause of the problem and respond accordingly. We suggest that brands must embrace such a process orientation to successfully survive in the marketplace.

The remainder of this chapter is divided into three parts. First, it explains the importance of shifting from an action-oriented mindset to a process-oriented mindset. Second, it introduces a framework for guiding the development of process-driven insight that leads to a workable solution. Third, it discusses how digital platforms offer a potentially rich landscape for enriching a process-driven orientation to produce more effective marketing and brand-building solutions.

Action-Oriented versus Process-Oriented Approaches

The Action-Oriented Approach

The action-oriented approach refers to the propensity to observe data and take an action in response to those data. This approach is necessarily backward looking and reactive, not forward looking or proactive. For example, a brand manager might receive data that suggest they are losing share in a market; in response, they might reduce prices, run a promotion, or try to copy the customer experience the competitor offers. But competitors get ahead when they do things based on their strengths; by following a stronger competitor, success of the me-too tactician manager is doubtful.

In a data-poor world, the lack of a multitude of constantly emerging data can actually facilitate data integration—albeit of impoverished data—as well as a focus on and prioritization of key issues. The irony of a data-rich world is that the constant stream of newly emerging data from a variety of sources can obscure the true problem at hand from managers; as data flood in, managers feel a need to act with a greater urgency. Faced with these pressures, managers seek simple solutions, such as outsourcing their decision making to algorithms and AI. Although algorithms certainly have value, they can also come with a cost: In many cases they prompt backward-looking decisions. At issue is that the quality of future outcomes depends on how valid the past conditions will continue to be. Moreover, in the case of competition, managers invite becoming trend followers rather than trend setters.

Take, for instance, Art Henks. For two years after he became CEO at Gap Inc. in 2015, the company struggled with declining sales, the rise of highly successful fast-fashion competitors such as Zara that commoditized fashionwear through their reliance on big data and predictive algorithms, and the growth of e-commerce. As a result, Henks fired all creatives and, copying his competitors, turned his efforts toward big data instead.[1] As history revealed, simply turning toward big data and AI would not solve the problem. The following year Gap's profitability decreased even further. While Henks took immediate action, the action itself neither identified nor solved the true problem: that Gap Inc. had failed to update its iconic 1990s positioning of being a classic, all-American, understated, uber-cool brand that was a trend setter.

By reacting to and imitating its major competitor, Zara, which had ten times the revenue at the time as Gap, Henks possibly set Gap up for failure. Henks copied competitors' strengths, at which Gap was not set up to excel. Unlike Gap, Zara was successful because its core business model was to commoditize fashion as a trend follower. Every aspect from its retail and production to promotion and distribution was geared toward this differentiating advantage. With factories located close to fashion capitals, Zara was able to identify trends early. By retailing in the plushest locations next to the most high-end fashion wear, it benefited from an aura of luxury and saved on advertising costs. By only producing limited batches, it offered reasonably priced products but with strong margins. Most of all, in its reliance on big data—unlike Gap, which had a history of trying to push underselling products at discount—Zara had extensive records of successful products that would sell out because every aspect of its business was set up to ensure this success. Thus, unless Gap changed all aspects of its business to become exactly like Zara, it was unlikely to have chosen the right path to become successful. Moreover, even if Gap changed its entire business model to imitate Zara, it would not have the data pertaining to decades of successful sales growth. As such, it's unclear whether reacting to its problems by copying Zara could ever lead to a differentiating advantage.

Over the past two decades, this action-oriented approach increasingly reflects the most prevalent decision-making style that marketing managers and business managers appear to use. Managers seem to gravitate toward an action-oriented approach for a couple of reasons. First, action-oriented approaches have an immediacy to them; that is, they are responsive to data and can produce the feeling of instant progress. Second, in some cases, an immediate corrective action can certainly help brands solve a problem. Indeed, value exists in taking actions in response to data. However, the problem with an action-orientated approach is that it is reactive as opposed to generative. When managers react, their actions reflect a disproportionate weight on whatever information they received first (the primacy effect), whatever is most recent (the recency effect), and whatever is most salient (the prominence effect). Factors that increase the availability and cognitive accessibility of some information over other information are not necessarily what should be used to cull or prioritize information. Unfortunately, by creating a sense of progression, the action orientation also reduces managers' ability to learn from mistakes—to recognize that the solution they enacted was one of several they could have undertaken. As such, an action orientation can lead managers to fail to generate and consider better alternatives.

An action orientation also can fail to produce an insight that is generative in nature. By taking immediate action, a manager may not truly understand the root of a problem (e.g., slipping sales), which impedes their ability to ultimately solve it. Consider a brand of tax-filing software that has lost share to a competitor. The brand runs advertisements on Facebook and finds that its sales increased 5% a week after running the ads. The brand, with proper controls and modeling, might find evidence that suggests its action—running the Facebook advertisements—increased sales. However, notice what this observation does not tell us. It does not tell us why the Facebook campaign was the right response to the brand's problem. It does not tell us that a similar campaign will work the next week, the next month, or the next year. It does not tell us whether a similar campaign will work on another platform, such as display ads on websites or against a higher-income target. It does not tell us that it was the best option for the brand to take. Put simply, by focusing on taking an action (e.g., advertising) in response to data (e.g., loss of share), managers leave a lot on the table when it comes to obtaining insight about the cause of a problem. As a result, the action (e.g., advertising) might offer a short-term gain that does not actually solve the underlying problem.

The Process-Oriented Approach

We propose the process-oriented approach as an alternative to the action-oriented approach. With this approach, managers use data to understand, test, and explain *why* a problem is occurring. Rather than react immediately to data, managers first generate alternative, and a broader range of, explanations for why something is being observed. A focus on explanations—the process underlying a problem or behavior—is central to the process-oriented approach.

To illustrate, consider a situation where a competitor advertises on a new social media platform. Consistent with the action-oriented approach, a brand manager could respond immediately by also advertising on the platform, increasing their advertising presence elsewhere, running price promotions, and so forth. In contrast, the process-oriented approach encourages a brand manager to consider what problem the competitor's action introduces. That is, rather than react with action, the manager identifies what problem, if any, is introduced by the data. If a problem is identified—for example, the new platform suggests share may be stolen—the process-oriented approach asks the manager to generate hypotheses to explain why this problem has arisen. Why does advertising in this channel lead to a potential loss of share? Is it because the channel itself is central to consumers' decision making? Is it because the advertisements convey a new benefit that undermines the brand's position?

Generating hypotheses allows for discussion and testing that offers insight to researchers on how to prioritize data. In fact, hypothesis generation can reveal the importance of data that may not have been prominent or available when the problem first arose. Thus, we advocate that managers investigate their data to check which of their hypotheses may be the most viable, rather than allow themselves to be pushed by data that happen to be momentarily salient or react based on a sliver of data. If a new competitor is entering the market, a brand manager should ask whether, why, and how consumers might change their behavior in response to the competitor, and which consumers are more likely to react in the proposed manner. Although this argument might come across as simple in form, at its core it represents a philosophical shift from asking *what* marketing lever to pull in response to data (i.e., an action orientation) to focusing on the right data and understanding what the data say in response to the hypotheses generated (i.e., a process orientation).

To further illustrate this difference, consider a government that is concerned about the number of accidents its citizens have around trains. The action-oriented approach would likely lead the government to consider, for example, posting warning signs near train tracks, advertising the number of fatalities that occur every year, using social media channels to encourage train safety, or even changing safety regulations. These actions could be meaningful in changing year-over-year accidents and fatalities. However, the emphasis is on the levers that can be pulled to produce an effect of interest; taking these actions ultimately requires little insight, if any insight at all, as to what causes accidents around trains in the first place.

In contrast, a process-oriented approach would go deeper by asking *why* people are having accidents around trains. Focusing on the explanation for the consumer behavior essentially calls for generating hypotheses about the *process* that explains why a behavior occurs. Rather than ask what it can do in response to accidents, the government asks why accidents or fatalities happen. Have previous efforts to educate people around train safety failed? Do people realize trains are dangerous? Do people enjoy danger? Notice that as we start to ask about the explanation or process, we have more enriched questions that can serve to generate hypotheses to inform our marketing efforts. Even if we want to pull a particular marketing lever—such as advertising—it is not the act of spending on advertising that reduces accidents. Advertising must influence behavior by solving a particular problem. And, as one begins to ask why advertising or any marketing activity exerts an effect, it becomes possible to understand what lever out of a potentially unlimited number of levers one must pull, and when one should pull that lever.

Implications of Process-Oriented Approaches

On its surface our line of argumentation may seem straightforward. However, it represents a significant departure from current marketing practice. To conclude the story on train safety, an action-oriented approach may lead to the simple and relatively easy-to-implement conclusion that the government should advertise being safe, so it simply needs to think about what venues to use. In contrast, a process-oriented relationship would force the government to think about what is causing the problem and thus why and under what conditions an action such as advertising would be valuable. In essence, a process-oriented approach demands that practitioners obtain insight about the consumer.

In the case of train safety, one reason accidents occur is that people believe they know how to be safe; consequently, directly advertising to them about train safety would fall on deaf ears. While they might need to be educated, they do not want to listen to information they believe they already know. As a consequence, simply pulling the "advertising lever" would not be effective. Rather, it is necessary to figure out how to bypass the belief people have that they already know about train safety.

Although this example is illustrative, it has a real-world analog. In Australia, a public safety campaign was run to encourage train safety. However, rather than just place signs or advertise being safe, the advertisements discussed "Dumb Ways to Die." The campaign featured a catchy song about numerous dumb ways to die; only at the end of several minutes did the campaign reveal that being stupid around trains is also a dumb way to die. The campaign waited to identify the true message so that consumers did not disengage because of content they believed they already knew. The campaign was reported to be associated with double-digit reductions in accidents after its launch.

The distinction between action-oriented and process-oriented approaches has a fundamental implication for how data should be used. In its strongest form, an action-oriented approach takes in data and reacts to that data. The problem is that, as depicted in Figure 22.1, although some of that data might be particularly useful (e.g., high relevance), some data might be moderately useful (e.g., moderate relevance), and some might be relatively useless (e.g., low relevance). Because an action-oriented approach prioritizes

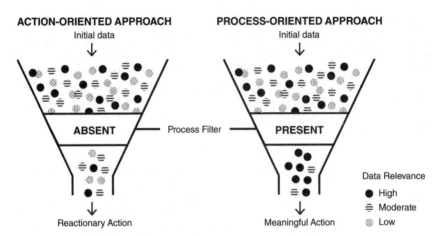

FIGURE 22.1 Action-Oriented versus Process-Oriented Approaches

action, it sacrifices the prioritization of what data should be used. Thus, it may end up employing more data, more irrelevant data, and responding in a sporadic and noncoherent way to more salient data. In contrast, a process-oriented approach challenges managers to think about the underlying problem and thus prioritizes the use of data that informs that problem. Doing so helps managers sift through the data and reduces the quantity of data used, facilitates the use of more relevant data, and removes less relevant data. The result is that a process-oriented approach helps managers formulate a course of action that is hard-hitting, coherent, and incisive at hammering out the root cause of a problem.

In summary, the first major proposition of this chapter is that marketers must move from an action-oriented approach to a process-oriented approach. Essential to accomplishing this objective, marketers must pivot from thinking about what actions they should take and toward understanding the consumer. However, a common question that typically follows the discussion of a process-oriented approach is: How does one even begin to think about explaining or extracting an insight about people? The next section addresses this matter.

The INSIGHT Framework

Part of a process-oriented approach is understanding the underlying motivations of the target customer as opposed to simply focusing on the actions a manager can take. Thus, a process-oriented approach relies on obtaining insight into the psychology of the target. But to uncover these insights, managers, entrepreneurs, and nonprofits are often uncertain of where to even begin.

To be fair, uncovering insights about the psychology of the consumer can be an arduous process. Yet, when done properly, insights can be a powerful means to understand how levers influence behaviors, which can result in a much more judicious use of marketing dollars. But let us take a step back and start by understanding what an *insight* is. We adopt the definition of an insight as a *meaningful human truth* associated with motivations and perceptions that guide action, or inaction, of target consumers.[2,3] To expand on this definition, an insight is about the consumer (i.e., human), it can be used by the brand in an informative way (i.e., meaningful), and it is accurate (i.e., truth). This definition can be a check that one is working with an insight as opposed to a piece of misinformation.

Recognizing the importance of insight, as well as the difficulty in doing research to uncover insight, the INSIGHT Framework, depicted in Figure 22.2, involves the consideration of six critical factors or pivot points: individual (I), network (N), situation (S), importance (I), generating hypotheses (GH), and testing (T). These factors collectively tie together the definition of an insight as a meaningful human truth. The first three factors involve the *human*-focused nature of insights. That is, they direct managers to ask questions that illuminate the target consumer's individual-level goals and motives, how the consumer is affected by their network, and/or how the consumer is influenced by the situation. The next factor, importance, focuses on weighting the available information about the individual, their network of influence, and the situational context to understand which information about the target is most *meaningful*. Finally, the last two factors involve generating hypotheses to test whether the ultimate information is *truthful*. Again, one can only be said to be operating with an insight when all these criteria are met.

The following discussion of the INSIGHT framework offers a brief primer of the core ideas as opposed to a deep tutorial on implementation and usage. Indeed, proper execution and application of the framework often requires multiple consults, workshops, or sessions. This is a way of thinking that becomes honed via experience. The objective here is simply to offer some

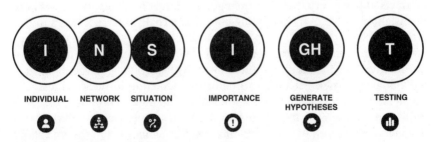

FIGURE 22.2 The INSIGHT Framework

exposure to these critical steps that facilitate the insight process. Each of these steps is supported by its own academic body of research and can be explored further at the reader's discretion.

Individual (I)

The first part of the framework involves understanding the *individual* consumer. Whether our brand is a consumer brand or a business-to-business brand, managers are talking to another human being. And human beings differ in a lot of ways! Thinking about the individual can be aided by more than a century of research in psychology and marketing on consumer goals, motivations, and beliefs. While people vary in numerous ways, the most important ones concern their goals, motivations, and beliefs. Indeed, we often focus on understanding beliefs in terms of how consumers think about the category and brands within the category.

Asking questions about people's goals, motivations, and/or beliefs can provide a first important basis for insight that can inform marketing efforts. For example, research in the persuasion literature suggests that people are more persuaded by messages that are tailored to their specific psychological needs. To illustrate, research by Fabrigar and Petty suggests that whether people are persuaded by information can depend on whether they hold attitudes that are based more around emotion or cognition.[4] Specifically, individuals who have more emotional attitudes, relative to more cognitive attitudes, are more persuaded by emotional arguments compared to logical facts. This knowledge helps determine how consumers' attitudes about a product can inform the type of information they would be receptive to. Thus, one set of questions for managers to ask, based on the individual aspect of the INSIGHT framework, involves understanding what the most prominent and pertinent consumer beliefs are, whether these beliefs have an emotional or cognitive basis, and/or how closely these beliefs inform the identity of the consumer.

For example, consider Merrick Pet Care, which produces pet products with high-quality ingredients. The brand has a fundamental understanding of the beliefs of its target. While the brand has an entire portfolio of dog food products, it has a very specific psychographic target on which it focuses both its insight efforts and its marketing efforts. Internally, Merrick refers to this group as "pet parents."[5] These pet parents love and treat their dogs as if they are their children. They want only the best for their pets, which means that the quality of the food is important to them. By recognizing this belief in such individuals, Merrick Pet Care can tailor its marketing to these targets. For example, one of the brand's innovations was to change its product packaging to list the high-quality ingredients on the *front* of the package. Part of this change was the result of understanding that the pet parent target cared about specialized ingredients. While these consumers would have put in sufficient effort to read ingredient information even when presented on the back of the package, putting it on the front conveyed to the consumer that the brand is in sync with them and their priorities.

Going beyond beliefs, managers could similarly ask questions regarding goals and motivations of their target consumer. For example, brands can ask what the consumer's primary goals are, why these goals are more important than other goals, what transcendental benefit these goals provide to the consumer, and so forth. By asking these and other pertinent questions, and peeling back the layers of insight, a manager might find solutions to their problems. For instance, for health-conscious consumers, highlighting the same cut of meat as 95% lean is likely to direct thoughts to the favorable qualities of the meat and increase purchase. However, stating that the same cut of meat contains 5% fat is likely to direct thoughts to the unhealthfulness of the meat cut and reduce purchase of that product. Of course, if the target consumer cares more about taste but is struggling to be healthy, highlighting the 5% fat may be a good strategy to convey that the cut will be tasty but still healthy.

Network (N)

Most consumers do not live life in isolation; as social animals, most belong to groups. That is, consumers have a *network* of other consumers who are part of their lives. This aspect has become particularly and increasingly important with the technological revolution and growth of social media. Interpersonal factors—ranging from the influence of strangers, to acquaintances, to close others—impact the choices consumers make. These sources can serve different roles as well. Ratings from strangers on Airbnb might provide a consumer with useful information, but the personal recommendations of close others might be more valuable when choosing a home remodeling contractor.

Moreover, some purchases can be influenced by multiple networks. For instance, the purchase of a car might be influenced by an individual's spouse but also by the opinions of friends or even by what a neighbor owns. Thus, asking the right questions to uncover deep insights regarding influences from interpersonal relationships with others can be vital to understand how consumers form their consideration sets as well as what might influence their ultimate purchase behaviors. The network part of our framework essentially places an emphasis on understanding the role of others in a consumer's decision making and behavior. It directs managers to ask questions such as how important a network influence is for a consumer, how big this network is and who is in it, and in what manner the network influence operates.

Numerous examples illustrate the potentially potent impact of others. As one example of the role of a network, consumers are likely to hold their beliefs with greater certainty when they learn that others share their opinions.[6] This certainty can be important, as people who have more certainty in their beliefs are more likely to act on those beliefs. As an additional example, people might also purchase (or abandon) products when they become adopted by a desirable (undesirable) referent group.[7] As these examples illustrate, understanding consumer behavior requires understanding those around the consumer as well.

A brand that understands the influence of consumer networks well is the United States Marines. In developing their website, they offer content directed to the consumer considering joining the Marines. This content informs the individual of what to expect and what the experience offers. However, their website also includes separate webpages built to house information for the *parents* of potential recruits that explains the life of a Marine and how their children will be treated. Clearly, the brand understands that a person's decision to join the Marines might involve, or even require, consultation with their family. In essence, decisions aren't always made in isolation, which is increasingly the case in a highly interconnected world. As such, value can be created by attending to the network that surrounds a target.

Situation (S)

Situation reflects the fact that individual preferences and network effects do not take place in a vacuum but exist within a context. Separate from factors of the individual or their network, their situation and their environment can change. For example, seasonal factors, such as weather, can affect what consumers value. A consumer might be more prone to value a thirst-quenching beverage on a hot summer day than on a cold winter night. Similarly, consumers might be willing to pay more for a bottle of wine when ordering it at a fancy restaurant than when purchasing it from a grocery store or online for home consumption. Although the product is identical, the nature of the situation can shape consumer behavior. A discussion of situation in the INSIGHT framework asks what is going on in consumers' environment that might either shape or interact with individual and network factors.

As an example of being sensitive to the power of the situation, consider the Godiva chocolate company. Godiva is a premium chocolatier; a box of a dozen truffles can retail for over $50. When a recession limited the brand's sales, presumably because of its high cost, it sought to better understand the consumer by creating a forum for Godiva lovers to discuss their passion for chocolate; this forum also offered an opportunity for the brand to engage with consumers and hear about their pain points. Of interest, the brand learned that during the recession these Godiva consumers missed their chocolate, but they felt the price point of a box of chocolate was too high to justify it to themselves without feeling guilty. The brand responded by shifting its portfolio to offer *smaller* boxes of chocolates that could be obtained below a $20 price point. This change in promotion offered consumers the indulgent experience they craved at a price point that assuaged their guilt.

Importance (I)

Of note, the individual, network, and situation elements of the INSIGHT framework all focus attention on the consumer in some form. That is, they ask about factors directly tethered to the individual, their network, or their situation. As such, these three factors are all focused on the *human*, a first check on whether one has an insight. However, recall that an insight must also be meaningful. A fact about the individual—such as whether they like warm weather—may hold little or no importance when it comes to marketing a brand's product. Thus, after asking a range of questions and gathering appropriate data, the manager must sift through and prioritize that data, placing decision weights on the collected information so that meaningful hypotheses can be distinguished from less meaningful ones.

Two independent sets of questions guide the analysis regarding placing decision weights on information. The first is the consumer perspective on the relative chronic and temporal importance of individual, network, and situational factors. This aspect focuses on the consumer's natural state of equilibrium as well as on recent changes in these three factors. To take the example of business attire, the network effect (i.e., what others think of the attire) may outweigh situational and individual goals. In contrast, in a looming recession, the situation might guide a target consumer's goals, while motivations and network influences may become less important. In essence, the temporal weighting of individual, network, and situational factors can vary; brand managers have to understand how important they are in the context of interest.

A second set of questions pertains to how important the information obtained is to the brand. In some cases, a brand might discover information that has value to the consumer or to a competitor but that cannot be used by the brand. For example, in the dietary supplement category, a brand might learn that as consumers age, they begin to have back pain. This observation might be important to the consumer, but it is of little value to the brand unless it can offer a remedy to this problem, and one that is better than what competitors already offer. Alternatively, if another brand has already executed against an insight, it may not be of value to a new brand. Indeed, when Old Spice deodorant tried to speak to its ability to make people attractive, it failed; one explanation for this is that the category leader, Axe, already owned this insight.

In short, gathering information about individual-level, network-level, and situational influences on consumers is an essential first step to gathering insight, but all data are not equally valuable. The information must be meaningful in that it is important to the consumer and can be used by the brand in some capacity. The aspect of the INSIGHT framework on importance serves to foster discussion of such matters.

Generate Hypotheses (GH)

The next aspect of the INSIGHT framework is to generate hypotheses. Assigning decision weights to factors pertaining to the individual, networks, and situation based on consumer and brand priorities encourages managers to generate hypotheses about which solutions are likely to be most effective in resolving the key problem. For example, consider a beer brand that identified a target segment of young millennials in America. At the individual level, these consumers aspire to achieve their dreams. Signaling that the American dream is still alive is something of importance to these consumers, and something that other brands are not talking about. This insight allows managers to act and leverage the opportunity to communicate to the consumer that the American dream is obtainable, especially for those who hold the highest aspirations.

This insight could then be used to generate different hypotheses. One hypothesis could take the form that networks can facilitate aspirational dreams collectively for the group. Thus, the brand can launch an advertising campaign speaking to the possibility that consumers' need to accomplish their dreams is achievable through the right networks of like-minded consumers, and their preferred beer is a way to identify, grow with, and share dreams with other aspirational consumers. An alternative hypothesis is that these consumers are highly individualistic and believe that although the dream is difficult to obtain, it is worth fighting for, and this beer is for those who have a fighting spirit. This hypothesis would result in a very different action by the brand manager, focusing not on collective strength to achieve one's dreams but on moments of individual grit. This latter hypothesis is consistent with what the Modelo beer company executed on in their "Fighting Spirit Campaign."[8] Specifically, Modelo identified a target that was, or desired to be, a *self-made* person, then used the stories of Hispanic immigrants who had come from little to become war heroes, astronauts, and the first female Hispanic military pilot. The advertising struck a chord, and the brand doubled sales from 50 million cases to 100 million cases in less than three years.

Test (T)

The final phase of the INSIGHT framework is testing. Testing is a means to assess which, if any, of the hypotheses that have been generated about the consumer is true. While the prior steps facilitate identification and articulation of an insight, testing facilitates the choice of the potentially most influential insight and guards against executing on insight that is misguided. Testing the hypotheses generated can be done in several ways. For example, "pet parents" might lead a manager to generate the hypothesis that their consumers want their dogs to have more than clean teeth; they want their dogs to have fresh breath so they can kiss them. To test this hypothesis, a brand could conduct focus groups with consumers to discuss and unpack the accuracy of this insight. A brand could also show early copy to consumers to see how they react to a change in price, an advertisement, or a promotion. Indeed, it is also possible to use digital platforms to test ads among a select set of consumers.

One can also test a hypothesis via market performance. While testing a hypothesis in the market might have the advantage of focusing on the actual behavior of interest, it can be costly, especially to learn that the hypothesis was wrong. In a well-known flounder, Tropicana repackaged its product to have a fresher and more contemporary image. The brand was reported to have lost millions in sales as consumers did not respond well to the new packaging. This example contains two additional observations of importance. First, the brand appeared to be operating largely with an action-oriented approach that they assumed would lead to a positive response and possibly greater sales. Second, even the brand's assumption of this simple relationship was wrong, which highlights the value of testing. Testing completes the definition of an insight by demonstrating that the meaningful human truth is, in fact, true.

Obtaining and Testing Insight in a Digitally Supersonic World

Insights allow managers to better understand, innovate, and communicate value to a target. While the rapid development of technology has created more ways to communicate with consumers, this does not mean insight should be forsaken. In fact, our argument is that the volume, velocity, and variety of data create an additional need to first garner insight. Technology, when used properly, offers additional opportunities to obtain and test insight. This section does not provide tutorials on the use of specific technological tools to obtain and test insight; rather, it provides exemplars of how technology can do so. Although various approaches exist, we focus on the distinction between observational and experimental methods.

The Observational Approach

The explosion of technology has created a wealth of publicly available data. This data can be used to understand consumer behavior and factors related to the individual, network, and situation. For example, Google Trends allows users to look at the type of information consumers are searching for. As such, it can be used as a means to both obtain data and test hypotheses. For example, L'Oréal used Google Trends to evaluate competing hypotheses about the next home haircare treatment of interest to consumers. L'Oréal had seen the development of three different styles among celebrities—splat, ombré, and tie-dye. Splat involved patches of different colors in one's hair, ombré involved dyeing the tips of one's hair, and tie-dye involved rainbow-colored hairtails. Were these fads or trends? The brand used search behavior to see whether some of these styles were taking on more value to consumers (i.e., increased search over time). They found that ombré showed a much stronger increase in search, which suggested it may be more important for the brand. This led the brand to produce a home haircare solution for ombré styles that led to successful growth.[9]

In the business-to-business context, Air Gas provides hydrogen and nitrogen cylinders, among other products, to small businesses such as metal welders, contractors, and mechanics. These consumers use the gas to cut, weld, disinfect, and shape metal. The firm learned from its sales force that businesses refer to cylinders as bottles. Before reacting and rebranding all cylinders as bottles, they did a Google Trends search and found that while referring to hydrogen cylinders as hydrogen bottles was indeed more common among customers, the reverse was true for nitrogen cylinders, which customers referred to as cylinders rather than as bottles.

Another form of observation involves content or sentiment analysis—that is, analyzing the language in text. Indeed, tools exist that can now be used to analyze large datasets to extract and understand both the positivity as well as the emotionality of the text.[10] However, it is possible to use such approaches more qualitatively; for example, one might look at headlines for common themes that reveal how consumers feel or think. Indeed, in the Modelo example referenced earlier, one way the brand obtained insight was to look at online newspaper headlines. The brand saw a theme of concern about the loss of the American dream surface time and time again. In the Gap example referred to previously, sentiment analysis could have been used to identify future fashion trends among target consumers that would fit with the Gap brand identity.

Brands can also use online interfaces to learn about consumers. For example, brands can invite questions and conversations that may allow them to learn about the pain points of their target. We shared the example of Godiva earlier. However, such an approach can also be powerful for business-to-business brands. For example, Maersk Line, which competes in the shipping industry, established itself on various social platforms where it could have conversations with customers. These channels allowed them to ask questions, such as what was bothering or of concern to consumers. Such conversations, if properly utilized, can be a powerful means to leverage social platforms to obtain insight for both business-to-consumer and business-to-business firms.

The Experimental Approach

The experimental approach can also be leveraged to obtain and test insight. For example, Facebook allows for A/B testing where brands can test different creative concepts against one another and see how they perform in the market. One less effective data-mining execution of the experimental approach is to run a large number of experiments without any hypothesis but alter minute aspects of advertising to different consumers and compare across all executions to see what works. The problem is that one can devise a literally infinite number of experiments, which is neither cognitively tractable nor empirically affordable. Indeed, this risks creating a situation of dustbowl empiricism, where managers are largely blind to whether they are even testing the right variations. Moreover, any observation uncovered through such testing is specific to the population, execution, and timing.

Credible science requires the identification of replicable generalizable truths and not momentary whims specific to the observations that happened to be tested at a given time, place, and circumstance. Of course, such concerns are addressed by focusing on tests driven by a process-oriented approach that emphasizes the generation of hypotheses.

To illustrate, consider Kellogg graduate Nicole Cuervo, creator of the Springrose brand. One offering of the brand is an adaptive bra meant to make the process of putting on a bra easier for those who have limited mobility (e.g., from arthritis, stroke, paralysis). Nicole had an insight around the target's experience of pain, but she had different ideas about how to best communicate this insight. For example, should the pain be depicted with some form of visual image? Or might depicting pain directly cause people to react negatively? Was presenting pain sufficient, or should she combine the problem with solution imagery? To address these competing hypotheses empirically, she could use the Facebook platform to test ad copy that described the product benefits (e.g., Figure 22.3, left image) and another ad that more directly featured an image of pain (e.g., Figure 22.3, right image). In essence, she could start with competing hypotheses—whether showing the pain image might be more or less effective—and bring empirical evidence to bear upon this matter. Indeed, Nicole found that depictions of physical pain accompanied with solution imagery outperformed other ads tested. However, ads that featured pain without the solution imagery were inferior to ads that didn't show the pain visually.

Having found that depicting pain with solution imagery was the most effective, Nicole could now quickly develop other executions that showcased concrete instances of pain along with solution imagery, consider speaking to such issues on her website, and even seek blogs and online groups to connect with her brand. Thus, testing for insight results in greater confidence in the observed data outcomes and can be utilized to cover an expanded range of marketing solutions around that insight.

FIGURE 22.3 Hypothesis Testing of Different Concepts for the Springrose Brand

Insight is a competitive advantage that facilitates the maximization of returns on brand spending. That there is no time or money to drill for insight is a fallacy. As an analogy, imagine a restaurant where consumers complain about the service or that the menu is bland. The manager could say, "Well, we don't have time right now to improve those issues," but the reality is that the restaurant may well lose to one across the street that established itself as having great service and an exciting menu. In a similar regard, if managers do not invest time in understanding their target, a competitor eventually will, and this outcome can be far more costly than the time and money spent on developing an insight.

Conclusion

In the modern world, managers are inundated with data that can help them build their brands. However, the danger is that data tend to drive action rather than understanding. The challenge to marketers is to move their thinking from an action-oriented approach to a process-oriented one. Central to this process is obtaining insights—meaningful human truths—that steer brands to better understand, innovate, and communicate with their targets. The INSIGHT framework facilitates asking the right questions to gather this insight. While the expanding digital landscape offers various challenges to marketers, it also offers a potentially rich opportunity to obtain insights. Through the strong application of insights, new brands can emerge to stand alongside the likes of Porsche, Hershey, DuPont, and others.

Author Biographies

Derek D. Rucker is the Sandy & Morton Goldman Professor of Entrepreneurial Studies in Marketing at the Kellogg School of Management at Northwestern University. He holds a PhD in psychology from The Ohio State University. His research focuses broadly on social rank, compensatory consumption, persuasion, and consumer behavior. His work asks, and seeks answers to, what makes for effective advertising and what motives underlie consumer consumption. To answer these questions, Dr. Rucker draws on his rich training in social psychology. His work has appeared in leading journals, including the *Journal of Personality and Social Psychology*, *Psychological Science*, the *Journal of Consumer Research*, the *Journal of Marketing Research*, and the *Journal of Consumer Psychology*.

Aparna A. Labroo is a professor of marketing at the Kellogg School of Management at Northwestern University. She has an MBA from the Indian Institute of Management (Ahmedabad) and her PhD is from Cornell. An exceptional educator and an expert on branding and marketing strategy, she teaches courses in Kellogg's EMBA, Executive Education, and MBA programs, and is winner of the J. Keith Murnighan Outstanding Professor Award and the Chair's Core Course Teaching Award. Through her career, she has worked with over 5,000 executives, has served on advisory boards of startups and nonprofits, and has consulted in the pharmaceutical and nonprofit space. Her research on consumer decision making, including health decisions, financial decisions, prosocial behaviors, and creativity has been featured in the *New York Times*, *Time*, *MSN*, *Forbes*, the *Financial Times*, *BusinessWeek*, *Scientific American*, and other leading media outlets, and she has presented this worldwide. She is the recipient of the Society for Consumer Psychology Early Career Award and is or has served as editor-in-chief, associate editor, or on editorial boards of leading marketing and psychology journals.

CHAPTER 23

Personalization— Today and Tomorrow

Tom O'Toole

In the previous chapter, we discussed customer centricity as the most effective business strategy and marketing approach to achieve the goal of growing customer value. If we carry customer centricity all the way to the individual customer level, we end up at personalization. The aim of personalization is to grow customer value by working to detect, anticipate, and predict specific needs, desires, and preferences, and act proactively to customize our marketing activity to be most effective for individual customers.

This concept is not new. Its roots can be traced back to 1993 when the book *The One to One Future: Building Relationships One Customer at a Time* by Don Peppers and Martha Rogers laid out many of the one-to-one customer marketing concepts that we know today as personalization.[1] That was a few decades ago, and while the view that they presented was engaging, it wasn't really doable at scale in practice yet because the technology had not matured enough. Yet the potential clearly was already there.

Personalization hit the radar again when McKinsey declared it the "holy grail" of marketing in a November 2016 article. Personalization—which McKinsey defined as "the tailoring of messages or offers to individuals based on their actual behavior"—showed compelling promise for increasing marketing effectiveness and was developing rapidly. A growing range of progressive companies was working to enable and adopt personalization.[2] The required customer data systems, analytics tools, and marketing practices were coming into wide use. Six months later, McKinsey declared that the technology "has finally advanced to the point where marketers can use real-time data in a way that is both meaningful to customers and profitable for companies." With this combination of advances in technology and marketing processes, data activation and personalization became nothing less than what McKinsey called the "heartbeat of modern marketing."[3] Two years later, in 2019, McKinsey predicted, "Personalization will be the prime driver of marketing success within five years . . . Advances in technology, data, and analytics will soon allow marketers to create much more personal and 'human' experiences across moments, channels, and buying stages."[4] (McKinsey has done a lot of good work on this subject, and so have BCG, Deloitte, Accenture, and many other firms.)

As this timeline shows, what was a breakthrough concept three decades ago has become doable and scalable, thanks to advanced technology for data and analytics, digital media, and marketing methods that allow marketers not only to identify customers and predict their behaviors, needs, and wants but also to reach them individually with relevant messages and offerings. Indeed, over the past five years, personalization has taken off, led now by the use of artificial intelligence (AI) to further advance marketing differentiation in real time across customer touchpoints at the individual level. The era of personalization has arrived, with more and more companies investing in enabling and using it at scale in a growing range of product and service categories. As this chapter will show, while personalization is a mainstay for leading marketers today, there are fascinating opportunities for advancing future practices that are now being developed.

Before continuing this discussion, though, we need to ask: What exactly do we mean by personalization? As I define it:

Personalization is delivering the right message, offer, or content at the right price to the right person at the right time through the right channel.

That's a lot of "rights"—and it's intentional. It means personalization allows the delivery of the most *relevant* message, offer, or content to a particular customer—what is most meaningful and desirable for that individual. *Relevance is the key that unlocks the potential of personalization.* As McKinsey stated in its July 2018 report, personalization at scale could drive 5–15% revenue growth for retail, travel, entertainment, telecom, and financial services companies.[5] Earlier, Ariker et al., in *Harvard Business Review*, reported that personalization could increase revenues by 5–15% while reducing customer acquisition costs by as much as 50%, and improving the efficiency of marketing spend by 10–30%.[6] Given numbers such as these, it's no surprise that chief marketing officers have been very interested in personalization in recent years, and their marketing initiatives increasingly aim to utilize this approach.

Technically, personalized offers can be made through a variety of methods and media—for example, by direct mail. (Ask anyone who has had a baby, turned 65, moved, or listed a house, and they'll tell you of being flooded with direct mail offers.) But today, the primary vehicles for personalization are digital channels, especially email, mobile apps, and targeted content on websites. While personalization involves differentiating customers at the most granular level—Fred is different from Jane is different from Mary—digital channels enable us to scale this approach to personalize messages and offers to millions of customers—individually, simultaneously, and often in real time. Plus, digital channels enable us to do so at a much lower cost. This makes it economical to target and personalize much more specifically than would be feasible through direct mail or other conventional media.

Thanks to data and analytics technology, digital media, and advanced marketing practices, the value of personalization continues to grow. Not only do marketers now employ personalization regularly, but customers have come to expect and like it. According to McKinsey, the vast majority (nearly three-quarters) of consumers now expect companies to deliver more personalized interactions. In 2021, McKinsey declared personalization to be a key engine driving performance and customer outcomes, observing: "Companies that grow faster drive 40 percent more of their revenue from personalization than their slower-growing counterparts." Further, it noted: "Across US industries, shifting to top-quartile performance in personalization would generate over $1 trillion in value. Players who are leaders in personalization achieve outcomes by tailoring offerings and outreach to the right individual at the right moment with the right experiences."[7]

The value of personalization is being realized today across multiple industries, which include not only retail, travel, telecom, and financial services but also consumer products, insurance, healthcare systems, pharmaceuticals, medical products and, soon, utilities and even waste management. It's important to note that personalization isn't just for, or being used only by, consumer marketers (i.e., B2C). Businesses marketing to businesses (i.e., B2B) can and do employ personalization, with growing effect; and, again, customers increasingly expect them to do so.

For B2B businesses, personalization often is applied at the account level (think of the account, rather than an individual person, as the customer), the distributor or retailer level (the distributor or retailer as the customer) and, increasingly, through B2B2C personalization. In B2B2C personalization, the marketer personalizes services, messaging, offers, and interactions for the individual end user of the product or service provided to its business customers.

For example, a corporate travel agency whose customers are large businesses with many travelers can differentiate the service, information, and offers that it provides to a corporation's individual travelers. John and Mary are employees of the same company, and both search for flights from Chicago to London and hotels in London, arriving on the same Wednesday and departing on Friday. However, the corporate travel management company knows that John's preferred airline is British Airways and Mary's is United Airlines, that John prefers an aisle seat and Mary likes a window, that John usually stays at Marriott and Mary likes to stay at Intercontinental, that John often calls a travel counselor personally while Mary books through her digital app, and that John never extends his stay while Mary will often extend her Friday stay over the weekend and depart on Sunday night.

Thus, in response to the same booking request, the corporate travel management company can propose a flight, seat, and hotel that meet John's preferences and do the same with a different flight, seat, and hotel for Mary. Plus, it can offer John an incentive to use the mobile app for his next booking (thus reducing costs for both the corporation and the corporate travel management company), but not a hotel offer to stay the weekend. At the same time, it can offer Mary a special offer from the local hotel to extend her stay over the weekend (thus generating additional revenue for the hotel, the corporate travel management company, and possibly the corporation) and perhaps also purchase theater tickets—offers that may appeal to Mary but that John would find irrelevant and possibly annoying. (This assumes that British Airways, United Airlines, Marriott, and Intercontinental are all approved for use in the corporation's travel policy and that the corporation permits personalized marketing and additional offers to its travelers.) This realistic example illustrates that personalization in B2B2C marketing can be a win–win–win, generating greater value for all three parties involved.

B2B businesses are also increasingly enabling personalization by their customers. In other words, a growing focus of B2B marketers is enabling their customers (businesses) to do personalized B2C marketing to their customers. For example, a company that makes gasoline pumps for truck stops (a B2B manufacturer) may build in greater features and capabilities to enable users of its product to direct personalized marketing to their customers (truckers and individual travelers) at the pump.

Tapping the Power of Predictive Analytics

If data and advanced analytics provide the customer insights that make personalization work, the question then becomes: How do companies harvest such insights from their customer data? The answer: predictive analytics.

Predictive analytics are used to *anticipate outcomes*. As described by Kellogg colleagues Eric Anderson and Florian Zettelmeyer, predictive analytic models enable us to anticipate future business outcomes.[8] In other words, predictive analytics enable us to determine what is likely to happen. (Predictive analytics aren't the same as causal analytics, which enable us to change the outcome of what happens.)

Predictive analytics are an important tool for marketing today because they enable us to answer, and thus act on, practical questions:

We use *predictive analytics* to know...

- What product is a customer most likely to purchase *next*?
- What product may a customer have a *propensity* to purchase?
- *When* to offer the next product?
- How to present the next product? What *messages*? What *image*? *Where* in the purchase path?
- When is a customer at growing *risk of attrition*?

The answers to these questions, and many related questions, help us take the right action (for example, the right product offer with the right message) at the right time to maximize our marketing effectiveness, secure and grow customer value, and produce the intended business outcomes. At the individual customer level, the practical insights provided by predictive analytics enable us to personalize.

Let's take the example of a financial services company that offers a range of products. It offers checking accounts, savings accounts, credit cards, different types of investment accounts and instruments, auto loans, home loans, auto insurance, car insurance, wealth management, estate planning, and more. What product(s) should it offer to a particular customer and when? The more it knows about each customer, their stage of life, their transaction history, what financial products they now use, and so on, the more it can determine the next product to offer and when to offer it. Offering a debit card to a young couple, perhaps bundled with a low-interest car loan and certain basic investment products, may be very appealing, and yet would be totally irrelevant to that same couple years later when they are affluent empty nesters. At that point, wealth management, tax management, and estate planning services may be very important, which would have not been of interest to them at an earlier point in life. And, along the way, college loans, second home loans, and other offerings would be very relevant at certain points and of no interest at others.

Moreover, at times there were probably indications that the risk of losing the customer (in other words, of customer churn or attrition) was growing. Perhaps the couple began adding credit cards from other issuers offering more compelling features. The couple's charge volume and the company's share of wallet were declining. They were using less and less of the company's services and transacting less often (and doing more with competitors). Proactive marketing activity could be the difference between keeping and losing these customers (and thus between continuing to grow their value and losing their future value). In short, the more the company knows about its customers—their transaction history, behavior patterns, experiences, characteristics, and preferences—and can employ predictive analytics to anticipate and act on specific needs, opportunities, and risks, the more it can secure and grow the customer's value.

What makes personalization so effective? It comes down to one word: *relevance*. Here's a shorthand formula to capture this:

Data

enables

Relevance

increases

Effectiveness

produces

Value

"Data" here includes predictive analytics and now artificial intelligence. What's important is that while data and analytics enable relevance, it is the *relevance*—in terms of offer, messaging, and timing—that produces greater effectiveness and value.

Here's a simple example. Imagine that the marketing team for an Arizona golf resort is marketing to me personally. My age, income, stage of life, travel patterns, and other characteristics fit the profile of a golfer and suggest that I am an ideal target for the Arizona golf resort. Despite all that, I am not a golfer. I don't enjoy golf. I definitely would not travel to a high-end resort to play golf. Thus, despite the fact that based on customer segment and profile I seem like an ideal prospect, if the golf resort targeted me with a great offer for a golf stay in March, it would be totally irrelevant to me. They can offer me a discount, a suite, a free massage, free breakfast . . . I don't care and am just going to ignore it.

Now suppose this golf resort knows more about me individually, including that I love to take my young grandchildren to vacation destinations. Let's say that based on this insight they change their targeted messaging for me to say: "Our resort isn't just a great place to golf—it's also a great place to bring your family. We offer fun and engaging kids' programs for your grandchildren. Plus, there are lots of other activities and amenities for the rest of your family." Suddenly that message is far more relevant to me, and I'm interested. I'm likely to pay attention, invest time in getting more information on the resort, check their rates and room availability, and seriously consider a vacation there. And, they may not even need to offer me a discount or other incentives. If they do, the best features to offer would be those that make the stay better for my family, especially my grandchildren.

As noted earlier, not only must the messaging be relevant, but so should the timing. Let's say that someone is an avid golfer, goes to a resort destination with a group of golfing buddies every March, and is a perfect target for our Arizona golf resort. He probably starts planning that trip in about January. Sending him a message in late December, right in the middle of holiday busyness, may greatly diminish the likelihood that he pays attention to it. However, if that same message arrives in the right window—probably in early January—it's going to hit at the right time, with the right message, to produce the intended outcome: that he books a golf trip to the Arizona resort.

This simple example is not at all hypothetical. Thinking about it from the point of view of someone who actually did resort marketing, a series of other questions immediately comes to mind for how to refine the personalized marketing: When did he book last year? How far in advance of his stay did he book? Did he respond to a promotional offer? Did he use other resort services (such as the spa)? Does he search for information on Google? When? What sites does he visit? Does he book directly with us or through an online travel agent? Has he visited our website? How often? What did he search on? Is he a member of our loyalty program? Has he stayed at our other golf properties? And more. Plus, virtually all elements of this example are testable. How far in advance of the intended stay date should we contact the person? What promotional offer will be most effective for whom? What messaging should be used? In actual practice today, marketers are doing exactly this: using data and predictive analytics to personalize and then track, test, and optimize continuously, not just at the customer-segment level or by profile but for individual customers.

Delta Airlines: Increasing Customer Lifetime Value

To show that actual companies are using these concepts and practices in the real world to grow customer value and thus create business value, let's review the 2018 Delta Airlines' Investor Day presentation.[9] One graphic in particular highlighted Delta's goal of "growing loyalty to unlock value"—specifically, customer lifetime value. (As defined in Chapter 5, customer lifetime value, or CLV, is the total of the past and projected future profit generated by a customer.) Delta's SkyMiles loyalty program, particularly in combination with its cobrand credit card, is key to achieving its aim of growing customer lifetime value.

But that's not all. Delta's investor presentation also highlighted its focus on making the right product available to the right customer at the right time with the right offer, a narrative that should sound familiar. In a word—personalization! Delta goes on to specify personalization of offers and service as a key element of its multi-year strategy to improve all aspects of the customer experience and, thus, grow customer value. Finally, Delta directly relates personalization to increased customer loyalty, leading to greater revenue and profit for the company.

This is a great example of how a leading company in a major industry explicitly described its use of personalization as a means to increase customer loyalty and grow customer lifetime value, which in turn increases the company's revenue, profit, and, thus, its business value. It makes clear that personalization is not just a marketing practice but a key element of the company's business strategy. And, this example is from 2018. The personalization capabilities and expertise of leading firms, such as Delta Airlines, have advanced considerably since then and are still progressing, as we will see.

Auto Mercado: Personalization on a Smaller Scale

You might be thinking that personalization sounds great for a huge international airline with millions of customers, extensive customer data systems, and deep technical resources, but how applicable is it for a smaller company? One of my favorite examples is a regional grocery store chain in San José, Costa Rica, named Auto Mercado. A family-owned business, it began as a bar and coffee shop established by Guillermo Alonso Rodríguez in 1917 and grew into a regional grocery store chain specializing in imported groceries. Today, there are about 25 Auto Mercado stores located in the San José area and expanding outward in the country. In short, Auto Mercado is a high-quality grocery store chain, with excellent service and fine products, but not a large company by any means.

Auto Mercado established its successful Auto Frecuente loyalty program in 1998. Around 2017, the company's marketing team wanted to go further and use personalization to strengthen and grow its customer relationships. They built a centralized data platform that captures transactions and other data from multiple customer touchpoints and enables using it to tailor their marketing and customer interactions. By knowing what products the customers in their loyalty program are purchasing, they can send relevant messaging that is individualized to personal product preferences. For example, the company emails recipes to its customers, as many do. In this case, Auto Mercado can send egg recipes to a customer who buys a lot of eggs and let them know when eggs are on sale. On the other hand, a customer who has never purchased any meat or meat products (suggesting that the customer may be a vegetarian or vegan) can receive meatless recipes. It probably wouldn't be relevant to this customer, nor a worthwhile marketing activity, to send them recipes for short ribs and emails telling them that pot roast and hamburger are on sale; it may actually annoy the customer. Again, it's all about relevance. With greater relevancy in the messaging (e.g., recipes and food specials), enabled by customer data on purchase history and other information, Auto Frecuente seeks to enhance the customer experience and increase customer lifetime value through personalization. And, this isn't a global company with a big staff, elaborate customer data systems, and large budgets.

Customer Triggers to Optimize Timing and Content

At this point, let's turn our attention to one particular method of personalization: customer triggers (also known as trigger marketing). As the name implies, *triggers are specific occasions or events when a particular message will likely be most relevant to a customer.* As such, these triggers are opportunities to optimize the timing, content, offer, and design of customer interactions. McKinsey has found that trigger-based marketing efforts are three to four times more effective than standard communication.[10]

Trigger marketing allows messaging and timing to be personalized based on what's going on in the customer's life — for example, from buying a house to starting a new fitness regimen. But it's not limited to such tangible events. *An event can also be a change in behavior,* such as purchasing patterns—which can involve buying different product categories or, conversely, decreasing frequency of purchases. Or, the event may have the characteristics of a particular transaction, such as an indication that a consumer is purchasing for a family. The event also may be a series of service experiences with a telecommunication company or electric utility that might involve a certain number of service outages in a period of time. In other words, *the event may be revealed in data as opposed to being an observable life occurrence.*

I define trigger marketing as:

> *Event-driven marketing practices through which a marketing activity is automatically executed when a specific event or situation occurs.*

Some typical examples of events that often are triggers for marketing activity include:

- **First order from an online retailer.** The retailer may automatically send a welcome message with a promotional offer to incent another purchase soon.

- **New mobile app download.** The marketer will likely send a message to encourage creating and using an account, perhaps with a promotional offer for referring a friend to become a user.
- **A life event.** A graduation, a new job, a move to a new place, getting married, having a baby . . . all of these events are likely to trigger offers from a range of retailers to celebrate, furnish, or get ready for the new development.

Triggering a Renewal

A customer may subscribe to or contract for a product or service with multiple features, such as enterprise software, but then not use many of the features that they are paying for. The data may show that, if a customer is using only using 3 out of 10 features, for example, then there is a high likelihood that they will not renew when the time comes. The customer's limited use should trigger a proactive marketing message in advance of the renewal date to encourage, support, or incent using the dormant features to reduce the otherwise likely customer attrition. This example shows that trigger marketing applies to B2B business, not just B2C.

You can think of many other examples, and probably have some examples in your email on your phone right now. But, going further, there are other, less obvious examples of trigger marketing events based on high-propensity characteristics drawn from the customer's profile and transaction history. Perhaps a customer started using a product and then stopped; it might be a subscription service that was canceled or an app that is now seemingly ignored. For example, after listening to a mindfulness app for several days in a row, the person has stopped using it. This often triggers a message such as, "We noticed you haven't listened in a while. Here's some new audio content and exercises that we think you will like."

An event familiar to most of us is "searched but did not buy"—spending time on a website but deciding, for whatever reason, not to make a purchase. We've all received a message from an online retailer saying, "You left something in your cart." A more advanced version of the "searched but did not buy" event trigger is when we observe that the same customer has returned to our website or mobile app (or Google) multiple times to search for information on the same subject. If I search for men's athleisure shoes multiple times over a two-week period, but never buy any, that's a good signal that I may respond to an offer for the product.

Now, let's get into more interesting examples. Decreasing frequency of usage is also an "event" that can trigger a proactive marketing intervention.

In this case, it's not that we've lost the customer. It's that the data indicate that *we are in the process of losing a customer* or that *the likelihood of losing the customer completely is growing.* (In the meantime, the customer's value is steadily diminishing.) A timely purchase incentive for a product that the customer likes and has purchased in the past, or may like based on previous purchases, can lead to growing customer activity and value instead of losing that customer.

The Bad Experiences Trigger

A series of dissatisfying experiences for the same customer can be a trigger event. If the cable goes out once in a year, that's aggravating but probably doesn't cause a big jump in customer loss or warrant extraordinary marketing action. If a customer experiences three cable outages in a month, the data may show that the company's likelihood of losing the customer spikes. A "dissatisfaction score" can be used as a trigger for proactive marketing to mitigate the loss of customer value, and even customer attrition, resulting from an accumulation of negative service experiences. This dissatisfaction score, and/or the marketing investment to rectify the customer relationship, can be weighted or based on the customer value and other factors.

The Timely Reminder

We can use customer data and predictive analytics to reveal changes in a customer's behavior pattern and, thus, anticipate and act on likely customer outcomes and key inflection points in the customer relationship. An example is Audible, the audio book service, which awards subscribers with credits every month that they can use to "purchase" a book. When a customer approaches or reaches the maximum of six unused credits, Audible will send a reminder—a "don't forget to use your credits" message—encouraging people to use their credits for free audiobooks.

A question that came up in a class discussion was why Audible would remind people to spend their credits to get a free audio book that has a cost to Audible. "Why not just let the credits expire and save the cost?" While cost of the digital audio book is minimal, if we imagine that Audible was giving people a free physical book that cost $10, I could still see a rationale for the company encouraging the credit use and choosing to incur the cost. People not using their credits is probably a leading indicator of their not buying any additional books and, possibly, canceling their monthly Audible subscription.

In other words, when subscribers stop taking their free books, it's likely a predictor that they will stop buying paid books, and then not renew their subscription. Diminishing customer engagement and customer value are likely to follow. In other words, it's a signal that the company is in the process of losing this customer, or at least that their CLV is headed downward. The investment in awarding free audio books is well worth the cost to save a customer, stimulate their engagement, and maintain their CLV. Depending on their CLV, a promotional incentive that goes beyond just encouraging a customer to use their earned credits may be a good investment. Would it be worth giving that customer three free credits (perhaps contingent on their purchasing one audio book in the next 30 days)? If the customer is valuable, with lots of future value to come, it may well be. Again, all of this needs to be triggered based on (1) customer data and predictive analytics revealing that not using credits (taking free books) is a predictor of a customer's declining future purchases and/or subscription attrition and (2) the fact that a particular customer has stopped using credits and is signaling disengagement.

Another example is a fitness app such as "MapMyWalk," which tracks the number and duration of walks taken, distance covered, calories expended, and other metrics. It even provides lifetime stats of total distance, number and duration of workouts, and more. Fitness enthusiasts are probably familiar with the congratulatory messages that pop up after a certain distance or number of workouts. But there may be more to the messaging than seems evident. If a user stops after, say, 13 workouts, that person may get an encouraging "keep going" message. It may seem random that 13 completed walks trigger an encouraging coaching message to keep going. But the company's data may very well show that after 13 workouts (or whatever the number may be), people reach a threshold and their activity starts to drop off—as if telling themselves, "Okay, I'm good; I've done this." That's the inflection point, predicted from the data, to trigger a personalized message to the customer to get them past that plateau and keep them engaged.

It's easy to extend this example with a lot more specificity. The data, predictive analytics, and messaging can take many more factors into account—the type of workouts; the frequency, duration and intensity of workouts; the profile of the customer; and so on—to personalize the timing and messaging more precisely and relevantly. And, using AI, we could refine this much more.

AI for Personalization

Up to this point, we've talked about the use of data and predictive analytics to inform personalization and identify key events for it. As said earlier, it's all about relevance. Now, let's shift from predictive analytics to AI , and thus to the leading edge of personalization today. AI enables us to scale predictive analytics broadly, economically, accurately, and in real time.

We often hear that AI and machine learning are becoming essential to the practice of marketing and being used increasingly by a growing range of companies. That is true, but one may wonder: What are companies really using AI for in marketing? What are they actually doing with it? The answer is largely personalization. In *The AI Marketing Canvas*,[11] Raj Venkatesan and Jim Lecinski describe how marketers are using and can use AI to optimize their marketing and customer relationships. A theme throughout the book is personalization.

Personalization was among the first AI applications in marketing and is among the biggest. For example, a recent survey of 323 top marketers at for-profit companies revealed that more than half are already using AI in content personalization and predictive analytics for customer insights.[12] These findings are corroborated by McKinsey's 2021 report about marketers that outperform in personalization. "[These high performers] invest in rapid activation capabilities powered by advanced analytics. Leaders develop at-scale content creation and AI-driven decisioning capabilities so they can respond to customer signals in real time."[13] AI takes predictive analytics, and thus personalization, to its extreme.

Early adopters have been in this space for several years already. For example, in 2019, JPMorgan Chase said it was using AI to improve the impact and effectiveness of its marketing messages, such as emails to prospective borrowers. The financial giant signed a five-year deal with Persado, a software company, to put the power of AI behind its marketing copy. In its story about the AI marketing venture, the *Wall Street Journal* gave a comparison of the promotion offerings composed by human copywriters and the AI-powered Persado. Humans suggested: "Access cash from the equity in your home" with "take a look" as the call to action. Persado wrote: "It's true—You can unlock cash from the equity in your home" with "click to apply" as the action. Which did consumers respond to better? The data told a clear story. Persado brought in nearly twice as many applications for home equity lines of credit compared to the human-generated messaging.[14]

While using AI and machine learning for personalization is powerful, is it only available to companies with the scale and resources of JPMorgan Chase? What about smaller companies? Is using AI for personalization beyond their reach? No. It's within reach today and steadily becoming more so. AI and machine learning for personalization are available to companies of all sizes from cloud-based software-as-a-service (SaaS) providers. These include Google, Amazon, and a rapidly growing set of smaller providers such as Offer-Fit, a firm that offers AI-based personalization for small and mid-sized companies. The OfferFit AI personalization engine can learn and optimize the personalization of customer messaging to maximize response and, thus, marketing effectiveness and business outcomes.

Brinks Home Security is an OfferFit customer. According to an OfferFit customer case study, Brinks used the service to personalize contract renewal offers for each customer. Within two weeks, the AI-generated offers were out-performing the control; within a month, Brinks had improved its profit (measured by incremental customer lifetime value or CLV) by more than 200%.[15] As this compelling example shows, sophisticated AI and machine learning capabilities are increasingly available to and usable by smaller companies, putting powerful personalization tools into the hands of their marketers.

The Connected Strategy

A customer-centric business strategy (as discussed in Chapter 5) leads us ultimately to personalization. The aim of personalization is to grow customer value through relevance. Data and predictive analytics enable relevance. AI-driven personalization is now the leading edge of marketing practice. So, what comes next? It is personalization in a world of *connected* customer relationships.

Nicolaj Siggelkow and Christian Terwiesch articulate the nature and potential of connected customer relationships in their book *Connected Strategy*. As they describe, we are shifting from episodic transactions to continuous, connected customer interaction.[16] They write: "A connected customer relationship is a relationship between a customer and a firm in which episodic interactions are replaced by frequent, low-friction and customized interactions enabled by rich data exchange." Connected customer relationships provide an ongoing flow of information that enables companies to sense customer needs, wants, and opportunities and act before customers ask—often before the customer is even aware of the need. This takes personalization to the next level. The business can personalize its offerings, messaging, and interactions to meet customer needs, solve customer problems, and improve the customer's well-being before the customer even knows of the problem or opportunity.

The authors outline four levels of connectivity strategies for engaging customers:

1. **Respond to desire:** As customers search and select products and services, companies respond with reduced friction and increased speed—for example, Amazon's "1-click" setting to complete a transaction and check out.

2. **Curate offerings:** Companies recommend products and services with customized and personalized suggestions. An example is Netflix's what-to-watch-next recommendations based on a customer's previous selections.

The third and fourth levels are where it really gets interesting for personalization going forward.

3. **Coach behavior:** This includes guidance, reminders, encouragement, suggestions, and even gamification. These can be based on trends and patterns in customers' behaviors, which the data reveal but customers may not even realize. And, most important, it enables marketers to act *prospectively* rather than *retrospectively*. Fitbit is a prime example of continuous customer data enabling coaching behavior. As James Park, founder and CEO of Fitbit, said, "Our users don't want to be told what they did. They want to be told what to do . . . how to get better."[17]

4. **Automatic execution:** Now we are at the point of acting before a customer is cognizant, or perhaps even knows, that there is a need. Automatic execution opens a huge range of possibilities in personalization. For example, one can envision continuous blood glucose monitors, as worn today by people with diabetes, which can signal a change, trend, or pattern in blood glucose level that result in a new insulin formulation before the individual is even aware of it: in other words, product personalization and, in this case, personalized medicine. (It's very important to note, particularly for this example, that customer data provision and uses must be subject to and require the customer's knowledge, intentional participation, and approval.)

With connected customer relationships, marketers can move to *predictive personalization* that will enable coaching guidance and customization of messaging, offerings, products, and services more proactively and precisely than ever before. And these applications aren't limited to business-to-consumer enterprises or personal diagnostics.

Consider farming. Deere is a world leader in precision agriculture. Today, a Deere tractor can be a smart technological device that collects a continuous stream of data to "monitor, manage, and maximize" farm operations.[18] In other words, Deere is in a continuous data relationship with the farmer through his tractor, just as Fitbit is with him through the device on his wrist. The day is imminent when changes in soil composition and moisture content are detected as they occur, enabling the customization of inputs from seed to fertilizer, as well as personalized coaching and guidance on farming techniques to maximize crop yield.

The opportunities for advances in predictive personalization will abound in the world of interconnected devices with sensors, known as the Internet of Things (IoT). IoT integration is a natural extension of customer centricity and personalization, and is just in its nascent stages. As one IoT expert observed recently: "In fact, if connected products are aligned with production systems as early as the product creation phase, they subsequently allow the processes themselves to be modified according to actual customer needs."[19] With personalization extending back into product design and production systems and forward into predictive personalization in connected customer relationships, the growth of customer lifetime value will be enabled and advanced to an unprecedented extent.

Connected customer relationship

+

AI

↓

Personalization

↓

Customer value growth

The combination of connected customer relationships, providing continuous customer data flow, and AI will advance the practice of personalization to enable a growing range of businesses to accomplish more effectively than ever before the aim of marketing—customer value growth.

Conclusion

Relevance is the key to personalization, which is now doable and scalable for a broad range of companies, using advanced technology for data and analytics, digital media, and marketing methods that enable identifying customers, predicting their behaviors, needs, and wants, and then reaching them individually and economically with relevant messages and offerings. *Predictive analytics* can personalize, track, test, and optimize continuously at the individual customer level. *Trigger marketing,* automatically executed when a specific event or situation occurs, effectively targets individuals when a particular message is likely to be most relevant, affording opportunities to optimize the timing, content, offer, and design of customer interactions.

Customer data and predictive analytics reveal changes in a specific customer's behavior pattern or situation and, thus, anticipate and act on likely customer outcomes and key inflection points in the customer relationship. *Artificial intelligence* (AI) enables us to scale predictive analytics broadly, economically, accurately, and in real time. *Connected* customer relationships facilitate personalization by providing an ongoing flow of information that enables companies to sense customer needs, wants, and opportunities—often before the customer is even aware of the need. The combination of digital channels, AI, and connected customer relationships is advancing the practice of personalization to enable businesses to grow customer value more effectively than ever before.

Author Biography

Thomas F. (Tom) O'Toole is the associate dean for Executive Education and clinical professor of marketing at the Kellogg School of Management at Northwestern University. He previously served as the executive director of the Program for Data Analytics at Kellogg. His work and teaching focus on customer value growth and related subjects. He developed and teaches a popular Kellogg MBA course on customer loyalty strategy and practices. He is the author of "Branding Services in the Digital Era" in *Kellogg on Branding in a Hyper-Connected World* (Wiley, 2019). O'Toole is a senior advisor for McKinsey and Company. He has served and currently serves on the board of directors of public and private companies in a range of industries. He writes for *Forbes* on subjects spanning academia and business. Until his retirement, O'Toole was chief marketing officer of United Airlines and president of its MileagePlus business unit. Before United, O'Toole was chief marketing officer and chief information officer of Hyatt Hotels Corporation.

Notes

Chapter 1: Marketing in the Age of Disruption

1. This chapter is largely based on the content published in *Strategic Marketing Management: Theory and Practice* by Alexander Chernev (Chicago, IL: Cerebellum Press, 2019).

Chapter 2: The Fall of the Four Ps and the Rise of Strategic Marketing

1. This chapter is largely based on the content published in *Strategic Marketing Management: Theory and Practice* by Alexander Chernev (Chicago, IL: Cerebellum Press, 2019).
2. E. Jerome McCarthy and William Perreault, *Basic Marketing: A Managerial Approach*, 12th ed. (Homewood, IL: Irwin, 1996).
3. Philip Kotler, *Kotler on Marketing: How to Create, Win, and Dominate Markets*, 4th ed. (Free Press, 1999).

Chapter 3: The Framework for Marketing Management

1. This chapter is largely based on the content published in *Strategic Marketing Management: Theory and Practice* by Alexander Chernev (Chicago, IL: Cerebellum Press, 2019) and *The Business Model* by Alexander Chernev (Chicago, IL: Cerebellum Press, 2017).
2. The 5-C framework stems from the 3-C framework (corporation, competition, customers) introduced by Kenichi Ohmae in his book *The Mind of the Strategist: The Art of Japanese Business* (New York: McGraw-Hill, 1982).

Chapter 4: Creating Value to Disrupt Markets

1. No one has written with greater clarity and insight about market disruptions than Clayton Christensen. See *The Clayton Christensen Reader* (Harvard Business Review Press, 2015) and "Disruption 2020: An Interview with Clayton Christensen," *Sloan Management Review* (Spring 2020).
2. Phil Wahba, "Walgreens Pumps Another $5.2 Billion into Its Health Clinic War with CVS and Walmart," *Forbes* (October 14, 2021).
3. Analysis of collaborators is often done as part of go-to-market in Steps 4 and 5.
4. Mathematically, product (i) is chosen if surplus (i) > Max [surplus (j), for $\forall$ j ≠ i].
5. The offering could be a product, service, app, or whatever. The word "product" or "brand" will be used going forward.
6. If interested in quantification, each of the three dimensions can be scaled from 0 to 10 and multiplied to get disruptive value ranging from 0 to 1,000. This number can be scaled by 100 to produce a range of disruptive values from 0 to 10.
7. The customer faced other pain points such as getting rid of the old mattress and sending back the Casper mattress if it proved unsatisfactory. Over time, Casper started to address these pain points.
8. Amanda Butcher, "A Brief History of Lab-Grown Diamonds," International Gem Society, https://www.gemsociety.org/article/brief-history-of-lab-grown-diamonds/
9. "Delivering the Future of Diamond, Our Story," Diamond Foundry, https://diamondfoundry.com/pages/about-diamond-foundry
10. The United States joined the Paris Climate Agreement in 2016, withdrew in 2020, and rejoined in 2021.
11. Bruce Lieberman, "1.5 or 2 Degrees Celsius of Additional Global Warming: Does It Make a Difference?" *Yale Climate Connections* (August 4, 2021).
12. Hannah Ritchie, "How Much of the World's Land Would We Need in Order to Feed the Global Population with the Average Diet of a Given Country?" Our World in Data (October 3, 2017).
13. "Do You Consider Yourself to be a Vegetarian or Vegan?" Statista (March 31, 2021). A 2018 survey found that 6% claimed to be vegetarian and 2% vegan. These numbers have undoubtedly risen since.
14. Of course, social media also amplifies the opposite.
15. Courtesy of Brian Sternthal.
16. As of this writing, McDonald's and KFC are testing Beyond in their U.S. restaurants. Denny's and Carl's Junior and many others sell Beyond burgers. Called McPlant, Beyond is widely available in McDonald's restaurants in the UK and Ireland. Beyond is also in talks with Pepsico to develop plant-based snack and beverage products.
17. VRBO, then and largely now, only rents stand-alone vacation properties.
18. Sam Kemmis, "Airbnb vs. Vrbo: Which Is Better for Travelers?" NerdWallet (May 3, 2022).
19. Donald Padgett, "New Study Compares Airbnb versus Hotels with Surprising Results," Yahoo! News (November 4, 2021.)
20. Verbatim from Airbnb 2021 annual report.

21. Cable is used to represent pay TV, including receiving signals via satellite transmission.
22. "Number of Pay TV Households in the United States from 2013 to 2026," Statista.
23. "Road Traffic Injuries and Deaths—A Global Problem," Centers for Disease Control and Prevention (December 14, 2020); "Road Traffic Injuries," World Health Organization (June 20, 2022).

Chapter 5: Customer Centricity as a Business Strategy

1. Natalie Robehmed, "Peter Drucker on Marketing," *Forbes* (July 3, 2006).
2. Kelsie Feeney, "Marketing IS Business: The Wisdom of Peter Drucker," *Marketing Insider Group* (April 13, 2022).
3. Peter Fader, *Customer Centricity: Focus on the Right Customers for Strategic Advantage* (Philadelphia: Wharton School Press, 2011).
4. Peter Fader, *Customer Centricity: Focus on the Right Customers for Strategic Advantage,* 39.
5. 2020 Letter to Amazon Shareholders (April 15, 2021).
6. Peter Fader, *Customer Centricity: Focus on the Right Customers for Strategic Advantage,* (Philadelphia: Wharton School Press, 2011), 41.
7. Peter Fader, *Customer Centricity: Focus on the Right Customers for Strategic Advantage,* 72.
8. Daniel McCarthy and Fernando Pereda, "Assessing the Role of Customer Equity in Corporate Valuation: A Review and a Path Forward," SSRN (February 7, 2020).

Chapter 6: Emptor Cognita: Competitive Advantage through Buyer Learning

1. Peter F. Drucker, *The Practice of Management* (New York: Harper & Row, 1954).
2. Bernard J. Jaworski and Ajay K. Kohli, "Market Orientation: Antecedents and Consequences," *Journal of Marketing* 57 (1993): 53–70.
3. Rohit Deshpandé and John U. Farley, "The Market Orientation Construct: Correlations, Culture, and Comprehensiveness," *Journal of Market-Focused Management* 2, no. 3 (1998): 237–239; Gary F. Gebhardt, Gregory S. Carpenter, and John F. Sherry Jr., "Creating a Market Orientation: A Longitudinal, Multifirm, Grounded Analysis of Cultural Transformation," *Journal of Marketing* 70 (October 2006): 37–55.
4. Christian Homburg and Christian Pflesser, "A Multiple-Layer Model of Market-Oriented Organizational Culture: Measurement Issues and Performance Outcomes," *Journal of Marketing Research* 37 (2000): 449–462.

5. Walter Isaacson, *Steve Jobs* (New York: Simon & Schuster, 2001).

6. Ken Gross, "Desperately Seeking Status," *Automotive Industries* (September 18, 2001).

7. Howard Schultz and Dori Jones Yang, *Pour Your Heart into It: How Starbucks Built a Company One Cup at a Time* (New York: Hyperion, 1997).

8. Bernard J. Jaworski, Ajay K. Kohli, and Arvind Sahay, "Market-Driven Versus Driving Markets," *Journal of the Academy of Marketing Science* 28, no. 1 (2000): 45–54.

9. Joseph A. Schumpeter, *The Theory of Economic Development: An Inquiry into Profits, Capital, Credit, Interest, and the Business Cycle* (London: Oxford University Press, 1934), 65.

10. Gregory S. Carpenter, Rashi Glazer, and Kent Nakamoto, "Meaningful Brands from Meaningless Differentiation: The Dependence on Irrelevant Attributes," *Journal of Marketing Research* 26 (August 1994): 339–350; Gregory S. Carpenter and Kent Nakamoto, "Consumer Preference Formation and Pioneering Advantage," *Journal of Marketing Research* 26 (August 1989): 285–298; Ashlee Humphreys and Gregory S. Carpenter, "Status Games: Market Driving through Social Influence in the U.S. Wine Industry," *Journal of Marketing* 82, no. 5 (2018): 141–159; Andre Maciel and Melanie Wallendorf, "Taste Engineering: An Extended Model of Cultural Competence Constitution," *Journal of Consumer Research* 43, no. 5 (2017): 726–746; Subha Patvardhan and J. Ramachandran, "Shaping the Future: Strategy Making as Artificial Evolution," *Organization Science* 31, no. 3 (2020): 671–697.

11. Gregory S. Carpenter and Kent Nakamoto, "Consumer Preference Formation and Pioneering Advantage," *Journal of Marketing Research* 26 (August 1989): 285–298.

12. Gregory S. Carpenter, "We Uber Yet We Google: Gaining Early- and Late-Entry Advantage," in *The Routledge Companion to Strategic Marketing*, edited by Russell S. Winer and Bodo Schlegelmilch (Abingdon, UK: Routledge, 2021), 163–174.

13. Peter N. Golder and Gerard J. Tellis, "Pioneering Advantage: Marketing Logic or Marketing Legend?," *Journal of Marketing Research* 30 (1993): 158–170.

14. William T. Robinson and Claes Fornell (1985), "Sources of Market Pioneering Advantages in Consumer Goods Industries," *Journal of Marketing Research* 22 (1985): 305–318.

15. Glen L. Urban, Theresa Carter, Steven Gaskin, and Zofia Mucha, "Market Share Rewards to Pioneering Brands: An Empirical and Strategic Analysis," *Management Science* 32 (1986): 645–669.

16. Gregory S. Carpenter and Kent Nakamoto, "Competitive Strategies for Late Entry into a Market with a Dominant Brand," *Management Science* 36 (October 1990): 1268–1278.

17. Glenn R. Carroll and Anand Swaminathan, "Why the Microbrewery Movement? Organizational Dynamics of Resource Partitioning in the U.S. Brewing Industry," *American Journal of Sociology* 106, no. 3 (November 2000): 715–762.

18. Colman Andrews and Grant Suneson, "America's 26 Top-Selling Beers Show That the Country Still Likes a Cold One Now and Then," *USA Today* (October 27, 2018).

19. L. V. Anderson, "Beer Companies Love to Brag about How Cold Their Beer Is. But It's All Meaningless Posturing," *Slate* (January 29, 2014).

20. Gregory S. Carpenter, Rashi Glazer, and Kent Nakamoto, "Meaningful Brands from Meaningless Differentiation: The Dependence on Irrelevant Attributes," *Journal of Marketing Research*, 26 (August 1994), 339–50.

21. Ashlee Humphreys and Gregory S. Carpenter, "Status Games: Market Driving through Social Influence in the U.S. Wine Industry," *Journal of Marketing* 82, no. 5 (2018): 141–15.
22. Elin McCoy, *The Emperor of Wine: The Rise of Robert M. Parker, Jr. and the Reign of the American Taste* (New York: HarperCollins, 2005).
23. Patricia M. West, Christina L. Brown, and Stephen J. Hoch, "Consumption Vocabulary and Preference Formation," *Journal of Consumer Research* 23, no. 2 (1996): 120–1935.
24. Howard S. Becker, "Becoming a Marihuana User," *American Journal of Sociology* 19, no. 3 (1953): 235–242.
25. Michael B. Beverland, "Crafting Brand Authenticity: The Case of Luxury Wines," *Journal of Management Studies* 42, no. 5 (2005): 1003–1029.
26. Robert K. Merton, "The Matthew Effect in Science," *Science* 159, no. 3810 (1968): 56–63.
27. Matthew S. Bothner, Joel M. Podolny, and Edward Bishop Smith, "Organizing Contests for Status: The Matthew Effect vs. the Mark Effect," *Management Science* 57, no. 3 (2011): 439–457; Ashlee Humphreys and Gregory S. Carpenter, "Status Games: Market Driving through Social Influence in the U. S. Wine Industry," *Journal of Marketing* 82, no. 5 (2018): 141–159; Joel M. Podolny, "A Status-Based Model of Market Competition," *American Journal of Sociology* 98 (1993): 829–872; Marvin Washington and Edward J. Zajac, "Status Evolution and Competition: Theory and Evidence," *Academy of Management Journal* 48, no. 2 (2005): 282–296.

Chapter 7: Defensive Market Strategy

1. D. D. Rucker, M. Hu, and A. D. Galinsky, "The Experience versus the Expectations of Power: A Recipe for Altering the Effects of Power on Behavior," *Journal of Consumer Research* 41, no. 2 (2014): 381–396.
2. Karen Dillon, "I Think of My Failures as a Gift," *Harvard Business Review,* April 2011.
3. Paul Blustein, "Italy Loses the Pasta Wars," *The Washington Post,* July 31, 1996.
4. Sui Ling Phang, "First Valemax to Unload at China Port for Two Years Will Discharge Iron Ore," *S&P Global,* July 1, 2015.

Chapter 10: Crafting a Positioning Strategy: Capturing the Customer Mindshare

1. J. Trout, "'Positioning' Is a Game People Play in Today's Me-Too Market Place," *Industrial Marketing* 54, no. 6 (June 1969): 51–55.

2. A. Ries and J. Trout, *Positioning: The Battle for Your Mind* (New York: Warner Books–McGraw-Hill Inc., 1981).
3. The "who we're for and why we're better" concept is from the teachings of Julie Hennessy and referenced in K. McTigue and D. Rucker, *The Creative Brief Blueprint* (BookBaby, 2021).
4. Michael Porter, "What Is Strategy?" *Harvard Business Review* (November–December 1996).

Chapter 11: Building Strong Brands

1. This chapter is largely based on the content published in *Strategic Brand Management* by Alexander Chernev (Chicago, IL: Cerebellum Press, 2020) and *Strategic Marketing Management: Theory and Practice* by Alexander Chernev (Chicago, IL: Cerebellum Press, 2019).
2. Phillip Nelson, "Information and Consumer Behavior," *Journal of Political Economy* 78 (March–April 1970): 311–339.
3. Nader Tavassoli, Alina Sorescu, and Rajesh Chandy, "Employee-Based Brand Equity: Why Firms with Strong Brands Pay Their Executives Less," *Journal of Marketing Research* 51, no. 6 (2014): 676–690; C. B. Bhattacharya, Sankar Sen, and Daniel Korschun, "Using Corporate Social Responsibility to Win the War for Talent," *MIT Sloan Management Review* 49 (January 2008): 37–44.
4. The accounting rules regarding the inclusion of brand equity on the balance sheets of a company vary across countries. Thus, in the United States, companies do not list brand equity on their balance sheets, whereas in the United Kingdom and Australia balance sheets include the value of the company's brands.
5. Kevin Lane Keller, *Strategic Brand Management: Building, Measuring, and Managing Brand Equity*, 4th ed. (Upper Saddle River, NJ: Prentice Hall, 2012).
6. Interbrand, *Interbrand Best Global Brands* (2015), www.bestglobalbrands.com

Chapter 12: Creating a Meaningful Brand Image

1. Sascha Lehmann, Nils Liedtke, Phyllis Rothschild, and Eloy Trevino, "The Future of Brand Strategy: It's Time to 'Go Electric,'" *McKinsey & Company* (May 27, 2020); see also Emanuel Bagna, Grazia Dicuonzo, Andrea Perrone, and Vittorio Dell'Atti, "The Value Relevance of Brand Valuation," *Applied Economics* 49, no. 58 (2017): 5865–5876.
2. Leonardo Bursztyn, Bruno Ferman, Stefano Fiorin, Martin Kanz, and Gautam Rao, "Status Goods: Experimental Evidence from Platinum Credit Cards," *The Quarterly Journal of Economics* 133, no. 3 (August 2018): 1561–1595.

3. B. Tolinski and A. di Pern, *Play It Loud: An Epic History of the Style, Sound, and Revolution of the Electric Guitar* (New York: Anchor, 2017).
4. N. J. Roese and W. L. Gardner, "Building Strong Connections between Brands and the Self," in *Kellogg on Branding in a Hyper-Connected World*, ed. A. Tybout and T. Calkins (Hoboken, NJ: Wiley, 2019), 129–142.
5. G. L. Leonardelli, C. L. Pickett, and M. B. Brewer, "Optimal Distinctiveness Theory: A Framework for Social Identity, Social Cognition, and Intergroup Relations," *Advances in Experimental Social Psychology* 43 (2010): 66–115.
6. Aron Culotta and Jennifer Cutler, "Mining Brand Perceptions from Twitter Social Networks," *Marketing Science* 35, no. 3 (2016): 343–362.
7. Douglas L. Medin, William D. Wattenmaker, and Sarah E. Hampson, "Family Resemblance, Conceptual Cohesiveness, and Category Construction," *Cognitive Psychology* 19, no. 2 (April 1987): 242–279.
8. Alexander Krasnikov and Satish Jayachandran, "Building Brand Assets: The Role of Trademark Rights," *Journal of Marketing Research* (June 9, 2022).
9. Ryan Hamilton and Alexander Chernev, "Low Prices Are Just the Beginning: Price Image in Retail Management," *Journal of Marketing* (November 1, 2013).
10. Eric T. Anderson and Duncan Simester, "Mind Your Pricing Cues," *Harvard Business Review* (September 2003).
11. *The Hire*, eight-film series with BMW-branded content produced in 2001–2002.
12. Tim Calkins, *Defending Your Brand: How Smart Companies Use Defensive Strategy to Deal with Competitive Attacks* (New York: Palgrave Macmillan, 2012).

Chapter 13: Brand Resilience: Surviving a Brand Crisis

1. Aaron Bernabll, "Behind the Red Triangle: The Bass Pale Ale Brand and Logo," Logoworks (2013).
2. Kantar Group, "The Kantar BrandZ 2022 Global Brands."
3. This perspective describes highly developed economies in which customers have choices and high discretionary income levels. The role of brands in communicating quality is more important in less developed economies and among less privileged customers.
4. Kendra Cherry, "Maslow's Hierarchy of Needs," Verywell mind (August 14, 2022).
5. Bain & Company suggest a similar framework: Eric Almquist, John Senior, and Nicholas Bloch, "The Elements of Value," *Harvard Business Review* (September 2016).
6. "Brand Voice," Salesforce. https://brand.salesforce.com/content/verbal-brand-voice__1
7. Brian Solis, "Nearly Half of U.S. Consumers Have Lost Trust in a Brand This Past Year," Salesforce (June 1, 2021).
8. ACSI, "The American Customer Satisfaction Index 2000–2022."

9. Corrin Jones, "Warnings (& Lessons) of the 2013 Target Data Breach," Red River (October 26, 2021). https://redriver.com/security/target-data-breach
10. Venky Anant, Lisa Donchak, James Kaplan, and Henning Soller, "The Consumer Data Opportunity and the Privacy Imperative," McKinsey & Company (April 27, 2020).
11. "The Trust 10," Edelman Trust Barometer 2022.
12. https://www.kinandcarta.com/en/brand-resilience-index-2020/
13. https://www.mbooth.com/blog/the-five-tiers-of-brand-resilience/
14. "Extraordinary Brand Transformation, by Design," Landor & Fitch.
15. International Trademark Association, 2021 Brand Resilience Conference: Practitioner Roadmap for Guiding Change (August 18, 2021).
16. The *Counterinsurgency Field Manual* was updated and republished in May 2014. The comments in this chapter are drawn from the 2006 version.
17. *The U.S. Army/Marine Corps Counterinsurgency Field Manual* (The University of Chicago Press, 2006).
18. https://www.jnj.com/credo/
19. https://brand.salesforce.com/content/who+we+are
20. https://www.personalsafetygroup.com/2009/02/threats-situational-awareness-and-perspective-from-stratfor/
21. https://www.annualreports.com/HostedData/AnnualReports/PDF/NYSE_CRM_2020.pdf

Chapter 14: Managing Advertising: From Strategic Planning to Creative Review

1. Derek D. Rucker, *Advertising Strategy*, 6th ed. (Acton, MA: Copley Custom Textbooks, 2022).
2. Bobby J. Calder, *Kellogg on Advertising and Media* (Hoboken, NJ: John Wiley & Sons, 2008).
3. Derek D. Rucker, "Old Spice: Revitalizing Glacial Falls," Kellogg School of Management Cases (2011).
4. Rucker, *Advertising Strategy*.
5. *Rucker, Advertising Strategy*.
6. Kevin McTigue and Derek D. Rucker, *The Creative Brief Blueprint* (Pennsauken, NJ: Bookbaby, 2021).
7. Brian Sternthal and Derek D. Rucker, *Advertising Strategy* (Acton, MA: Copley Custom Textbooks, 2010).
8. Rucker, *Advertising Strategy*.
9. McTigue and Rucker, *The Creative Brief Blueprint*.

Chapter 15: Developing an Impactful Communication Campaign

1. Derek D. Rucker, *Advertising Strategy*, 6th ed. (XanEdu Publishing Inc., 2022).
2. Jim Lecinski, *The AI Marketing Canvas: A Five-Stage Road Map to Implementing Artificial Intelligence in Marketing* (Stanford Business Books, 2021).
3. Daniel Kahneman, *Thinking, Fast and Slow* (New York: Farrar, Straus and Giroux, 2011).

Chapter 16: Marketing in the Metaverse

1. Casey Newton, "Mark in the Metaverse," *The Verge* (July 22, 2021).
2. Mark Sullivan, "Microsoft's Metaverse Vision Is Becoming Clear—and Makes Sense," *Fast Company* (January 27, 2022).
3. Jordan Novet, "Mark Zuckerberg Envisions a Billion People in the Metaverse Spending Hundreds of Dollars Each," *CNBC.com* (June 22, 2022).
4. Eric Hazan, Greg Kelly, Hamza Kham, Dennis Spillecke, and Lareina Yee, "Marketing in the Metaverse: An Opportunity for Innovation and Experimentation," *McKinsey Quarterly* (May 24, 2022).
5. Taylor Hatmaker, "Fortnite's Ariana Grande Concert Offers a Taste of Music in the Metaverse," *Tech Crunch* (August 9, 2021).
6. Sam Desatoff, "Fortnite's Travis Scott Concert Attracts More Than 12 Million Concurrent Players," *GameDaily.biz* (April 24, 2020).
7. Jon Radoff, "The Metaverse Value-Chain," *Medium.com* (April 7, 2021).
8. Sanjana Shivdas, "Into the Metaverse: Nike Creates 'NIKELAND' on Roblox," Reuters (November 18, 2021).
9. Godwin Ariguzo, Efrem Mallach, and D. Steven White, "The First Decade of e-Commerce," *Internal Journal of Business Information Systems* 1, no. 3 (January 2006): 239–255.
10. Khee Hoon Chan, "Facebook's Horizon Worlds Is a Broken Metaverse Filled with Unimaginative Games," *TheGamer* (January 4, 2022).
11. Crypto.com, "NFTs: The Metaverse Economy," *Financial Times*, Partner Content. https://www.ft.com/partnercontent/crypto-com/nfts-the-metaverse-economy .html
12. Stephanie Glen, "The Metaverse Enters Ancient Egypt," *Data Science Central* (November 8, 2021).
13. Sarah Doughty, "What the Metaverse Means for B2B Companies," *Inc.* (April 11, 2022).
14. Musadiq Bidar, "Companies Race to Build 'Digital Twins' in the Metaverse," *CBSNews.com* (March 17, 2022).

15. Nike, "Nike Acquires RTFKT" (December 13, 2021).
16. Andrew Hayward, "Adidas Enters Metaverse with Bored Ape Yacht Club Ethereum NFT," *Decrypt.co* (December 2, 2021).

Chapter 18: Go-to-Market Omnichannel Design

1. https://info.dacgroup.com/dac-forrester-omnichannel-report-2021
2. H&R Block Press Release (November 27, 2001). https://investors.hrblock.com/news-releases/news-release-details/taxcut-hr-block-guides-do-it-yourselfers-through-tax-law-changes
3. https://www.hrblock.com/tax-center/newsroom/around-block/about-us/qa-jeff-jones-incoming-president-ceo-hr-block/
4. Stock Titan (June 16, 2022). https://www.stocktitan.net/news/HRB/h-r-block-continues-to-drive-transformation-and-business-growth-with-fcvsomv272jj.html.
5. David C. Edelman and Mark Abraham, "Customer Experience in the Age of AI: The Case for Building 'Intelligent Experience Engines,'" *Harvard Business Review* (March-April 2022).
6. Bradley Seth McNew, "4 Reasons Nike Inc Has Such a High Profit Margin," *The Motley Fool* (October 16, 2018).
7. Amy Lamare, "A Brief History of Away: From Suitcases to Scandals," *The Business of Business* (September 4, 2020).
8. Scott Brinker and Frans Riemersma, "State of Martech 2022."
9. Michael Vizard, "Salesforce Boosts Customer Data Platform Strategy as Rivals Circle," Venture Beat (June 2, 2021).
10. "What is a Customer Data Platform?" Bloomreach (2021). https://drive.google.com/file/d/1TMPq4_FPS64cj5G7XYSoyU_Wu6nlGCLt/view
11. "Treasure Data CDP at Subaru." https://tinyurl.com/yrkkwbcc
12. John P. Kotter, *Leading Change* (Boston: Harvard Business Review Press, 2012).

Chapter 19: Sales as Storytelling

1. B. Fryer, "Storytelling That Moves People," *Harvard Business Review* (2003).
2. W. Suzuki, M.I. Feliú-Mójer, U. Hasson, R. Yehuda, and J. M. Zarate, "Dialogues: The Science and Power of Storytelling," *Journal of Neuroscience* 38, no. 44 (October 2018): 9468–9470.
3. V. Boris, "What Makes Storytelling So Effective for Learning?" *Harvard Business Review* (2017).
4. G. Bower and M. Clark, "Narrative Stories as Mediators for Serial Learning," *Psychonomic Science* 15, no. 4 (1980): 181–182.
5. A. Simmons, *The Story Factor: Inspiration, Influence, and Persuasion through the Art of Storytelling* (New York: Basic Books, 2019), p. 62.

6. D. Small, G. Loewenstein, and P. Slovic, "Sympathy and Callousness: The Impact of Deliberative Thought on Donations to Identifiable and Statistical Victims," *Organizational Behavior and Human Decision Processes* 102 (2007): 143–153.
7. Rick Moody, "Tiny Jar of Mayo" SignificantObjects.com (March 26, 2010).
8. C. Tse and K. Porter, "Mars Is Said to Acquire PrettyLitter for Under $1 Billion," *Bloomberg* (September 7, 2021).

Chapter 20: Leading with AI and Analytics

1. The CMO Survey, www.cmosurvey.org, accessed May 15, 2022.
2. Much of this chapter's content was adapted from Eric Anderson and Florian Zettelmeyer, *Leading with AI and Analytics: Build Your Data Science IQ to Drive Business Value* (McGraw-Hill, 2020).
3. Michael Lewis, *Moneyball* (Norton, 2004).
4. Baseball Almanac offers data for teams and players starting in the mid-1870s, www.baseball-almanac.com, accessed May 20, 2022.

Chapter 21: Leveraging Technology to Manage the Customer Experience

1. Don Peppers and Martha Rogers, *Managing Customer Experience and Relationships: A Strategic Framework*, 3rd ed. (Hoboken, NJ: Wiley, 2017).
2. Jeffrey M. O'Brien, "The Netflix Effect," *Wired* (December 2002).
3. Tom Huddleston Jr., "Netflix Didn't Kill Blockbuster—How Netflix Almost Lost the Movie Rental Wars," CNBC (September 22, 2020).
4. Rachel Dornhelm, "Netflix Expands Indie Film Biz," Marketplace American Public Media (December 8, 2006).
5. Minaya and Amol Sharma, "Netflix Expands to 190 Countries," *Wall Street Journal* (January 6, 2016).
6. Reed Hastings and Erin Meyer, *No Rules Rules: Netflix and the Culture of Reinvention* (New York: Penguin Press, 2020).
7. Gavin Bridge, "Netflix Released More Originals in 2019 Than the Entire TV Industry Did in 2005," *Variety* (December 17, 2019),
8. Meghan Murray, "Starbucks Loyalty Reigns," University of Virginia, Darden Business Publishing, Case M-0903 (February 9, 2016).
9. David Dubois, Inyoung Chae, Joerg Niessing, and Jean Wee, "AccorHotels and the Digital Transformation: Enriching Experiences through Content Strategies along the Customer Journey," INSEAD Case 1251 (August 26, 2016).
10. David Dubois and Jean-Michel Moslonka, "Digitally-powered Customer-centricity in the Industrial Gas Sector: The Air Liquide-Airgas Merger," INSEAD Case 6446 (2019).

Chapter 22: The Consumer INSIGHT Framework: A Hypothesis-Driven Approach to Data Analytics

1. Ayelet Israeli and Jill Avery, "Predicting Consumer Tastes with Big Data at Gap," Harvard Business School Case #9-517-115 (2018).
2. Derek D. Rucker, *Advertising Strategy*, 6th ed. (Acton, MA: Copley Custom Textbooks, 2022).
3. Kevin McTigue and Derek D. Rucker, *The Creative Brief Blueprint* (Pennsauken, NJ: Bookbaby, 2021).
4. Leandre R. Fabrigar and Richard E. Petty, "The Role of the Affective and Cognitive Bases of Attitudes in Susceptibility to Affectively and Cognitively Based Persuasion," *Personality and Social Psychology Bulletin* 25, no. 3 (1999): 363–381.
5. Derek D. Rucker, "Merrick Pet Care: Trial, Error, and Success," Kellogg School of Management Case 5-420-754 (April 29, 2022).
6. Zakary L. Tormala, Victoria L. DeSensi, Joshua J. Clarkson, and Derek D. Rucker, "Beyond Attitude Consensus: The Social Context of Persuasion and Resistance," *Journal of Experimental Social Psychology* 45, no. 1 (2009): 149–154.
7. Jonah Berger and Chip Heath, "Who Drives Divergence? Identity Signaling, Outgroup Dissimilarity, and the Abandonment of Cultural Tastes," *Journal of Personality and Social Psychology* 95, no. 3 (2008): 593.
8. Derek D. Rucker and Ann Legan, "Modelo: Finding a Fighting Spirit," Case 5-321-500 (2021).
9. David Dubois and Katrina Bens, "Ombre, Tie-Dye, Splat Hair: Trends or Fads? 'Pull' and 'Push' Social Media Strategies at L'Oréal Paris," INSEAD Case 06/2014-6060 (2014).
10. Matthew D. Rocklage, Derek D. Rucker, and Loran F. Nordgren, "Mass-Scale Emotionality Reveals Human Behaviour and Marketplace Success," *Nature Human Behaviour* (2021): 1–7.

Chapter 23: Personalization—Today and Tomorrow

1. Don Peppers and Martha Rogers, *The One to One Future: Building Relationships One Customer at a Time* (New York: Crown Business, 1993).
2. Brian Gregg, Hussein Kalaoui, Joel Maynes, and Gustavo Schüler, "Marketing's Holy Grail: Digital Personalization at Scale," *McKinsey Digital* (November 18, 2016).
3. Julien Boudet, Brian Gregg, Jason Heller, and Caroline Tufft, "The Heartbeat of Modern Marketing: Data Activation and Personalization," McKinsey & Company (March 22, 2017).

4. Julien Boudet, Brian Gregg, Kathryn Rathje, Eli Stein, and Kai Vollhardt, "The Future of Personalization—and How to Get Ready for It," McKinsey & Company (June 18, 2019).

5. Julien Boudet, Lars Fiedler, Brian Gregg, Jason Heller, Mathias Kulman, Kelsey Robinson, and Kai Vollhardt, "Perspectives on Personalization @ Scale," Vol. 1, McKinsey & Company (July 2018).

6. Matt Ariker, Jason Heller, Alejandro Diaz, and Jesko Perry, "How Marketers Can Personalize at Scale," *Harvard Business Review* (November 23, 2015).

7. Nidhi Arora, Daniel Ensslen, Lars Fiedler, Wei Wei Liu, Kelsey Robinson, Eli Stein, and Gustavo Schüler, "The Value of Getting Personalization Right—or Wrong—Is Multiplying," McKinsey & Company (November 12, 2021).

8. Eric Anderson and Florian Zettelmeyer, *Leading with AI and Analytics: Build Your Data Science IQ to Drive Business Value* (New York: McGraw-Hill, 2021).

9. Delta Airlines, Investor Day Presentation (2018). https://s2.q4cdn.com/181345880/files/doc_presentations/Investor-Day-2018-Presentation.pdf

10. Boudet et al., "Perspectives on Personalization @ Scale."

11. Raj Venkatesan and Jim Lecinski, *The AI Marketing Canvas: A Five-Stage Road Map to Implementing Artificial Intelligence in Marketing* (Stanford, CA: Stanford University Press, 2021).

12. MarketingCharts.com, "How US CMOs Are Using AI in Marketing". https://www.marketingcharts.com/charts/us-cmos-using-artificial-intelligence-marketing

13. Nidhi Arora, Daniel Ensslen, Lars Fiedler, Wei Liu, Kelsey Robinson, Eli Stein, and Gustavo Schüler, "The Value of Getting Personalization Right—or Wrong—Is Multiplying," McKinsey & Company (November 12, 2021).

14. Nat Ives, "JPMorgan Chase Taps AI to Make Marketing Messages More Powerful," *Wall Street Journal* (July 30, 2019).

15. OfferFit, "How Does a Leading Home Security Brand Use AI to Optimize Loyalty?". https://www.offerfit.ai/customers

16. Nicolaj Siggelkow and Christian Terwiesch, *Connected Strategy: Building Continuous Customer Relationships for Competitive Advantage* (Cambridge, MA: Harvard Business Review Press, 2019).

17. "Fitbit: James Park," *How I Built That*, produced by NPR (April 27, 2020).

18. John Deere, "Precision Ag Technology" (2022). https://www.deere.com/en/technology-products/precision-ag-technology/

19. Research and Markets, "Predictions and Growth Opportunities for the Global Internet of Things (IoT) Market, 2022–2023," Frost & Sullivan (April 2022).